COLONY PATTERN
No. 2412 LINE

2412—Sweetmeat
Diameter 5 in.
Height 1¾ in.

2412—Bon Bon
Length 5 in.
Width 6 in.

2412 Whip Cream
Diameter 4¾ in.
Height 1¾ in.

2412—3 Piece Ash Tray Set
Consisting of:
Min.—2¼ in. Ind. Ash Tray
Min.—3½ in. Small Ash Tray
Min.—4½ in. Large Ash Tray

Elegant Glassware
of the
Depression Era

TWELFTH EDITION

IDENTIFICATION
AND
VALUE GUIDE

Gene & Cathy Florence

On the front cover: Green Deerwood iced tea. $50.00.
                       Yellow Kashmir ice bucket. $85.00.
                       Pink Morgan candy. $595.00.

On the back cover: Queen Louise pink saucer champagne. $360.00.
                       Amber Seville grapefruit insert liner. $30.00.
                       Green Cleo candlestick. $30.00.

Cover design by Beth Summers
Book design by Allan Ramsey
Cover photography by Charles R. Lynch

COLLECTOR BOOKS
P.O. Box 3009
Paducah, Kentucky 42002-3009

www.collectorbooks.com

Gene & Cathy Florence

P.O. Box 22186   P.O. Box 64
Lexington, KY 40522   Astutula, FL 34705

Copyright © 2007 Gene & Cathy Florence

The current values in this book should be used only as a guide. They are not intended to set prices, which vary from one section of the country to another. Auction prices as well as dealer prices vary greatly and are affected by condition as
well as demand. Neither the authors nor the publisher assumes responsibility for
any losses that might be incurred as a result of consulting this guide.

SEARCHING FOR A PUBLISHER?

We are always looking for people knowledgeable within their fields. If you feel
that there is a real need for a book on your collectible subject and have a large
comprehensive collection, contact Collector Books.

Proudly printed and bound in the
United States of America

About the Author 4
Acknowledgments 4
Preface 5

Achilles 6
Adonis 7
Alexis 9
American 11
American Beauty 17
Apple Blossom 18
"Balda" 21
Baroque 22
Black Forest 25
Bo Peep 27
Brocade, Fostoria 28
Brocade, Mckee 30
"Bubble Girl" Etching 31
Cadena 32
Candlelight 33
Candlewick 35
Canterbury, No 115 42
Cape Cod 45
Caprice 49
Caribbean 52
Catalonian 55
Chantilly 57
Charter Oak 59
Cherokee Rose 61
Chintz 62
Classic 64
Cleo 66
Colony 69
"Columbine Variant," Bluebell 73
Crystolite 74
Daffodil 76
"Dance of the Nudes," Dancing Nymph 77
Decagon 79
"Deerwood" or "Birch Tree" 81
Diane 83
Elaine 87
Elizabeth 91
Empire 92
Empress 93
Fairfax No. 2375 96
      Fostoria Stems and Shapes 98
First Love 99
Flanders 102
Fontaine 104
Fuchsia, Fostoria 105
Fuchsia, Tiffin 106
Gazebo 108
Glacier 109
Gloria 110
Golf Ball 113
Greek Key 115
"Harding" 117
Hermitage 118
Imperial Hunt Scene, #718 120
Ipswich 122
Janice 123
Julia 126
June 127
June Night 129
Jungle Assortment 130
Kalonyal 133
Kashmir 134
Lafayette 136
Lariat 137
Le Fleur 139
Lily of the Valley 140

"Lions" 141
Luciana 142
Mardi Gras 143
Marjorie 144
Meadow Wreath 145
Minuet 146
Morgan 148
Mt. Vernon 150
Narcissus 152
Nautical 153
Navarre 155
New Era 157
New Garland 158
Number 520, "Byzantine" 159
Number 703, "Florentine" 160
Number 704, "Windows Border" 161
Nymph 163
Octagon 164
Old Colony 166
Old Sandwich 168
Oriental 170
Persian Pheasant 172
Pioneer 173
Plaza 174
Pleat & Panel 175
Portia 176
Princess Feather 179
Priscilla 180
Provincial, Whirlpool 181
Psyche 183
Puritan 184
Queen Louise 185
Ridgeleigh 186
Rogene 188
Rosalie 189
Rose Point 191
Royal 197
Ruba Rombic 199
Sandwich 201
Saturn 203
Seville 205
"Spiral Flutes" 206
Shirley 208
Sparta 210
Stanhope 211
Sunburst 213
Sun Ray 215
Sunrise Medallion 217
Sylvan 219
Tally Ho 220
Tear Drop 223
Terrace 225
Thistle 227
Thistle Cut 228
Thousand Eye 229
"Tinkerbell" 230
Trojan 231
Turkey Tracks 233
Twist 234
Valencia 237
Versailles 239
Vesper 241
Victorian 244
Waverly 246
Wildflower 248
Woodland 250
Yeoman 251

Index by Company 225

ABOUT THE AUTHOR

Gene M. Florence, Jr., a native Kentuckian, graduated from the University of Kentucky in 1967. He held a double major in mathematics and English that he immediately put to use in industry and subsequently, in teaching junior and senior high school.

A collector since childhood, Mr. Florence progressed from baseball cards, comic books, coins, and bottles to glassware. His buying and selling glassware "hobby" began to override his nine-year teaching career. In the summer of 1972, he wrote a book on Depression glassware that was well received by collectors in the field, persuading him to leave teaching in 1976 and pursue the antique glass business full time. This allowed time to travel to glass shows throughout the country, where he assiduously studied the prices of glass being sold… and of that remaining unsold.

Cathy Gaines Florence, also a native Kentuckian, graduated with honors and a coveted voice award from high school, attended Georgetown College where she obtained a French major and an English minor, then married her middle-school sweetheart Gene Florence.

She taught for four years at the middle school level, then worked part-time while raising two boys. It was then that she typed her husband's first manuscript, written in "chicken scratch." The first three or four letters of each word would be legible and then it was up to her to guess what the last was. To their astonishment, the book sold well and a new career was born for her husband and their lives took different turns from the teaching careers they'd planned. In the mid-80s she authored a book on collecting quilts, harking back to skills taught her by her grandmothers; and she has since co-authored books on glass with husband Gene.

Books written by the Florences include the following titles: *Collector's Encyclopedia of Depression Glass*, *Stemware Identification*, *Collector's Encyclopedia of Akro Agate*, *Pocket Guide to Depression Glass & More*, *Kitchen Glassware of the Depression Years*, *Collectible Glassware from the 40s, 50s, and 60s*, two volumes of *Glass Candlesticks of the Depression Era*, *Anchor Hocking's Fire-King & More*, four volumes of *Florences' Glassware Pattern Identification Guide*, *Florences' Big Book of Salt and Pepper Shakers*, *Florences' Glass Kitchen Shakers, 1930 – 1950s*, *Standard Baseball Card Price Guide*, six editions of *Very Rare Glassware of the Depression Years*, and *Treasures of Very Rare Depression Glass*. They have also written six volumes of *Collector's Encyclopedia of Occupied Japan*, *Occupied Japan Collectibles*, and a book on Degenhart glassware for that museum. Mr. and Mrs. Florence's most recent books are *The Hazel-Atlas Glass Identification and Value Guide* and *Florences' Ovenware from the 1920s to the Present*.

ACKNOWLEDGMENTS

Behind the production of every book, there are a multitude of helpful people, many of whom often go unrecognized. We get the credit but others contribute much of the work. Some lent glass, some, their time; others lent their talents and expertise. These people have unrelentingly remained friends and contributors even after grueling hours of packing, unpacking, arranging, sorting, and repacking glass. Some traveled hundreds of miles to bring valuable glass of theirs and their friends to photograph for you. Some spent hours thrashing out and listing prices, often late at night after long show hours. This has been a difficult chore this time with the advent of price adjustments in a downward mode in the present economy. Others sent lists of additional pieces from their personal collections that we had not yet acknowledged. Without these generous and remarkable people, this book would not be the quality their assistance made it.

An extraordinary note of gratitude is due Dick and Pat Spencer. It was Dick who talked us into doing this book 25 years ago by volunteering to furnish glass (in particular Heisey, Fenton, Duncan, and Cambridge) and to help in pricing it. Little did he know how much time that would involve all these years later. Today, the Legend pictorials for the glass take as long to do as writing and pricing the glass. Dick and Pat bring their wares and gather other collectors' patterns for the photography sessions. They provide their vast knowledge of pricing and experiences in the wonderful world of glass. We hope you will benefit from all our long, tedious days of numbering, researching, and labeling pieces herein. Requests have been received over the years for the legends, and responses to our doing it have been well received — but do know it is quite an additional chore!

More generous people helping us with this book include John and Evelyn Knowles, Dan and Geri Tucker, Charles and Maxine Larson, Ray Sibley, Jr., and numerous nameless readers from all over the U.S., Canada, and beyond who shared pictures and morsels of information about their collections and discoveries. Richard Walker and Charles R. Lynch, with help arranging by Jane White and Zibby Walker, did most of the photography for this book. Thanks, also, to Allan Ramsey of Collector Books for laying out the photos you see herein.

This year's books have been an extra challenge due to Cathy's stroke last October. We had already been trying to slow down but life seems to be telling us that more vividly of late. Cathy, who has always worked long hours as editor, sounding board, and proofreader, had worked even harder filling in to overcome my health problems for several manuscripts. This didn't exactly help her stress level, and a mild, but debilitating stroke was evidently the result. Yet, somehow, we made it through days of doctor visits, therapy, and energy wipeouts. If we even knew the names of all the people who prayed for us both, we couldn't thank them enough! Now, we try to live each day in greater appreciation and hope to continue writing a few more years; but our travels to shows will necessarily be curtailed to a great extent. Thanks to all the readers whose generous responses to our books have made our writing careers possible. Moreover, many pieces and information have been added to lists over the years simply via your efforts, and collectors as a whole have benefited. If you have sent a postcard or e-mail with prices or a particular bit of knowledge, give yourself a well-deserved pat on the back!

Elegant glassware, as defined in this book, refers mostly to the hand worked, acid etched glassware that was sold by better department and jewelry stores during the Depression era through the 1960s, separating it from the colored dime store and give-away glass that has become known as Depression glass.

The elevation in acquiring Elegant glassware has been astonishing in recent years. Many dealers who would not gamble on stockpiling that type glass a few years ago are currently buying more Elegant than basic Depression glass. Our glass shows used to only display 15% to 20% Elegant glass; now, most shows have more than 50% and that percentage is growing. Some collectors who have completed sets of Depression glassware are now acquiring sets of Elegant while it is still available in the market.

There are nine new patterns in this book after adding 46 the last three editions. These 55 patterns are really pushing the limits of 256 pages in order to keep the price of the book affordable.

A few patterns were mostly produced after 1940 making them candidates for transferring them into our *Collectible Glassware from the 40s, 50s, and 60s.* This will be determined by how many new patterns we can fit into the prearranged number of pages for the books.

Six photography sessions for this book were spread over a two-year period with one session requiring ten days. We hope you enjoy this book, and will feel our 36 years of working to furnish you the best glassware books possible were worth the efforts of countless people also involved with the endeavor.

PRICING

All prices quoted are retail for mint condition glassware. This book is intended only as a guide to prices. There continue to be regional price disparities that cannot be adequately dealt with herein.

You may expect dealers to pay approximately 30 to 60 percent less than the prices listed. My personal knowledge of prices comes from buying and selling glass for 36 years and from traveling to and selling at shows in various parts of the United States. Strangely, I am working even harder at markets and shows, today, to remain current with the ever-fluctuating prices. You can find me on the Internet at www.geneflorence.com. I readily admit that I solicit price information from persons known to be authorities in certain wares in order to provide you with the latest, most accurate pricing information. However, final pricing judgments are always mine.

MEASUREMENTS AND TERMS

All measurements and terminology in this book are from factory catalogs and advertisements or actual measurements from the piece. It has been our experience that actual measurements vary slightly from those listed in most factory catalogs; so, do not get unduly concerned over slight variations. For example, Fostoria always seems to have measured plates to the nearest inch, but we have found that most Fostoria plates are never exact inches in measurement.

HOW TO USE THE PHOTO LEGENDS

To make this book easier to use and to provide more information, you will find photo legends with each pattern. Each piece is now identified either through the use of photo legends or through the use of numbers on shelf shots and individual shots. Each piece is numbered in the photo legends with corresponding numbers alongside the listings. Now you can tell exactly which piece is in the photo, and then refer to the listing to find size, color, price, and other information.

	Candlestick, 3⅛", #7951 Stafford	100.00
	Pitcher, 48 oz. 8"	195.00
5	Plate, 7½", #1511	12.50
	Stem, ¾ oz. cordial, #7565 Astrid	55.00
3	Stem, 3 oz., 5" cocktail, Monroe cut stem	45.00
1	Stem, 3½ oz. cocktail, #7669 Grandure	20.00
2	Stem, 5½ oz. saucer champagne, #7565 Astrid	20.00
	Stem, 6 oz., champagne	20.00
	Stem, 8½ oz. #7565 Astrid	30.00
4	Stem, 9 oz., 7", water	32.50

COLOR: CRYSTAL

After adding the Cambridge engraved patterns Achilles and Adonis to the last book, we were surprised by the number of readers who thanked us for explaining the differences between the two patterns. It seemed that these two are often confused with each other as are those of Valencia and Minerva. Achilles has a "shield" type design with a floral cut at its top. Think of "hill" within the name Achilles and the point of the shield as a "hill." That may help you distinguish between Achilles and Adonis.

The 18" vase pictured here has created some envious thoughts among collectors. There are not many of these found today. Can you imagine how long it would have taken to engrave such a large piece?

Achilles is a wonderful design, and it remains difficult to find in quantity today. Obviously, cut patterns were expensive at the time and more devotees were buying Rose Point because that pattern was so heavily promoted by Cambridge.

#	Item	Price		#	Item	Price
	Bonbon, 7½", 2-hdld., ftd. bowl, 3900/130	50.00			Plate, 13½", 2-hdld. cake, #3900/35	85.00
	Bowl, 12", 4-toed, flared, #3900/62	75.00			Plate, 14", rolled edge, #3900/166	75.00
	Candlestick, double, #399/72	65.00		5	Saucer, demi, #3400/69	20.00
	Candy box & cover, #3900/165	145.00			Stem, 1 oz., cordial, #3121	80.00
	Celery & relish, 8", 3-pt, #3900/125	65.00			Stem, 3½ oz., wine, #3121	65.00
	Celery & relish, 12", 3-pt, #3900/126	75.00			Stem, 3 oz., cocktail, #3121	35.00
	Celery & relish, 12", 5-pt, #3900/120	85.00			Stem, 4½ oz., claret, #3121	65.00
1	Cigarette holder, oval, #1066	85.00			Stem, 4½ oz., oyster cocktail, #3121	25.00
	Cocktail icer w/liner, #968	85.00			Stem, 5 oz., café parfait, #3121	65.00
	Comport, 5⅜", blown, #3121	75.00			Stem, 6 oz., high sherbet, #3121	17.00
	Comport, 5½", #3900/136	65.00			Stem, 6 oz., low sherbet, #3121	27.00
	Creamer, #3900/41	25.00			Stem, 10 oz., water goblet, #3121	55.00
5	Cup, demi, #3400/69	75.00			Sugar, #3900/41	25.00
	Mayonnaise, 2 part, #3900/11	35.00			Tumbler, 5 oz., ftd. juice, #3121	35.00
2	Mayonnaise liner, #3900/11	15.00			Tumbler, 10 oz., ftd. water, #3121	40.00
3	Mayonnaise, #3900/129	35.00			Tumbler, 12 oz., ftd. tea, #3121	45.00
	Mayonnaise liner, #3900/129	15.00			Vase, 11", ftd., #278	225.00
4	Pitcher, 80 oz., ball jug, #3400/38	265.00			Vase, 11", floral, ftd., #278	225.00
	Plate, 8", 2-hdld. ftd. bonbon, #3900/111	50.00		6	Vase, 18", floor vase, #1336	1,100.00
	Plate, 8½", luncheon, #3900/22	16.00				

COLOR: CRYSTAL

Adonis is another beautiful Cambridge pattern, but it seems to be easier to find than Achilles. You can recognize it by an oval in the design with a flower within the oval. Most tumblers and stems in Adonis are found on the #3500 line as pictured below. As with most glass patterns of this era, you will find stems more abundant than any serving pieces. Thankfully, we had friends who collected both Adonis and Achilles so we were fortunate to borrow many hard to find pieces.

Cut patterns are usually found in sets or a partial set kept in a family for years. Rarely do you find individual pieces for sale.

19	Bonbon, 7½", 2-hdld., ftd. bowl, 3900/130	45.00	10	Plate, 13", ftd., #3500/110	75.00
18	Bowl, 9" ram's head, #3500/25	395.00		Plate, 13½", 2-hdld. cake, #3900/35	85.00
14	Bowl, 12", 4-toed, #3400/4	95.00		Plate, 14", rolled edge, #3900/166	75.00
	Bowl, 12", 4-toed, flared, #3900/62	95.00	23	Relish, 2-hdld., 2-pt.	85.00
13	Candlestick, #627	35.00	15	Saucer, demi, #3400	15.00
	Candlestick, double, #399/72	65.00	22	Shaker, pr.	85.00
12	Candlestick, double, ram's head, #657	95.00	6	Stem, 1 oz., cordial, #3500	80.00
	Candy box & cover, #3900/165	135.00		Stem, 2 oz., sherry, #7966	65.00
	Celery & relish, 8", 3-pt, #3900/125	65.00	4	Stem, 2½ oz., wine, #3500	65.00
	Celery & relish, 12", 3-pt, #3900/126	75.00	5	Stem, 3 oz., cocktail, #3500	35.00
	Celery & relish, 12", 5-pt, #3900/120	85.00		Stem, 4½ oz., claret, #3500	65.00
	Cocktail icer w/liner, #968	85.00		Stem, 4½ oz., oyster cocktail, #3500	25.00
	Comport, 5⅜", blown, #3500	75.00		Stem, 5 oz., café parfait, #3500	65.00
	Comport, 5½", #3900/136	65.00	7	Stem, 7 oz., high sherbet, #3500	17.00
17	Comport, 8", 2-hdld., #3500	125.00	8	Stem, 7 oz., low sherbet, #3500	27.00
	Creamer, #3900/41	25.00	1	Stem, 10 oz., water goblet, #3500	55.00
15	Cup, demi, #3400	75.00		Sugar, #3900/41	25.00
9	Decanter, 28 oz., #1321	295.00		Tumbler, 5 oz., ftd. juice, #3500	35.00
11	Ice pail, #1402/52	150.00	2	Tumbler, 10 oz., ftd. water, #3500	40.00
	Mayonnaise, 2 pt., #3900/11	35.00	3	Tumbler, 13 oz., ftd. tea, #3500	45.00
	Mayonnaise liner, #3900/11	15.00	16	Urn, 10" w/cover, #3500/41	395.00
	Mayonnaise, #3900/129	35.00		Vase, 10", ftd., bud, #274	85.00
	Mayonnaise liner, #3900/129	15.00		Vase, 11", ftd., #278	225.00
20	Plate, 6", bread, #3500	12.00		Vase, 20", ftd.	1,295.00
	Plate, 8", 2-hdld. ftd. bonbon, #3900/111	50.00			
21	Plate, 8½", luncheon, #3500	16.00			

COLOR: CRYSTAL

Alexis is an older Fostoria pattern that was finishing its manufacturing cycle about the time that the most of patterns in this book were beginning production. Alexis has a classic simplicity that sells well for us at shows across the country. To our amazement, it has not become an expensive pattern to accumulate. As with most patterns, there are hard to find items that will be pricey. Among these are pitchers, water bottles, and syrups or cruets. Many pressed and earlier glasswares are gaining impetus in the collectibles market especially now that they are a century old. Production of Alexis began in 1909 and it was a long-lived pattern of a major company. Alexis serves as a link from the pattern glass era to that of Depression glass.

You can find Alexis at glass shows, antique malls, and antique shows as well as listed on Internet auctions.

4

#	Item	Price
1	Bowl, 4½", high foot	15.00
9	Bowl, 4½", nappy	12.50
	Bowl, 5", nappy	15.00
	Bowl, 7", nappy	20.00
	Bowl, 8", nappy	22.50
10	Bowl, 8", nappy, shallow	22.50
12	Bowl, 9", nappy	25.00
	Bowl, crushed ice	25.00
	Bowl, finger (flat edge)	15.00
	Butter dish w/cover	75.00
	Catsup bottle	65.00
	Celery, tall	32.50
	Comport, 4½" high	22.50
4	Cream, short, hotel	25.00
	Cream, tall	22.50
11	Cup, hdld. custard	10.00
	Decanter w/stopper	110.00
	Horseradish jar w/spoon	60.00
	Molasses can ewer, drip cut	65.00
	Mustard w/slotted cover	35.00
	Nut bowl	15.00
	Oil, 2 oz.	30.00
	Oil, 4 oz.	35.00
7	Oil, 6 oz.	45.00
	Oil, 9 oz.	55.00
	Pitcher, 16 oz.	45.00
	Pitcher, 32 oz.	75.00
	Pitcher, 64 oz., ice	85.00
	Pitcher, 64 oz., tall	100.00
14	Plate, crushed ice liner	10.00
	Salt shaker, pr. (2 styles)	35.00
8	Salt, individual, flat	20.00
	Salt, individual, ftd.	15.00

#	Item	Price
	Salt, table, flat	15.00
2	Spooner	30.00
	Stem, claret, 5 oz.	15.00
	Stem, cocktail, 3 oz.	12.50
	Stem, cordial, 1 oz.	15.00
	Stem, crème de menthe, 2½ oz.	15.00
13	Stem, egg cup	12.50
5	Stem, ice cream, high foot	15.00
	Stem, pousse café, ¾ oz.	16.00
	Stem, sherbet, high	13.00
	Stem, sherbet, low	12.00
	Stem, water, 10 oz.	15.00
6	Stem, wine, 2½ oz.	14.00
	Stem, wine, 3 oz.	14.00
	Sugar shaker	65.00
	Sugar, hdld., hotel	25.00
	Sugar, no handles w/lid	40.00
16	Sugar lid only	10.00
	Toothpick	30.00
	Tray, celery	25.00
	Tray, olive	20.00
	Tray, pickle	22.50
	Tumbler, ice tea	17.50
	Tumbler, ice tea, ftd., 10 oz.	20.00
15	Tumbler, water	15.00
	Tumbler, water, ftd., 8½ oz.	20.00
	Tumbler, whiskey	15.00
	Tumbler, wine	15.00
	Vase, 7", sweet pea, ftd.	50.00
3	Vase, 9", ftd.	60.00
	Vase, Nasturtium (sic)	37.50
	Water bottle	85.00

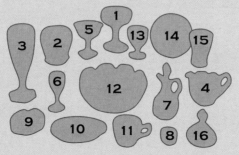

Colors: crystal; some amber, blue, green, yellow, pink tinting to purple in late 1920s; white, red in 1980s; and being newly made in crystal for Lancaster Colony

American is Fostoria's most identifiable pattern, having been made from 1915 until Fostoria's closing in 1986. Since then, American has continued to be produced under the guidance of the new owner, Lancaster Colony. Many items (particularly red colored) were subcontracted to Viking Glass Company (later Dalzell-Viking) and sold labeled Fostoria American by Lancaster Colony. Don't be confused by the recently designed Whitehall pattern that was fashioned by Indiana Glass Company and is similar to American. Whitehall's traits are inferior to that of American and shapes and sizes are dissimilar as well. Still, neophytes often fail to differentiate between the two patterns.

American, though respected by collectors, is beginning to be snubbed by a few dealers because it is, presently, a slow seller due to its substantial availability. Rarely found items continue to sell if priced within reason, but many of the expensively priced items are faltering due, in part, to the economy and collectors choosing to do without. In addition, the ongoing production of normally found pieces by Lancaster Colony keeps adding to the abundant supply. A wealth of Whitehall is found in pink, avocado green, and several shades of blue. The glassware section of your local discount store is a good place to scrutinize colors and items currently being made. Numerous specialty catalogs insinuate this new colored glassware to be Depression glass in an effort to enhance its value. Whitehall's pink colored ware is frequently confused with Jeannette's Depression era Cube pattern judging by the numerous letters and e-mails we receive. There are no footed pitchers or tumblers in Jeannette's Cube. Current American or look-alike American pieces are not marked in any way. American pieces that have been produced in recent years are indicated with an asterisk (*) in the price listing below.

Auction advertisements publicize Fostoria is being sold when they actually mean American as that is what is recognized rather than the hundreds of other Fostoria patterns that were made. These were the "Sunday" dishes used by Mom or Grandma. When Fostoria was no longer available in the department or jewelry stores, the secondary market (glass shows, flea markets, local antique or thrift shops) became the way to replace absent wares. The Internet has added to the adventure of finding American, but the risk there is that many sellers are inexperienced or unscrupulous regarding glass condition (or identification). Realize that most auctions on the Internet that proclaim colored American for bidding are not Fostoria's American, although recently an original green pitcher and iced teas were offered and found new homes. Try to buy only from those who guarantee their merchandise. We have been told frequently that the shysters will not offer returns.

Today, a copious supply of American pattern keeps a majority of the prices within the range of the average collector. Harder to find pieces are almost out of the realm of the general collector. There are noticeable price adjustments for American items being found in England. The Internet has European antique dealers observant of our glass collecting proclivities. Those once hard-to-find English Fostoria American pieces are easier to find here, since so many have been imported. Reissued cookie jars continue to create a problem. A majority of the newer issues have wavy lines in the pattern itself and crooked knobs on the top. Old cookie jars do not. (A telling point that works more than half the time is to try to turn the lid around while it rests inside the cookie jar. The new lids seem to hang up and stop somewhere along the inside, making the whole cookie jar turn. The old jars will allow you to turn the lid completely around without catching on the sides.)

If you get pleasure from the beauty the American pattern radiates, then definitely buy it. Collecting what you like has always been a primary criterion; and little pleasures in life should be catered to whenever possible.

		*Crystal				*Crystal
	Appetizer, tray, 10½", w/6 inserts	275.00			Bottle, cordial, w/stopper, 7¼", 9 oz.	80.00
	Appetizer, insert, 3¼"	32.50			Bottle, water, 44 oz., 9¼"	625.00
	Ashtray, 2⅞", sq.	7.50	22		Bowl, banana split, 9" x 3½"	595.00
	Ashtray, 3⅞", oval	9.00			Bowl, finger, 4½" diam., smooth edge	40.00
	Ashtray, 5", sq.	45.00			Bowl, 3½", rose	20.00
	Ashtray, 5½", oval	20.00			Bowl, 3¾", almond, oval	18.00
	Basket, w/reed handle, 7" x 9"	95.00			Bowl, 4¼", jelly, 4¼" h.	15.00
	Basket, 10", new in 1988 (glass handle)	40.00			Bowl, 4½", 1 hdld.*	10.00
	Bell	495.00	18		Bowl, 4½", 1 hdld., sq.	11.00
	Bottle, bitters, w/tube, 5¼", 4½ oz.	70.00			Bowl, 4½", jelly, w/cover, 6¾" h.	30.00
	Bottle, condiment/ketchup w/stopper	125.00			Bowl, 4½", nappy*	12.00
	Bottle, cologne, w/stopper, 6 oz., 5¾"	65.00			Bowl, 4½", oval	15.00
26	Bottle, cologne, w/stopper, 7¼", 8 oz.	70.00			Bowl, 4¾", fruit, flared	15.00

* See note in second paragraph above.

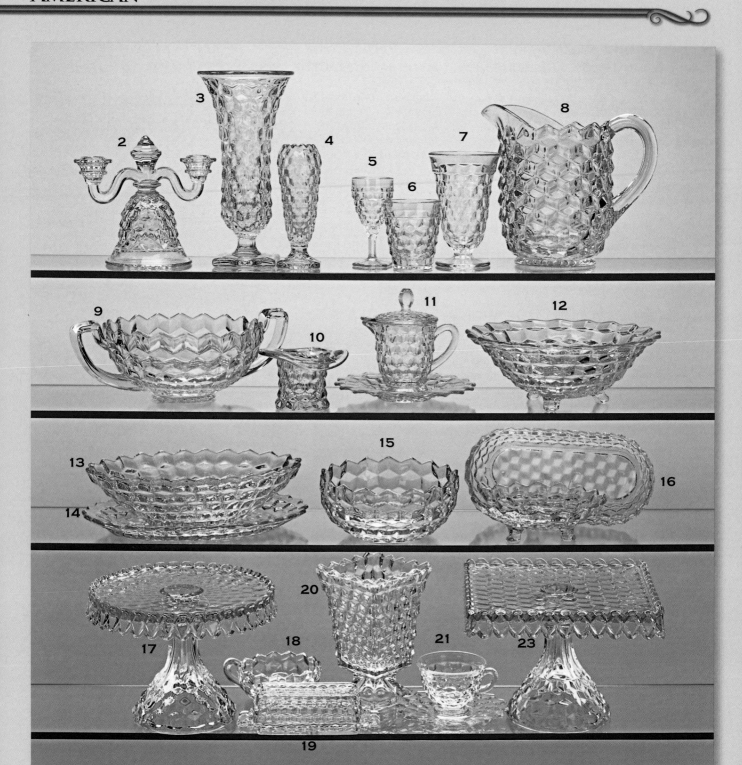

	*Crystal
Bowl, 5", cream soup, 2 hdld.	45.00
Bowl, 5", 1 hdld., tri-corner	12.00
Bowl, 5", nappy*	10.00
Bowl, 5", nappy, w/cover	30.00
Bowl, 5", rose	30.00
Bowl, 5½", lemon, w/cover	50.00

	*Crystal
Bowl, 5½", preserve, 2 hdld., w/cover	90.00
Bowl, 6", bonbon, 3 ftd.	15.00
Bowl, 6", nappy*	15.00
Bowl, 6", olive, oblong	12.00
Bowl, 6½", wedding, w/cover, sq., ped. ft., 8" h.	100.00
Bowl, 6½", wedding, sq., ped. ft., 5¼" h.	70.00

		*Crystal
	Bowl, 7", bonbon, 3 ftd.	13.00
	Bowl, 7", cupped, 4½" h.	55.00
	Bowl, 7", nappy*	25.00
	Bowl, 8", bonbon, 3 ftd.	17.50
	Bowl, 8", deep	60.00
	Bowl, 8", ftd.	90.00
	Bowl, 8", ftd., 2 hdld., "trophy" cup	110.00
15	Bowl, 8", nappy*	25.00
	Bowl, 8", pickle, oblong*	15.00
9	Bowl, 8½", 2 hdld.	50.00
	Bowl, 8½", boat*	16.00
	Bowl, 9", boat, 2 pt.	12.50
	Bowl, 9", oval veg.*	30.00
	Bowl, 9½", centerpiece	50.00
	Bowl, 9½", 3 pt., 6" w.	37.50
16	Bowl, 10", celery, oblong	22.00
	Bowl, 10", deep*	35.00
	Bowl, 10", float	45.00
	Bowl, 10", oval, float	32.50
	Bowl, 10", oval, veg., 2 pt.	35.00
12	Bowl, 10½", fruit, 3 ftd.	40.00
	Bowl, 11", centerpiece	45.00
	Bowl, 11", centerpiece, tri-corner	45.00
	Bowl, 11", relish/celery, 3 pt.	30.00
	Bowl, 11½", float	65.00
	Bowl, 11½", fruit, rolled edge, 2¾" h.	42.50
	Bowl, 11½", oval, float	45.00
	Bowl, 11½", rolled edge	50.00
13	Bowl, 11¾", oval, deep	42.50
	Bowl, 12", boat	20.00
	Bowl, 12", fruit/sm. punch, ped. ft. (Tom & Jerry)*	235.00
	Bowl, 12", lily pond	60.00
	Bowl, 12", relish "boat," 2 pt.	20.00
	Bowl, 13", fruit, shallow	80.00
	Bowl, 14", punch, w/high ft. base (2 gal.)	350.00
	Bowl, 14", punch, w/low ft. base	300.00
	Bowl, 15", centerpiece, "hat" shape	175.00
	Bowl, 16", flat, fruit, ped. ft.	200.00
	Bowl, 18", punch, w/low ft. base (3¾ gal.)	400.00
	Box, pomade, 2" square	295.00
27	Box, w/cover, puff, 3⅛" x 2¾"	195.00
	Box, w/cover, 4½" x 4½"	195.00
25	Box, w/cover, handkerchief, 5⅝" x 4⅝"	275.00
	Box, w/cover, hairpin, 3½" x 1¾"	295.00
28	Box, w/cover, jewel, 5¼" x 2¼"	300.00
	Box, w/cover, jewel, 2 drawer, 4¼" x 3¼"	6,000.00
31	Box, w/cover, glove, 9½" x 3½"	295.00
	Butter, w/cover, rnd. plate, 7¼"*	100.00
19	Butter, w/cover, ¼ lb.*	22.00
	Cake stand (see salver)	
	Candelabrum, 6½", 2-lite, bell base w/bobeche & prisms	135.00

		*Crystal
	Candle lamp, 8½", w/chimney, candle part, 3½"	135.00
	Candlestick, twin, 4⅛" h., 8½" spread	50.00
	Candlestick, 2", chamber with fingerhold	40.00
	Candlestick, 3", rnd. ft.**	15.00
	Candlestick, 4⅜", 2-lite, rnd. ft.	40.00
	Candlestick, 6", octagon ft.	25.00
2	Candlestick, 6½", 2-lite, bell base	110.00
	Candlestick, 6¼", round ft.	195.00
	Candlestick, 7", sq. column*	115.00
	Candlestick, 7¼", "Eiffel" tower	150.00
	Candy box, w/cover, 3 pt., triangular	90.00
	Candy, w/cover, ped. ft.	37.50
	Cheese (5¾" compote) & cracker (11½" plate)	65.00
	Cigarette box, w/cover, 4¾"	35.00
	Coaster, 3¾"	8.00
	Comport, 4½", jelly	12.00
	Comport, 5", jelly, flared*	12.00
	Comport, 6¾", jelly, w/cover*	35.00
	Comport, 8½", 4" high	45.00
	Comport, 9½", 5¼" high	85.00
	Comport, w/cover, 5"	25.00
	Cookie jar, w/cover, 8⅞" h.**	275.00
	Creamer, tea, 3 oz., 2⅜" (#20561/2)	8.00
	Creamer, individual, 4¾ oz.	8.00
	Creamer, 9½ oz.	11.00
	Crushed fruit, w/cover & spoon, 10"	2,500.00
	Cup, flat	7.00
21	Cup, ftd., 7 oz.	7.00
	Cup, punch, flared rim	10.00
	Cup, punch, straight edge	9.00
	Decanter, w/stopper, 24 oz., 9¼" h.	85.00
	Dresser set: powder boxes w/covers & tray	475.00
1	Flower pot, w/perforated cover, 9½" diam., 5½" h.	1,995.00
5	Goblet, #2056, 2½ oz., wine, hex ft., 4½" h.	9.00
	Goblet, #2056, 4½ oz., oyster cocktail, 3½" h.	13.00
	Goblet, #2056, 4½ oz., sherbet, flared, 4⅜" h.	7.00
	Goblet, #2056, 4½ oz., fruit, hex ft., 4¾" h.	7.00
	Goblet, #2056, 5 oz., low ft., sherbet, flared, 3¼" h.	7.00
	Goblet, #2056, 6 oz., low ft., sundae, 3⅛" h.	7.00
	Goblet, #2056, 7 oz., claret, 4⅞" h.	50.00
	Goblet, #2056, 9 oz., low ft., 4⅜" h.*	9.00
	Goblet, #2056, 10 oz., hex ft., water, 6⅞" h.	10.00
	Goblet, #2056, 12 oz., low ft., tea, 5¾" h.	14.00
	Goblet, #2056½, 4½ oz., sherbet, 4½" h.	8.00
	Goblet, #2056½, 5 oz., low sherbet, 3½" h.	8.00
	Goblet, #5056, 1 oz., cordial, 3⅛", w/plain bowl	40.00
	Goblet, #5056, 3½ oz., claret, 4⅝", w/plain bowl	16.00
	Goblet, #5056, 3½ oz., cocktail, 4", w/plain bowl	10.00
	Goblet, #5056, 4 oz., oyster cocktail, 3½", w/plain bowl	10.00
	Goblet, #5056, 5½ oz., sherbet, 4⅛", w/plain bowl	8.00

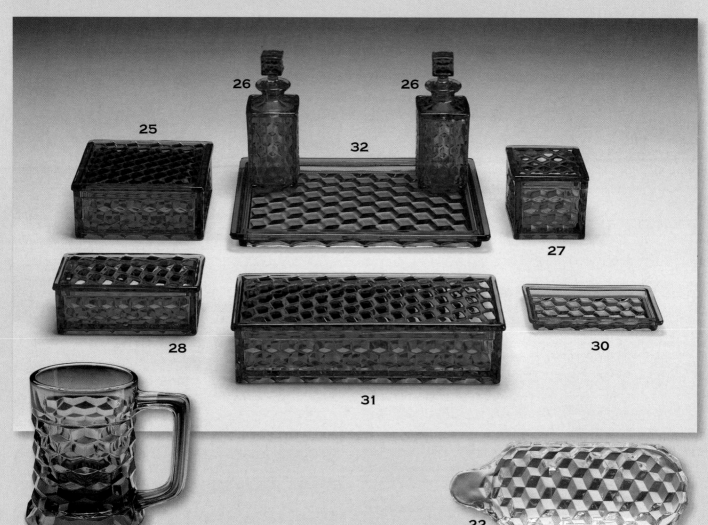

		*Crystal
	Goblet, #5056, 10 oz., water, 6⅛", w/plain bowl	14.00
	Hair receiver, 3" x 3"	395.00
	Hat, 2⅛" (sm. ashtray)	16.00
10	Hat, 3" tall	27.50
24	Hat, 4" tall	65.00
	Hat, western style	295.00
	Hotel washbowl and pitcher	3,300.00
	Hurricane lamp, 12" complete w/chimney	175.00
	Hurricane lamp base	50.00
	Ice bucket, w/tongs	60.00
	Ice cream saucer (2 styles)	45.00
	Ice dish for 4 oz. crab or 5 oz. tomato liner	30.00
	Ice dish insert	8.00
	Ice tub, w/liner, 5⅝"	90.00
	Ice tub, w/liner, 6½"	95.00
	Jam pot, w/cover	55.00
	Jar, pickle, w/pointed cover, 6" h.	295.00
	Marmalade, w/cover & chrome spoon	50.00
	Mayonnaise, div.*	15.00
	Mayonnaise, w/ladle, ped. ft.	55.00
	Mayonnaise, w/liner & ladle	35.00
	Molasses can, 11 oz., 6¾" h., 1 hdld.	400.00
	Mug, 5½ oz., Tom & Jerry, 3¼" h.*	35.00
32	Mug, 12 oz., beer, 4½" h.*	60.00
	Mustard, w/cover	35.00
	Napkin ring	15.00
	Oil, 5 oz.	35.00
	Oil, 7 oz.	35.00
	Picture frame	15.00
	Pitcher, ½ gal. w/ice lip, 8¼", flat bottom	85.00
	Pitcher, ½ gal., w/o ice lip, 69 oz. (2056½)	275.00
8	Pitcher, ½ gal., 8", ftd.	70.00
	Pitcher, 1 pt., 5⅜", flat	27.50
	Pitcher, 2 pt., 7¼", ftd.	65.00
	Pitcher, 3 pt., 8", ftd.	70.00
	Pitcher, 3 pt., w/ice lip, 6½", ftd., "fat"	60.00
	Pitcher, 1 qt., flat*	30.00
	Plate, cream soup liner	10.00
	Plate, 6", bread & butter	10.00
	Plate, 7", salad	10.00
	Plate, 7½" x 4⅜", crescent salad	50.00
	Plate, 8", sauce liner, oval	18.00
	Plate, 8½", salad	10.00
	Plate, 9", sandwich (sm. center)	14.00
	Plate, 9½", dinner	18.00
	Plate, 10", cake, 2 hdld.	25.00
	Plate, 10½", sandwich (sm. center)	20.00
	Plate, 11½", sandwich (sm. center)	20.00
	Plate, 12", cake, 3 ftd.	25.00
	Plate, 13½", oval torte	50.00
	Plate, 14", torte	75.00
	Plate, 18", torte	135.00
	Plate, 20", torte	195.00
	Plate 24", torte	225.00

		*Crystal
	Platter, 10½", oval*	40.00
14	Platter, 12", oval	55.00
	Ring holder	200.00
	Salad set: 10" bowl, 14" torte, wood fork & spoon	135.00
	Salt, individual	9.00
23	Salver, 10", sq., ped. ft. (cake stand)	140.00
17	Salver, 10", rnd., ped. ft. (cake stand)	110.00
	Salver, 11", rnd., ped. ft. (cake stand)*	35.00
	Sauce boat & liner	50.00
21	Saucer	3.00
	Set: 2 jam pots w/tray	150.00
	Set: decanter, six 2 oz. whiskeys on 10½" tray	245.00
	Set: toddler, w/baby tumbler & bowl	100.00
	Set: youth, w/bowl, hdld. mug, 6" plate	110.00
	Set: condiment, 2 oils, 2 shakers, mustard w/ cover & spoon w/tray	350.00
	Shaker, 3", ea.	10.00
	Shaker, 3½", ea.*	7.00
	Shaker, 3¼", ea.	10.00
	Shakers w/tray, individual, 2"	20.00
	Sherbet, handled, 3½" high, 4½ oz.	95.00
	Shrimp bowl, 12¼"	325.00
29	Soap dish	995.00
	Spooner, 3¾"	35.00
	Strawholder, 10", w/cover**	275.00
	Sugar, tea, 2¼" (#2056½)	13.00
	Sugar, hdld., 3¼" h.	12.00
	Sugar shaker	65.00
	Sugar, w/o cover	10.00
	Sugar, w/cover, no hdl., 6¼" (cover fits strawholder)	65.00
	Sugar, w/cover, 2 hdld.	20.00
	Syrup, 6½ oz., #2056½, Sani-cut server	65.00
	Syrup, 6 oz., non pour screw top, 5¼" h.	225.00
11	Syrup, 10 oz., w/glass cover & 6" liner plate	195.00
	Syrup, w/drip proof top	35.00
	Toothpick	20.00
	Tray, cloverleaf for condiment set	155.00
	Tray, tidbit, w/question mark metal handle	40.00
	Tray, pin, oval, 5½" x 4½"	195.00
30	Tray, 5" x 2½", rect.	80.00
	Tray, 6" oval, hdld.	35.00
	Tray, 6½" x 9" relish, 4 part	40.00
	Tray, 9½", service, 2 hdld.	32.00
	Tray, 10", muffin (2 upturned sides)	32.50
	Tray, 10", square, 4 part	75.00
	Tray, 10", square	175.00
	Tray, 10½", cake, w/question mark metal hdl.	32.00
32	Tray, 10½" x 7½", rect.	70.00
	Tray, 10½" x 5", oval hdld.	45.00
	Tray, 10¾", square, 4 part	155.00
	Tray, 12", sand. w/ctr. handle	37.50
	Tray, 12", round	150.00

29

	*Crystal
Tray, 13½", oval, ice cream	165.00
Tray for sugar & creamer, tab. hdld., 6¾"	12.00
Tumbler, hdld. iced tea	395.00
Tumbler, #2056, 2 oz., whiskey, 2½" h.	10.00
Tumbler, #2056, 3 oz., ftd. cone, cocktail, 2⅞" h.	11.00
Tumbler, #2056, 5 oz., ftd., juice, 4¾"	11.00
6 Tumbler, #2056, 6 oz., flat, old-fashion, 3⅜" h.	14.00
Tumbler, #2056, 8 oz. flat, water, flared, 4⅛" h.	14.00
7 Tumbler, #2056, 9 oz. ftd., water, 4⅞" h.*	11.00
Tumbler, #2056, 12 oz., flat, tea, flared, 5¼" h.	15.00
Tumbler, #2056½, 5 oz., straight side, juice	13.00
Tumbler, #2056½, 8 oz., straight side, water, 3⅞" h.	12.00
Tumbler, #2056½, 12 oz., straight side, tea, 5" h	18.00
Tumbler, #5056, 5 oz., ftd., juice, 4⅛" w/plain bowl	8.00
Tumbler, #5056, 12 oz., ftd., tea, 5½" w/plain bowl	8.00
Urn, 6", sq., ped. ft	30.00
20 Urn, 7½", sq. ped. ft.	37.50
Vase, 4½", sweet pea	80.00

	*Crystal
4 Vase, 6", bud, ftd., cupped	18.00
Vase, 6", bud, flared*	18.00
Vase, 6", straight side	35.00
Vase, 6½", flared rim	15.00
Vase, 7", flared	80.00
Vase, 8", straight side*	40.00
Vase, 8", flared*	80.00
Vase, 8", porch, 5" diam.	495.00
Vase, 8½", bud, flared	25.00
Vase, 8½", bud, cupped	25.00
3 Vase, 9", w/sq. ped. ft.	45.00
Vase, 9½", flared	150.00
Vase, 10", cupped in top	295.00
Vase, 10", porch, 8" diam.	795.00
Vase, 10", straight side*	90.00
Vase, 10", swung	225.00
Vase, 10", flared	90.00
Vase, 12", straight side	250.00
Vase, 12", swung	250.00
Vase, 14", swung	250.00
Vase, 20", swung	395.00

29

COLORS: AMBER, BLUE, CRYSTAL, GREEN, AND PINK

American Beauty is one of those patterns that used to be brought into shows for us to identify until it was included in this book. It seems evident that it was widely dispersed in a quantity of stems and colors. The cordial pictured illustrates stem #7575 which has a rose vine climbing along the stem.

		*Crystal				*Crystal
	Candlestick, 3⅛", #7951 Stafford	110.00	1	Stem, 3½ oz. cocktail, #7669 Grandure		20.00
	Compote, 5" w/8" diameter	40.00		Stem, 4½ oz. parfait, #7565 Astrid		20.00
	Compote, 6½" high, w/cover, #7941 Helena	195.00		Stem, 4½ oz., 5⅝", tall champagne, #7565 Astrid		20.00
	Custard liner, 5⅛"	15.00		Stem, 4¼ oz. claret, #7565 Astrid		25.00
	Custard, hdld. #8851	75.00		Stem, 5 oz. deep champagne, #7565 Astrid		20.00
	Finger bowl liner	10.00		Stem, 5 oz. hot whiskey, #7565 Astrid		15.00
	Finger bowl, 4⅜", #2927	45.00		Stem, 5 oz. sherbet, #7565 Astrid		15.00
	Nappy, 6" diameter, w/cover, #7557 Savoy	155.00	2	Stem, 5½ oz. saucer champagne, #7565 Astrid		20.00
	Nut, 4½" master w/cover, #7556	165.00		Stem, 6 oz., champagne		20.00
	Pitcher, 48 oz. 8"	210.00		Stem, 6½ oz., 4⅝" bowl champagne, #7565 Astrid		20.00
	Pitcher, 54 oz. w/lid, #2 Arcadia	325.00		Stem, 8½ oz., #7565 Astrid		30.00
	Plate, 7¼"	12.50	4	Stem, 9 oz., 7" water		32.50
5	Plate, 7½", #1511	12.50		Stem, 10 oz. water, #7565 Astrid		40.00
	Stem, ¾ oz. cordial, #7565 Astrid	55.00		Stem, 11 oz., 7½" water, #7695 trumpet		45.00
6	Stem, ¾ oz., 4⅜" cordial, #7575	85.00		Tumbler, 2¾ oz., 2¼" bar, #8107 Sherman		38.00
	Stem, 1½ oz. port, #7565 Astrid	30.00		Tumbler, 8 oz., 4⅛" water, #9001 Billings		30.00
	Stem, 1 oz. pousse cafe, #7565 Astrid	50.00		Tumbler, 9 oz. ftd. w/handle, #9069 Hopper		50.00
	Stem, 2½ oz. sherry, #7565 Astrid	25.00		Tumbler, 9 oz., 4⅝" water, #8701 Garrett		30.00
	Stem, 3 oz., 6" sherry, #7695 trumpet	50.00		Tumbler, 12 oz. 4⅞", #9715 Calhoun		30.00
3	Stem, 3 oz., 5" cocktail, Monroe cut stem	45.00		Tumbler, 12 oz., ftd. w/handle, #9069 Hopper		60.00
	Stem, 3 oz. wine, #7565 Astrid	25.00		Vase, 10", #25 Olympic		165.00
	Stem, 3½ oz. cocktail, #7565 Astrid	15.00		Vase, 12" #25 Olympic		200.00

* Add 40% for colors.

COLORS: AMBER, AMETHYST, CRYSTAL, CRYSTAL W/ EBONY STEM, LIGHT AND DARK EMERALD, GOLD KRYSTOL, HEATHERBLOOM, PEACH BLO, ROYAL BLUE, WILLOW BLUE

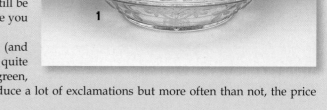

Apple Blossom mainly appeals to new collectors in Cambridge's yellow, called Gold Krystol. That color of Apple Blossom is found regularly and is the most moderately priced except for crystal. You can attain a small set reasonably; however, difficult to find items and serving pieces are now expensive. Notice the round casserole pictured. Luckily, we were able to obtain a photo, because it was destroyed on its way to us. We would have loved to own it undamaged. Beverage items including tumblers and stems can still be found in most colors. Buy any serving pieces or dinner plates every time you have the opportunity.

Colors, excluding yellow and crystal, can be found with patience (and funds); although, availability of pink, green, blue, and Heatherbloom is quite insufficient in contrast to yellow or crystal. Very little dark Emerald green, amethyst, or amber is found. Settings of blue displayed at shows, produce a lot of exclamations but more often than not, the price makes viewers vacillate at buying.

Apple Blossom is found on several Cambridge stemware lines, but the #3130 line is mainly found and collected. Some collectors intermingle stemware lines, but since bowl shapes differ, many will not combine them. One collector informed us that she was mixing several stem lines simultaneously. She liked Apple Blossom and bought anything she could find. That collecting mode may become more and more routine in the future, predominantly in Elegant patterns like this.

		Crystal	Yellow Amber	Pink *Green
	Ashtray, 6", heavy	40.00	100.00	135.00
	Bowl, #3025, ftd., finger, w/plate	45.00	65.00	75.00
	Bowl, #3130, finger, w/plate	40.00	60.00	70.00
	Bowl, 3", indiv. nut, 4 ftd.	50.00	70.00	75.00
	Bowl, 5¼", 2 hdld., bonbon	25.00	40.00	45.00
	Bowl, 5½", 2 hdld., bonbon	25.00	40.00	40.00
	Bowl, 5½", fruit "saucer"	20.00	28.00	30.00
	Bowl, 6", 2 hdld., "basket" (sides up)	30.00	48.00	50.00
	Bowl, 6", cereal	30.00	45.00	50.00
18	Bowl, 9", pickle	30.00	55.00	60.00
2	Bowl, 10", 2 hdld.	55.00	95.00	110.00
	Bowl, 10", baker	60.00	100.00	110.00
3	Bowl, 10", oval baker	30.00	60.00	75.00
6	Bowl, 11", fruit, tab hdld.	65.00	110.00	125.00
	Bowl, 11", low ftd.	60.00	100.00	120.00
	Bowl, 12", relish, 5 pt.	45.00	70.00	75.00
	Bowl, 12", 4 ftd.	60.00	100.00	125.00
5	Bowl, 12", flat	55.00	90.00	95.00
	Bowl, 12", oval, 4 ftd.	65.00	95.00	125.00
	Bowl, 12½", console	55.00	75.00	80.00
	Bowl, 13"	55.00	90.00	100.00
14	Bowl, cream soup, w/liner plate	35.00	55.00	60.00
19	Butter w/cover, 5½"	150.00	300.00	410.00
	Candelabrum, 3-lite, keyhole	35.00	50.00	75.00
	Candlestick, 1-lite, keyhole	24.00	35.00	40.00
	Candlestick, 2-lite, keyhole	30.00	45.00	50.00
	Candy box w/cover, 4 ftd. "bowl"	85.00	145.00	195.00
1	Casserole, 10½", #912	195.00	400.00	
	Cheese (compote) & cracker (11½" plate)	45.00	85.00	110.00
	Comport, 4", fruit cocktail	20.00	28.00	30.00
	Comport, 7", tall	45.00	70.00	95.00

* Blue prices 25% to 30% more.

		Crystal	Yellow Amber	Pink *Green
	Creamer, ftd., 3400/68	20.00	26.00	30.00
	Creamer, tall, ftd.	22.00	30.00	35.00
	Cup, 3400/75	16.00	28.00	35.00
17	Cup, A.D., 3400/83	45.00	65.00	90.00
	Ice bucket	75.00	135.00	195.00
	Fruit/oyster cocktail, #3025, 4½ oz.	20.00	25.00	30.00
	Mayonnaise, w/liner & ladle (4 ftd. bowl)	45.00	65.00	80.00
	Pitcher, 50 oz., ftd., flattened sides	195.00	295.00	395.00
	Pitcher, 64 oz., #3130	215.00	325.00	400.00
	Pitcher, 64 oz., #3025	215.00	325.00	400.00
	Pitcher, 67 oz., squeezed middle, loop hdld.	225.00	375.00	425.00
	Pitcher, 76 oz.	125.00	350.00	425.00
	Pitcher, 80 oz., ball	225.00	395.00	550.00
	Pitcher w/cover, 76 oz., ftd., #3135	250.00	395.00	595.00
8	Plate, 6", bread/butter	8.00	10.00	12.00
	Plate, 6", sq., 2 hdld.	10.00	20.00	22.00
7	Plate, 7½", tea	12.00	22.00	25.00
	Plate, 8½"	20.00	25.00	30.00
9	Plate, 9½", dinner	45.00	75.00	100.00
	Plate, 10", grill, 3400/66, club luncheon	35.00	55.00	75.00

* Blue prices 25% to 30% more.

20

		Crystal	Yellow Amber	Pink *Green
	Plate, sandwich, 11½", tab hdld.	30.00	45.00	50.00
	Plate, sandwich, 12½", 2 hdld.	32.00	50.00	60.00
	Plate, sq., bread/butter	8.00	10.00	12.00
	Plate, sq., dinner	55.00	90.00	115.00
	Plate, sq., salad	12.00	22.00	25.00
	Plate, sq., servce	30.00	45.00	50.00
4	Platter, 11½	55.00	95.00	120.00
13	Platter, 13½" rect., w/tab handle	65.00	125.00	195.00
	Salt & pepper, pr., 3400/77	50.00	95.00	125.00
	Saucer, 3400/540 rnd.	5.00	7.00	8.00
	Saucer, A.D., squared, 3400/83	20.00	30.00	35.00
11	Stem, #1066, parfait	45.00	100.00	130.00
10	Stem, #3025, 7 oz., low fancy ft., sherbet	17.00	25.00	28.00
	Stem, #3025, 7 oz., high sherbet	18.00	30.00	33.00
12	Stem, #3025, 10 oz.	24.00	35.00	45.00
	Stem, #3130, 1 oz., cordial	50.00	90.00	150.00
	Stem, #3130, 3 oz., cocktail	18.00	32.00	35.00
	Stem, #3130, 6 oz., low sherbet	14.00	22.00	25.00
	Stem, #3130, 6 oz., tall sherbet	18.00	30.00	33.00
	Stem, #3130, 8 oz., water	22.00	30.00	45.00
	Stem, #3135, 3 oz., cocktail	18.00	32.00	35.00
	Stem, #3135, 6 oz., low sherbet	14.00	20.00	25.00
	Stem, #3135, 6 oz., tall sherbet	18.00	30.00	33.00
	Stem, #3135, 8 oz., water	22.00	30.00	33.00
	Stem, #3400, 6 oz., ftd., sherbet	15.00	20.00	25.00
	Stem, #3400, 9 oz., water	22.00	35.00	50.00
	Sugar, ftd., 3400/68	20.00	26.00	30.00
	Sugar, tall ftd.	20.00	30.00	35.00
	Tray, 7", hdld. relish	25.00	40.00	45.00
	Tray, 11", ctr. hdld. sand., 3400/10	35.00	50.00	60.00
	Tumbler, #3025, 4 oz.	16.00	24.00	28.00
	Tumbler, #3025, 10 oz.	20.00	30.00	35.00
	Tumbler, #3025, 12 oz.	25.00	40.00	45.00
	Tumbler, #3130, 5 oz., ftd.	16.00	28.00	33.00
	Tumbler, #3130, 8 oz., ftd.	22.00	30.00	35.00
	Tumbler, #3130, 10 oz., ftd.	25.00	35.00	40.00
	Tumbler, #3130, 12 oz., ftd.	30.00	40.00	50.00
	Tumbler, #3135, 5 oz., ftd.	16.00	30.00	35.00
	Tumbler, #3135, 8 oz., ftd.	22.00	35.00	40.00
	Tumbler, #3135, 10 oz., ftd.	25.00	35.00	45.00
	Tumbler, #3135, 12 oz., ftd.	30.00	40.00	50.00
16	Tumbler, #3400, 2½ oz., flat	35.00	75.00	85.00
	Tumbler, #3400, 12 oz., flat	22.00	30.00	35.00
	Tumbler, #3400, 14 oz., flat	30.00	40.00	50.00
	Tumbler, 12 oz., flat (2 styles) – 1 mid indent to match 67 oz. pitcher	25.00	50.00	60.00
	Tumbler, 6"	25.00	45.00	50.00
20	Vase, 5"	65.00	110.00	145.00
	Vase, 6", rippled sides	95.00	145.00	195.00
	Vase, 8", 2 styles	100.00	175.00	225.00
	Vase, 12", keyhole base w/neck indent	125.00	195.00	265.00

* Blue prices 25% to 30% more.

COLORS: AMBER, AMETHYST, BLACK, BLUE, CRYSTAL, GREEN, PINK

We recognize "Balda" to be a Central Glass Works pattern that was designed by Joseph Balda who was widely acclaimed for his Heisey designs. No one has uncovered a bona fide name from Central Glass Works except Etch #410; hence its designer's designation thus far. As with most Elegant patterns, stems are the most found items. Amethyst (lilac) as pictured here is the most often found color and consequently the most collected.

The Internet auctions exposed this pattern quickly to collectors. At first, there was a flurry of activity with rapidly rising prices. Now things have settled into more stabilized pricing and the collectors searching for "Balda" are able to shop around for suitable prices. There are likely additional pieces and/or colors to those currently listed. It is doubtful you will discover large batches of "Balda," except for stemware or plates, but it does happen every so often.

Another Central Glass pattern, Morgan, is also found on the same #1428 stem and tumbler line shown here in Amethyst. The Morgan pattern is etched on at least two additional stem lines (page 148), but may be found etched on several other Central lines. Let us know if you find additional stemware lines or pieces of "Balda."

1

		Blue Amethyst	Pink Green Amber
7	Bowl, 7" soup	65.00	45.00
	Candy and lid, cone shaped, 7⅝" tall	250.00	195.00
	Candlestick	65.00	45.00
	Cup	25.00	20.00
1	Decanter and stopper	450.00	325.00
	Ice bucket	295.00	195.00
	Pitcher	795.00	595.00
3	Plate, 6"	12.50	10.00
8	Plate, lunch	20.00	14.00
4	Plate, dinner	65.00	45.00
	Platter	95.00	65.00
	Saucer	6.00	4.00

		Blue Amethyst	Pink Green Amber
	Shaker, pr		150.00
9	Stem, champagne/sherbet	25.00	20.00
	Stem, claret	75.00	40.00
6	Stem, cordial	95.00	65.00
	Stem, water	45.00	30.00
5	Stem, wine	45.00	30.00
	Tumbler, ftd. juice	25.00	20.00
	Tumbler, ftd. tea	35.00	30.00
2	Tumbler, ftd. water	30.00	25.00
	Tumbler, ftd. whiskey	50.00	35.00
	Vase, 9"	195.00	135.00

COLORS: CRYSTAL, AZURE BLUE, TOPAZ YELLOW, AMBER, GREEN, PINK, RED, COBALT BLUE, BLACK AMETHYST

Baroque cream soups and individual shakers are elusive in colors, and to some extent, crystal. They have always been expensive. Speaking of shakers, the regular size came with both metal and glass tops. Today, most collectors prefer glass lids, but they are found sporadically. Glass lids were easily broken by over tightening them. Fostoria changed to metal lids before Baroque production was halted. Replacement lids were always metal. Metal tops are normally found on the later crystal patterns of Navarre, Chintz, Lido, and Meadow Rose that were etched onto Baroque blanks. Pitchers and punch bowls are not abundant; but blue ones are virtually impossible to find. Straight tumblers are more burdensome to find than footed ones, but are preferred over cone-shaped, footed pieces even though they are more expensive. The photo above illustrates two larger 9" sweetmeats compared to the smaller covered 7½" jelly.

28   29   28

Baroque has seven different candlesticks, and candles are one item that new collectors seek regardless of the pattern. There are many books out addressing this candlestick-collecting phenomenon, two of which are ours. These are called *Glass Candlesticks of the Depression Era*, volume 1 and volume 2.

You will find both 4" and 5½" single light candles and a 4½" double candle. The 6" three-light (triple) candlesticks are called candelabra when prisms are attached. Some collectors desire these elusive candelabra with original prism wires attached. Many collectors are exchanging modern wires for the old, rusty ones. Once prisms are secured properly (try needle nose pliers or medical hemostats), they rarely come off, even if moved. New prisms and wires are obtainable at lamp and hardware stores.

Triple candlesticks without the prisms have been located in all the colors listed above, but matching console bowls have yet to be found in red, cobalt blue, or amethyst. Some pieces of Azure Baroque appear to be light green (bad batches of blue that were sold anyhow). This light green color is not as prized as Azure. Fewer collectors track color variances; you likely could not find enough pieces of light green to complete a set and it would be challenging to try.

We have received several letters and e-mails about Wisteria Baroque vases, bowls, and candlesticks being discovered. Lancaster Colony produced a few pieces of Baroque in a color similar to Fostoria's Wisteria for Tiara. We have seen the bowl and vase, but not the candle. Our old Tiara catalogs do not show the candle. These items do have a purple/pink tint; do not pay collectible prices for Baroque pieces in this color. Baroque was never made in the original Fostoria Wisteria, which, by the way, does change tints in natural or artificial light.

		Crystal	Blue	Yellow
	Ashtray	10.00	22.00	15.00
	Bowl, cream soup	35.00	85.00	77.50
	Bowl, ftd., punch, 1½ gal., 8¼" x 13¼"	450.00	1,200.00	
20	Bowl, 3¾", rose	32.00	110.00	70.00
8, 12	Bowl, 4", hdld. (4 styles: sq., rnd., tab hdld. mint, 4⅝" tricorn)	12.50	28.00	22.00
	Bowl, 5", fruit	15.00	38.00	30.00
	Bowl, 6", cereal	20.00	50.00	38.00
	Bowl, 6", sq., sweetmeat	12.00	30.00	25.00
22	Bowl, 6", 3-toe nut	12.00	33.00	20.00
11	Bowl, 6", 2-part relish, sq.	14.00	30.00	22.00
	Bowl, 6½", oblong sauce	14.00	30.00	20.00
	Bowl, 6½", 2 pt. mayonnaise, oval tab hdl.	15.00	35.00	23.00
	Bowl, 7", 3 ftd.	12.50	25.00	25.00
29	Bowl, 7½", jelly, w/cover	45.00	145.00	85.00
	Bowl, 8", pickle	15.00	32.50	25.00
	Bowl, 8½", hdld.	30.00	65.00	45.00
23	Bowl, 9½", veg., oval	40.00	85.00	60.00
	Bowl, 10", hdld.	35.00	100.00	70.00
	Bowl, 10" x 7½", hdld.	30.00		
14	Bowl, 10", relish, 3 pt.	22.00	45.00	30.00
5	Bowl, 10½", hdld., 4 ftd.	35.00	85.00	65.00
	Bowl, 11", celery	28.00	45.00	35.00

		Crystal	Blue	Yellow
7	Bowl, 10½", salad	35.00	75.00	65.00
	Bowl, 11", rolled edge	30.00	80.00	60.00
	Bowl, 12", flared	30.00	45.00	35.00
	Candelabrum, 8¼", 2-lite, 16 lustre	100.00	200.00	150.00
	Candelabrum, 9½", 3-lite, 24 lustre	160.00	250.00	195.00
	Candle, 7¾", 8 lustre	50.00	90.00	80.00
	Candlestick, 4"	15.00	52.50	35.00
	Candlestick, 4½", 2-lite	20.00	55.00	45.00
9	Candlestick, 5½"	30.00	60.00	40.00
13	Candlestick, 6", 3-lite*	32.50	90.00	65.00
	Candy, 3 part w/cover	55.00	140.00	95.00
	Comport, 4¾"	20.00	50.00	33.00
	Comport, 6½"	22.00	55.00	40.00
2	Creamer, 3¼", indiv.	10.00	25.00	20.00
	Creamer, 3¾", ftd.	12.00	30.00	20.00
1	Cup	10.00	33.00	24.00
	Cup, 6 oz., punch	15.00	30.00	
19	Ice bucket	60.00	135.00	85.00
	Mayonnaise, 5½", w/liner	30.00	85.00	60.00
	Mustard, w/cover	50.00	110.00	85.00
	Oil, w/stopper, 5½"	85.00	350.00	200.00
	Pitcher, 6½"	100.00	800.00	450.00
	Pitcher, 7", ice lip	100.00	750.00	550.00
	Plate, 6"	5.00	12.00	10.00
	Plate, 7½"	8.00	17.00	11.00
	Plate, 8½"	9.00	22.50	18.00
	Plate, 9½"	20.00	67.50	47.50
18	Plate, 10", cake, hdld.	30.00	45.00	35.00
	Plate, 11", ctr. hdld., sandwich	30.00		
6	Plate, 14", torte	28.00	65.00	40.00
	Platter, 12", oval	40.00	85.00	52.50
	Salt & pepper, 2¾", pr.	50.00	150.00	105.00
	Salt & pepper, indiv., 2", pr.	50.00	210.00	160.00
26	Sauce dish	30.00	65.00	50.00
21	Sauce dish, divided	25.00	55.00	45.00
1	Saucer	2.00	7.00	6.00
24	Sherbet, 3¾", 5 oz.	12.00	25.00	18.00
	Stem, 6¾", 9 oz., water	18.00	38.00	25.00
3	Sugar, 3", indiv.	10.00	25.00	20.00
	Sugar, 3½", ftd.	12.00	30.00	20.00
28	Sweetmeat, covered, 9"	90.00	175.00	150.00
15	Tidbit, 3-toe flat	20.00	35.00	30.00
	Tray, 8" oblong, 7" w, tab hdl.	25.00	45.00	35.00
	Tray, 12½", oval	40.00	85.00	52.50
4	Tray, 6¼" for indiv. cream/sugar	15.00	25.00	20.00
25	Tumbler, 3½", 6½ oz., old-fashion	22.50	95.00	60.00
	Tumbler, 3", 3½ oz., ftd., cocktail	12.00	30.00	22.00
10	Tumbler, 6", 12 oz., ftd., tea	20.00	40.00	30.00
	Tumbler, 3¾", 5 oz., juice	15.00	50.00	33.00
	Tumbler, 5½", 9 oz., ftd., water	12.00	30.00	25.00
27	Tumbler, 4¼", 9 oz., water	25.00	55.00	37.50
	Tumbler, 5¾", 14 oz., tea	35.00	95.00	62.00
16	Vase, 6½"	50.00	125.00	100.00
17	Vase, 7"	60.00	160.00	115.00

* Red $150.00; Green $120.00; Black Amethyst $140.00; Cobalt Blue $140.00; Amber $75.00

BLACK FOREST, POSSIBLY PADEN CITY FOR VAN DEMAN & SON, LATE 1920S – EARLY 1930S

COLORS: AMBER, BLACK, ICE BLUE, CRYSTAL, GREEN, PINK, RED, COBALT

Black Forest items are continuing to attract attention on Internet auctions, but prices have settled down and are reaching more reasonable levels than they were exhibiting two years ago. Internet auctions had blown the former standard prices of Black Forest out of the water. Internet activity has also encouraged sales of Deerwood, a pattern often promoted incorrectly as Black Forest. The Black Forest design consists of moose and trees, while Deerwood shows deer and trees.

We are frequently asked about the etched, heavy goblets pictured on the right that were made in the 1970s in amber, amberina, dark green, blue, crystal, and ruby by L. G. Wright. These are retailing in the $18.00 to $30.00 range with red and blue on the upper side of that price although you may see them priced for more by sellers who do not know their manufacturing history. These newer goblets have a heavy, prevalent "Daisy and Button" cubed stem and are not accepted as Black Forest by most long-time collectors. Notice the three styles of ice containers pictured on the bottom of page 26. The blue one sold to an avid collector for a tidy sum — but it is the only one known!

		Amber	*Black	Crystal	Green	Pink	Red
	Batter jug			295.00			
	Bowl, 4½", finger				40.00		
	Bowl, 9¼", center hdld.				125.00	125.00	
4	Bowl, 11", console	95.00	150.00	65.00	125.00	125.00	
	Bowl, 11", fruit		150.00		125.00	125.00	
	Bowl, 13", console		195.00				
	Bowl, 3 ftd.			100.00			
	Cake plate, 2" pedestal	95.00	150.00		125.00	125.00	
2	Candlestick, mushroom style, Line 210, 2⅜"		50.00	95.00	50.00	85.00	85.00
	Candlestick double			100.00			
3	Candy dish, w/cover, several styles	155.00	250.00		225.00	225.00	
	Creamer, 2 styles, Line 210 shown	50.00	75.00	35.00	65.00	65.00	
	Comport, 4", low ftd.				75.00	75.00	
	Comport, 5½", high ftd.		125.00		100.00	100.00	
	Cup and saucer, 3 styles		125.00		100.00	100.00	150.00
	Decanter, w/stopper, 8½", 28 oz., bulbous				395.00	395.00	395.00
	Decanter w/stopper, 8¾", 24 oz., straight				295.00	395.00	395.00
	Egg cup, Line 210				195.00		
6	Ice bucket		225.00		125.00	125.00	
1	Ice pail, 6", 3" high	150.00					
7	Ice tub, 3 styles (ice blue $1,000.00), Line 210	160.00	250.00		195.00	195.00	
	Mayonnaise, with liner		175.00		125.00	125.00	
	Night set: pitcher, 6½", 42 oz. & tumbler				795.00	795.00	
	Pitcher, 8", 40 oz. (cobalt $1,500.00)						
	Pitcher, 8", 62 oz., night set			295.00			
	Pitcher, 9", 80 oz.					500.00	
	Pitcher, 10½", 72 oz., T-neck, bulbous bottom				625.00	625.00	
	Plate, 6½", bread/butter		35.00		30.00	30.00	
	Plate, 8", luncheon		50.00		40.00	40.00	
	Plate, 10", dinner		175.00				
	Plate, 11", 2 hdld.		125.00		65.00	65.00	
	Plate, 13¾", 2 hdld., Line 210				100.00	100.00	
	Relish, 10½", 5 pt. covered				595.00	595.00	
	Salt and pepper, pr.			125.00		175.00	
5	Server, center hdld.	50.00	40.00	35.00	50.00	35.00	
	Shot glass, 2 oz., 2½"	40.00					
	Stem, 2 oz., wine, 4¼"			17.50	50.00		
	Stem, 6 oz., champagne, 4¾"			17.50		30.00	
	Stem, 9 oz., water, 6"			22.50			
	Sugar, 2 styles, Line 210 shown	50.00	75.00	35.00	65.00	65.00	

*Add 20% for gold decorated.

25

	Amber	*Black	Crystal	Green	Pink	Red
Tumbler, 3 oz., juice, flat or footed, 3½"			50.00	95.00	95.00	
Tumbler, 8 oz., old fashion, 3⅞"				95.00	95.00	
Tumbler, 9 oz., ftd., 5½"	50.00					
Tumbler, 12 oz., tea, 5½"				125.00	125.00	
Vase, 6½" (cobalt $300.00)		195.00	100.00	175.00	175.00	
Vase, 8½", Line 210				150.00	150.00	
Vase, 10", 2 styles in black, Line 210		250.00		195.00	195.00	
Whipped cream pail	95.00					

COLORS: PINK, AMBER, PINK AND GREEN WITH CRYSTAL, GREEN, ALL WITH OPTIC

We saw one large set of pink Bo Peep for sale in an antique mall about ten years ago. Prices were more than we were willing to pay for stems at that time. Even today, we would have trouble selling for the prices being asked. We did buy the vase and pitcher shown here. The pitcher lid is undecorated, as are Tiffin pitcher lids. Another collector was pleased we left that set; he eventually bought it. One of the toughest lessons as a dealer is a desire to buy pieces you like. You have a tendency to pay too much and not be able to rapidly profit.

Last year we were contacted by a lady who said she had a set of green Tinkerbell which got us really excited, but it turned out to be Bo Peep. That was fine since it had pieces we had never seen before including parfaits, footed finger bowls, and juice tumblers. The only major concern was the amount of damaged pieces in the set. It had been used by a relative as everyday ware and it showed.

Monongah was forced out of business in the economic decline of the late 20s by the larger, more mechanized glass firms who were able to "hang on" after the Depression. It was absorbed by Hocking Glass Company. Bo Peep was made by Monongah, although the shapes are very analogous to those we identify as Tiffin. Perhaps these moulds were sold to Tiffin in an effort to stay afloat or maybe Hocking sold them after the takeover, as they did not then make glass of this quality.

		Pink Green
	Finger bowl, ftd., #6102	95.00
7	Jug w/cover, #20	995.00
	Jug w/o cover, #20	895.00
3	Plate, 7½", salad	25.00
	Stem, cocktail, #6102	65.00
4	Stem, high sherbet, #6102	65.00
9	Stem, low sherbet, #6102	60.00
	Stem, parfait, #6102	125.00
1	Stem, water, #6102	125.00
	Stem, wine, #6102	95.00
8	Tumbler, 5 oz., ftd., juice/seltzer, #6102	75.00
5	Tumbler, 9 oz., ftd., water/table, #6102	65.00
6	Tumbler, 12 oz., ftd., iced tea, #6102	85.00
2	Vase, 9", ruffled edge, #0713	595.00

Grape

COLORS: AZURE BLUE, CRYSTAL, EBONY, GREEN, ORCHID, ROSE

Pictured are a few of the more collected Fostoria Brocades, demonstrating that you can intermingle different designs rather than buy only one. Designs are shown independently here and on pages 29 and 30. Hopefully, the categorizing of small group shots will make recognition simple. You should know that Oak Leaf pattern with iridescence is correctly referred to as Oakwood and Paradise with iridescence is called Victoria, Decoration #71.

		Crystal	#290 Oakleaf Green/Rose	Ebony	#72 Oakwood Orchid/Azure	#289 Paradise Green/Orchid	#73 Palm Leaf Rose/Green	Blue	#287 Grape Green	Orchid
	Bonbon, #2375	30.00	45.00		50.00		50.00		40.00	
	Bowl, finger, #869	60.00	70.00		75.00					
	Bowl, 4½", mint, #2394	30.00	40.00							
	Bowl, 7½", "D," cupped rose, #2339							85.00	60.00	110.00
	Bowl, 10", scroll hdld, #2395	90.00	155.00	145.00			200.00			
12	Bowl, 10", 2 hdld, #2375	80.00	125.00		175.00		165.00			
	Bowl, 10½", "A," 3 ftd., #2297					95.00		95.00	70.00	120.00
	Bowl, 10½", "C," sm roll rim, deep, #2297							95.00	70.00	120.00
	Bowl, 10½", "C," pedestal ftd., #2315					95.00				
	Bowl, 11", roll edge ctrpiece, #2329					100.00		155.00	135.00	175.00
	Bowl, 11", ctrpiece, #2375				195.00		155.00			
	Bowl, 11", cornucopia hdld, #2398	100.00	135.00							
8	Bowl, 12", 3 toe, flair rim, #2394	100.00	125.00		195.00		150.00			
	Bowl, 12", console, #2375	85.00	115.00							
2	Bowl, 12" low, "saturn rings," #2362					85.00		115.00	90.00	135.00
	Bowl, 12", hexagonal, 3 tab toe, #2342	110.00	135.00		210.00	100.00				
4	Bowl, 12", "A," 3 tab toe, #2297					115.00		125.00	110.00	135.00
	Bowl, 12½", "E," flat, shallow, #2297							125.00	100.00	135.00
	Bowl, 13", center piece rnd., #2329					140.00		225.00	195.00	235.00
	Bowl, center piece oval, #2375½		135.00		175.00		250.00			
	Bowl, 13", oval, roll edge w/grid frog, #2371					175.00		225.00	185.00	250.00
	Bowl, #2415 comb, candle hdld.	120.00	175.00	185.00	295.00		250.00			
	Candlestick, 2", mushroom, #2372					25.00		35.00	30.00	35.00
	Candlestick, 2", 3 toe, #2394	40.00	55.00				70.00			
	Candlestick, 3", scroll, #2395	50.00	65.00	75.00						
	Candlestick, 3", #2375	45.00	60.00		65.00		75.00			
	Candlestick, 3", stack disc, #2362					40.00		35.00	30.00	35.00
1	Candlestick, 4", #2324					35.00		35.00	30.00	35.00
13	Candlestick, 5", 2395½						95.00			
	Candlestick, hex mushroom, #2375½	45.00	55.00		75.00					
	Candlestick, trindle, #2383 ea.						145.00			
9	Candy box, cov., 3 pt, #2331	100.00	150.00	200.00	250.00			185.00	145.00	200.00
11	Candy, box, cone lid, #2380	100.00	145.00			115.00				
	Candy, cov., oval, #2395		135.00		200.00					
	Cheese & cracker, #2368	65.00	75.00							
	Cigarette & cov. (small), #2391	65.00	135.00	120.00	175.00					

Oakwood

Oak Leaf

14

8

7

3

9

	Crystal	#290 Oakleaf Green/Rose	Ebony	#72 Oakwood Orchid/Azure	#289 Paradise Green/Orchid	#73 Palm Leaf Rose/Green	Blue	#287 Grape Green	Orchid
Cigarette & cov. (large), #2391	85.00	135.00	125.00	185.00					
Comport, 6", #2400						125.00			
Comport, 7" tall, twist stem, #2327					75.00		75.00	55.00	75.00
Comport, 8", short, ftd., #2350					65.00				
Comport, 8", pulled stem, #2400				115.00					
Comport, 11", stack disc stem, ftd., #2362					100.00		125.00	100.00	120.00
10 Ice bucket, #2378	100.00	145.00		225.00		155.00	100.00	90.00	95.00
Ice bucket, w/drainer, handle & tongs, #2378				150.00		140.00	125.00	130.00	
Jug, #5000	395.00	595.00		995.00	695.00				
Lemon, "bow" or open hdld, #2375	30.00	45.00		65.00	60.00	40.00		40.00	
Mayonnaise, #2315	55.00	70.00		225.00					
Plate, mayonnaise, #2332	20.00	30.00		35.00					
Plate, 6", #2283	15.00	20.00							
Plate, 7", #2283	20.00	25.00		35.00					
Plate, 8", sq., #2419						35.00			
Plate, 8", #2283	22.00	30.00		45.00					
Plate, 10", cake, #2375	65.00	90.00		125.00		155.00			
Plate, 12", salver, #2315	100.00	125.00		160.00					
Plate, 13", lettuce, #2315	60.00	90.00		145.00					
Stem, ¾ oz., cordial, #877	65.00			165.00					
Stem, 2¾ oz., wine, #877	35.00			95.00					
Stem, 3½ oz., cocktail, #877	25.00			65.00					
Stem, 4 oz., claret, #877	35.00			95.00					
Stem, 6 oz., high sherbet, #877	32.50			65.00					
Stem, 6 oz., low sherbet, #877	22.50			55.00					
Stem, 10 oz., water, #877	45.00			100.00					
Sugar pail, #2378	105.00	150.00		225.00		250.00			
7 Sweetmeat, hex 2 hdld bowl, #2375	35.00	45.00		50.00		60.00		40.00	
Tray, rnd, fleur de lis hdld., #2387							95.00	90.00	95.00
3 Tray, ctr, hdld., #2342, octagonal	65.00	95.00		150.00	75.00	140.00	95.00	90.00	95.00
Tumbler, 2½ oz., ftd. whiskey, #877	30.00	75.00							
Tumbler, 4½ oz., ftd. oyster cocktail	22.50								
Tumbler, 5 oz., ftd. juice, #877	30.00								
Tumbler, 5½ oz., parfait, #877	40.00	65.00							
Tumbler, 9 oz., ftd., #877				90.00	60.00				
Tumbler, 12 oz., ftd. tea, #877				120.00	65.00				

Paradise

Palm Leaf

		Crystal	#290 Oakleaf Green/Rose	Ebony	#72 Oakwood Orchid/Azure	#289 Paradise Green/Orchid	#73 Palm Leaf Rose/Green	Blue	#287 Grape Green	Orchid
	Urn & cover, #2413		200.00		425.00		495.00			
	Vase, 3", 4", #4103, bulbous	50.00	60.00	75.00		70.00		85.00	70.00	80.00
	Vase, 5", 6", #4103, optic					75.00		105.00	90.00	100.00
	Vase, 6", #4100, flat straight side optic					85.00		105.00	90.00	100.00
	Vase, 6", #4105, scallop rim	65.00	85.00		140.00	85.00				
	Vase, 7", 9", ftd. urn, #2369	85.00	100.00		140.00	120.00	150.00			
14	Vase, 8", cupped melon, #2408						255.00			
	Vase, 8", #2292, ftd. flair flat, straight side	85.00	100.00	125.00						
	Vase, 8", #4100					95.00		125.00	115.00	135.00
	Vase, 8", #4105	70.00	95.00		265.00		250.00			
	Vase, 8", melon, #2387	90.00	115.00		210.00					
	Vase, 8½" fan, #2385	150.00	200.00		450.00		285.00			
	Vase, 10½" ftd., #2421						295.00			
	Vase, sm. or lg. window & cov., #2373	150.00	200.00	350.00	365.00		350.00			
	Whip cream, scallop 2 hdld. bowl, #2375	35.00	50.00		55.00		40.00			
	Whip cream pail, #2378	90.00	135.00		195.00				40.00	

BROCADE, MCKEE, 1930S

COLORS: PINK AND GREEN

McKee's Brocade only came in the one design unlike Fostoria's multitude. We usually hear it referred to by collectors as "Poinset-tia" and sometimes "Palm Tree" though we have found no official designation for either appellation. We have found a few more pieces but no one seems to price Brocade reasonably. Usually sellers of this pattern assume it to be rare or hard to get and price it accordingly.

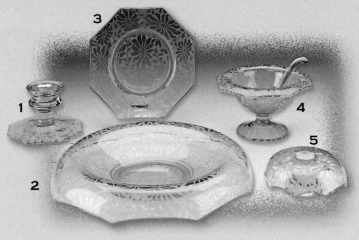

		Pink/Green
	Bowl, 12", flared edge	50.00
	Bowl, center, hdld. nut	40.00
2	Bowl, 12", console, rolled edge	50.00
5	Candlestick, roll edge, octagonal	18.00
1	Candlestick, octagonal ft.	22.00
	Candy box/cover	75.00
	Candy jar, ftd., w/cover	65.00
	Cheese and cracker	55.00
	Compote, 10", flared edge	50.00
	Compote, cone shape, octagonal	50.00
3, 4	Mayonnaise, 3 pc., w/liner & spoon	45.00
	Salver, ftd. (cake stand)	45.00
	Server, center hdld.	35.00
	Vase, 11", bulbous	175.00

COLORS: PINK, CRYSTAL

"Bubble Girl" has been a mysterious pattern for glass dealers and collectors for over 25 years. The best guess now is that an etching company used different mould blanks from several companies to illustrate this pattern. In the early 80s, several dealers discussed this pattern over dinner. Plates were showing up marked Cambridge, but the stems all were Fry blanks which confused us terribly then. "Bubble Girl" was the name proposed as the reclining woman looks to be blowing bubbles. We had jokes about Lawrence Welk and several other references to bubbles and champagne, but "Bubble Girl" seemed to win over "Champagne Lady."

We bought several different Fry stems hoping to research it someday, but they were stored for future use and forgotten. A few years ago, we found a Heisey candle and a friend found a Heisey Octagon bowl for us. It took some diligent searching to unearth the stems, but during the interim we found some footed water and tea tumblers which appear to be Fry also.

A collector in Georgia has since uncovered additional pieces on Cambridge blanks including cups and saucers. We have listed the newly found items and wonder how many others await discovery. The Internet has exposed pieces that may never have been uncovered for years; so in that way, it has helped our business.

Most plates are unmarked, but others have Cambridge's triangle in a "C." Stems and tumblers are Fry with bowls and candles being Heisey. This pattern needs your input; so if you see additional items, let us know.

		Pink/Crystal			Pink/Crystal
1	Bowl, 5⅜", 2-hdld., Heisey, Octagon, 1229 Jelly	55.00		Saucer, 5¾"	20.00
3	Bowl, 11½", Octagon, 1229 Floral	65.00		Shaker	125.00
	Bowl, 12", oval	125.00		Stem, 3 oz., 4¾", wine	37.50
4	Candlestick, 3½", Heisey, Pluto #114	37.50	5	Stem, 3½ oz., 4⅜", cocktail	30.00
	Cup	100.00		Stem, 6 oz., 6¼", parfait	50.00
	Plate, 6¼", sherbet	12.50	6	Stem, 7 oz., 5⅛", Fry stem, high sherbet	22.50
	Plate, 6⅝", Octagon, 2-hdld.	45.00	7	Stem, 9 oz., 7", Fry stem, water	35.00
2	Plate, 8½" luncheon	18.00	8	Tumbler, 10 oz., 5⅛", Fry blank, ftd. water	25.00
	Relish, 5-part	75.00	9	Tumbler 15 oz., 6¼", Fry blank, ftd. ice tea	35.00

COLORS: CRYSTAL, YELLOW; SOME PINK

Cadena stemware is a collector's dream, but finding serving pieces is a nightmare. Even if you may be willing to pay the price for them, they will only appear infrequently. Even Internet auctions have been void of items save the omnipresent stems. We have seen a few bowls occasionally in 27 years of searching, but they have been more highly cherished by their owners even with a thumb-sized piece missing in one case. Never leave a rare piece if you come across it at a reasonable price. Someone desires it, even if you do not.

A few pieces of pink have been surfacing, but they have all been stems. Tiffin pitchers were sold either with or without a lid. The top edge of pitchers without lids were often curved in or "cupped" so much that a lid will not fit inside the lip. We found this out by buying a yellow lid separately for the pitcher shown. The only way it would have fit inside the rim would have involved cutting it down. Remember that the pitcher cover does not have an etching, even though the Cadena pitcher itself will.

		Crystal	Pink Yellow
	Bowl, cream soup, #5831	25.00	45.00
	Bowl, finger, ftd., #041	25.00	45.00
	Bowl, grapefruit, ftd., #251	50.00	110.00
	Bowl, 6", hdld., #5831	20.00	30.00
	Bowl, 10", pickle, #5831	30.00	45.00
	Bowl, 12", console, ftd., #5831	35.00	65.00
	Candlestick, #5831	30.00	50.00
1	Creamer, #5831	20.00	30.00
	Cup, #5831	40.00	100.00
	Decanter w/stopper	140.00	300.00
	Mayonnaise, ftd., w/liner, #5831	50.00	85.00
	Oyster cocktail, #065	20.00	32.00
3	Pitcher, ftd., #194	200.00	300.00
	Pitcher, ftd., w/cover, #194	250.00	400.00
	Plate, 6", #8814	8.00	12.00

		Crystal	Pink Yellow
	Plate, 7¾", #5831	10.00	20.00
	Plate, 9¼"	45.00	75.00
	Saucer, #5831	10.00	25.00
9	Stem, 4¾", sherbet/sundae	16.00	25.00
6	Stem, 5¼", cocktail	22.00	30.00
	Stem, 5¼", ¾ oz., cordial	65.00	130.00
	Stem, 6", wine	30.00	50.00
	Stem, 6⁵⁄₁₆", 8 oz., parfait	35.00	60.00
5	Stem, 6½", champagne	22.00	28.00
4	Stem, 7½", water, #065	30.00	35.00
2	Sugar, #5831	20.00	25.00
	Tumbler, 3¼", ftd., bar, #065	20.00	32.00
8	Tumbler, 4¼", ftd., juice, #065	22.00	28.00
7	Tumbler, 5¼", ftd., water, #065	25.00	30.00
	Vase, 9"	115.00	165.00

Colors: crystal, crystal and Crown Tuscan with gold decoration

Pictured are pages from a 1951 Candlelight pamphlet of the type frequently given to people who were registering a crystal pattern for bridal gifts. We have copied it to show you the #3776 stems typically found in Candlelight. Through these brochure pages and the legends for each item in the photograph, we hope we have solved some identification questions asked us over the years.

The photo below shows the Candlelight stem line #3114. Candlelight is not as plentiful as other Cambridge patterns. Candlelight was designed in two ways. The pattern was cut into some pieces, but was acid etched on others. The cut items are sparse, but a wine and water goblet is pictured. There are fewer collectors for cut pieces due to scarcity. Etching was accomplished by covering the glass except where the design was desired and then dipping the glass into acid. Cutting was accomplished by a skilled hand on a wheel turning to form the design.

With many collectors hunting for this pattern, there is a lack of shakers (both footed and flat), butter dishes, basic serving pieces, candlesticks, and even cups and saucers. Do not pass any of those items if you have a chance to buy them. Again, even if you don't want them, someone does.

Dealers should note that, today, when people ask for wine goblets, you might need to find out if they want water goblets. Formerly, wine goblets held 2½ to 4 ounces; but now, many people think of wine goblets as holding 8 or 9 ounces. Thus, what they want for serving wine is actually a water goblet.

		Crystal
	Bonbon, 7", ftd., 2 hdld., #3900/130	40.00
	Bowl, 10", 4 toed, flared, #3900/54	85.00
	Bowl, 11", 2 hdld., #3900/34	95.00
	Bowl, 11", 4 ftd., fancy edge, #3400/48	100.00
	Bowl, 11½", ftd., 2 hdld., #3900/28	85.00
	Bowl, 12", 4 ftd., flared, #3400/4	85.00
	Bowl, 12", 4 ftd., oblong, #3400/160	90.00
	Bowl, 12", 4 toed, flared, #3900/62	90.00
	Bowl, 12", 4 toed, oval, hdld., #3900/65	110.00
	Butter dish, 5", #3400/52	295.00
	Candle, 5", #3900/67	60.00
	Candle, 6", 2-lite, #3900/72	75.00
	Candle, 6", 3-lite, #3900/74	95.00
	Candlestick, 5", #646	65.00
	Candlestick, 6", 2-lite, #647	75.00
	Candlestick, 6", 3-lite, #1338	95.00
	Candy box and cover, 3-part, #3500/57	165.00
15	Candy jar, 10", #3500/41	195.00
	Candy w/lid, rnd., div., #3900/165	60.00
	Cocktail shaker, 36 oz., #P101	225.00
	Comport, 5", cheese, #3900/135	45.00
	Comport, 5⅜", blown, #3121	80.00
	Comport, 5½", #3900/136	70.00
	Creamer, #3900/41	25.00
	Creamer, indiv., #3900/40	25.00
	Cruet, 6 oz., w/stopper, #3900/100	175.00
	Cup, #3900/17	33.00
	Decanter, 28 oz., ftd., #1321	265.00
6	Ice bucket, #3900/671	175.00
5	Icer, 2 pc., cocktail, #968	120.00
	Lamp, hurricane, #1617	225.00
	Lamp, hurricane, keyhole, w/bobeche, #1603	275.00
	Lamp, hurricane, w/bobeche, #1613	325.00
	Mayonnaise, 3 pc., #3900/129	75.00
	Mayonnaise, div., 4 pc., #3900/111	85.00
	Mayonnaise, ftd., 2 pc., #3900/19	75.00
	Nut cup, 3", 4 ftd., #3400/71	70.00

		Crystal
	Oil, 6 oz., #3900/100	125.00
11	Pitcher, Doulton, #3400/141	435.00
	Plate, 6½", #3900/20	14.00
	Plate, 8", 2 hdld., #3900/131	30.00
	Plate, 8", salad, #3900/22	22.00
	Plate, 10½", dinner, #3900/24	85.00
	Plate, 12", 4 toed, #3900/26	75.00
	Plate, 13", torte, 4 toed, #3900/33	85.00
	Plate, 13½", cake, 2 hdld., #3900/35	85.00
	Plate, 13½", cracker, #3900/135	75.00
	Plate, 14", rolled edge, #3900/166	85.00
	Relish, 7", 2 hdld., #3900/123	45.00
	Relish, 7", div., 2 hdld., #3900/124	50.00
8	Relish, 8", 3 part, #3400/91	65.00
	Relish, 9", 3 pt., #3900/125	65.00
	Relish, 12", 3 pt., #3900/126	75.00
	Relish, 12", 5 pt., #3900/120	85.00
	Salt & pepper, pr., #3900/1177	140.00
13	Salt & pepper, ftd., #3400/77	130.00
	Saucer, #3900/17	7.00
	Stem, 1 oz., cordial, #3776	95.00
1	Stem, 1 oz., cordial cut	150.00
	Stem, 2 oz., sherry, trumpet, #7966	90.00
15, 2	Stem, 2½ oz., wine, #3111, w/ball, 3114, w/rings	70.00
	Stem, 3 oz., cocktail, #3114	35.00
	Stem, 3 oz., cocktail, #3776	35.00
	Stem, 3½ oz., wine, #3776	65.00
	Stem, 4 oz., cocktail, #7801	32.00
	Stem, 4½ oz., claret, #3776	75.00
	Stem, 4½ oz., oyster cockt ail, #3114	35.00
	Stem, 4½ oz., oyster cocktail, #3776	35.00
	Stem, 7 oz., low sherbet, #3114	20.00
	Stem, 7 oz., low sherbet, #3776	20.00
	Stem, 7 oz., tall sherbet, #3114	28.00
	Stem, 7 oz., tall sherbet, #3776	26.00
	Stem, 9 oz., water, #3776	50.00
16	Stem, 9 oz., water, cut	75.00
10	Stem, 10 oz., water, #3114	50.00
7	Sugar, #3900/41	25.00
	Sugar, indiv., #3900/40	35.00
4	Tumbler, 5 oz., ftd., juice, #3114	30.00
	Tumbler, 5 oz., juice, #3776	30.00
3	Tumbler, 10 oz., ftd., #3114	37.50
14	Tumbler, 12 oz., ftd., iced tea, #3114	45.00
	Tumbler, 12 oz., iced tea, #3776	45.00
	Tumbler, 13 oz., #3900/115	50.00
	Vase, 5", ftd., bud, #6004	95.00
12	Vase, 5", globe, #1309	85.00
	Vase, 6", ftd., #6004	100.00
	Vase, 8", ftd., #6004	120.00
	Vase, 9", ftd., keyhole, #1237	125.00
	Vase, 10", bud, #274	95.00
	Vase, 11", ftd., pedestal, #1299	185.00
9	Vase, 11", ftd., #278	135.00
	Vase, 12", ftd., keyhole, #1238	175.00
	Vase, 13", ftd, #279	195.00

Cut Candlelight

COLORS: CRYSTAL, BLUE, PINK, YELLOW, BLACK, RED, COBALT BLUE, GREEN, CARAMEL SLAG

New collectors should know that not all Candlewick has a ball in its stem. Note the Ritz blue oyster cocktail shown on page 38. After explaining the story of finding a dozen of these at an antique show where no one recognized them, we showed one in the previous book so you would know what they were. Lo and behold, we lately spotted four more in an antique mall in Ohio for a very inexpensive price.

Tumbler and stemware identification is a principal concern of new collectors of Candlewick. Stemware line 400/190 comes with a hollow stem. Although not pictured this time, hollow stem should be easy to understand. The tumblers designated 400/19 have flat bases with knobs around that base (page 40) as opposed to 400/18 that has a domed foot. The 400/... was Imperial's factory designation for each piece. If you can find a copy of the first *Elegant Glassware of the Depression Era* book, there is a 15-page reprint of Imperial's Catalog B showing Candlewick listings as distributed by the factory. Room does not permit the liberty of that catalog now.

The mid 30s Viennese Blue (light blue) Candlewick continues to sell well if priced appropriately, but higher priced red and black items have presently leveled off. One of the problems has been the many colored reproductions of Candlewick coming into the market. Candlewick was never made by Imperial in Jadite, but numerous Jadite pieces continue to plague the market from an Ohio glass company. Dalzell Viking made red and cobalt blue pieces before they went bankrupt a few years ago and many investors (and we use that word reluctantly,) rushed to their outlet store to buy these pieces including punch sets.

Ruby and black fancy bowls sell in the ballpark of $225.00 to $250.00 with the Viennese blue pieces bringing 50% to 60% of that. Ruby stems continue to be found in the 3400 and 3800 lines with most of these selling in the $85.00 to $120.00 range. However, cordials are selling in Ruby and Ritz blue (cobalt) from $125.00 to $175.00. Other Ritz blue stems are fetching $125.00 to $175.00. All of these original colors of Candlewick were presented before 1943.

Collectors and non-collectors alike admire the 72-hole birthday cake plate. Imperial made these cake plates in Cape Cod and Tradition also. Candlewick ones are difficult to find without scratches or gouges from cake cuttings over the years. Be sure to notice the hanging lamp on page 36. There is a cutting on the shades and the matching center piece. This was one of a pair found in Louisville, Kentucky, several years ago. It was intriguing watching the photographers figure how to suspend it for a photo, although intriguing is not one of the adjectives we heard used while trying to hang it. It was more cumbersome than it looked.

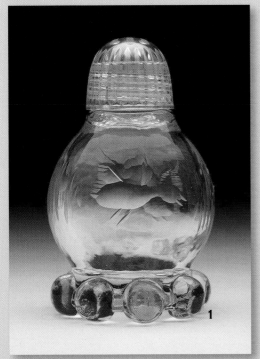

CANDLEWICK

		Crystal
8	Ashtray, eagle, 6½", 1776/1	50.00
	Ashtray, heart, 4½", 400/172	8.00
	Ashtray, heart, 5½", 400/173	10.00
	Ashtray, heart, 6½", 400/174	12.00
	Ashtray, indiv., 400/64	8.00
6	Ashtray, oblong, 4½", 400/134/1	5.00
56	Ashtray, round, 2¾", 400/19	8.00
57	Ashtray, round, 4", 400/33	10.00
58	Ashtray, round, 5", 400/133	12.00
	Ashtray, square, 3¼", 400/651	30.00
	Ashtray, square, 4½", 400/652	30.00
	Ashtray, square, 5¾", 400/653	40.00
	Ashtray, 6", matchbook holder center, 400/60	165.00
	Ashtray set, 3 pc. rnd. nesting (crystal or colors), 400/550	33.00
	Ashtray set, 3 pc. sq. nesting, 400/650	105.00
69	Ashtray set, 4 pc. bridge (cigarette holder at side), 400/118	50.00
	Basket, 5", beaded hdld., 400/273	225.00
	Basket, 6½", hdld., 400/40/0	32.50
	Basket, 11", hdld., 400/73/0	265.00
	Bell, 4", 400/179	85.00
	Bell, 5", 400/108	95.00
67	Bottle, bitters, w/tube, 4 oz., 400/117	75.00
61	Bottle, cologne, 4 bead, E408	75.00
	Bowl, bouillon, 2 hdld., 400/126	45.00
	Bowl, #3400, finger, ftd.	35.00
	Bowl, #3800, finger	35.00
	Bowl, 4½", nappy, 3 ftd., 400/206	80.00
	Bowl, 4¾", round, 2 hdld., 400/42B	12.50
	Bowl, 5", cream soup, 400/50	40.00
	Bowl, 5", fruit, 400/1F	12.00
	Bowl, 5", heart w/handle, 400/49H	22.00
	Bowl, 5", square, 400/231	95.00
51	Bowl, 5½", heart, 400/53H	20.00
	Bowl, 5½", jelly, w/cover, 400/59	75.00
	Bowl, 5½", sauce, deep, 400/243	40.00
	Bowl, 6", baked apple, rolled edge, 400/53X	35.00
	Bowl, 6", cottage cheese, 400/85	25.00
	Bowl, 6", fruit, 400/3F	12.00

		Crystal
	Bowl, 6", heart w/hand., 400/51H	32.00
	Bowl, 6", mint w/hand., 400/51F	22.00
20	Bowl, 6", round, div., 2 hdld., 400/52	22.00
	Bowl, 6", 2 hdld., 400/52B	15.00
	Bowl, 6", 3 ftd., 400/183	60.00
	Bowl, 6", sq., 400/232	125.00
	Bowl, 6½", relish, 2 pt., 400/84	25.00
	Bowl, 6½", 2 hdld., 400/181	30.00
	Bowl, 7", round, 400/5F	25.00
	Bowl, 7", round, 2 hdld., 400/62B	17.50
	Bowl, 7", relish, sq., div., 400/234	150.00
	Bowl, 7", ivy, high, bead ft., 400/188	245.00
	Bowl, 7", lily, 4 ft., 400/74J	80.00
	Bowl, 7", relish, 400/60	25.00
	Bowl, 7", sq., 400/233	155.00
	Bowl, 7¼", rose, ftd. w/crimp edge, 400/132C	550.00
	Bowl, 7½", pickle/celery, 400/57	27.50
	Bowl, 7½", lily, bead rim, ftd., 400/75N	350.00
	Bowl, 7½", belled (console base), 400/127B	75.00
	Bowl, 8", round, 400/7F	37.50
	Bowl, 8", relish, 2 pt., 400/268	20.00
	Bowl, 8", cov. veg., 400/65/1	375.00
	Bowl, 8½", rnd., 400/69B	35.00
	Bowl, 8½", nappy, 4 ftd., 400/74B	75.00
	Bowl, 8½", 3 ftd., 400/182	145.00
	Bowl, 8½", 2 hdld., 400/72B	22.00
	Bowl, 8½", pickle/celery, 400/58	20.00
	Bowl, 8½", relish, 4 pt., 400/55	22.00
	Bowl, 9", round, 400/10F	50.00
	Bowl, 9", crimp, ftd., 400/67C	185.00
	Bowl, 9", sq., fancy crimp edge, 4 ft., 400/74SC	85.00
	Bowl, 9", heart, 400/49H	125.00
	Bowl, 9", heart w/hand., 400/73H	150.00
	Bowl, 10", 400/13F	45.00
	Bowl, 10", banana, 400/103E	1,750.00
	Bowl, 10", 3 toed, 400/205	175.00
	Bowl, 10", belled (punch base), 400/128B	95.00
	Bowl, 10", cupped edge, 400/75F	45.00
	Bowl, 10", deep, 2 hdld., 400/113A	165.00
	Bowl, 10", divided, deep, 2 hdld., 400/114A	165.00
	Bowl, 10", fruit, bead stem (like compote), 400/103F	210.00
	Bowl, 10", relish, oval, 2 hdld., 400/217	40.00
	Bowl, 10", relish, 3 pt., 3 ft., 400/208	115.00
	Bowl, 10", 3 pt., w/cover, 400/216	600.00
	Bowl, 10½", belled, 400/63B	60.00
	Bowl, 10½", butter/jam, 3 pt., 400/262	255.00
50	Bowl, 10½", salad, 400/75B	40.00
21	Bowl, 10½", relish, 3 section, 400/256	30.00
	Bowl, 11", celery boat, oval, 400/46	65.00
	Bowl, 11", centerpiece, flared, 400/13B	55.00
	Bowl, 11", float, inward rim, ftd., 400/75F	40.00
	Bowl, 11", oval, 400/124A	300.00
	Bowl, 11", oval w/partition, 400/125A	325.00
	Bowl, 12", round, 400/92B	45.00
	Bowl, 12", belled, 400/106B	100.00

73

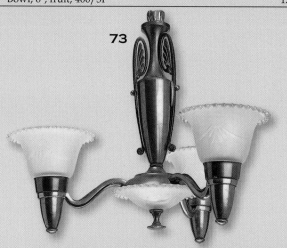

30

	Crystal
Bowl, 12", cupped, float, console, rnd., 400/92F	40.00
Bowl, 12", hdld., 400/113B	150.00
Bowl, 12", shallow, 400/17F	47.50
Bowl, 12", relish, oblong, 4 sect., 400/215	110.00
Bowl, 13", centerpiece, mushroom, 400/92L	60.00
Bowl, 13", float, 1½" deep, 400/101	65.00
Bowl, 13½", relish, 5 pt., 400/209	82.50
Bowl, 14", belled, 400/104B	95.00
Bowl, 14", oval, flared, 400/131B	325.00
Butter and jam set, 5 piece, 400/204	495.00
Butter, w/cover, rnd., 5½", 400/144	35.00
Butter, w/cover, no beads, California, 400/276	140.00
Butter, w/bead top, ¼ lb., 400/161	30.00
53 Cake stand, 10", low foot, 400/67D	60.00
Cake stand, 11", high foot, 400/103D	75.00
68 Calendar, 1947, desk	275.00
Candleholder, 3 way, beaded base, 400/115	135.00
Candleholder, 2-lite, 400/100	24.00
Candleholder, flat, 3½", 400/280	40.00
Candleholder, 3½", rolled edge, 400/79R	17.50
Candleholder, 3½", w/fingerhold, 400/81	60.00
Candleholder, flower, 4", 2 bead stem, 400/66F	65.00
Candleholder, flower, 4½", 2 bead stem, 400/66C	65.00
Candleholder, 4½", 3 toed, 400/207	120.00
Candleholder, 3-lite on cir. bead. ctr., 400/147	45.00
Candleholder, 5", hdld./bowled up base, 400/90	65.00
Candleholder, 5", heart shape, 400/40HC	125.00
Candleholder, 5½", 3 bead stems, 400/224	150.00
Candleholder, flower, 5" (epergne inset), 400/40CV	210.00
Candleholder, 5", flower, 400/40C	35.00
Candleholder, 6½", tall, 3 bead stems, 400/175	175.00
Candleholder, flower, 6", round, 400/40F	40.00
Candleholder, urn, 6", holders on cir. ctr. bead, 400/129R	185.00
Candleholder, flower, 6½", square, 400/40S	85.00
Candleholder, mushroom, 400/86	40.00
Candleholder, flower, 9", centerpiece, 400/196FC	265.00
Candy box, round, 5½", 400/59	50.00
Candy box, sq., 6½", rnd. lid, 400/245	395.00
Candy box, w/cover, 7", 400/259	150.00

		Crystal
	Candy box, w/cover, 7" partitioned, 400/110	130.00
	Candy box, w/cover, round, 7", 3 sect., 400/158	250.00
	Candy box, w/cover, beaded, ft., 400/140	550.00
	Cigarette box w/cover, 400/134	35.00
66	Cigarette holder, Bicentennial	35.00
44	Cigarette holder, 3", bead ft., 400/44	40.00
	Cigarette set: 6 pc. (cigarette box & 4 rect. ashtrays), 400/134/6	67.50
7	Clock, 4", round	310.00
	Coaster, 4", 400/78	10.00
	Coaster, w/spoon rest, 400/226	18.00
	Cocktail, seafood w/bead ft., 400/190	90.00
	Cocktail set: 2 pc., plate w/indent; cocktail, 400/97	40.00
	Compote, 4½", 400/63B	40.00
	Compote, 5", 3 bead stems, 400/220	90.00
	Compote, 5½", 4 bead stem, 400/45	30.00
	Compote, 5½, low, plain stem, 400/66B	22.00
	Compote, 5½", 2 bead stem, 400/66B	22.00
	Compote, 8", bead stem, 400/48F	110.00
	Compote, 10", ftd. fruit, crimped, 40/103C	225.00
	Compote, ft. oval, 400/137	1,750.00
31	Condiment set, 4 pc., 400/1769	80.00
	Creamer, domed foot, 400/18	125.00
	Creamer, 6 oz., bead handle, 400/30	8.00
	Creamer, indiv. bridge, 400/122	9.00
49	Creamer, plain ft., 400/31	9.00
33	Creamer, flat, bead handle, 400/126	35.00
29	Cruet set, 3 pc., 400/2911	95.00
39	Cruet w/stopper, 4 oz., 400/70	55.00
	Cup, after dinner, 400/77	20.00
10	Cup, coffee, 400/37	6.00
	Cup, punch, 400/211	7.00
	Cup, tea, 400/35	7.00
	Decanter, w/stopper, 15 oz. cordial, 400/82/2	450.00
	Decanter, w/stopper, 18 oz., 400/18	350.00
	Decanter, w/stopper, 26 oz., 400/163	395.00
28	Deviled egg server, 12", ctr. hdld., 400/154	120.00
65	Eagle bookend, 777/3	350.00
	Egg cup, bead. ft., 400/19	60.00
	Fork & spoon, set, 400/75	35.00
	Hurricane lamp, 2 pc. candle base, 400/79	135.00
	Hurricane lamp, 2 pc., hdld. candle base, 400/76	210.00
	Hurricane lamp, 3 pc. flared & crimped edge globe, 400/152	225.00
	Ice tub, 5½" deep, 8" diam., 400/63	135.00
	Ice tub, 7", 2 hdld., 400/168	250.00
	Icer, 2 pc., seafood/fruit cocktail, 400/53/3	100.00
	Icer, 2 pc., seafood/fruit cocktail, #3800 line, one bead stem	75.00
	Jam set, 5 pc., oval tray w/2 marmalade jars w/ladles, 400/1589	135.00
60	Jar tower, 3 sect., 400/655	495.00
	Knife, butter, 4000	525.00
	Ladle, marmalade, 3 bead stem, 400/130	12.00
	Ladle, mayonnaise, 3 knob, 400/165	12.00

		Crystal
	Ladle, mayonnaise, 6¼", 400/135	12.00
73	Lamp shade	85.00
	Marmalade set, 3 pc., beaded ft. w/cover & spoon, 400/1989	45.00
	Marmalade set, 3 pc. tall jar, domed bead ft., lid, spoon, 400/8918	100.00
43	Marmalade set, 4 pc., liner saucer, jar, lid, spoon, 400/89	55.00
	Mayonnaise set, 2 pc. scoop side bowl, spoon, 400/23	40.00
	Mayonnaise set, 3 pc. hdld. tray/hdld. bowl/ladle, 400/52/3	55.00
	Mayonnaise set, 3 pc. plate, heart bowl, spoon, 400/49	40.00
	Mayonnaise set, 3 pc. scoop side bowl, spoon, tray, 400/496	150.00
	Mayonnaise, 4 pc., plate, divided bowl, 2 ladles, rnd., 400/84	45.00
64	Mirror, 4½", rnd., standing	165.00
55	Muddler, 400/19	15.00
	Mustard jar, w/spoon, 400/156	40.00
	Oil, 4 oz., bead base, 400/164	55.00
	Oil, 6 oz., bead base, 400/166	75.00
62	Oil, 4 oz., 400/177	55.00
26	Oil, 4 oz., bulbous bottom, 400/274	55.00
	Oil, 4 oz., hdld., bulbous bottom, 400/278	75.00
	Oil, 6 oz., hdld., bulbous bottom, 400/279	90.00
	Oil, 6 oz., bulbous bottom, 400/275	65.00
	Oil, w/stopper, etched "Oil," 400/121	75.00
	Oil, w/stopper, etched "Vinegar," 400/121	75.00

		Crystal
	Party set, 2 pc., oval plate w/indent for cup, 400/98	27.50
	Pitcher, 14 oz., short rnd., 400/330	210.00
37	Pitcher, 16 oz., low ft., Liliputian, 400/19	245.00
	Pitcher, 16 oz., no ft., 400/16	200.00
	Pitcher, 20 oz., plain, 400/416	40.00
71	Pitcher, 40 oz., juice/cocktail, 400/19	215.00
38	Pitcher, 40 oz., manhattan, 400/18	250.00
	Pitcher, 40 oz., plain, 400/419	50.00
	Pitcher, 64 oz., plain, 400/424	60.00
	Pitcher, 80 oz., plain, 400/424	70.00
	Pitcher, 80 oz., 400/24	150.00
	Pitcher, 80 oz., beaded ft., 400/18	250.00
	Plate, 4½", 400/34	8.00
	Plate, 5½", 2 hdld., 400/42D	12.00
	Plate, 6", bread/butter, 400/1D	7.00
	Plate, 6", canape w/off ctr. indent, 400/36	18.00
	Plate, 6¾", 2 hdld. crimped, 400/52C	30.00
47	Plate, 7", salad, 400/3D	8.00
	Plate, 7½", 2 hdld., 400/52D	12.00
	Plate, 7½", triangular, 400/266	100.00
	Plate, 8", oval, 400/169	25.00
	Plate, 8", salad, 400/5D	10.00
	Plate, 8", w/indent, 400/50	12.00
	Plate, 8¼", crescent salad, 400/120	60.00
	Plate, 8½", 2 hdld., crimped, 400/62C	30.00
	Plate, 8½", 2 hdld., 400/62D	12.00
	Plate, 8½", salad, 400/5D	10.00
	Plate, 8½", 2 hdld. (sides upturned), 400/62E	30.00
	Plate, 9", luncheon, 400/7D	15.00

		Crystal
	Plate, 9", oval, salad, 400/38	40.00
	Plate, 9", w/indent, oval, 400/98	22.00
	Plate, 10", 2 hdld., sides upturned, 400/72E	40.00
	Plate, 10", 2 hdld. crimped, 400/72C	40.00
	Plate, 10", 2 hdld., 400/72D	35.00
	Plate, 10½", dinner, 400/10D	42.00
	Plate, 12", 2 hdld., 400/145D	45.00
	Plate, 12", 2 hdld. crimp., 400/145C	55.00
	Plate, 12", service, 400/13D	35.00
	Plate, 12½", cupped edge, torte, 400/75V	35.00
	Plate, 12½", oval, 400/124	90.00
	Plate, 13½", cracker, 400/145	40.00
	Plate, 13½", cupped edge, serving, 400/92V	47.00
	Plate, 14" birthday cake (holes for 72 candles), 400/160	595.00
	Plate, 14", 2 hdld., sides upturned, 400/113E	50.00
	Plate, 14", 2 hdld., torte, 400/113D	50.00
	Plate, 14", service, 400/92D	50.00
	Plate, 14", torte, 400/17D	50.00
	Plate, 17", cupped edge, 400/20V	95.00
	Plate, 17", torte, 400/20D	95.00
	Platter, 13", 400/124D	110.00
	Platter, 16", 400/131D	225.00
63	Puff box, E - 409	65.00
	Punch ladle, small 2 lip, 400/259	30.00
	Punch set, family, 8 demi cups, ladle, lid, 400/139/77	795.00

		Crystal
	Punch set, 15 pc. bowl on 18" plate, 12 cups, ladle, 400/20	275.00
	Relish & dressing set, 4 pc. (10½" 4 pt. relish w/marmalade), 400/1112	115.00
16	Relish, 10½", 5 pt., 5 hdld., 400/56	75.00
15	Relish, 10½", 6 pt., 5 hdld., 400/112	50.00
18	Relish, 13", 5 pt., 400/102	75.00
22	Relish, 6½", 2 pt., 400/54	20.00
23	Relish, 7" sq., div., 2 pt., 400/234	110.00
19	Relish, 10½", oval, 400/256	30.00
	Salad set, 4 pc. (buffet; lg. rnd. tray, div. bowl, 2 spoons), 400/17	135.00
	Salad set, 4 pc. (rnd. plate, flared bowl, fork, spoon), 400/75B	110.00
35	Salt & pepper pr., bead ft., straight side, chrome top, 400/247	20.00
1	Salt & pepper pr., bead ft., bulbous, chrome top, 400/96	18.00
42	Salt & pepper, 400/167	16.00
	Salt & pepper pr., bulbous w/bead stem, plastic top, 400/116	100.00
45	Salt & pepper, pr., indiv., 400/109	15.00
	Salt & pepper, pr., ftd. bead base, 400/190	65.00
41	Salt dip, 2", 400/61	11.00
	Salt dip, 2¼", 400/19	10.00
40	Salt "type" dip, 2¾", nut or sugar, 400/64	12.00
	Salt spoon, 3, 400/616	11.00
	Salt spoon, w/ribbed bowl, 4000	11.00

		Crystal
	Sauce boat, 400/169	115.00
	Sauce boat liner, 400/169	40.00
	Saucer, after dinner, 400/77AD	5.00
10	Saucer, tea or coffee, 400/35 or 400/37	2.50
	Set: 2 pc. hdld. cracker w/cheese compote, 400/88	65.00
	Set: 2 pc. rnd. cracker plate w/indent; cheese compote, 400/145	65.00
36	Snack jar w/cover, bead ft., 400/139/1	795.00
	Stem, 1 oz., cordial, 400/190	90.00
	Stem, 4 oz., cocktail, 400/190	20.00
	Stem, 5 oz., tall sherbet, 400/190	15.00
	Stem, 5 oz., wine, 400/190	22.00
	Stem, 6 oz., sherbet, 400/190	15.00
	Stem, 10 oz., water 400/190	22.00
27	Stem, #3400, 1 oz., cordial	40.00
13	Stem, #3400, 4 oz., cocktail	16.00
30	Stem, #3400, 4 oz., oyster cocktail	14.00
14	Stem, #3400, 4 oz., wine	20.00
24	Stem, #3400, 5 oz., claret	55.00
	Stem, #3400, 5 oz., low sherbet	9.00
	Stem, #3400, 6 oz., parfait	60.00
	Stem, #3400, 6 oz., sherbet/saucer champagne	14.00
25	Stem, #3400, 9 oz., goblet, water	18.00
	Stem, #3800, low sherbet	28.00
	Stem, #3800, brandy	60.00
	Stem, #3800, 1 oz., cordial	50.00
	Stem, #3800, 4 oz., cocktail	24.00
	Stem, #3800, 4 oz., wine	30.00
	Stem, #3800, 6 oz., champagne/sherbet	28.00
	Stem, #3800, 5 oz., claret	75.00
	Stem, #3800, 9 oz., water goblet	38.00
	Stem, #4000, 1¼ oz., cordial	36.00
	Stem, #4000, 4 oz., cocktail	22.00
	Stem, #4000, 5 oz., wine	28.00
	Stem, #4000, 6 oz., tall sherbet	22.00
	Stem, #4000, 11 oz., goblet	32.00
	Stem, #4000, 12 oz., tea	32.00
	Strawberry set, 2 pc. (7" plate/sugar dip bowl), 400/83	50.00
	Sugar, domed foot, 400/18	135.00
	Sugar, 6 oz., bead hdld., 400/30	8.00
	Sugar, flat, bead handle, 400/126	35.00
32	Sugar, indiv. bridge, 400/122	9.00
52	Sugar, plain ft., 400/31	7.00
	Tete-a-tete 3 pc. brandy, a.d. cup, 6½" oval tray, 400/111	125.00
	Tidbit server, 2 tier, cupped, 400/2701	60.00
	Tidbit set, 3 pc., 400/18TB	225.00
	Toast, w/cover, set, 7¾", 400/123	365.00
	Tray, 5½", hdld., upturned handles, 400/42E	25.00
	Tray, 5½", lemon, ctr. hdld., 400/221	35.00
	Tray, 5¼" x 9¼", condiment, 400/148	48.00
	Tray, 6½", 400/29	18.00
	Tray, 6", wafer, handle bent to ctr. of dish, 400/51T	25.00
34	Tray, 9", oval, 400/159	40.00

		Crystal
70	Tray, 10", circular rings	
	Tray, 10½", ctr. hdld. fruit, 400/68F	135.00
	Tray, 11½", ctr. hdld. party, 400/68D	65.00
48	Tray, 11½", 2 hdld., 400/145E	50.00
	Tray, 13½", 2 hdld., celery, oval, 400/105	35.00
	Tray, 13", relish, 5 sections, 400/102	65.00
	Tray, 14", hdld., 400/113E	95.00
	Tumbler, 3½ oz., cocktail, 400/18	55.00
	Tumbler, 3½ oz., juice, 400/112	12.00
	Tumbler, 5 oz., juice, 400/18	60.00
	Tumbler, 6 oz., sherbet, 400/18	60.00
	Tumbler, 7 oz., old-fashion, 400/18	70.00
	Tumbler, 7 oz., parfait, 400/18	85.00
	Tumbler, 9 oz., water, 400/18	75.00
	Tumbler, 12 oz., tea, 400/18	80.00
	Tumbler, 3 oz., ftd., cocktail, 400/19	16.00
72	Tumbler, 3 oz., ftd., wine, 400/19	22.00
59	Tumbler, 5 oz., low sherbet, 400/19	14.00
9	Tumbler, 5 oz., juice, 400/19	10.00
74	Tumbler, 7 oz., old-fashion, 400/19	38.00
	Tumbler, 10 oz., 400/19	12.00
	Tumbler, 12 oz., 400/19	22.00
11	Tumbler, 14 oz., 400/19, tea	22.00
54	Tumbler, 12 oz., 400/195	
17	Tumbler, #3400, 5 oz., ft., juice	18.00
	Tumbler, #3400, 6 oz., parfait	70.00
	Tumbler, #3400, 9 oz., ftd.	20.00
	Tumbler, #3400, 10 oz., ftd.	20.00
12	Tumbler, #3400, 12 oz., ftd.	20.00
	Tumbler, #3800, 5 oz., juice	30.00
	Tumbler, #3800, 9 oz.	28.00
	Tumbler, #3800, 12 oz.	35.00
	Vase, 4", bead ft., sm. neck, ball, 400/25	65.00
	Vase, 5¾", bead ft., bud, 400/107	65.00
	Vase, 5¾", bead ft., mini bud, 400/107	65.00
	Vase, 6", flat, crimped edge, 400/287C	50.00
	Vase, 6", ftd., flared rim, 400/138B	195.00
	Vase, 6" diam., 400/198	350.00
	Vase, 6", fan, 400/287 F	40.00
	Vase, 7", ftd., bud, 400/186	310.00
	Vase, 7", ftd., bud, 400/187	325.00
	Vase, 7", ivy bowl, 400/74J	165.00
	Vase, 7", rolled rim w/bead hdld., 400/87 R	45.00
2	Vase, 7", rose bowl, 400/142 K	300.00
	Vase, 7¼", ftd., rose bowl, crimped top, 400/132C	525.00
4	Vase, 7½", ftd., rose bowl, 400/132	495.00
	Vase, 8", fan, w/bead hdld., 400/87F	35.00
	Vase, 8", flat, crimped edge, 400/143C	95.00
46	Vase, 8", fluted rim w/bead hdlds., 400/87C	40.00
3	Vase, 8½", bead ft., bud, 400/28C	110.00
	Vase, 8½", bead ft., flared rim, 400/21	325.00
	Vase, 8½", bead ft., inward rim, 400/27	325.00
	Vase, 8½", hdld. (pitcher shape), 400/227	595.00
5	Vase, 10", bead ft., straight side, 400/22	295.00
	Vase, 10", ftd., 400/193	295.00

COLORS: CRYSTAL, SAPPHIRE BLUE, CAPE COD BLUE, CHARTREUSE, RUBY, CRANBERRY PINK, JASMINE YELLOW

Canterbury production began in 1937, but it had its primary manufacturing output through the 1940s and early 1950s. Canterbury exemplifies that 50s love of fluid shapes. Later, moulds were transferred to Tiffin where most of the colored Canterbury was made. We see the yellow-green colored Canterbury (called Chartreuse) more than any other color in our travels. Maybe the few collectors of Chartreuse haven't found all those nooks and crannies where we shop. Those items being found in this color are Tiffin pieces manufactured from Duncan's moulds sometime after 1955. Often, you will find Tiffin labels still attached to these.

Canterbury, issued as Line No. 115, was the mould blank Duncan incorporated for some of their etched patterns; First Love is the most well-known. You can find First Love listed in our *Collectible Glassware of the 40s, 50s, and 60s* book and on page 99. In order to have space for the additional patterns in this book we've removed all of the copies of original catalog pages of Canterbury that were integrated in previous editions. If you are a new collector and wish to see Canterbury catalog listings by Duncan, you will have to track down one of those earlier editions. You need to know that older editions have become collectible themselves and sell at a premium price.

Duncan's light blue was called Sapphire and the opalescent blue was christened Cape Cod blue. The red was Ruby. You may find opalescent pieces of Canterbury in pink, called Cranberry, or yellow, called Jasmine. In Florida, crystal Canterbury pieces are habitually found cloudy or stained, which almost certainly indicates the hard water from wells here leaves residue that cannot be removed easily. Be aware of this problem especially when buying in the early morning dew by flashlight. Moisture hides the cloudiness until it dries out later and you observe your fundamental mistake. If you know of additional pieces not listed or wish to share prices on colored wares, just drop us a postcard. The 64-ounce water pitcher and candlesticks have been the quick sell items for us.

We have mostly shown Canterbury crystal which is the most sought "color." We have not seen enough Canterbury in colors to get a feel for those prices although 15% to 20% more than crystal seems to be normal except for Chartreuse and amber which sell in the range of crystal. We see Ruby pieces priced either very high or rather low. There does not seem to be any consensus. Time will determine whether Ruby is rare. Opalescent items seem to be priced three to four times those for crystal, but we have not found many customers for those either.

Reasonably priced when compared to patterns made by Cambridge, Heisey, or Fostoria, Canterbury is beginning to inch up in price with new collectors on the lookout for it. Pieces are heavier than most patterns, which bothers some, but which has also meant greater survival over the years. Another major concern is scratches from heavy use. This pattern seems to have been bought for everyday use — and it shows.

		Crystal
	Ashtray, 3"	5.00
	Ashtray, 3", club	7.00
	Ashtray, 4½", club	9.00
	Ashtray, 5"	12.00
	Ashtray, 5½", club	14.00
	Basket, 3" x 3" x 3¼", oval, hdld.	22.00
	Basket, 3" x 4", crimped, hdld.	30.00
	Basket, 3½", crimped, hdld.	35.00
	Basket, 3½", oval, hdld.	26.00
	Basket, 4½" x 4¾" x 4¾", oval, hdld.	42.00
	Basket, 4½" x 5" x 5", crimped, hdld.	48.00
	Basket, 9¼" x 10" x 7¼"	55.00
	Basket, 10" x 4¼" x 7", oval, hdld.	75.00
	Basket, 10" x 4½" x 8", oval, hdld.	78.00
	Basket, 11½", oval, hdld.	78.00
	Bowl, 4¼" x 2", finger	12.00
	Bowl, 5" x 3¼", 2 part, salad dressing	12.50
	Bowl, 5" x 3¼", salad dressing	12.50
	Bowl, 5½" x 1¾", one hdld., heart	9.00
	Bowl, 5½" x 1¾", one hdld., square	9.00
	Bowl, 5½" x 1¾", one hdld., star	10.00
	Bowl, 5½" x 1¾", one hdld., fruit	7.00
22	Bowl, 5½" x 1¾", one hdld., round	7.00
	Bowl, 5", fruit nappy	8.00
	Bowl, 6" x 2", 2 hdld., round	10.00
	Bowl, 6" x 2", 2 hdld., sweetmeat, star	15.00
	Bowl, 6" x 3¼", 2 part, salad dressing	14.00
	Bowl, 6" x 3¼", salad dressing	14.00

		Crystal
	Bowl, 6" x 5¼" x 2¼", oval olive	10.00
	Bowl, 7½" x 2¼", crimped	15.00
	Bowl, 7½" x 2¼", gardenia	17.50
6	Bowl, 8" x 2¾", crimped	20.00
	Bowl, 8" x 2½", flared	17.50
	Bowl, 8½" x 4"	22.00
	Bowl, 9" x 2", gardenia	27.50
12	Bowl, 9" x 4¼", crimped	27.50
	Bowl, 9" x 6" x 3", oval	30.00
	Bowl, 10" x 5", salad	30.00
	Bowl, 10" x 8½" x 5", oval	27.50
	Bowl, 10¾" x 4¾"	27.50
8	Bowl, 10½" x 5", crimped	32.50
7	Bowl, 11½" x 8¼", oval	32.50
	Bowl, 12" x 2¾", gardenia	30.00
	Bowl, 12" x 3½", flared	30.00
16	Bowl, 12" x 3¾", crimped	32.50
	Bowl, 13" x 8½" x 3¼", oval, flared	35.00
	Bowl, 13" x 10" x 5", crimped, oval	40.00
	Bowl, 15" x 2¾", shallow salad	42.00
20	Candle, 3", low	12.50
	Candle, 3½"	15.00
	Candlestick, 6", 3-lite	39.00
	Candlestick, 6"	25.00
	Candlestick, 7", w/U prisms	75.00
	Candy and cover, 8" x 3½", 3 hdld., 3 part	35.00
	Candy, 6½", w/5" lid	32.50
	Celery and relish, 10½" x 6¾" x 1¼", 2 hdld., 2 pt.	32.50

	Crystal			Crystal
Celery and relish, 10½" x 6¾" x 1¼", 2 hdld., 3 pt.	32.50		Cigarette box w/cover, 3½" x 4½"	22.50
Celery, 9" x 4" x 1¼", 2 hdld.	22.50		Cigarette jar w/cover, 4"	30.00
Cheese stand, 5½" x 3½" high	15.00		Comport, high, 6" x 5½" high	20.00

		Crystal
	Comport, low, 6" x 4½" high	18.00
	Creamer, 2¾", 3 oz., individual	8.00
5	Creamer, 3¾", 7 oz.	8.00
	Cup	8.00
	Decanter w/stopper, 12", 32 oz.	80.00
28	Ice bucket or vase, 6"	40.00
	Ice bucket or vase, 7"	45.00
	Lamp, hurricane, w/prisms, 15"	135.00
	Marmalade, 4½" x 2¾", crimped	20.00
	Mayonnaise, 5" x 3¼"	20.00
1	Mayonnaise, 5½" x 3¼", crimped	22.00
	Mayonnaise, 6" x 3¼"	24.00
	Pitcher, 16 oz., pint	55.00
	Pitcher, 9¼", 32 oz., hdld., martini	90.00
	Pitcher, 9¼", 32 oz., martini	80.00
	Pitcher, 64 oz.	250.00
	Plate, 6½", one hdld., fruit	6.00
15	Plate, 6", finger bowl liner	6.00
	Plate, 7½"	9.00
18	Plate, 7½", 2 hdld., mayonnaise	12.00
19	Plate, 8½"	12.00
	Plate, 11¼", dinner	25.00
	Plate, 11", 2 hdld. w/ring, cracker	20.00
17	Plate, 11", 2 hdld., sandwich	22.00
	Plate, 13½", cake, hdld.	40.00
	Plate, 14", cake	25.00
	Relish, 6" x 2", 2 hdld., 2 part, round	14.00
	Relish, 6" x 2", 2 hdld., 2 part, star	14.00
14	Relish, 7" x 5¼" x 2¼", 2 hdld., 2 part, oval	16.00
21	Relish, 8" x 1¾", 3 hdld., 3 part	17.50
23	Relish, 9" x 1½", 3 hdld., 3 part	22.00
	Relish, 11" x 2", 5 part	33.00
	Rose bowl, 5"	20.00
	Rose bowl, 6"	25.00
	Salt and pepper	22.50
	Sandwich tray, 12" x 5¼", center handle	50.00
	Saucer	3.00
	Sherbet, crimped, 4½", 2¾" high	10.00

		Crystal
	Sherbet, crimped, 5½", 2¾" high	11.00
25	Stem, 3¾", 6 oz., ice cream	6.00
	Stem, 4", 4½ oz., oyster cocktail	12.50
	Stem, 4¼", 1 oz., cordial, #5115	25.00
	Stem, 4¼", 3½ oz., cocktail	12.00
	Stem, 4½", 6 oz., saucer champagne	12.00
	Stem, 5", 4 oz., claret or wine	20.00
	Stem, 5¼", 3 oz., cocktail, #5115	14.00
	Stem, 5½", 5 oz., saucer champagne, #5115	12.00
	Stem, 6", 3½ oz., wine, #5115	27.50
24	Stem, 6", 9 oz., water	15.00
	Stem, 6¾", 5 oz., claret, #5115	27.00
	Stem, 7¼", 10 oz., water, #5115	20.00
	Sugar, 2½", 3 oz., individual	8.00
9	Sugar, 3", 7 oz.	8.00
	Top hat, 3"	20.00
26	Tray, 6", cream/sugar, shakers	15.00
13	Tray, 9", individual cream/sugar	10.00
	Tray, 9" x 4" x 1¼", 2 part, pickle and olive	17.50
3	Tumbler, 2½", 1½ oz., whiskey	12.50
	Tumbler, 2½", 5 oz., ftd., ice cream, #5115	10.00
4	Tumbler, 3¼", 4 oz., ftd., oyster cocktail, #5115	12.50
	Tumbler, 3¾", 5 oz., flat, juice	8.00
	Tumbler, 4¼", 5 oz., ftd., juice	10.00
	Tumbler, 4¼", 5 oz., ftd., juice, #5115	12.00
10	Tumbler, 4½", 9 oz., flat, table, straight	14.00
	Tumbler, 4½", 10 oz., ftd., water, #5115	14.00
	Tumbler, 5½", 9 oz., ftd., luncheon goblet	14.00
	Tumbler, 5¾", 12 oz., ftd., ice tea, #5115	17.50
11	Tumbler, 6¼", 13 oz., flat, ice tea	18.00
	Tumbler, 6¼", 13 oz., ftd., ice tea	20.00
	Urn, 4½" x 4½"	15.00
	Vase, 3", crimped violet	15.00
	Vase, 3½", clover leaf	15.00
	Vase, 3½", crimped	15.00
	Vase, 3½", crimped violet	15.00
	Vase, 3½", oval	15.00
	Vase, 4", clover leaf	17.50
	Vase, 4", crimped	17.50
	Vase, 4", flared rim	17.50
	Vase, 4", oval	17.50
	Vase, 4½" x 4¾"	15.00
	Vase, 4½", clover leaf	20.00
2	Vase, 4½", crimped violet	17.50
	Vase, 4½", oval	17.50
	Vase, 5" x 5", crimped	17.50
	Vase, 5", clover leaf	25.00
	Vase, 5", crimped	17.50
	Vase, 5½", crimped	20.00
	Vase, 5½", flower arranger	27.50
	Vase, 6½", clover leaf	38.00
	Vase, 7", crimped	35.00
	Vase, 7", flower arranger	45.00
	Vase, 8½" x 6"	55.00
	Vase, 12", flared	80.00

28

COLORS: AMBER, ANTIQUE BLUE, AZALEA, BLACK, CRYSTAL, EVERGREEN, MILK GLASS, RITZ BLUE, RUBY, VERDE

Crystal Cape Cod is most hunted, since it can still be found while colored wares besides stems are difficult to gather. Our picture below illustrates the variety of colors found. In the top row is Ruby and crystal with red flashing as well as the pink that was called Azalea by Imperial. The trimmed pieces were made in the early 1940s and are difficult to find with that red flashing intact.

The second row shows pieces in Ebony, milk glass, Antique and Ritz blue, Emerald (dark) and Verde (light) green, and amber in that order. Colored items were mostly made in the late 1960s and 1970s although Ruby and Ritz Blue first appeared in the 1930s.

There are several hundred different pieces in crystal giving collectors a wide range of choices. As can be seen by our photos, stems and tumblers are what turn up regularly in color as well as crystal. This massive amount of crystal stems being unearthed is causing them to sell for lower prices than a few years ago. Rarely found items continue to soar in price, but those commonly found have diminished in price due to lack of demand.

Possibly, the color in which you could collect a small set would be Ruby. Most of the Ritz blue has disappeared into collections. Ruby won't come cheaply, but there was enough made to find some. If you like the Verde or Azalea, you could find enough stems to use, but other than that, it would be a chore to find. You can buy most of the fundamental pieces of crystal Cape Cod inexpensively. How long that will hold true is a question. If you like it, buy it now.

43

		Crystal
	Ashtray, 4", 160/134/1	14.00
	Ashtray, 5½", 160/150	17.50
	Basket, 9", handled, crimped, 160/221/0	225.00
	Basket, 11" tall, handled, 160/40	175.00
	Bottle, bitters, 4 oz., 160/235	60.00
	Bottle, cologne, w/stopper, 1601	60.00
	Bottle, condiment, 6 oz., 160/224	65.00
	Bottle, cordial, 18 oz., 160/256	110.00
	Bottle, decanter, 26 oz., 160/244	135.00
	Bottle, ketchup, 14 oz., 160/237	225.00
	Bowl, 3", handled mint, 160/183	20.00
	Bowl, 3", jelly, 160/33	12.00
33	Bowl, 4½", finger, 1604½A	15.00
	Bowl, 4½", handled spider, 160/180	22.50
	Bowl, 4½", dessert, tab handled, 160/197	24.00
	Bowl, 5", dessert, heart shape, 160/49H	22.00
30	Bowl, 5", finger, 1602	15.00

		Crystal
	Bowl, 5", flower, 1605N	25.00
31	Bowl, 5½", fruit, 160/23B	10.00
	Bowl, 5½", handled spider, 160/181	25.00
40	Bowl, 5½", tab handled, soup, 160/198	22.50
	Bowl, 6", fruit, 160/3F	10.00
	Bowl, 6", baked apple, 160/53X	11.00
	Bowl, 6", handled, round mint, 160/51F	22.00
	Bowl, 6", handled heart, 160/40H	25.00
	Bowl, 6", handled mint, 160/51H	22.00
	Bowl, 6", handled tray, 160/51T	30.00
	Bowl, 6½", handled portioned spider, 160/187	27.50
	Bowl, 6½", handled spider, 160/182	32.50
	Bowl, 6½", tab handled, 160/199	30.00
	Bowl, 7", nappy, 160/5F	22.00
	Bowl, 7½", 160/7F	22.00
	Bowl, 7½", 2-handled, 160/62B	27.50

	Crystal
Bowl, 8¾", 160/10F	33.00
Bowl, 9", footed fruit, 160/67F	65.00
Bowl, 9½", 2 handled, 160/145B	40.00
Bowl, 9½", crimped, 160/221C	100.00
Bowl, 9½", float, 160/221F	65.00
Bowl, 10", footed, 160/137B	75.00
Bowl, 10", oval, 160/221	80.00
Bowl, 11", flanged edge, 1608X	165.00
Bowl, 11", oval, 160/124	80.00
Bowl, 11", oval divided, 160/125	85.00
Bowl, 11", round, 1608A	95.00
Bowl, 11", salad, 1608D	60.00
Bowl, 11¼", oval, 1602	80.00
Bowl, 12", 160/75B	40.00
Bowl, 12", oval, 160/131B	95.00
Bowl, 12", oval crimped, 160/131C	175.00
Bowl, 12", punch, 160/20B	65.00
Bowl, 13", console, 160/75L	42.50
Bowl, 15", console, 1601/0L	75.00
Butter, 5", w/cover, handled, 160/144	30.00
Butter, w/cover, ¼ lb., 160/161	45.00
Cake plate, 10", 4 toed, 160/220	90.00
Cake stand, 10½", footed, 160/67D	50.00
Cake stand, 11", 160/103D	85.00
Candleholder, twin, 160/100	95.00
Candleholder, 3", single, 160/170	17.50
Candleholder, 4", 160/81	27.50
Candleholder, 4", Aladdin style, 160/90	150.00
Candleholder, 4½", saucer, 160/175	30.00
Candleholder, 5", 160/80	20.00
Candleholder, 5", flower, 160/45B	60.00
Candleholder, 5½", flower, 160/45N	110.00
Candleholder, 6", centerpiece, 160/48BC	100.00
Candy, w/cover, 160/110	85.00
Carafe, wine, 26 oz., 160/185	235.00
Celery, 8", 160/105	30.00

		Crystal
	Celery, 10½", 160/189	55.00
	Cigarette box, 4½", 160/134	45.00
	Cigarette holder, ftd., 1602	12.50
	Cigarette holder, Tom & Jerry mug, 160/200	32.50
	Cigarette lighter, 1602	30.00
	Coaster, w/spoon rest, 160/76	12.00
	Coaster, 3", square, 160/85	20.00
29	Coaster, 4", round, 160/78	15.00
	Coaster, 4½", flat, 160/1R	10.00
	Comport, 5¼", 160F	27.50
	Comport, 5¾", 160X	30.00
	Comport, 6", 160/45	25.00
	Comport, 6", w/cover, ftd., 160/140	85.00
	Comport, 7", 160/48B	37.50
	Comport, 11¼", oval, 1602, 6½" tall	200.00
	Creamer, 160/190	30.00
36	Creamer, 160/30	8.00
	Creamer, ftd., 160/31	15.00
	Cruet, w/stopper, 4 oz., 160/119	22.00
	Cruet, w/stopper, 5 oz., 160/70	30.00
	Cruet, w/stopper, 6 oz., 160/241	40.00
	Cup, tea, 160/35	6.00
	Cup, coffee, 160/37	6.00
23	Cup, bouillon, 160/250	50.00
	Decanter, bourbon, 160/260	100.00
	Decanter, rye, 160/260	100.00
39	Decanter w/stopper, 30 oz., 160/163	65.00
	Decanter w/stopper, 24 oz., 160/212	70.00
43	Decanter, 26 oz., 160/244	110.00
	Egg cup, 160/225	28.00
	Epergne, 2 pc., plain center, 160/196	265.00
	Fork, 160/701	12.00
	Gravy bowl, 18 oz., 160/202	85.00
	Horseradish, 5 oz. jar, 160/226	95.00
	Ice bucket, 6½", 160/63	185.00
	Icer, 3 pc., bowl, 2 inserts, 160/53/3	60.00
	Jar, 12 oz., hdld. peanut w/lid, 160/210	75.00
	Jar, 10", "Pokal," 160/133	85.00
	Jar, 11", "Pokal," 160/128	90.00
	Jar, 15", "Pokal," 160/132	150.00
	Jar, candy w/lid, wicker hand., 5" h., 160/194	125.00
	Jar, cookie, w/lid, wicker hand., 6½" h., 160/195	150.00
	Jar, peanut butter w/lid, wicker hand., 4" h., 160/193	110.00
	Ladle, marmalade, 160/130	10.00
	Ladle, mayonnaise, 160/165	10.00
	Ladle, punch	25.00
	Lamp, hurricane, 2 pc., 5" base, 160/79	100.00
	Lamp, hurricane, 2 pc., bowl-like base, 1604	145.00
37	Marmalade, 3 pc. set, 160/89/3	32.50
	Marmalade, 4 pc. set, 160/89	40.00
	Mayonnaise, 3 pc. set, 160/52H	37.50
	Mayonnaise, 3 pc., 160/23	27.50

		Crystal
	Mayonnaise, 12 oz., hdld., spouted, 160/205	55.00
15	Mug, 12 oz., handled, 160/188	60.00
	Mustard, w/cover & spoon, 160/156	35.00
	Nut dish, 3", hdld., 160/183	30.00
	Nut dish, 4", hdld., 160/184	30.00
	Pepper mill, 160/236	30.00
	Pitcher, milk, 1 pt., 160/240	55.00
	Pitcher, 36 oz., refrig. jug open lip, Tiars pro.	60.00
24	Pitcher, ice lipped, 40 oz., 160/19	85.00
	Pitcher, martini, blown, 40 oz., 160/178	200.00
	Pitcher, ice lipped, 2 qt., 160/239	85.00
	Pitcher, 2 qt., 160/24	85.00
	Pitcher, blown, 5 pt., 160/176	200.00
	Plate, 4½" butter, 160/34	8.00
	Plate, 6", cupped (liner for 160/208 salad dressing), 160/209	25.00
	Plate, 6½", bread & butter, 160/1D	7.00
	Plate, 7", 160/3D	8.00
	Plate, 7", cupped (liner for 160/205 mayo), 160/206	30.00
	Plate, 8", center handled tray, 160/149D	40.00
	Plate, 8", crescent salad, 160/12	80.00
	Plate, 8" cupped (liner for gravy), 160/203	30.00
	Plate, 8", salad, 160/5D	9.00
	Plate, 8½", 2 handled, 160/62D	28.00
	Plate, 9", 160/7D	20.00
	Plate, 9½", 2 hdld., 160/62D	40.00
	Plate, 10", dinner, 160/10D	37.50
	Plate, 11½", 2 handled, 160/145D	40.00
	Plate, 12½" bread, 160/222	70.00
	Plate, 13", birthday, 72 candle holes, 160/72	425.00
	Plate, 13", cupped torte, 1608V	35.00
	Plate, 13", torte, 1608F	40.00
	Plate, 14", cupped, 160/75V	50.00
	Plate, 14", flat, 160/75D	50.00
	Plate, 16", cupped, 160/20V	80.00
	Plate, 17", 2 styles, 160/10D or 20D	95.00
34	Platter, 13½", oval, 160/124D	80.00
	Puff box, w/cover, 1601	60.00
	Relish, 8", hdld., 2 part, 160/223	37.50
	Relish, 9½", 4 pt., 160/56	35.00
	Relish, 9½", oval, 3 part, 160/55	25.00
	Relish, 11", 5 part, 160/102	55.00
	Relish, 11¼", 3 part, oval, 1602	75.00
	Salad dressing, 6 oz., hdld., spouted, 160/208	65.00
	Salad set, 14" plate, 12" bowl, fork & spoon, 160/75	110.00
	Salt & pepper, individual, 160/251	18.00
10	Salt & pepper, pr., ftd., 160/117	18.00
	Salt & pepper, pr., ftd., stemmed, 160/243	40.00
	Salt & pepper, pr., 160/96	16.00
	Salt & pepper, pr. square, 160/109	25.00
	Salt dip, 160/61	20.00

		Crystal
	Salt spoon, 1600	8.00
	Saucer, tea, 160/35	2.00
	Saucer, coffee, 160/37	2.00
	Server, 12", ftd. or turned over, 160/93	75.00
	Spoon, 160/701	12.00
14	Stem, 1½ oz., cordial, 1602	6.00
21	Stem, 3 oz., wine, 1600	30.00
5	Stem, 3 oz., wine, 1602	5.00
18	Stem, 3½ oz., cocktail, 1602	5.00
28	Stem, 3½ oz., cocktail, 160B	5.00
7	Stem, 3½ oz., cocktail, 1600	5.00
12	Stem, 5 oz., claret, 1602	6.00
3	Stem, 6 oz., low sundae, 1602	3.00
	Stem, 6 oz., ftd., juice, 1602	5.00
20	Stem, 6 oz., parfait, 1602	8.00
	Stem, 6 oz., sherbet, 1600	12.00
25	Stem, 6 oz., sherbet, 3600	20.00
13	Stem, 6 oz., tall sherbet, 1602	5.00
	Stem, 8 oz., goblet, 160	7.00
4	Stem, 9 oz., water, 1602	5.00
	Stem, 10 oz., water, 1600	15.00
8	Stem, 11 oz., dinner goblet, 1602	7.00
27	Stem, 11 oz., goblet, 3600	20.00
26	Stem, 12 oz., tea, 3600	20.00
16	Stem, 14 oz., goblet, magnum, 160	40.00
42	Stem, oyster cocktail, 1602	8.00
	Sugar, 160/190	30.00
35	Sugar, 160/30	7.00
	Sugar, ftd., 160/31	15.00
	Toast, w/cover, 160/123	235.00
	Tom & Jerry footed punch bowl, 160/200	375.00
	Tray, sq. cov. sugar & creamer, 160/25/26	150.00
	Tray, 7", for creamer/sugar, 160/29	15.00
	Tray, 11", pastry, center hdld., 160/68D	65.00
	Tumbler, 2½ oz., whiskey, 160	10.00
11	Tumbler, 6 oz., ftd., juice, 1602	5.00
19	Tumbler, 6 oz., ftd., juice, 1600	20.00
2	Tumbler, 6 oz., juice, 160	5.00
1	Tumbler, 7 oz., old-fashion, 160	6.00
	Tumbler, 10 oz., ftd., water, 1602	5.00
41	Tumbler, 10 oz., water, 160	5.00
22	Tumbler, 12 oz., ftd., ice tea, 1600	6.00
9	Tumbler, 12 oz., ftd., tea, 160	11.00
6	Tumbler, 12 oz., ice tea, 160	11.00
32	Tumbler, 14 oz., double old-fashion, 160	30.00
38	Tumbler, 14 oz., 160	32.00
	Vase, 6¼", ftd., 160/22	35.00
	Vase, 6½", ftd., 160/110B	70.00
	Vase, 7½", ftd., 160/22	40.00
	Vase, 8", fan, 160/87F	215.00
	Vase, 8½", flip, 160/143	60.00
	Vase, 8½", ftd., 160/28	45.00
	Vase, 10", cylinder, 160/192	75.00
	Vase, 10½", hdld., urn, 160/186	200.00

IMPERIAL GLASS CORPORATION, BELLAIRE, OHIO

IMPERIAL
CAPE COD

160/73/0
11" Basket

160/186   10½"
2 Handled Urn Vase

160/79   2 pc.
Hurrican Lamp 9 inches Overall

160/24   60 oz.
Ice Lipped Pitcher

160/19   40 oz.
Ice Lipped Pitcher

160/196   2 pc. Epergne
Height-12 inches Overall

160/40   11"
Basket

160/63   6½"
Ice Bucket with Handle & Ice Tongs

Page 10

		Crystal	Blue/Pink
	Mayonnaise, 6½", 3 pc. set, #129*	42.00	110.00
	Mayonnaise, 8", 3 pc. set, #106*	55.00	110.00
26	Mustard, w/cover, 2 oz., #87	60.00	160.00
	Nut Dish, 2½", #93	22.00	40.00
	Nut dish, 2½", divided, #94	25.00	40.00
25	Oil, 3 oz., w/stopper, #101*	35.00	75.00
28	Oil, 3 oz., w/stopper, belled skirt, #117*	35.00	75.00
	Oil, 3 oz., w/stopper, #98*	35.00	75.00
19	Oil, 5 oz., w/stopper, #100*	70.00	210.00
	Pitcher, 32 oz., ball shape, #179	135.00	295.00
	Pitcher, 80 oz., ball shape, #183	125.00	300.00
	Pitcher, 90 oz., tall Doulton style, #178	600.00	3,750.00
	Plate, 5½", bread & butter, #20	10.00	18.00
	Plate, 6½", bread & butter, #21	10.00	18.00
	Plate, 6½", hdld., lemon, #152	12.00	25.00
11	Plate, 7½", salad, #23	12.00	22.00
12	Plate, 8½", luncheon, #22	13.00	25.00
	Plate, 9½", dinner, #24*	40.00	165.00
	Plate, 11", cabaret, 4 ftd., #32	30.00	60.00
	Plate, 11½", cabaret, #26	30.00	60.00
	Plate, 14", cabaret, 4 ftd., #33	40.00	75.00
	Plate, 14", 4 ftd., #28	35.00	70.00
	Plate, 16", #30	45.00	135.00
	Punch bowl, ftd., #498	2,750.00	
	Salad dressing, 3 pc., ftd. & hdld., 2 spoons, #112*	195.00	400.00
31	Salt & pepper, pr., ball, #91	45.00	110.00
	Salt & pepper, pr., flat, #96*	35.00	80.00
	Salt & pepper, indiv., ball, pr., #90	50.00	120.00
	Salt & pepper, indiv., flat, pr., #92	40.00	110.00
	Salver, 13", 2 pc. (cake pedestal), #31	165.00	600.00
15	Saucer, #17	2.50	5.00
17	Stem, #300, blown, 1 oz., cordial	52.50	125.00
	Stem, #300, blown, 2½ oz., wine	25.00	60.00
32	Stem, #300, blown, 3 oz., cocktail	25.00	40.00
	Stem, #300, blown, 4½ oz., claret	80.00	135.00
	Stem, #300, blown, 4½ oz., low oyster cocktail	20.00	35.00
	Stem, #300, blown, 5 oz., parfait	95.00	160.00
	Stem, #300, blown, 6 oz., low sherbet	12.00	18.00
8	Stem, #300, blown, 6 oz., tall sherbet	12.00	24.00
	Stem, #300, blown, 9 oz., water	18.00	40.00
	Stem, #301, blown, 1 oz., cordial	40.00	
	Stem, #301, blown, 2½ oz., wine	20.00	
	Stem, #301, blown, 3 oz., cocktail	20.00	
	Stem, #301, blown, 4½ oz., claret	38.00	
	Stem, #301, blown, 6 oz., sherbet	12.00	
	Stem, #301, blown, 9 oz., water	16.00	
	Stem, 3 oz., wine, #6*	35.00	90.00
	Stem, 3½ oz., cocktail, #3*	20.00	50.00
	Stem, 4½ oz., claret, #5*	70.00	175.00
	Stem, 4½ oz., fruit cocktail, #7	25.00	65.00
	Stem, 5 oz., low sherbet, #4	20.00	35.00
	Stem, 7 oz., tall sherbet, #2*	15.00	30.00

		Crystal	Blue/Pink
	Stem, 10 oz., water, #1	22.00	40.00
	Sugar, large, #41*	10.00	22.00
1	Sugar, medium, #38*	9.00	18.00
29	Sugar, indiv., #40*	10.00	20.00
4	Tray, for sugar & creamer, #37*	15.00	30.00
	Tray, 9" oval, #42	20.00	45.00
	Tumbler, 2 oz., flat, #188*	25.00	70.00
	Tumbler, 3 oz., ftd., #12	27.50	75.00
	Tumbler, 5 oz., ftd., #11	18.00	55.00
23	Tumbler, 5 oz., flat, #180	18.00	50.00
	Tumbler, #300, 2½ oz., whiskey	45.00	160.00
	Tumbler, #300, 5 oz., ftd., juice	18.00	35.00
	Tumbler, #300, 10 oz., ftd. water	18.00	40.00
	Tumbler, #300, 12 oz., ftd. tea	18.00	40.00
	Tumbler, #301, blown, 4½ oz., low oyster cocktail	16.00	
	Tumbler, #301, blown, 5 oz., juice	13.00	
	Tumbler, #301, blown, 12 oz., tea	18.00	
	Tumbler, 9 oz., straight side, #14*	35.00	100.00
	Tumbler, 10 oz., ftd., #10*	18.00	35.00
18	Tumbler, 12 oz., flat., #184	45.00	50.00
	Tumbler, 12 oz., ftd., #9	20.00	40.00
	Tumbler, 12 oz., straight side, #15*	35.00	90.00
	Tumbler, #310, 5 oz., flat, juice	20.00	70.00
21	Tumbler, #310, 7 oz., flat, old-fashion	35.00	125.00
	Tumbler, #310, 10 oz., flat, table	20.00	60.00
	Tumbler, #310, 11 oz., flat, tall, 4¹³⁄₁₆"	20.00	75.00
	Tumbler, #310, 12 oz., flat, tea	25.00	110.00
	Vase, 3½", #249	60.00	150.00
	Vase, 4", blown, #251, blown	60.00	150.00
	Vase, 4¼", #241, ball	55.00	95.00
	Vase, 4½", #237, ball	65.00	175.00
	Vase, 4½", #252, blown	45.00	150.00
	Vase, 4½", #337, crimped top	45.00	120.00
	Vase, 4½", #344, crimped top	75.00	150.00
	Vase, 4½", #244	50.00	135.00
	Vase, 5", ivy bowl, #232	80.00	195.00
22	Vase, 5½", #245	50.00	150.00
	Vase, 5½", #345, crimped top	75.00	195.00
	Vase, 6", #242, ftd.	70.00	175.00
	Vase, 6", blown, #254	175.00	395.00
	Vase, 6", #342, crimped top	85.00	175.00
	Vase, 6", #235, ftd., rose bowl	65.00	135.00
13	Vase, 6½", #238, ball	50.00	150.00
	Vase, 6½", #338, crimped top	85.00	225.00
	Vase, 7½", #246	55.00	175.00
	Vase, 7½", #346, crimped top	95.00	295.00
	Vase, 8", #236, ftd., rose bowl	85.00	225.00
	Vase, 8½", #243	95.00	195.00
	Vase, 8½", #239, ball	110.00	295.00
	Vase, 8½", #339, crimped top	110.00	275.00
	Vase, 8½", #343, crimped top	135.00	275.00
	Vase, 9¼" #240, ball	130.00	295.00
	Vase, 9½" #340, crimped top	165.00	420.00

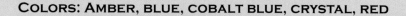

COLORS: AMBER, BLUE, COBALT BLUE, CRYSTAL, RED

6

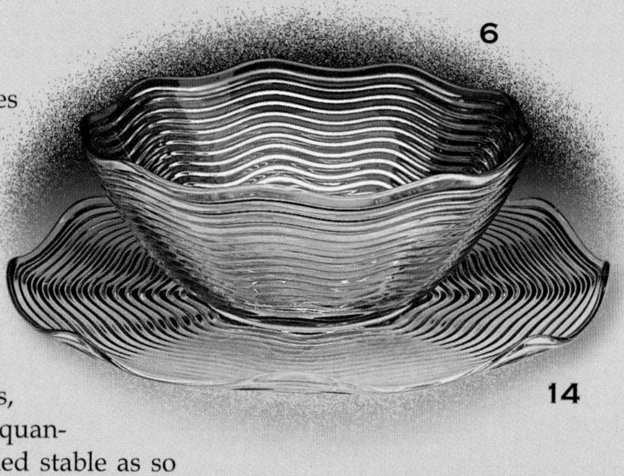

Caribbean is one pattern where a combination of blue and crystal makes a delightful display. Collectors started combining colors due to a decorating influence introduced in women's magazines. At this moment in time, mixing glass colors has come about from necessity (due to lack of finding just one color) as much as anything. However, it's generating some delightfully creative collections. We've been sent photos of imaginative table arrangements using this wonderful older glassware.

Blue Caribbean dinner plates are taxing to find, but even more infuriating is finding them worn and mutilated with mint condition prices on them. Collectors shopping for basic Caribbean dinnerware items (dinner plates, cups, and saucers) are not finding many. When fundamental items are not found in quantity, new collectors tend to sidestep the pattern. Prices for blue have remained stable as so little is available for sale. Neither do we see the crystal on the market that we once did. Of course, dealers have a propensity to avoid buying patterns that few collectors seek, creating a second difficulty for collecting crystal Caribbean. The blue punch bowl, pitchers, and some of the stemware, particularly cordials, will all cost you big time, if you can find them.

14

Amber Caribbean is rarely seen except for the cigarette jar and ashtrays. Other pieces are unusual; keep that in mind.

Crystal punch sets can be found with all crystal cups or with crystal cups with colored handles of red, cobalt blue, or amber. With the colored handled punch cup and ladle, these sets sell for about $75.00 more than the plain crystal set priced below. Red and cobalt blue handled pieces appear to be more desirable than amber. Many collectors mix the colored punch cups so that they have four of each colored handle with their set. In fact, we have seen so many with four of each cup that they may have been promoted like that in some areas.

		Crystal	Blue
	Ashtray, 6", 4 indent	15.00	30.00
	Bowl, 3¾" x 5", folded side, hdld.	16.00	33.00
17	Bowl, 4½", finger	16.00	30.00
	Bowl, 5", fruit nappy (takes liner), hdld.	12.50	25.00
	Bowl, 5" x 7", folded side, hdld.	20.00	35.00
18	Bowl, 6½", soup (takes liner)	16.00	40.00
	Bowl, 7", hdld.	25.00	45.00
	Bowl, 7¼", ftd., hdld., grapefruit	20.00	45.00
19	Bowl, 8½"	30.00	75.00
	Bowl, 9", salad	30.00	75.00
	Bowl, 9¼", veg., flared edge	32.50	75.00
	Bowl, 9¼", veg., hdld.	40.00	90.00
	Bowl, 9½", epergne, flared edge	37.50	95.00
	Bowl, 10", 6¼ qt., punch	90.00	495.00
6	Bowl, 10", 6¼ qt., punch, flared top (catalog lists as salad)	90.00	400.00
	Bowl, 10¾", oval, flower, hdld.	40.00	95.00
	Bowl, 12", console, flared edge	50.00	110.00
	Candelabrum, 4¾", 2-lite	40.00	95.00
	Candlestick, 7¼", 1-lite, w/blue prisms	65.00	195.00
	Candy dish w/cover, 4" x 7"	50.00	120.00
	Cheese/cracker crumbs, 3½" h., plate 11", hdld.	50.00	100.00
	Cigarette holder (stack ashtray top)	35.00	75.00
	Cocktail shaker, 9", 33 oz.	100.00	300.00
	Creamer	10.00	22.00
	Cruet	40.00	95.00
5	Cup, tea	15.00	55.00
	Cup, punch	10.00	20.00
	Epergne, 4 pt., flower (12" bowl, 9½" bowl, 7¾" vase, 14" plate)	225.00	450.00
	Ice bucket, 6½", hdld.	75.00	210.00

		Crystal	Blue
	Ladle, punch	35.00	100.00
	Mayonnaise, w/liner, 5¾", 2 pt., 2 spoons, hdld.	42.50	100.00
	Mayonnaise, w/liner, 5¾", hdld., 1 spoon	35.00	80.00
	Mustard, 4", w/slotted cover	35.00	55.00
	Pitcher, 4¾" 16 oz., milk	95.00	235.00
	Pitcher, w/ice lip, 9", 72 oz., water	225.00	595.00
	Plate, 6", hdld., fruit nappy liner	4.00	10.00
13	Plate 6¼", bread/butter	5.00	10.00
	Plate, 7¼", rolled edge, soup liner	5.00	12.50
	Plate, 7½", salad	8.00	18.00
	Plate, 8", hdld., mayonnaise liner	6.00	14.00
15	Plate, 8½", luncheon	12.00	30.00
4	Plate, 10½", dinner	50.00	125.00
	Plate, 11", hdld., cheese/cracker liner	20.00	45.00
14	Plate, 12", salad liner, rolled edge	22.00	50.00
	Plate, 14"	25.00	80.00
	Plate, 16", torte	35.00	110.00
	Plate, 18", punch underliner	40.00	125.00
	Relish, 6", round, 2 pt.	12.00	25.00
	Relish, 9½", 4 pt., oblong	30.00	60.00
	Relish, 9½", oblong	25.00	60.00
	Relish, 12¾", 5 pt., rnd.	40.00	95.00
	Relish, 12¾", 7 pt., rnd.	40.00	95.00
	Salt dip, 2½"	11.00	25.00
	Salt & pepper, 3", metal tops	32.00	95.00
16	Salt & pepper, 5", metal tops	37.50	125.00
5	Saucer	3.00	8.00
	Server, 5¾", ctr. hdld.	13.00	40.00
	Server, 6½", ctr. hdld.	22.00	50.00
	Stem, 3", 1 oz., cordial	50.00	210.00
3	Stem, 3½", 3½ oz., ftd., ball stem, wine/cocktail	20.00	65.00
1	Stem, 3⅝", 2½ oz., wine (egg cup shape)	20.00	35.00
	Stem, 4", 6 oz., ftd., ball stem, champagne	12.00	27.50
8	Stem, 4¼", ftd., sherbet	10.00	25.00
7	Stem, 4¾", 3 oz., ftd., ball stem, wine	20.00	60.00
2	Stem, 5¾", 8 oz., ftd., ball stem	20.00	50.00
9	Sugar	10.00	22.00
	Syrup, metal cutoff top	110.00	250.00
	Tray, 6¼", hand., mint, div.	14.00	30.00
	Tray, 12¾", rnd.	25.00	50.00
12	Tumbler, 2¼", 2 oz., shot glass	20.00	60.00
10	Tumbler, 3½", 5 oz., flat	20.00	55.00
11	Tumbler, 5¼", 11½ oz., flat	20.00	55.00
	Tumbler, 5½", 8½ oz., ftd.	22.00	55.00
	Tumbler, 6½", 11 oz., ftd., ice tea	25.00	60.00
	Vase, 5¾", ftd., ruffled edge	22.00	55.00
	Vase, 7¼", ftd., flared edge, ball	27.50	75.00
	Vase, 7½", ftd., flared edge, bulbous	32.50	85.00
	Vase, 7¾", flared edge, epergne	40.00	125.00
	Vase, 8", ftd., straight side	40.00	85.00
21	Vase, 9", ftd., ruffled top	50.00	225.00
	Vase, 10", ftd.	55.00	195.00

21

BRILLIANT COLORS: EMERALD GREEN, SPANISH ROSE, AND CRYSTAL (COLOR OF THE GLASS ITSELF)
SOFT COLORS: HONEY, AMETHYST, AND JADE (CERAMIC WASH OVER CRYSTAL)
RARE COLORS: RUBY STAINED (ON CRYSTAL), RED (RUBY GLASS), BLUE (CERAMIC WASH), AND RAINBOW (MULTIPLE COLOR WASHED ON CRYSTAL)

Catalonian was handmade glass introduced in January 1927 and advertised as "a replica of seventeenth-century glass." Original labels read "Catalonian, A Reproduction of Old Spanish Glass."

Catalonian is distinguished by bubbled and spiral ridges on the exterior surface of each piece. The gather of glass was sprinkled with raw "batch" and then dipped back into the molten glass. This caused the granules to bubble. As the glassmaker worked the glass, the bubbles would stretch and become larger.

Blown items always have a rough pontil mark on the base. The edges of Catalonian were generally not polished or shaped. The only exception to this is Ruby glass items, which commanded higher prices at the time of production and thus demanded extra attention. If you find a piece of Catalonian other than Ruby with a ground edge, someone tried to repair a chip and didn't understand how it was made.

8

The Spanish Knobs line was based on the Catalonian shapes and glass formula. In addition to the bubbles, Spanish Knobs pieces have raised knobs molded into the glass. This line was sold along with Catalonian and original company ads combine the two in table settings. Today it's regarded as part of the Catalonian line, not a separate pattern.

As a rule, vases, candlesticks, and 8" plates are commonly located. Other tableware is harder to find, and cup and saucer sets, decanters, toilet bowls, covered cigarette boxes, and the whiskey set trays are rarely seen.

Crystal pieces are highlighted with one or more colors making a Rainbow color in the early 1940s. These colors were applied in bands, so that crystal became one of the colors in the "Rainbow." Rare Rainbow items illustrate three colors: blue, green, and red with no crystal band.

13

Pricing is the same for all the brilliant and soft colors (with crystal about 50% less than the others). Spanish Rose is the hardest of the regular production colors to find. We find mostly green in our travels. Ruby Stained items are about 50% higher than listed prices. Blue ceramic, Rainbow colors, and Ruby glass are at least 100% more. Rare colors are primarily found on vases and occasional pieces such as console sets and pitchers.

Milk glass vases in Catalonian shapes were made in the 1950s, but are not accepted as Catalonian. Catalonian has been known to fetch higher prices in art glass markets than in Depression glass ones.

	Ashtray, #1125	45.00		1	Goblet, 10 oz., low ftd., #1120	40.00
	Basket (made from fingerbowl), #1114	125.00			Goblet, 10 oz., low ftd., SK, #1142	65.00
	Bottle, toilet water w/lid, #1175	135.00		2	Goblet, 12 oz., low ftd. iced tea, #1121	40.00
	Bowl, bulb, #1178	70.00			Jug, 20 oz., 6", triangular, #1102P	150.00
10	Bowl, 4½", finger or mayo, #1114	45.00			Jug, 72 oz., cylindrical, #1100P	225.00
11	Bowl, 9", straight-sided salad, #1115	125.00			Jug, 72 oz., 10", triangular, #1101P	225.00
	Bowl, 9½", flared salad, #1115B	125.00			Jug, 72 oz., squat triangular, #1109	225.00
	Bowl, 12", Lily, cupped, #1108	350.00			Jug, whiskey decanter & stopper, #1127	300.00
	Bowl, 12¾", flared, #1185	200.00			Plate, 6", bread & butter, #1181	20.00
	Bowl, flower or low centerpiece, SK, #1130	375.00			Plate, 7", bread & butter, #1113	26.00
	Candlestick, mushroom, SK, #1131, pr.	150.00		3	Plate, 8", salad, #1112	30.00
7	Candlestick, ftd., #1124, pr.	100.00			Plate, 10", service, #1177	75.00
	Cigarette box and cover, #1107	165.00			Plate, 13", charger, #1111	125.00
	Comport, 6½", SK, #1145	85.00			Plate, 16", #1194	175.00
	Creamer or mayonnaise boat, #1106	40.00			Relish tray, 3 part, #1191	350.00
	Creamer, 7 oz., triangular, #1103P	45.00			Relish tray, 6 part, #1192	450.00
	Creamer, footed, SK, #1147	65.00			Saucer, #1180	50.00
	Cup, #1179	75.00			Sugar, no handles, #1105B	35.00
	Goblet, parfait, low ftd., SK, #1141	75.00			Sugar, two handles, #1105	45.00

	Sugar, footed, SK, #1146	65.00
12	Sundae (sherbet), 7 oz., ftd., #1123	45.00
	Sundae (sherbet), ftd. SK, #1140	65.00
	Tray, round whiskey set, #1128	300.00
9	Tumbler, 2 oz., whiskey, flat, #1119	40.00
	Tumbler, 2½ oz., whiskey, ftd., #1122	55.00
	Tumbler, 7 oz., flat, #1118	35.00
	Tumbler, 8 oz., flat, SK, #1138	75.00
6	Tumbler, 9 oz., flat, #1110	35.00
13	Tumbler, 12. oz., tea, flat, #1117	45.00
5	Tumbler, 12. oz., hdld. tea, flat, #1117B	65.00
	Vase, 3 bulge rolled edge, #1182	300.00
	Vase, 3 bulge cupped edge, #1183	300.00
	Vase, 3 bulge flared edge, #1184	300.00
8	Vase, Nasturtium, 4 openings, bulbous, #1170	300.00
	Vase, 3¾", Violet, SK, #1171	110.00
	Vase, 4", fan, SK, #1174	110.00
	Vase, 4", flared (hat), SK, #1153	110.00

	Vase, 4", Sweet Pea SK, #1154	110.00
	Vase, 4", triangular, #1103	65.00
	Vase, 6", flared (hat shape), #1116C	100.00
	Vase, 6", ftd., flared, SK, #1148	125.00
	Vase, 6", pillow (oblong), #1104	100.00
	Vase, 6", pinch bottle, triangular, SK, #1167	175.00
	Vase, 6", pinch bottle, 4-sided, SK, #1166	175.00
	Vase, 6", pinch bottle, 4 openings, SK, #1169	225.00
4	Vase, 6", triangular, #1102	90.00
	Vase, 6½", ftd. fan, #1172	90.00
	Vase, 7", fan, #1168	100.00
	Vase, 7", tumbler, #1116	100.00
	Vase, 8", fan, #1100B	125.00
	Vase, 8", flared (hat shape), #1100C	125.00
	Vase, 8", rose jar, #1109B	175.00
	Vase, 8", rose jar, SK, #1173	225.00
	Vase, 8", tumbler, #1100	125.00
	Vase, 10", triangular, #1101	175.00

COLORS: CRYSTAL, EBONY (GOLD ENCRUSTED)

There is a more complete accounting for etched Cambridge items under Rose Point later in this book (pgs. 191 – 196). Many Chantilly pieces are not listed here, as our foremost concern is to make you acquainted with the pattern itself. When pricing missing Chantilly items using the Rose Point list, you must remember that Rose Point items are currently a minimum of 40% to 60% higher due to collector demand.

Although Chantilly was made and sold along with the well-liked Rose Point, it never enthralled the magnitude of customers then or today as did Rose Point. We have included a couple of fold out pages from a pamphlet showing the readily available #3625 Chantilly stems and an array of vases at the top of page 58. Maybe this will help those having trouble differentiating stems or line numbers.

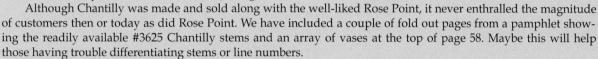

		Crystal
	Bowl, 7", bonbon, 2 hdld., ftd.	25.00
	Bowl, 7", relish/pickle, 2 pt.	30.00
	Bowl, 7", relish/pickle	32.00
	Bowl, 9", celery/relish, 3 pt.	35.00
	Bowl, 10", 4 ftd., flared	50.00
	Bowl, 11", tab hdld.	50.00
	Bowl, 11½", tab hdld. ftd.	55.00
	Bowl, 12", celery/relish, 3 pt.	50.00
	Bowl, 12", 4 ftd., flared	55.00
	Bowl, 12", 4 ftd., oval	60.00
	Bowl, 12", celery/relish, 5 pt.	50.00
	Butter, w/cover, round	195.00
	Butter, ¼ lb.	295.00
	Candlestick, 5"	28.00
	Candlestick, 6", 2-lite, "keyhole"	40.00
	Candlestick, 6", 3-lite	50.00
	Candy box, w/cover, ftd.	75.00
	Candy box, w/cover, rnd.	95.00
	Cocktail icer, 2 pc.	60.00
	Comport, 5½"	35.00
	Comport, 5⅜", blown	40.00
	Creamer	16.00
	Creamer, indiv., #3900, scalloped edge	15.00
20	Cup, #3900/17	15.00
	Decanter, ftd.	210.00
	Decanter, ball	250.00
	Hat, small	225.00
	Hat, large	325.00
	Hurricane lamp, candlestick base	160.00
	Hurricane lamp, keyhole base w/prisms	295.00
3	Ice bucket, w/chrome handle	125.00
	Marmalade & cover	60.00
	Mayonnaise (sherbet type bowl w/ladle)	35.00
	Mayonnaise, div. w/liner & 2 ladles	65.00
	Mayonnaise, w/liner & ladle	50.00
	Mustard & cover	95.00
	Oil, 6 oz., hdld., w/stopper	125.00
	Pitcher, ball	195.00
	Pitcher, Doulton	350.00
	Pitcher, upright	250.00
8	Pitcher, 32 oz., martini jug, #3900/114	175.00
	Plate, crescent, salad	135.00
	Plate, 6½", bread/butter	7.00
7	Plate, 8", salad	11.00
	Plate, 8", tab hdld., ftd., bonbon	20.00

		Crystal
	Plate, 10½", dinner	65.00
	Plate, 12", 4 ftd., service	50.00
	Plate, 13", 4 ftd.	60.00
	Plate, 13½", tab hdld., cake	65.00
	Plate, 14", torte	45.00
	Salad dressing bottle	165.00
	Salt & pepper, pr., flat	30.00
	Salt & pepper, footed	35.00
	Salt & pepper, handled	35.00
20	Saucer, #3900/17	3.00
9	Stem, #3080, 9 oz., water	40.00
12	Stem, #3138, 6 oz., tall sherbet	16.00
	Stem, #3600, 1 oz., cordial	45.00
	Stem, #3600, 2½ oz., cocktail	20.00
	Stem, #3600, 2½ oz., wine	30.00
	Stem, #3600, 4½ oz., claret	35.00
	Stem, #3600, 4½ oz., low oyster cocktail	14.00
	Stem, #3600, 7 oz., tall sherbet	16.00
	Stem, #3600, 7 oz., low sherbet	14.00
	Stem, #3600, 10 oz., water	28.00
	Stem, #3625, 1 oz., cordial	45.00
	Stem, #3625, 3 oz., cocktail	22.00
	Stem, #3625, 4½ oz., claret	35.00
	Stem, #3625, 4½ oz., low oyster cocktail	14.00
	Stem, #3625, 7 oz., low sherbet	14.00
	Stem, #3625, 7 oz., tall sherbet	16.00
	Stem, #3625, 10 oz., water	28.00
	Stem, #3775, 1 oz., cordial	45.00
19	Stem, #3775, 2½ oz., wine	30.00
16	Stem, #3775, 3 oz., cocktail	22.00
	Stem, #3775, 4½ oz., claret	35.00
	Stem, #3775, 4½ oz., oyster cocktail	14.00
17	Stem, #3775, 6 oz., low sherbet	14.00
18	Stem, #3775, 6 oz., tall sherbet	16.00
6	Stem, #3779, 1 oz., cordial	55.00
4	Stem, #3779, 2½ oz., wine	30.00
5	Stem, #3779, 3 oz., cocktail	22.00
	Stem, #3779, 4½ oz., claret	35.00
	Stem, #3779, 4½ oz., low oyster cocktail	14.00
1	Stem, #3779, 6 oz., tall sherbet	16.00
	Stem, #3779, 6 oz., low sherbet	14.00
2	Stem, #3779, 9 oz., water	28.00
	Stem, #7801, 10 oz., goblet	28.00
	Sugar	16.00
	Sugar, indiv., #3900, scalloped edge	15.00

		Crystal
14	Syrup, 1670, drip cut top	250.00
	Tumbler, #3600, 5 oz., ftd., juice	16.00
	Tumbler, #3600, 12 oz., ftd., tea	22.00
11	Tumbler, #3625, 5 oz., ftd., juice	16.00
10	Tumbler, #3625, 10 oz., ftd., water	18.00
	Tumbler, #3625, 12 oz., ftd., tea	24.00
	Tumbler, #3775, 5 oz., ftd., juice	16.00
	Tumbler, #3775, 10 oz., ftd., water	18.00
	Tumbler, #3775, 12 oz., ftd., tea	22.00
	Tumbler, #3779, 5 oz., ftd., juice	18.00
	Tumbler, #3779, 12 oz., ftd., tea	22.00
	Tumbler, 13 oz.	25.00
	Vase, 5", globe	55.00
	Vase, 6", high ftd., flower	45.00
	Vase, 8", high ftd., flower	50.00
	Vase, 9", keyhole base	60.00
	Vase, 10", bud	95.00
	Vase, 11", ftd., flower	95.00
	Vase, 11", ped. ftd., flower	115.00
	Vase, 12", keyhole base	110.00
	Vase, 13", ftd., flower	165.00
21	Cordial, Sterling base	65.00
15	Wine, Farberware Trims	25.00
22	Sugar, Farberware Trims	25.00
13	Creamer, Farberware Trims	30.00

COLORS: CRYSTAL, FLAMINGO, MOONGLEAM, HAWTHORNE, MARIGOLD

Flamingo (pink) Charter Oak pieces are offered periodically, but we rarely find other colors. Notice, we have been able to show Flamingo for years but other colors seem not to appear. Stemware, however, seems to materialize in small batches of pink rather than a piece or two. Prices have remained steady over the last few years, which means there has been sufficient supply to meet collector demand. Price increases often indicate not enough being found to supply all who want it. Many pieces of Charter Oak are unmarked, however, and bargains can still be revealed to an astute eye. Acorns are the hallmark of the pattern. Plantation with its pineapple and Charter Oak with its acorn stems ought to be hard to miss.

You can see that clever "Acorn" #130, one lite candleholder in our *Florences' Glassware Pattern Identification Guide, Volume 2*. The base is an oak leaf with stem curled up and an acorn for the candle cup. Honestly, this candle is not Charter Oak pattern, but most Charter Oak collectors try to obtain these to go with their sets.

Heisey designed a number of candles to "blend" (their words) with numerous patterns. This candle was made during the same time as Charter Oak and mostly in the same colors. Yeoman cups and saucers are often used with this set since there were no cups and saucers made. A Yeoman cup and saucer set is pictured here, and used with Charter Oak.

		Crystal	Flamingo	Moongleam	Hawthorne	Marigold
	Bowl, 11", floral, #116 (oak leaf)	50.00	50.00	70.00	85.00	
4	Bowl, finger, #3362	10.00	17.50	20.00		
	Candleholder, 1-lite, #130, "Acorn"	150.00	400.00	500.00		
	Candlestick, 3", #116 (oak leaf)	25.00	35.00	45.00	100.00	
1	Candlestick, 5", 3-lite, #129, "Tricorn"	60.00	110.00	120.00	160.00	200.00+
11	Coaster, #10 (Oak Leaf)	10.00	20.00	25.00	35.00	
	Comport, 6", low ft., #3362	45.00	55.00	60.00	80.00	100.00
18	Comport, 7", ftd., #3362	50.00	65.00	70.00	120.00	175.00
7	Cup and saucer (#1231 Yeoman)	15.00	25.00	25.00	35.00	
	Lamp, #4262 (blown comport/water filled to magnify design & stabilize lamp)	1,000.00	1,500.00	1,500.00		
14	Pitcher, flat, #3362		160.00	180.00		
	Plate, 6", salad, #1246 (Acorn & Leaves)	5.00	10.00	12.50	20.00	
2	Plate, 7", luncheon/salad, #1246 (Acorn & Leaves)	8.00	12.00	17.50	22.50	
	Plate, 8", luncheon, #1246 (Acorn & Leaves)	10.00	15.00	20.00	25.00	
17	Plate, 10½", dinner, #1246 (Acorn & Leaves)	30.00	45.00	55.00	70.00	

		Crystal	Flamingo	Moongleam	Hawthorne	Marigold
12	Stem, 3 oz., cocktail, #3362	10.00	25.00	25.00	45.00	40.00
10	Stem, 3½ oz., low ft., oyster cocktail, #3362	8.00	20.00	20.00	40.00	35.00
15	Stem, 4½ oz., parfait, #3362	15.00	25.00	35.00	60.00	50.00
6	Stem, 6 oz., saucer champagne, #3362	10.00	15.00	20.00	50.00	40.00
5	Stem, 6 oz., sherbet, low ft., #3362	10.00	15.00	22.00	50.00	40.00
16	Stem, 8 oz., goblet, high ft., #3362	15.00	30.00	30.00	95.00	50.00
3	Stem, 8 oz., luncheon goblet, low ft., #3362	15.00	35.00	35.00	95.00	50.00
13	Tumbler, 10 oz., flat, #3362	10.00	20.00	25.00	35.00	30.00
9	Tumbler, 12 oz., flat, #3362	12.50	20.00	25.00	40.00	35.00

COLOR: CRYSTAL

Cherokee Rose stemware line #17399 is the teardrop style in the photo, while the #17403 stem is represented by the footed juice in the center. Should you find a Cherokee Rose cup or saucer, please let us know. The #5902 line had scalloped and beaded edges on serving pieces. A few are found with gold trim, but that was called Laurel by Tiffin.

13

	Bowl, 5", finger	28.00
	Bowl, 6", fruit or nut, #5902	28.00
	Bowl, 7", nappy, #5902	45.00
	Bowl, 10", deep salad, cupped, #5902	70.00
	Bowl, 10½", celery, rectangular, #5902	50.00
	Bowl, 12", crimped, #5902	65.00
	Bowl, 12½", centerpiece, flared, #5902	65.00
	Bowl, 13", centerpiece, cone shape, #5902	75.00
	Cake plate, 12½", center hdld., #5902	55.00
5	Candlesticks, pr., double branch, 7¼"	100.00
	Comport, 6", #15082	52.50
6	Creamer, also bead hndl., #5902	20.00
	Icer w/liner	125.00
	Mayonnaise, liner and ladle, #5902	60.00
	Pitcher, sleek top dips to hndl., #5859	650.00
	Pitcher, 2 qt., straight top, ftd., #14194	500.00+
	Plate, 6", sherbet	8.00
4	Plate, 8", luncheon, plain or beaded rim, #5902	15.00
	Plate, 13½", turned-up edge, lily, #5902	50.00
	Plate, 14", sandwich, #5902	55.00
13	Relish, 6½", 3 pt., #5902	38.00
	Relish, 12½", 3 pt., #5902	60.00
	Shaker, pr.	160.00
	Stem, 1 oz., cordial, #17399	40.00

	Stem, 2 oz., sherry, #17399	30.00
10	Stem, 3½ oz., cocktail, #17399	16.00
7	Stem, 3½ oz., wine, #17399	30.00
9	Stem, 4 oz., claret, #17399	40.00
	Stem, 4½ oz., parfait	45.00
12	Stem, 5½ oz., sherbet/champagne, #17399	15.00
1	Stem, 9 oz., water, #17399	25.00
	Sugar, also w/beaded hndl., #5902	20.00
	Table bell, #9742 – lg.; #9743 – sm.	75.00
11	Tumbler, 4½ oz., oyster cocktail, #14198	20.00
8	Tumbler, 5 oz., ftd., juice, #17399	20.00
	Tumbler, 8 oz., ftd., water, #17399	22.00
	Tumbler, 10½ oz., ftd., ice tea, #17399	35.00
	Vase, 6", bud, #14185	25.00
3	Vase, 8", bud, #14185	35.00
	Vase, 8½", tear drop	75.00
	Vase, 9¼", tub, #17350, (1) ball stem, ftd.	95.00
2	Vase, 10", bud, #14185	40.00
	Vase, 11", bud, 6 beaded stem, flare rim	50.00
	Vase, 11", urn, #5943, (1) ball stem, ftd.	110.00
	Vase, 12", flared, #5855	135.00

COMPANY, 1931 – 1938

COLORS: CRYSTAL, SAHARA YELLOW (CHINTZ ONLY), MOONGLEAM GREEN, FLAMINGO PINK, AND ALEXANDRITE ORCHID (ALL COLORS MADE IN FORMAL CHINTZ)

Heisey's Chintz pattern is found as two distinct ornamentations on assorted Heisey blanks. Pieces pictured below are known as Chintz. Pieces with surrounding circles are pictured at the bottom of page 63 and are designated Formal Chintz. These patterns are similarly priced. We have never found any tumblers or stemware in Formal Chintz although they were supposedly made on the #3390 Carcassone stem line.

Collectors have informed us that Chintz shakers have been found on #1401 Empress line. Items do sneak by our listings until someone lets us know so we can correct omissions. Sahara is the color most desired, but a few collectors search for crystal. Alexandrite Formal Chintz is quite uncommon. It is very striking when displayed in quantity. There is so little Alexandrite color that putting a set together would be a tremendous challenge.

Do not confuse this pattern with the Fostoria or Tiffin Chintz; and realize that you must also specify the company name when you ask for any pattern named Chintz. It was a trendy trade name used by many glass and pottery companies for their wares.

		Crystal	Sahara				Crystal	Sahara
10	Bowl, cream soup	18.00	35.00	15	Bowl, 10", oval, vegetable		20.00	35.00
16	Bowl, finger, #4107	10.00	20.00		Bowl, 11", dolphin ft., floral		45.00	110.00
17	Bowl, nut, dolphin ftd., individual	40.00	60.00		Bowl, 13", 2 pt., pickle & olive		15.00	35.00
	Bowl, 5½", ftd., preserve, hdld.	15.00	30.00		Comport, 7", oval		45.00	85.00
	Bowl, 6", ftd., mint	20.00	32.00	7	Creamer, 3 dolphin ft.		20.00	50.00
	Bowl, 6", ftd., 2 hdld., jelly	17.00	35.00		Creamer, individual		12.00	30.00
	Bowl, 7", triplex relish	20.00	40.00	1	Cup		10.00	25.00
	Bowl, 7½", Nasturtium	20.00	40.00		Grapefruit, ftd., #3389, Duquesne		30.00	60.00
	Bowl, 8½", ftd., 2 hdld., floral	35.00	70.00		Ice bucket, ftd.		85.00	155.00

		Crystal	Sahara
	Mayonnaise, 5½", dolphin ft.	35.00	65.00
	Oil, 4 oz.	60.00	135.00
	Pitcher, 3 pint, dolphin ft.	200.00	300.00
	Plate, 6", sq. or rnd., bread	6.00	15.00
	Plate, 7", sq. or rnd., salad	8.00	18.00
12	Plate, 8", sq. or rnd., luncheon	10.00	22.00
	Plate, 10½", sq. or rnd., dinner	40.00	85.00
	Plate, 12", two hdld.	25.00	47.50
14	Plate, 13", hors d' oeuvre, two hdld.	30.00	65.00
13	Platter, 14", oval	35.00	90.00
	Salt and pepper, pr.	40.00	95.00
2	Saucer	3.00	5.00
	Stem, #3389, Duquesne, 1 oz., cordial	50.00	100.00
6	Stem, #3389, 2½ oz., wine	18.00	40.00
	Stem, #3389, 3 oz., cocktail	12.00	30.00

		Crystal	Sahara
	Stem, #3389, 4 oz., claret	18.00	40.00
	Stem, #3389, 4 oz., oyster cocktail	10.00	22.00
5	Stem, #3389, 5 oz., parfait	12.00	20.00
	Stem, #3389, 5 oz., saucer champagne	10.00	15.00
4	Stem, #3389, 5 oz., sherbet	7.00	10.00
3	Stem, #3389, 9 oz., water	15.00	35.00
	Sugar, 3 dolphin ft.	20.00	50.00
8	Sugar, individual	12.00	30.00
	Tray, 10", celery	15.00	30.00
	Tray, 12", sq., ctr. hdld., sandwich	35.00	65.00
	Tray, 13", celery	18.00	45.00
	Tumbler, #3389, 5 oz., ftd., juice	10.00	20.00
	Tumbler, #3389, 8 oz., soda	11.00	22.00
11	Tumbler, #3389, 10 oz., ftd., water	12.00	22.00
9	Tumbler, #3389, 12 oz., iced tea	14.00	25.00
18	Tumbler, #3390, 2½ oz., bar	10.00	
	Vase, 9", dolphin ft.	95.00	200.00

COLORS: CRYSTAL, PINK; CRYSTAL WITH NILE GREEN TRIM

Classic is an older pattern that I have had fun finding over the years. When you start with few listings, you can discover an assortment of surprises in your travels. Dinner plates shocked me several years ago, as did a pink cup. Alas, I have never found a saucer to go with it, but I'm confident it will turn up. Note the decorated vase that was found right at this book's deadline.

I prefer the pink Classic, but only stemmed beverage items are surfacing in that color. Tiffin pitchers (one pictured in pink) came with and without a lid. The one here has the top curved in so it will not take a lid. Remember that Tiffin pitcher lids have no pattern etched on them.

Note the crystal pitcher at the bottom of page 65, which is a different style, but holds approximately 60 ounces. I have priced both pitchers in the same listing. As with all glass dinner plates with no pattern in the center, you need to check for blemishes and scratches from use. Of course, finding any mint condition dinner plate 70 or 80 years after its manufacture is nearly impossible. I, personally, have found few serving pieces save for a two-handled bowl and a cheese and cracker.

Pink Classic stems are found on the #17024 line that is also found with Tiffin's Flanders pattern. Crystal stemmed items seem to surface on the #14185 line. There are some size discrepancies within these two stemware lines. We have measured both colors and noted them in the listings.

Nile green trim is found on the #15011 stem line which has a wafer beneath the flared rim bowl. On #15016, the bowl is cupped at the rim.

32

		Crystal	Pink
21	Bowl, 9½" Nouvelle, #15361	100.00	
	Bowl, 2 hdld., 8" x 9¼"	140.00	
	Bowl, 11" centerpiece, #14185	120.00	
	Bowl, 13" centerpiece, rolled edge	135.00	
	Candy jar w/cover, ½ lb., ftd	150.00	
	Candle, 5", #9758	50.00	
28	Cheese & cracker set	110.00	
	Comport, 6" wide, 3¼" tall	75.00	
	Creamer, flat, #6	40.00	90.00
24	Creamer, ftd., #5931	33.00	
	Creamer, ftd., cone, #14185	33.00	
27	Cup, #8869	75.00	
	Finger bowl, ftd., #14185	25.00	50.00
29	Mayonnaise, or whipped cream w/ladle, ftd.		75.00

		Crystal	Pink
	Pitcher, ftd., hld, #194 (bulbous)	225.00	
4	Pitcher, 61 oz., (2 qt.) #114	250.00	595.00
25, 15	Pitcher, 61 oz., w/cover, #145 (subtract $50 w/out cover)	325.00	595.00
7	Plate, 6 5/8", champagne liner, #23	8.00	
22	Plate, 7 1/2", #8814	12.50	
	Plate, 8", #8833	15.00	25.00
23	Plate, 10", dinner, #8818	100.00	125.00
27	Saucer, #8869	15.00	
6	Sherbet, 3 1/8", 6 1/2 oz., short	17.50	*38.00
18	Stem, 3 7/8", 1 oz., cordial	65.00	
19	Stem, 4 15/16", 3 oz., wine	30.00	*65.00
13	Stem, 4 7/8", 3 3/4 oz., cocktail	35.00	
	Stem, 4 7/8", 4 oz., cocktail	22.00	
14, 20	Stem, 6 1/2", 5 oz., parfait	35.00	*75.00
	Stem, 6", 7 1/2 oz., saucer champagne	20.00	*50.00
2	Stem, 7 1/4", 9 oz., water	33.00	*70.00
	Stem, 22 oz., grapefruit w/liner	75.00	
	Sugar, flat, #6	33.00	95.00
	Sugar, ftd.	33.00	
	Sugar, ftd., covered, #14185	35.00	
26	Tray, center handle	75.00	
5	Tumbler, 3 1/2", 5 oz., ftd., juice	20.00	
8	Tumbler, 4 1/2", 8 1/2 oz., ftd., water	22.00	60.00
11	Tumbler, 4 1/8", 10 1/2 oz., flat, water	25.00	
	Tumbler, 5 9/16", 14 oz., ftd., tea	30.00	
	Tumbler, 6", 13 oz., ftd., iced tea		75.00
3	Tumbler, 6 1/16", 14 oz., ftd., iced tea	33.00	
	Tumbler, 6 1/4", 6 1/2 oz., ftd., Pilsner	40.00	
12	Tumbler, 10 oz., flat, table	28.00	
10	Tumbler, 12 oz., flat, tea	33.00	
	Tumbler, tea, hdld., #14185	35.00	
30	Vase, bud, 6 1/2", #14185	35.00	
32	Vase, 8", wide optic	**175.00	
31	Vase, bud, 10 1/2", #14185	40.00	

*Slight variation in size 40.00
**with decoration 350.00

COLORS: AMBER, WILLOW BLUE, CRYSTAL, EBONY, EMERALD (LIGHT GREEN), GOLD KRYSTOL, PEACH BLO

Cleo Peach Blo (pink) and Emerald (light green) prices have stayed about the same since supplies of those colors continue to be found. Unfortunately, Emerald Cleo has been ignored by new collectors of late and is unchanging in dealer inventories. Cleo can be found in substantial sets of pink or green, but not all pieces were made in the other colors. The blue, a forerunner of Moonlight blue, was dubbed Willow by Cambridge and is pictured below. A few collections of Willow have surfaced in the market the last few years, and have quickly been absorbed into new collections. Original owners made a tidy profit at today's prices from their long years of patient collecting. Hopefully, you will encounter a large set for a reasonable price; but those probabilities are not as numerous as in the past.

There are more collectors looking for blue than quantities turning up. Thus, prices for Willow Cleo continue upward, although at a slower pace than in the past. Most blue is found on Cambridge's Decagon blank. Rarely found Cleo items garner some serious prices. There is always a market for any rare or unusual glassware.

When we have spotted rare pieces of Cleo in the past, they were usually amber rather than colors that charm collectors. Cleo will continue to attract new collectors as long as the supply lasts. You might consider mixing colors or even collecting one particular item such as the ice buckets and pails like those pictured on page 68.

	Blue	Pink Green Yellow Amber
Almond, 2½", individual	100.00	65.00
Basket, 7", 2 hdld. (up-turned sides), Decagon	60.00	30.00
Basket, 11", 2 hdld. (up-turned sides), Decagon	95.00	45.00
Bouillon cup, w/saucer, 2 hdld., Decagon	95.00	50.00
Bowl, 2 pt., relish	40.00	20.00
Bowl, 3½", cranberry	65.00	45.00
Bowl, 5½", fruit	40.00	22.00
Bowl, 5½" 2 hdld., bonbon, Decagon	60.00	22.00
Bowl, 6", 4 ft., comport	60.00	32.00

		Blue	Pink Green Yellow Amber
	Bowl, 6", cereal, Decagon	60.00	35.00
	Bowl, 6½", 2 hdld., bonbon, Decagon	40.00	22.00
	Bowl, 7½", tab hdld., soup	70.00	32.00
	Bowl, 8", miniature console		175.00
	Bowl, 8½"	90.00	38.00
	Bowl, 8½" 2 hdld., Decagon	100.00	42.00
	Bowl, 9", covered vegetable		295.00
	Bowl, 9½", oval veg., Decagon	135.00	70.00
8	Bowl, 9", pickle, Decagon, #1082	75.00	42.00

13

		Blue	Pink Green Yellow Amber
	Bowl, 10", 2 hdld., Decagon	125.00	70.00
3	Bowl, 11", oval, celery, #1083	125.00	70.00
	Bowl, 11½", oval	125.00	70.00
	Bowl, 12", console	140.00	70.00
7	Bowl, 12", #842	125.00	65.00
22	Bowl, 15½", oval, Decagon		210.00
	Bowl, cream soup w/saucer, 2 hdld., Decagon	90.00	55.00
	Bowl, finger w/liner, #3077	75.00	45.00
	Bowl, finger w/liner, #3115	75.00	45.00
5	Candlestick, 1-lite, 2 styles, 4", #627	40.00	30.00
	Candlestick, 2-lite	110.00	60.00
	Candlestick, 3-lite	150.00	80.00
	Candy box w/lid	295.00	175.00
	Candy & cover, tall	325.00	195.00
	Comport, 7", tall, #3115	110.00	70.00
1	Comport, 12", #877	145.00	85.00
11	Creamer, Decagon/"Lightning"	35.00	22.00
	Creamer, ewer style, 6"	195.00	110.00
9	Creamer, ftd., #867	40.00	20.00
14	Cup, Decagon, #865	30.00	12.50
	Decanter, w/stopper		325.00
13	Gravy boat, w/liner plate, Decagon, #1091	595.00	295.00
20	Gravy boat, 2 spout, #917	185.00	
21	Gravy boat liner, #167	75.00	
16	Ice bowl, #844		150.00
17	Ice pail, #851	225.00	115.00
15	Ice tub, #394	210.00	110.00
19	Mayonnaise, w/liner and ladle, Decagon, #983	145.00	80.00
	Mayonnaise, ftd.	75.00	45.00
	Oil, 6 oz., w/stopper, Decagon	750.00	195.00
	Pitcher, 3½ pt., #38		235.00
	Pitcher, w/cover, 22 oz.		275.00
	Pitcher, w/cover, 60 oz., #804		495.00
	Pitcher, w/cover, 62 oz., #955	675.00	375.00
	Pitcher, w/cover, 63 oz., #3077	995.00	395.00
	Pitcher, w/cover, 68 oz., #937		375.00
2	Plate, 6½", bread & butter, #809	12.00	9.00
	Plate, 7"	25.00	15.00
	Plate, 7", 2 hdld., Decagon	30.00	20.00
24	Plate, 8½", luncheon, Decagon	35.00	20.00
	Plate, 9½", dinner, Decagon	150.00	65.00
	Plate, 9½", grill		90.00
	Plate, 11", 2 hdld., Decagon	110.00	50.00
	Platter, 12"	175.00	110.00
23	Platter, 15", #1079	295.00	195.00
	Platter, w/cover, oval (toast)		425.00
	Platter, asparagus, indented, w/sauce & spoon		395.00
	Salt dip, 1½"	125.00	75.00
14	Saucer, Decagon, #865	8.00	5.00
	Server, 12", ctr. hand.	70.00	40.00
	Stem, #3077, 1 oz., cordial	195.00	175.00

		Blue	Pink Green Yellow Amber
	Stem, #3077, 2½ oz., cocktail		30.00
	Stem, #3077, 3½ oz., wine	95.00	55.00
	Stem, #3077, 6 oz., low sherbet	35.00	18.00
	Stem, #3077, 6 oz., tall sherbet	45.00	22.00
	Stem, #3115, 9 oz.		28.00
	Stem, #3115, 3½ oz., cocktail		22.00
	Stem, #3115, 6 oz., fruit		14.00
	Stem, #3115, 6 oz., low sherbet		14.00
	Stem, #3115, 6 oz., tall sherbet		16.00
	Stem, #3115, 9 oz., water		25.00
	Sugar cube tray		185.00
4	Sugar, Decagon/"Lightning"	35.00	22.00
10	Sugar, ftd., #867	40.00	20.00
	Sugar sifter, ftd., 6¾"	850.00	295.00
	Syrup pitcher, drip cut		175.00
	Syrup pitcher, glass lid		250.00
	Toast & cover, round		500.00
	Tobacco humidor		500.00
	Tray, 12", handled serving		155.00
	Tray, 12", oval service, Decagon	225.00	125.00
	Tray, creamer & sugar, oval		35.00
12	Tray, hdld. for creamer/sugar	35.00	20.00
	Tumbler, #3077, 2½ oz., ftd.	110.00	55.00
6	Tumbler, #3077, 5 oz., ftd.	60.00	22.00
	Tumbler, #3077, 8 oz., ftd.	60.00	25.00
	Tumbler, #3077, 10 oz., ftd.	65.00	28.00
	Tumbler, #3022, 12 oz., ftd.	95.00	35.00
	Tumbler, #3115, 2½ oz., ftd.		50.00
	Tumbler, #3115, 5 oz., ftd.		22.00
	Tumbler, #3115, 8 oz., ftd.		22.00
	Tumbler, #3115, 10 oz., ftd.		35.00
	Tumbler, #3115, 12 oz., ftd.		32.00
	Tumbler, 12 oz., flat		55.00
	Vase, 5½"		95.00
18	Vase, 9", ftd., #3450, Nautilis		225.00
	Vase, 9½"		155.00
	Vase, 11"		195.00

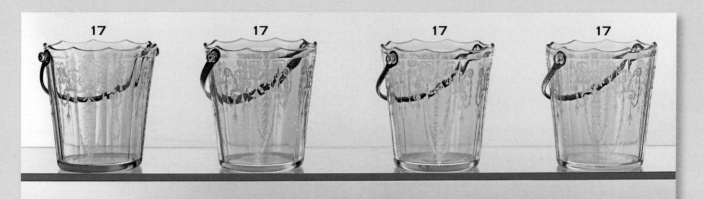

COLORS: CRYSTAL; SOME YELLOW, OPAQUE BLUE, GREEN, WHITE, AMBER, RED IN 1980S AS MAYPOLE

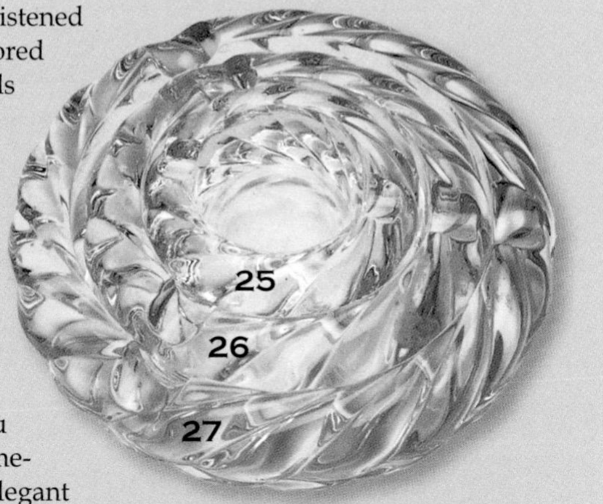

Fostoria's majestic Colony was developed from an earlier Fostoria pattern christened Queen Ann. A few Colony pieces were made as late as 1983. Fostoria listed colored pieces of Colony as Maypole in the 1980s catalogs. Red vases, candlesticks, and bowls now being found were produced by Viking for Fostoria in the early 1980s. Note the amber tall candle and red bowl pictured on page 70. Dalzell-Viking later made red for Lancaster Colony who now has possession of these Fostoria moulds.

Stems and tumblers with a thin, plain bowl and a Colony patterned foot (sold to go with this pattern) were called Colonial Dame. You might even find these stems with colored bowls in dark emerald green or amethyst.

Note the round stacking set of three ashtrays containing a 3", 4½", and 6", pictured on the right. Round ones are rarely found, though the square ones appear regularly.

Experimental pieces such as blue opaque goblets turn up sporadically, but you could never accumulate many pieces in that color. Colony prices have slowed somewhat indicating there is enough available for those searching for it. As with other Elegant patterns, stemware abounds. Some pieces you may have trouble locating include finger bowls, cream soups, punch bowl, and an ice tub with flat rim, flat tumblers, and cigarette boxes. The supply of pitchers is adequate for now and we just found one for $9.00 in an antique mall. Evidently, that labeled "old twist pitcher" was not recognized as Colony. All the flat pieces with plain centers need to be studied closely for abrasions, but that is true for any pattern with clear centers. When stacking flat pieces today, place a paper plate between each one to protect them for future generations.

		Crystal
	Ashtray, 2⅞", sq.	10.00
25	Ashtray, 3", round, #2412½	15.00
	Ashtray, 3½", sq.	16.00
26	Ashtray, 4½", round, #2412½	22.00
27	Ashtray, 6", round, #2412½	22.00
24	Bowl, 2¾" ftd., almond	15.00
10	Bowl, 4½", rnd.	10.00
	Bowl, 4¾", finger	45.00
	Bowl, 4¾", hdld., whip cream	10.00
	Bowl, 5", bonbon, rolled edge	10.00
	Bowl, 5", cream soup	55.00
	Bowl, 5", hdld., sweet meat	12.00
13	Bowl, 5½", sq.	20.00
	Bowl, 5⅝", 3 toe nut	18.00
	Bowl, 5¾", high ft.	14.00
6	Bowl, 5", rnd.	13.00
	Bowl, 6", rose	22.00
	Bowl, 7", 2 pt., relish, 2 hdld.	12.00
	Bowl, 7", bonbon, 3 ftd.	12.00
21	Bowl, 7", olive, oblong	12.00
	Bowl, 7¾", salad	22.00
	Bowl, 8", cupped	40.00
	Bowl, 8½", hdld.	35.00
	Bowl, 9", rolled console	35.00
17	Bowl, 9½", pickle	20.00
	Bowl, 9¾", salad	45.00
	Bowl, 8¾" x 9¾", w/rolled edge, muffin tray	30.00
	Bowl, 10", fruit	38.00
	Bowl, 10½", low ft.	65.00
	Bowl, 10½", high ft., #2412½, 6½" tall	110.00
	Bowl, 10½", oval	50.00
	Bowl, 10½", oval, 2 part	45.00

		Crystal
2	Bowl, 11", oval, ftd.	65.00
	Bowl, 11", flared	35.00
	Bowl, 11½", celery	30.00
	Bowl, 13", console	38.00
	Bowl, 13¼", punch, ftd.	395.00
	Bowl, 14", fruit	55.00
3	Butter dish, ¼ lb.	40.00
	Candlestick, 3½"	14.00
	Candlestick, 6½", double	38.00
	Candlestick, 7"	35.00
	Candlestick, 7½", w/8 prisms	100.00
1	Candlestick, 9"	38.00
	Candlestick, 9¾", w/prisms	125.00
	Candlestick, 14½", w/10 prisms	195.00
4	Candy, w/cover, 6½"	42.00
	Candy, w/cover, ftd., ½ lb.	70.00
	Cheese & cracker	50.00
	Cigarette box	50.00
	Comport, 4", low foot	15.00
	Comport, cover, 6½"	40.00
	Comport, 7"	55.00
	Comport, 7", w/plain top	85.00
	Creamer, 3¼", indiv.	10.00
23	Creamer, 3¾"	8.00
18	Cup, 6 oz., ftd.	5.50
	Cup, punch	13.00
	Ice bucket	90.00
	Ice bucket, plain edge	235.00
	Lamp, electric	195.00
	Mayonnaise, 3 pc.	35.00
	Oil w/stopper, 4½ oz.	38.00
14	Pitcher, 16 oz., milk	58.00

		Crystal
	Pitcher, 48 oz., ice lip	165.00
	Pitcher, 2 qt., ice lip	100.00
	Plate, ctr. hdld., sandwich	30.00
	Plate, 6", bread & butter	5.00
	Plate, 6½", lemon, hdld.	10.00
22	Plate, 7", salad	8.00
	Plate, 8", luncheon	10.00
19	Plate, 9", dinner	22.00
	Plate, 10", hdld., cake	25.00
	Plate, 12", ftd., salver	75.00
	Plate, 13", torte	28.00
	Plate, 15", torte	55.00
	Plate, 18", torte	85.00
	Platter, 12"	48.00
	Relish, 10", 3 part	22.00
	Salt, 2½" indiv., pr.	18.00
	Salt & pepper, pr., 3⅝"	24.00
18	Saucer	1.50
	Stem, 3½ oz., cocktail	8.00

		Crystal
5	Stem, 3⅜", 4 oz., oyster cocktail	8.00
	Stem, 3⅝", 5 oz., sherbet	6.00
	Stem, 4", 3½ oz., cocktail	9.00
7	Stem, 4¼", 3¼ oz., wine	16.00
8	Stem, 5¼", 9 oz., goblet	13.00
	Sugar, 2¾", indiv.	10.00
20	Sugar, 3½"	8.00
	Tray for indiv. sugar/cream, 6¾"	12.00
15	Tumbler, 3⅝", 5 oz., juice	22.00
12	Tumbler, 3⅞", 9 oz., water	20.00
16	Tumbler, 4⅞", 12 oz., tea	33.00
	Tumbler, 4½", 5 oz., ftd.	15.00
9	Tumbler, 5¾", 12 oz., ftd.	18.00
	Vase, 6", bud, flared	14.00
	Vase, 7", cupped	40.00
	Vase, 7½", flared	55.00
	Vase, 9", cornucopia	80.00
	Vase, 12", straight	175.00

COLONY PATTERN

No. 2412 LINE

Fostoria Glass Company, Moundsville, West Virginia, January 1, 1941

2412—Sweetmeat
Diameter 5 in.
Height 1½ in.

2412—Bon Bon
Length 5 in.
Width 6 in.

2412 Whip Cream
Diameter 4¾ in.
Height 1¾ in.

2412—Lemon
Diameter 6½ in.

2412—3 Piece Ash Tray Set
Consisting of:
1/12 Doz. 2412—3 in. Ind. Ash Tray
1/12 Doz. 2412—3½ in. Small Ash Tray
1/12 Doz. 2412—4½ in. Large Ash Tray

2412—Oblong Cigarette Box and Cover
Length 6 in.   Width 4¾ in.
Height 1⅜ in.   Holds 38 Cigarettes

2412—3 in. Individual Ash Tray

2412—3½ in. Small Ash Tray

2412—4½ in. Large Ash Tray

22A

COLORS: FOSTORIA BLUE, TIFFIN CRYSTAL WITH BLUE

"Columbine Variant" is a name we first used for this cutting, which is very close to Tiffin's Columbine and Double Columbine patterns. However, in researching, Cathy found the pattern called Bluebell in a 1928 Butler Brothers merchandising catalog. After this book, we will list it as Bluebell and not as "Columbine Variant."

This cutting was fashioned on both Fostoria and Tiffin mould blanks suggesting a separate decorating firm rather than either of these companies per se. This early Blue color of Fostoria and the blue of Tiffin are virtually identical, so a lot of pieces could be used for this cutting. The name apparently came from the bluebell-like cutting as well as the color. Frankly, there does not seem to be much of this offered in the marketplace today, which lends credibility to its not being a major company's production.

The candlestick and comport are Fostoria mould blanks, but all the other pieces we have found have been on Tiffin blanks. Additional pieces could be found, but our listing only includes those we could document. We've found additional pieces, but they were priced in groups of six or eight with over half of them damaged. A great idea for the seller, but not the buyer who does not want a group which forces you to own damaged items.

		Crystal
5	Candlestick, 4", #2324, Fostoria	25.00
4	Comport, 6¼" h x 7¼" w, #2327, Fostoria	65.00
	Creamer	37.50
2	Pitcher w/cover, 2 qt., #14194	250.00
3	Plate, 7⅛", #2350, Fostoria	12.50
	Stem, 3 oz., wine #50001	45.00
	Stem, 6 oz., low sherbet #50001	18.00
	Stem, 6 oz., high sherbet #50001	22.00
1	Stem, 9 oz., 7¼" water #50001	35.00
	Sugar	37.50

COLORS: CRYSTAL, ZIRCON/LIMELIGHT, SAHARA, AND RARE IN AMBER

Crystolite is one of the most recognizable Heisey patterns since nearly all pieces are marked with the well-known H inside a diamond. That prominent mark means you will seldom find a bargain on a piece of Crystolite in today's market. Many later patterns of Heisey were not marked. They had paper labels that were removed with use.

One question we received for years with an answer that seemed way too obvious was "What makes up the swan handled Crystolite pitcher?" To bring the "big bucks," it has to have the swan handle. It is found only in crystal and pictured below on the right, while the normally found pitcher is on the left. If you spot colored pitchers, they are reproductions by Imperial from Heisey's moulds bought when Heisey closed its plant in 1957.

You can recognize the harder to find items by their elevated prices. Non-scratched dinner plates, 5" comport, 6" basket, rye bottle, cocktail shaker, and pressed tumblers have always been difficult to locate, but they are presently priced more reasonably than in the past.

		Crystal				Crystal
	Ashtray, 3½", sq.	6.00			Bowl, 10", salad, rnd.	50.00
	Ashtray, 4½", sq.	6.00	17		Bowl, 11", w/attached mayonnaise (chip 'n dip)	200.00
9	Ashtray, 4" x 6", oblong	75.00			Bowl, 12", gardenia, shallow	65.00
12	Ashtray, 5", w/book match holder	35.00			Bowl, 13", oval floral, deep	60.00
	Ashtray (coaster), 4", rnd.	8.00			Candle block, 1-lite, sq.	20.00
15	Basket, 6", hdld.	450.00			Candle block, 1-lite, swirl	20.00
	Bonbon, 7", shell	22.00			Candlestick, 1-lite, ftd.	25.00
	Bonbon, 7½", 2 hdld.	15.00			Candlestick, 1-lite, w/#4233, 5", vase	35.00
2	Bottle, 1 qt., rye, #107 stopper	300.00			Candlestick, 2-lite	35.00
	Bottle, 4 oz., bitters, w/short tube	140.00			Candlestick, 2-lite, bobeche & 10 "D" prisms	65.00
	Bottle, 4 oz., cologne, w/#108 stopper	75.00			Candlestick and vase, 3-lite	45.00
	w/drip stop	140.00			Candlestick, w/#4233, 5", vase, 3-lite	55.00
	Bottle, syrup, w/drip & cut top	135.00			Candy, 5½", shell and cover	55.00
	Bowl, 7½ quart, punch	120.00			Candy box, w/cover, 7", 3 part	70.00
	Bowl, 2", indiv. swan nut (or ashtray)	20.00			Candy box, w/cover, 7"	60.00
	Bowl, 3", indiv. nut, hdld.	20.00			Cheese, 5½", ftd.	27.00
	Bowl, 4½", dessert (or nappy)	20.00			Cigarette box, w/cover, 4"	35.00
	Bowl, 5", preserve	20.00			Cigarette box, w/cover, 4½"	40.00
	Bowl, 5", 1000 island dressing, ruffled top	30.00	11		Cigarette holder, ftd.	35.00
	Bowl, 5½", dessert	14.00			Cigarette holder, oval	25.00
	Bowl, 6", oval jelly, 4 ft.	60.00			Cigarette holder, rnd.	25.00
	Bowl, 6", preserve, 2 hdld.	20.00			Cigarette lighter	45.00
19	Bowl, 7", shell praline	35.00			Coaster, 4"	12.00
	Bowl, 8", dessert (sauce)	30.00	3		Cocktail shaker, 1 qt. w/#1 strainer, #86 stopper	350.00
	Bowl, 8", 2 pt. conserve, hdld.	55.00			Comport, 5", ftd., deep, #5003, blown rare	300.00
	Bowl, 9", leaf pickle	30.00			Creamer, indiv.	20.00

		Crystal
	Creamer, reg.	30.00
	Creamer, round	40.00
	Cup	22.00
	Cup, punch or custard	9.00
	Hurricane block, 1-lite, sq.	40.00
	Hurricane block, w/#4061, 10" plain globe, 1-lite, sq.	120.00
	Ice tub, w/silver plate handle	100.00
	Jar, covered cherry	85.00
	Jam jar, w/cover	60.00
	Ladle, glass, punch	35.00
	Ladle, plastic	10.00
	Mayonnaise, 5½", shell, 3 ft.	35.00
	Mayonnaise, 6", oval, hdld.	40.00
	Mayonnaise ladle	12.00
	Mustard & cover	45.00
20	Nut, oval, footed	55.00
	Oil bottle, 3 oz.	45.00
	Oil bottle, w/stopper, 2 oz.	35.00
	Oval creamer, sugar, w/tray, set	70.00
1	Pitcher, ½ gallon, ice, blown	125.00
4	Pitcher, 2 quart swan, ice lip	700.00
	Plate, 7", salad	15.00
	Plate, 7", shell	32.00
	Plate, 7", underliner for 1000 island dressing bowl	20.00
	Plate, 7½", coupe	40.00
	Plate, 8", oval, mayonnaise liner	20.00
	Plate, 8½", salad	20.00
	Plate, 10½", dinner	100.00
	Plate, 11", ftd., cake salver	450.00
	Plate, 11", torte	40.00
	Plate, 12", sandwich	45.00
	Plate, 13", shell torte	100.00
	Plate, 14", sandwich	55.00
	Plate, 14", torte	50.00

		Crystal
	Plate, 20", buffet or punch liner	125.00
	Puff box, w/cover, 4¾"	75.00
	Salad dressing set, 3 pc.	38.00
	Salt & pepper, pr.	40.00
	Saucer	6.00
	Stem, 1 oz., cordial, wide optic, blown, #5003	95.00
	Stem, 3½ oz., cocktail, w.o., blown, #5003	18.00
	Stem, 3½ oz., claret, w.o., blown, #5003	28.00
	Stem, 3½ oz., oyster cocktail, w.o. blown, #5003	18.00
	Stem, 6 oz., sherbet/saucer champagne, #5003	10.00
7	Stem, 10 oz., water, #1503, pressed	500.00
	Stem, 10 oz., w.o., blown, #5003	30.00
	Sugar, indiv.	20.00
	Sugar, reg.	30.00
	Sugar, round	40.00
	Syrup pitcher, drip cut	135.00
	Tray, 5½", oval, liner indiv. creamer/sugar set	40.00
	Tray, 9", 4 pt., leaf relish	40.00
	Tray, 10", 5 pt., rnd. relish	45.00
	Tray, 12", 3 pt., relish, oval	35.00
	Tray, 12", rect., celery	38.00
	Tray, 12", rect., celery/olive	35.00
5	Tumbler, 5 oz., juice, blown	25.00
	Tumbler, 5 oz., ftd., juice, w.o., blown, #5003	38.00
6	Tumbler, 8 oz., blown	25.00
10	Tumbler, 8 oz., pressed, #5003	60.00
	Tumbler, 10 oz., pressed	70.00
8	Tumbler, 10 oz., iced tea, w.o., blown, #5003	30.00
	Tumbler, 12 oz., ftd., iced tea, w.o., blown, #5003	30.00
13	Urn, 7", flower	75.00
18	Vase, 3", short stem	45.00
21	Vase, 6", ftd.	40.00
14	Vase, 12"	225.00
16	Vase, spittoon (whimsey)	400.00

COLORS: CRYSTAL, CRYSTAL W/GOLD ENCRUSTING

Daffodil is a 50s Cambridge pattern that has started to appeal to a few collectors. We will be transferring it to our *Collectible Glassware from the 40s, 50s, and 60s* book with the next edition since it is one of the patterns that corresponds to that time frame.

1

		Crystal
	Basket, 6", 2 hdld., low ft., #55	40.00
	Bonbon, #1181	28.00
1	Bonbon, 5¼", 2 hdld., #3400/1180	40.00
2	Bowl, 11" oval, tuck hdld., #384	75.00
	Bowl, 12", belled, #430	85.00
	Candle, 2 lite, arch, #3900/72	65.00
	Candlestick, 3½", #628	50.00
	Candy box & cover, cut hexagon knob, #306	155.00
11	Celery, 11", #248	65.00
	Comport, 5½", ftd., #533	45.00
	Comport, 6½", 2 hdld., low ftd., #54	55.00
3	Comport, 6" tall, pulled stem, #532	65.00
	Creamer, #254	25.00
9	Creamer, indiv., #253	30.00
	Cup, #11770	25.00
	Jug, #3400/140	295.00
	Jug, 76 oz., #3400/141	325.00
	Mayonnaise, 3 pc., ftd., w/ladle & liner plate, #533	95.00
7	Mayonnaise, ftd., w/ladle and plate	95.00
	Oil, 6 oz., #293	145.00
	Plate, #1174	30.00
	Plate, 6", 2 hdld., bonbon, #3400/1181	20.00
	Plate, 8½", salad	18.00
4	Plate, 8", sq., #1176	20.00
	Plate, 8", 2 hdld., low ft., #56	30.00
	Plate, 11½" cake, #1495	80.00
	Plate, 13½", cabaret, #166	100.00
12	Relish, 10", 3 pt., #214	65.00
6	Salad dressing set, twin, 4 pc. w/ladles & liner, #1491	115.00
	Salt & pepper, squat, pr., #360	65.00
	Saucer, #1170	5.00

		Crystal
	Stem, brandy, ¾ oz., #1937	75.00
	Stem, claret, 4½ oz., #3779	55.00
	Stem, claret, 4½ oz., #1937	55.00
	Stem, cocktail, 3½ oz., #1937	30.00
	Stem, cocktail, 3 oz., #3779	30.00
13	Stem, cordial, 1 oz., #3779	100.00
	Stem, cordial, 1 oz., #1937	100.00
	Stem, oyster cocktail, 5 oz., #1937	18.00
	Stem, oyster cocktail, 4½ oz., #3779	18.00
	Stem, sherbet, 6 oz., low, #1937	16.00
	Stem, sherbet, 6 oz., low, #3779	16.00
	Stem, sherbet, 6 oz., tall, #1937	20.00
	Stem, sherbet, 6 oz., tall, #3779	20.00
	Stem, sherry, 2 oz., #1937	65.00
	Stem, water, 9 oz., low, #3779	30.00
	Stem, water, 9 oz., tall, #3779	35.00
	Stem, water, 11 oz., #1937	50.00
	Stem, wine, 2½ oz., #3779	55.00
	Stem, wine, 3 oz., #1937	50.00
	Sugar, #254	25.00
8	Sugar, indiv., #253	30.00
	Tumbler, ftd., 5 oz., #1937	22.00
10	Tumbler, ftd., 5 oz., #3779	22.00
	Tumbler, ftd., 10 oz., #1937	25.00
5	Tumbler, ftd., 12 oz., iced tea, #3779	38.00
	Tumbler, ftd., 12 oz., #1937	38.00
	Vase, 8", ftd., #6004	125.00
	Vase, 11", ftd., #278	150.00

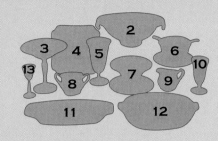

COLORS: CRYSTAL, FRENCH CRYSTAL, FROSTED CRYSTAL, GREEN AND FROSTED GREEN, PINK AND FROSTED PINK, RUBY FLASHED, WHITE, AND ASSORTED CERAMIC COLORS

Dancing Nymph is the Consolidated name for this pattern that has been referred to as "Dance of the Nudes" for as long as we have been researching glassware. Traditional names are practically impossible to pitch aside in the collecting world, once they have been recognized, even after the accurate name has become known. When Consolidated's Deco-looking Ruba Rombic was first listed in this book fourteen years ago, bargains in that pattern soon became few and far between. Dancing Nymph price escalations have not been quite so dramatic, since glassware illustrating nude women has always been popular and pricey. People may not have known its proper name, but it captured their attention and few priced it inexpensively. Dancing Nymph prices are actually reasonable when measured against other Consolidated patterns. This pattern is one of a few three-dimensional patterns that exist in this collecting field and was influenced by Lalique glassware and the graceful curves of the Art Nouveau period, fashionable at that time.

Dancing Nymph was introduced in 1926 and made until Consolidated closed in 1932. In 1936, the plant was restarted and a cupped saucer and sherbet plates were added to the line. These sherbet plates are like a shallow bowl and were often referred to as ice cream plates in other patterns of the period. The flatter version has no raised edge and is often used as sherbet liners. Salad plates usually came with basic sets, but sherbet plates were special order items, which makes them harder to find now. They should be priced more than the salad plates, but in this case, size does make a difference. Dancing Nymph candlesticks are rare. We have been advised that crystal items were never sold by the factory, but were intended to be frosted. We have seen enough crystal to wonder about that. On the other hand, one story informed us that the crystal was toted out of the factory when it finally closed in the 1940s. It had been programmed to be frosted, but had not received the treatment when the plant closed.

The green color has an aqua cast to it as shown in the photograph. French Crystal consists of clear nudes with satin background actually exemplifying the Lalique influence. Other colors are self-explanatory except for the atypical ceramic colors. Ceramic colors were obtained by covering the bottom of a crystal piece with color, wiping the nude designs clear, and firing the piece. The Honey (yellow) plate is an example. Older glassware often involved several hand processes that would be prohibitive to perform today due to labor costs. Ceramic colors are highly desirable and costly. Other colors with this process are Sepia (brown), white, dark blue, light blue, pinkish lavender, and light green.

		Crystal	Frosted Crystal French Crystal	*Frosted Pink or Green	Ceramic Colors
5	Bowl, 4½", #3098	30.00	60.00	75.00	110.00
1	Bowl, 8", #3098½	65.00	110.00	200.00	275.00
	Bowl, 16", palace, #2795B	600.00	1,250.00		1,600.00
9	Candle, pr., #2840	350.00	500.00		750.00
6	Cup, #3099	30.00	45.00	75.00	110.00
10	Plate, 6", cupped, #3099½	15.00	20.00	30.00	45.00
4	Plate, 6", sherbet, flat, #3099½	22.00	35.00	50.00	100.00
8	Plate, 8", salad, #3096	30.00	55.00		125.00
7	Plate, 10", #3097	60.00	75.00	150.00	195.00
	Platter, 18", palace	600.00	1,000.00		1,250.00
6	Saucer, coupe	12.00		30.00	
3	Sherbet, #3094	30.00	55.00	75.00	
12	Tumbler, 3½", cocktail, #3094½	40.00	55.00		
2	Tumbler, 5½", goblet, #3080	50.00	65.00	125.00	175.00
	Vase, 5½", crimped, #3080C	75.00	135.00		165.00
	Vase, 5½", fan, #3080F	75.00	135.00		165.00

*Subtract 10% to 15% for unfrosted.

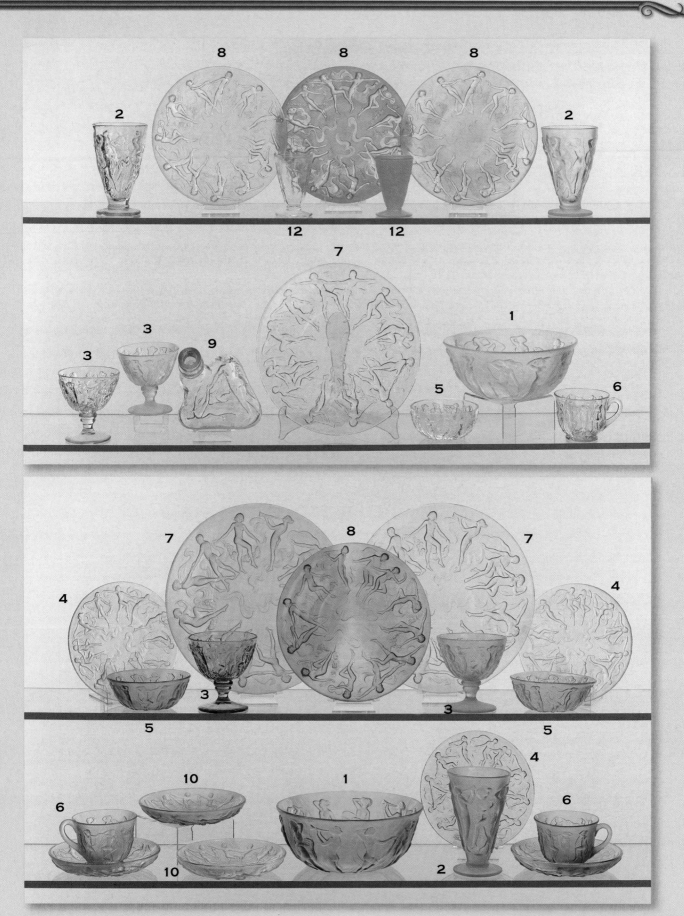

COLORS: AMBER, AMETHYST, CRYSTAL, EMERALD (LIGHT GREEN), PEACH-BLO, CARMEN, ROYAL BLUE, WILLOW BLUE, EBONY

Decagon is Cambridge's name for a ten-sided blank on which many of its etchings were decorated. The blank has added significance when etchings like Cleo, Rosalie, and Imperial Hunt Scene are decorated on it. Collectors then see the pattern decoration rather than its Decagon blank. Yet, there are some enthusiastic admirers of this plain, geometric Decagon "pattern." Amber Decagon has admirers too, but not as many as Willow (blue). Some Cleo collectors go for Decagon to supplement their etched collections. Why splurge $500.00 for a blue gravy and liner when you can buy an undecorated Decagon one for 25% of that?

You will find that Peach-Blo (pink), Emerald (light green), and amber are more plentiful, but Willow (blue) is the favored color, and therefore is more expensive to acquire. Pattern availability is only one influential issue in collecting. Color also plays an extremely important part, and blue colors repeatedly win collector interest.

Flat soups, cordials, and pitchers are not easily attained. Many collectors are on a quest for serving pieces for not only Decagon but the etched wares. This makes finding what you need doubly demanding.

		Pastels	Blue
	Basket, 7", 2 hdld. (upturned sides), #760	15.00	30.00
	Bowl, bouillon, w/liner, #866	15.00	35.00
	Bowl, cream soup, w/liner, #1075	22.00	35.00
	Bowl, 2½", indiv., almond, #611	30.00	50.00
	Bowl, 3¾", flat rim, cranberry	20.00	35.00
	Bowl, 3½" belled, cranberry, #1102	20.00	35.00
	Bowl, 5½", 2 hdld., bonbon, #758	12.00	22.00
	Bowl, 5½", belled, fruit, #1098	10.00	20.00
	Bowl, 5¾", flat rim, fruit, #1099	10.00	20.00
	Bowl, 6", belled, cereal, #1011	20.00	30.00
	Bowl, 6", flat rim, cereal, #807	22.00	40.00
	Bowl, 6", ftd., almond, #612	30.00	45.00
	Bowl, 6¼", 2 hdld., bonbon	12.00	22.00
20	Bowl, 8½", flat rim, soup, #808	25.00	45.00
	Bowl, 9", rnd., veg., #1085	30.00	55.00
	Bowl, 9", 2 pt., relish, #1067	30.00	40.00
	Bowl, 9½", oval, veg., #1087	35.00	50.00
	Bowl, 10", berry, #1087	35.00	50.00
	Bowl, 10½", oval, veg., #1088	35.00	50.00
	Bowl, 11", rnd. veg., #1086	40.00	48.00
	Bowl, 11", 2 pt., relish, #1068	38.00	40.00
	Comport, 5¾", #869	20.00	35.00
	Comport, 6½", low ft., #608	20.00	32.00
	Comport, 7", tall, #1090	25.00	45.00
	Comport, 9½", #877	35.00	60.00
15	Comport, 11½", #877	50.00	75.00
5	Creamer, ftd., #979	10.00	20.00
	Creamer, bulbous, ftd., #867	9.00	18.00
	Creamer, lightning bolt handles, #1096	10.00	15.00
	Creamer, tall, lg. ft., #814	10.00	22.00
11	Cup, #865	6.00	11.00
14	Finger bowl	20.00	25.00
	Gravy boat, w/2 hdld. liner (like spouted cream soup), #917/1167	100.00	125.00
	French dressing bottle, "Oil/Vinegar," #1263, ftd., #1261	90.00	150.00
10	Ice pail, #851	45.00	75.00
	Ice tub	40.00	65.00
	Mayonnaise, 2 hdld., w/2 hdld. liner and ladle, #873	35.00	45.00

		Pastels	Blue
	Mayonnaise, w/liner & ladle, #983	35.00	65.00
	Oil, 6 oz., tall, w/hdld. & stopper, #197	60.00	175.00
	Plate, 6¼", bread/butter	5.00	10.00
	Plate, 7", 2 hdld.	9.00	15.00
	Plate, 7½"	8.00	12.00
8	Plate, 8½", salad, #597	12.00	22.00
12	Plate, 8½", snack w/ring		35.00
	Plate, 9½", dinner	40.00	60.00
	Plate, 10", grill, #1200	35.00	50.00
4	Plate, 10", service, #812	30.00	50.00
2	Plate, 12½", service, #598	30.00	60.00
16	Relish, 6 inserts	90.00	110.00
	Salt dip, 1½", ftd., #613	25.00	40.00
7	Salt & pepper, #396	40.00	85.00
	Sauce boat & plate, #1091	90.00	110.00
11	Saucer, #866	3.00	4.00
	Stem, 1 oz., cordial, #3077	30.00	50.00
	Stem, 3½ oz., cocktail, #3077	12.00	20.00
	Stem, 6 oz., low sherbet, #3077	8.00	15.00
18	Stem, 6 oz., high sherbet, #3077	12.00	20.00
1	Stem, 9 oz., water, #3077	18.00	30.00
17	Sugar, lightning bolt handles, #1096	10.00	15.00
6	Sugar, ftd., #979	9.00	20.00
	Sugar, bulbous, ftd., #867	9.00	20.00
	Sugar, tall, sifter, #813	20.00	35.00
	Tray, 8", 2 hdld., flat pickle, #1167	25.00	40.00
	Tray, 9", pickle, #1082	25.00	40.00
	Tray, 11", oval, service	30.00	50.00
	Tray, 11", celery, #1083	30.00	50.00
19	Tray, 12", center handled, #870	30.00	45.00
3	Tray, 12", oval, service, #1078	25.00	45.00
	Tray, 13", 2 hdld., service, #1084	35.00	50.00
9	Tray, 15", oval, service, #1079	45.00	75.00
	Tumbler, 2½ oz., ftd., #3077	18.00	25.00
	Tumbler, 5 oz., ftd., #3077	12.00	20.00
	Tumbler, 8 oz., ftd., #3077	14.00	22.00
	Tumbler, 10 oz., ftd., #3077	16.00	25.00
13	Tumbler, 12 oz., ftd., #3077	18.00	30.00

COLORS: LIGHT AMBER, GREEN, PINK, BLACK, CRYSTAL

Look on page 25 for the Black Forest pattern photo if you have a tendency to confuse these two patterns. Deer and trees are illustrated on "Deerwood"; moose and trees are exhibited on Black Forest.

Know that some pieces similar to Deerwood (made at the Tiffin plant of U.S. Glass) have turned up on Paden City blanks.

Gold decorated, black "Deerwood" on Tiffin blanks is being acquired by admirers of that decorating genre who are not necessarily glass collectors per se, but who just admire this rich look. Those searching Internet auctions have also noticed "Deerwood." Auction results have caused some price modifications. "Deerwood" itself is not commonly found, but gold decoration on black really makes the pattern "pop." We found a black decorated creamer and sugar in a so-called antique mall in California where the oldest things in the mall were us. Remember that if gold is missing in the design, you will have to be cautious of the price you pay. Mint gold decorations are a must! Remember gold decoration disintegrates in the dishwasher especially if you use lemon enhanced detergent.

Large sets can only be assembled in green and pink with patience (and money). You will have to settle for an infrequent piece or two in other colors.

There is some catalog documentation for "Deerwood," but not nearly enough. That is why unlisted pieces keep turning up after 30 years of serious collecting.

The traditional mayonnaise was cataloged by Tiffin as a whipped cream rather than a mayonnaise. Jargon within the old glass companies often diverged from their competitors.

1

		*Black	Amber	Green	Pink
	Bowl, breakfast/cereal w/attched liner, #8133			60.00	60.00
	Bowl, 10", ftd.	185.00			
	Bowl, 10", straight edge, flat rim, salad, #8105			75.00	75.00
	Bowl, 12", centerpiece, flat rim ftd.	95.00			
9	Bowl, 12", centerpiece, #8177, cupped	125.00		85.00	80.00
	Cake plate, low pedestal, 10", #330, #8177			75.00	75.00
	Candlestick, 2½"	75.00		40.00	
6	Candlestick, 5"				65.00
1	Candy dish, w/cover, 3 part, flat, #329, 6"	195.00			140.00
	Candy jar, w/cover, ftd. cone, #330			150.00	150.00
	Celery, 12", #151			75.00	
	Cheese and cracker, #330			110.00	110.00
3	Comport, 7", #8177	110.00			65.00
5	Comport, 9", low, ftd.	150.00			
	Comport, 10", low, ftd., flared, #330	150.00			75.00
10	Creamer, 2 styles, #179	70.00		45.00	45.00
	Cup, #9395				85.00
	Plate, 5½", #8836			15.00	15.00
	Plate, 7½", salad, #8836				20.00
	Plate, 9½", dinner, #8859				100.00
	Plate, 10¼", 2 hdld., cake, #336	155.00			
	Saucer, #9395				15.00
	Server, center hdld., 10", #330			65.00	65.00
	Stem, 2 oz., cocktail, 4½", #2809				55.00
	Stem, 3 oz., wine, 4¾", #2809			30.00	
	Stem, 6 oz., saucer champagne, 5", #2809			35.00	
	Stem, 9 oz., water, 7", #2809			60.00	60.00
8	Sugar, 2 styles, #179	70.00		45.00	45.00
	Tumbler, 9 oz., ftd., table, #2808			35.00	37.50
2	Tumbler, 12 oz., ftd., tea, 5½", #2808			50.00	
4	Tumbler, 12 oz., flat, tea		50.00	65.00	
	Vase, 7", sweet pea, rolled edge, #151			195.00	195.00
	Vase, 10", ruffled top, #6471			195.00	195.00
7	Vase, 10", 2 handles, #15319	225.00			
	Whipped cream pail, w/ladle			75.00	75.00

*Add 20% for gold decorated.

COLORS: CRYSTAL; SOME PINK, YELLOW, BLUE, HEATHERBLOOM, EMERALD GREEN, AMBER, CROWN TUSCAN WITH GOLD

Cambridge's Diane pattern can be found in all the colors listed; but only crystal can be collected in a large set. You may be able to obtain a small luncheon set in color, but after that only an occasional bowl, candlestick, or tumbler will be seen. Notice the Willow Blue on the next page. This was part of a place setting for 24. It was ordered by two sisters who each received a 12 place setting. Seemingly, the price of making this colored, hand-made glass contributed to its scarcity. At any rate, colored Diane is in very short supply today.

On page 85 are samples of other colors found with Diane etchings and page 86 shows pages from an original Cambridge pamphlet. Hopefully these Diane listings and our legends will ease identification. As with other Cambridge patterns in this book, you will have to look at Rose Point listings for pricing any unlisted Diane items you come across. Diane will run 30% to 40% less than similar items listed in Rose Point. Remember that Rose Point is currently the highest priced Cambridge pattern and other patterns sell for less. Demand for Rose Point pushes prices to higher levels; other patterns increase in price slowly, if at all.

The bitters bottle, cabinet flask, and pitchers are in demand. You have several choices for stemware in Diane; pick whichever you like. Each line enhances the set. In our travels, we see more #3122 stems than other stem lines; they might be easier to find.

		Crystal				Crystal
	Basket, 6", 2 hdld., ftd.	30.00		17	Candy Jar, 12", #3500/42	200.00
19	Bottle, bitters	210.00		18	Cigarette urn	60.00
1	Bowl, #3106, finger, w/liner	45.00			Cocktail shaker, glass top	250.00
10	Bowl, #3122	25.00			Cocktail shaker, metal top	150.00
21	Bowl, #3400, cream soup, w/liner	50.00		3	Cocktail icer, 2 pc.	75.00
	Bowl, 3", indiv. nut, 4 ftd.	50.00			Comport, 5½"	40.00
14	Bowl, 4½", finger, blown	30.00			Comport, 5⅜", blown	60.00
	Bowl, 5", berry	30.00			Creamer, #3400	18.00
	Bowl, 5¼", 2 hdld., bonbon	22.00			Creamer, indiv., #3500 (pie crust edge)	20.00
	Bowl, 6", 2 hdld., ftd., bonbon	22.00			Creamer, indiv., #3900, scalloped edge	20.00
	Bowl, 6", 2 pt., relish	22.00		9	Creamer, scroll handle, #3400	22.00
	Bowl, 6", cereal	35.00		2	Cup	18.00
	Bowl, 6½", 3 pt., relish	35.00			Decanter, ball, 16 oz., cordial, #3400/92	250.00
	Bowl, 7", 2 hdld., ftd., bonbon	35.00			Decanter, lg. ftd.	225.00
	Bowl, 7", 2 pt., relish	32.00			Decanter, short ft., cordial	265.00
	Bowl, 7", relish or pickle	35.00			Hurricane lamp, candlestick base	195.00
	Bowl, 9", 3 pt., celery or relish	38.00			Hurricane lamp, keyhole base w/prisms	250.00
	Bowl, 9½", pickle (like corn)	35.00			Ice bucket, w/chrome hand	110.00
	Bowl, 10", 4 ft., flared	65.00			Mayonnaise, div., w/liner & ladles	65.00
	Bowl, 10", baker	60.00			Mayonnaise (sherbet type w/ladle)	45.00
7	Bowl, 10½", 3400/68	75.00			Mayonnaise, w/liner, ladle	40.00
	Bowl, 11", 2 hdld., 2 pt. relish, #3400/89	60.00		13	Oil, 6 oz., w/stopper	135.00
	Bowl, 11", 4 ftd., fancy top, #3400/45	60.00		16	Pitcher, ball	195.00
	Bowl, 11½", tab hdld., ftd.	60.00			Pitcher, Doulton	350.00
15	Bowl, 11½", hdld., 3900/34	60.00			Pitcher, martini	795.00
	Bowl, 12", 3 pt., celery & relish	50.00			Pitcher, upright	225.00
	Bowl, 12", 4 ft.	70.00			Plate, 6", 2 hdld., plate.	15.00
	Bowl, 12", 4 ft., flared	80.00			Plate, 6", sq., bread/butter	8.00
	Bowl, 12", 4 ft., oval	70.00			Plate, 6½", bread/butter	8.00
	Bowl, 12", 4 ft., oval, w/"ears," hdld.	75.00			Plate, 8", 2 hdld., ftd., bonbon	16.00
	Bowl, 12", 5 pt., celery & relish	65.00			Plate, 8", salad	12.00
	Bowl, 15", 3 pt. relish, #3500/112	65.00			Plate, 8½"	18.00
11	Butter, rnd.	150.00		6	Plate, 10½", dinner, #3900/24	75.00
	Cabinet flask	295.00			Plate, 12", 4 ft., service	55.00
	Candelabrum, 6", 2-lite, keyhole	40.00			Plate, 13", 4 ft., torte	60.00
	Candelabrum, 6", 3-lite, keyhole	50.00			Plate, 13½", 2 hdld.	60.00
8	Candlestick, 1-lite, keyhole	30.00			Plate, 14", torte	75.00
	Candlestick, 5"	30.00		5	Platter, 13½"	100.00
	Candy, 5½", blown, #3121/3	135.00			Salt & pepper, ftd., w/glass tops, pr.	40.00
	Candy box, w/cover, rnd.	125.00			Salt & pepper, pr., flat	40.00
12	Candy Jar, 10", #3500/41	175.00		2	Saucer	5.00

		Crystal
	Stem, #1066, 1 oz., cordial	55.00
	Stem, #1066, 3 oz., cocktail	22.00
	Stem, #1066, 3 oz., wine	30.00
	Stem, #1066, 3½ oz., tall cocktail	25.00
	Stem, #1066, 4½ oz., claret	40.00
	Stem, #1066, 5 oz., oyster/cocktail	20.00
	Stem, #1066, 7 oz., low sherbet	16.00
	Stem, #1066, 7 oz., tall sherbet	18.00
	Stem, #1066, 11 oz., water	30.00
	Stem, #3122, 1 oz., cordial	55.00
	Stem, #3122, 2½ oz., wine	30.00
	Stem, #3122, 3 oz., cocktail	20.00
	Stem, #3122, 4½ oz., claret	40.00
	Stem, #3122, 4½ oz., oyster/cocktail	18.00
	Stem, #3122, 7 oz., low sherbet	16.00
	Stem, #3122, 7 oz., tall sherbet	20.00
	Stem, #3122, 9 oz., water goblet	30.00
	Stem, #3575, tall sherbert/champagne	20.00
	Sugar, indiv., #3500 (pie crust edge)	20.00
	Sugar, indiv., #3900, scalloped edge	20.00
	Sugar, scroll handle, #3400	18.00
20	Sugar sifter	125.00
	Tumbler, 2½ oz., sham bottom	55.00
	Tumbler, 5 oz., ft., juice	35.00
	Tumbler, 5 oz., sham bottom	40.00
	Tumbler, 7 oz., old-fashion, w/sham bottom	50.00
	Tumbler, 8 oz., ft.	28.00
	Tumbler, 10 oz., sham bottom	33.00
	Tumbler, 12 oz., sham bottom	38.00

		Crystal
	Tumbler, 13 oz.	32.00
	Tumbler, 14 oz., sham bottom	40.00
	Tumbler, #1066, 3 oz.	26.00
	Tumbler, #1066, 5 oz., juice	22.00
	Tumbler, #1066, 9 oz., water	20.00
	Tumbler, #1066, 12 oz., tea	23.00
	Tumbler, #3106, 3 oz., ftd.	22.00
	Tumbler, #3106, 5 oz., ftd., juice	20.00
	Tumbler, #3106, 9 oz., ftd., water	18.00
	Tumbler, #3106, 12 oz., ftd., tea	24.00
	Tumbler, #3122, 2½ oz.	35.00
	Tumbler, #3122, 5 oz., juice	18.00
	Tumbler, #3122, 9 oz., water	22.00
	Tumbler, #3122, 12 oz., tea	26.00
	Tumbler, #3135, 2½ oz., ftd., bar	40.00
	Tumbler, #3135, 10 oz., ftd., tumbler	20.00
4	Tumbler, #3135, 12 oz., ftd., tea	28.00
	Tumbler, #3575, 5 oz., ftd., juice	18.00
	Tumbler, #3575, 12 oz., ftd., tea	25.00
	Vase, 5", globe	55.00
	Vase, 6", high ft., flower	50.00
	Vase, 8", high ft., flower	65.00
	Vase, 9", keyhole base	85.00
	Vase, 10", ftd., #1301	75.00
	Vase, 10", bud	65.00
	Vase, 11", flower	115.00
	Vase, 11", ped. ft., flower	110.00
	Vase, 12", keyhole base	115.00
	Vase, 13", flower	165.00

20

21

3

12

13

16

17

11

15

14

18

3

19

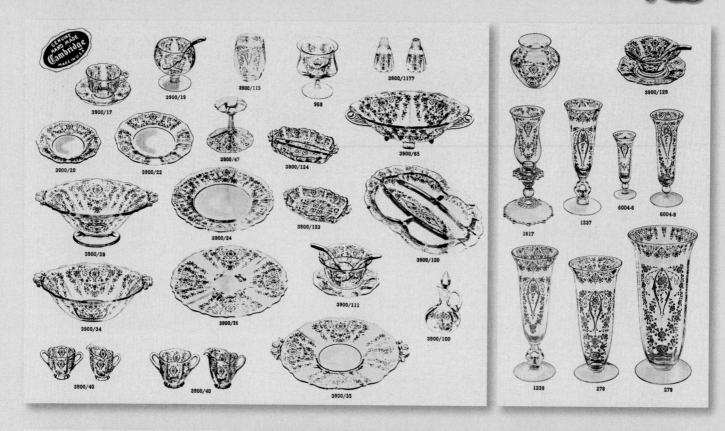

LIST OF DIANE ITEMS

3122	9 oz. Goblet	
3122	7 oz. Tall Sherbet	
3122	7 oz. Low Sherbet	
3122	3 oz. Cocktail	
3122	2½ oz. Wine	
3122	4½ oz. Claret	
3122	4½ oz. Oyster Cockta	
3122	1 oz. Cordial	
3122	12 oz. Ftd. Ice Tea	
3122	9 oz. Ftd. Tumbler	
3122	5 oz. Ftd. Tumbler	
477	9½ in. Pickle	
3400/1180	5¼ in. 2 Hdl. Bonbon	
3400/1181	6 in. 2 Hdl. Plate	
3400/90	6 in. 2 part Relish	
3500/15	Ind. Sugar & Cream	
3500/54	6 in. 2 Hdl. Ftd. Bonbon	
3500/55	6 in. 2 Hdl. Ftd. Basket	
3500/69	6½ in. 3 part Relish	
3500/161	8 in. 2 Hdl. Ftd. Plate	
3500/57	8 in. 3 part Candy Box & Cover (not illus.)	
3900/17	Cup & Saucer	
3900/19	2 pc. Mayonnaise Set	
3900/20	6½ in. Bread & Butter Plate	
3900/22	8 in. Salad Plate	
3900/24	10½ in. Dinner Plate	
3900/26	12 in. 4 Ftd. Plate	
3900/28	11½ in. Ftd. Bowl	
3900/33	13 in. 4 Ftd. Torte Plate, R.E.	
3900/34	11 in. 2 Handled Bowl	
3900/35	13½ in. 2 Handled Cake Plate	
3900/40	Ind. Sugar & Cream	
3900/41	Sugar & Cream	
3900/54	10 in. 4 Ftd. Bowl, flared	
3900/62	12 in. 4 Ftd. Bowl, flared	
3900/65	12 in. 4 Ftd. Oval Bowl	
3900/67	5 in. Candlestick	
3900/72	6 in. 2 lite Candlestick	
3900/74	6 in. 3 lite Candlestick	
3900/100	6 oz. Oil, g.s.	
3900/111	4 pc. Mayonnaise Set	
3900/115	13 oz. Tumbler	
3900/120	12 in. 5 part Celery & Relish	
3900/123	7 in. Relish or Pickle	
3900/124	7 in. 2 part Relish	
3900/125	9 in. 3 part Celery & Relish	
3900/126	12 in. 3 part Celery & Relish	
3900/129	3 pc. Mayonnaise Set	
3900/130	7 in. 2 handled Ftd. Bonbon	
3900/131	8 in. 2 handled Ftd. Bonbon Plate	
3900/136	5½ in. Comport	
3900/165	Candy Box & Cover	
3900/165	14 in. Plate, r.e.	
3900/671	Ice Bucket	
3900/671	Ice Bucket with chrome handle	
	Chrome Ice Tongs (long)	
3900/1177	Salt & Pepper Shaker (doz. pr.)	
274	10 in. Bud Flower Holder	
278	11 in. Ftd. Flower Holder	
279	13 in. Ftd. Flower Holder	
968	2 pc. Cocktail Icer	
1237	9 in. Ftd. Flower Holder	
1238	12 in. Ftd. Flower Holder	
1299	11 in. Ftd. Flower Holder	
1309	5 in. Glode Flower Holder	
1603	Hurricane Lamp (Etch. Chimney only)	
1617	Hurricane Lamp (Etch. Chimney only)	
3121	5-⅜ in. Blown Comport	
6004	6 in. Ftd Flower Holder	
6004	8 in. Ftd Flower Holder	

COLOR: CRYSTAL

Elaine is constantly mistaken with Chantilly. The Elaine design has a thin and angled scroll like the top of the capital script letter "E." Compare the design to the right with the one on the top of page 57.

Elaine is customarily found on Cambridge's #3500 Gadroon line that has the ornate "pie crust" edge. Several nationally known Cambridge dealers have found that description irritating, but most readers know to what it refers. You will find accessory pieces not listed here. Many pieces listed under Rose Point etch exist in Elaine. However, bear in mind that prices for Elaine will be 30% to 50% lower than those shown for Rose Point, which is more in demand in the market.

	Item	Price		Item	Price
	Basket, 6", 2 hdld. (upturned sides)	30.00		Pitcher, 78 oz., #3900/115	225.00
	Bowl, #3104, finger, w/liner	45.00		Plate, 6", 2 hdld.	15.00
	Bowl, 3", indiv. nut, 4 ftd.	50.00		Plate, 6½", bread/butter	10.00
	Bowl, 5¼", 2 hdld., bonbon	30.00		Plate, 7½", dessert, #3500/4, "Gadroon"	12.00
	Bowl, 5½", 2 pt., relish, #3500/60	30.00		Plate, 8", 2 hdld., ftd., bonbon, #3500/131	20.00
2	Bowl, 6", 1 hdld., 2 pt., relish, 3400/1093	30.00		Plate, 8", salad	18.00
	Bowl, 6", 2 hdld., ftd., bonbon	30.00		Plate, 8", tab hdld., bonbon	22.00
3	Bowl, 6", 2 pt., relish, "Gadroon"	28.00		Plate, 8½", salad, #3500, "Gadroon"	18.00
	Bowl, 6½", 3 pt., relish	30.00		Plate, 10½", dinner	70.00
	Bowl, 7", 2 pt., pickle or relish	33.00		Plate, 11½" 2 hdld., ringed "Tally Ho" sandwich	65.00
	Bowl, 7", ftd., tab hdld., bonbon	35.00		Plate, 12", 4 ftd., service	55.00
	Bowl, 7", pickle or relish	30.00		Plate, 13", 4 ftd., torte	60.00
	Bowl, 8", 3 pt., relish, #3400/91	45.00	9	Plate, 13", torte, 3500/38	90.00
	Bowl, 9", 3 pt., celery & relish, #3500/164 "Gadroon"	45.00		Plate, 13½", tab hdld., cake	65.00
	Bowl, 9½", pickle (like corn dish)	40.00		Plate, 14", service, #3900/166, rolled edge	65.00
	Bowl, 10", 4 ftd., flared	75.00	10	Salt & pepper, flat, pr.	40.00
	Bowl, 11", tab hdld.	85.00	5	Salt & pepper, ftd., pr	40.00
	Bowl, 11½", ftd., tab hdld.	80.00		Salt & pepper, hdld., pr	40.00
	Bowl, 12", 3 pt., celery & relish	60.00	4	Salt & pepper, individual	20.00
	Bowl, 12", 4 ftd., flared, #3400/4	70.00		Saucer	4.00
	Bowl, 12", 4 ftd., oval, "ear" hdld.	85.00		Stem, #1402, 1 oz., cordial	110.00
7	Bowl, 12", 5 pt., celery & relish	55.00		Stem, #1402, 3 oz., wine	38.00
	Candlestick, 5", #3400/646, "Keyhole"	35.00		Stem, #1402, 3½ oz., cocktail	30.00
	Candlestick, 6", 2-lite	40.00		Stem, #1402, 5 oz., claret	40.00
	Candlestick, 6", 3-lite	50.00		Stem, #1402, low sherbet	16.00
6	Candlestick, 7", #3121	85.00		Stem, #1402, tall sherbet	18.00
12	Candy box, w/cover, ftd., 3121/4	125.00		Stem, #1402, goblet	35.00
11	Candy box, 6", #306	110.00		Stem, #3035, cordial	55.00
	Candy jar, 10", #3500/41	195.00		Stem, #3104 (very tall stems), ¾ oz., brandy	225.00
	Candy jar, 12", #3500/42	250.00		Stem, #3104, 1 oz., cordial	225.00
	Cocktail icer, 2 pc.	85.00		Stem, #3104, 1 oz., pousse-cafe	225.00
1	Comport, 5½", 3600/136	40.00		Stem, #3104, 2 oz., sherry	225.00
	Comport, 5⅜", #3500 stem	45.00		Stem, #3104, 2½ oz., creme de menthe	175.00
	Comport, 5⅜", blown	55.00		Stem, #3104, 3 oz., wine	175.00
	Creamer (several styles)	20.00		Stem, #3104, 3½ oz., cocktail	110.00
	Creamer, indiv.	20.00		Stem, #3104, 4½ oz., claret	175.00
	Cup	18.00		Stem, #3104, 5 oz., roemer	175.00
	Decanter, lg., ftd.	235.00		Stem, #3104, 5 oz., tall hock	175.00
	Hat, 9"	395.00	15	Stem, #3104, 7 oz., tall sherbet	135.00
	Hurricane lamp, candlestick base	190.00		Stem, #3104, 9 oz., goblet	175.00
	Hurricane lamp, keyhole ft., w/prisms	250.00		Stem, #3121, 1 oz., cordial	55.00
8	Ice bucket, w/chrome handle	110.00		Stem, #3121, 3 oz., cocktail	25.00
	Mayonnaise (cupped sherbet w/ladle)	40.00		Stem, #3121, 3½ oz., wine	33.00
	Mayonnaise (div. bowl, liner, 2 ladles), #3900/111	55.00		Stem, #3121, 4½ oz., claret	38.00
	Mayonnaise, w/liner & ladle, #1532, "Pristine"	50.00		Stem, #3121, 4½ oz., oyster cocktail	22.00
	Oil, 6 oz., hdld., w/stopper	125.00		Stem, #3121, 5 oz., parfait, low stem	35.00
	Pitcher, ball, 80 oz.	225.00		Stem, #3121, 6 oz., low sherbet	18.00
	Pitcher, Doulton	350.00		Stem, #3121, 6 oz., tall sherbet	20.00

	Stem, #3121, 10 oz., water	30.00
	Stem, #3500, 1 oz., cordial	55.00
	Stem, #3500, 2½ oz., wine	33.00
	Stem, #3500, 3 oz., cocktail	25.00
	Stem, #3500, 4½ oz., claret	40.00
	Stem, #3500, 4½ oz., oyster cocktail	22.00
	Stem, #3500, 5 oz., parfait, low stem	35.00
	Stem, #3500, 7 oz., low sherbet	16.00
	Stem, #3500, 7 oz., tall sherbet	18.00
	Stem, #3500, 10 oz., water	32.00
14	Stem, #7801, champagne	125.00
	Sugar (several styles), #3500/14 (shown)	18.00
	Sugar, indiv.	18.00
	Tumbler, #1402, 9 oz., ftd., water	22.00
	Tumbler, #1402, 12 oz., tea	35.00
	Tumbler, #1402, 12 oz., tall ftd., tea	35.00
	Tumbler, #3121, 5 oz., ftd., juice	25.00
	Tumbler, #3121, 10 oz., ftd., water	35.00
	Tumbler, #3121, 12 oz., ftd., tea	35.00
	Tumbler, #3500, 5 oz., ftd., juice	25.00
	Tumbler, #3500, 10 oz., ftd., water	30.00
	Tumbler, #3500, 12 oz., ftd., tea	35.00
	Vase, 6", ftd.	65.00
	Vase, 8", ftd.	90.00
	Vase, 9", keyhole, ftd.	135.00
	Vase, 10", cornucopia, #3900/575	195.00
13	Vase, 11", #278	110.00
	Vase, 12", #3400	175.00

15

13

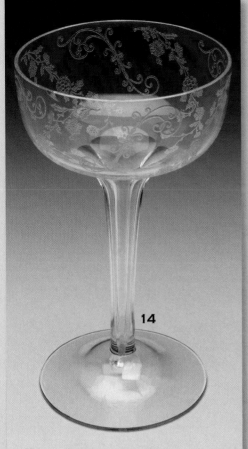

14

Elaine

LIST OF ELAINE ITEMS

3121	10 oz. Goblet
3121	6 oz. Tall Sherbet
3121	6 oz. Low Sherbet
3121	3 oz. Cocktail
3121	3½ oz. Wine
3121	4½ oz. Claret
3121	4½ oz. Oyster Cocktail
3121	1 oz. Cordial
3121	5 oz. Cafe Parfait
3121	12 oz. Ftd. Ice Tea
3121	10 oz. Ftd. Tumbler
3121	5 oz. Ftd. Tumbler
477	9½ in. Pickle
3400/1180	5¼ in. 2 Hdl. Bonbon
3400/1181	6 in. 2 Hdl. Plate
3400/90	6 in. 2 part Relish
3500/15	Ind. Sugar & Cream
3500/54	6 in. 2 Hdl. Ftd. Bonbon
3500/55	6 in. 2 Hdl. Ftd. Basket
3500/69	6½ in. 2 part Relish
3500/161	8 in. 2 Hdl. Plate
3500/57	8 in. 3 part Candy Box & Cover (not illus.)
3900/17	Cup & Saucer
3900/19	2 pc. Mayonnaise Set
3900/20	6½ in. Bread & Butter Plate
3900/22	8 in. Salad Plate
3900/24	10½ in. Dinner Plate
3900/26	12 in. 4 Ftd. Plate
3900/28	11½ in. Ftd. Bowl
3900/33	13 in. 4 Ftd. Torte Plate, R.E.
3900/34	11 in. 2 Handled Bowl
3900/35	13½ in. 2 Handled Cake Plate
3900/40	Ind. Sugar & Cream
3900/41	Sugar & Cream
3900/54	10 in. 4 Ftd. Bowl, flared
3900/62	12 in. 4 Ftd. Bowl, flared
3900/65	12 in. 4 Ftd. Oval Bowl
3900/67	5 in. Candlestick
3900/72	6 in. 2 lite Candlestick
3900/74	6 in. 3 lite Candlestick
3900/100	6 oz. Oil, g.s.
3900/111	4 pc. Mayonnaise Set
3900/115	13 oz. Tumbler
3900/120	12 in. 5 part Celery & Relish
3900/123	7 in. Relish or Pickle
3900/124	7 in. 2 part Relish
3900/125	9 in. 3 part Celery & Relish
3900/126	12 in. 3 part Celery & Relish
3900/129	3 pc. Mayonnaise Set
3900/130	7 in. 2 handled Ftd. Bonbon
3900/131	8 in. 2 handled Ftd. Bonbon Plate
3900/136	5½ in. Comport
3900/165	Candy Box & Cover
3900/166	14 in. Plate, r.e.
3900/671	Ice Bucket
3900/671	Ice Bucket with chrome Handle
	Chrome Ice Tongs (long)
3900/1177	Salt & Pepper Shaker (doz. pr.)
274	10 in. Bud Flower Holder
278	11 in. Ftd. Flower Holder
279	13 in. Ftd. Flower Holder
968	2 pc. Cocktail Icer
1237	9 in. Ftd. Flower Holder
1238	12 in. Ftd. Flower Holder
1299	11 in. Ftd. Flower Holder
1309	5 in. Glode Flower Holder
1603	Hurricane Lamp (Etch., Chimney only)
1617	Hurricane Lamp (Etch., Chimney only)
3121	5-⅜ in. Blown Comport
6004	6 in. Ftd. Flower Holder
6004	8 in. Ftd. Flower Holder

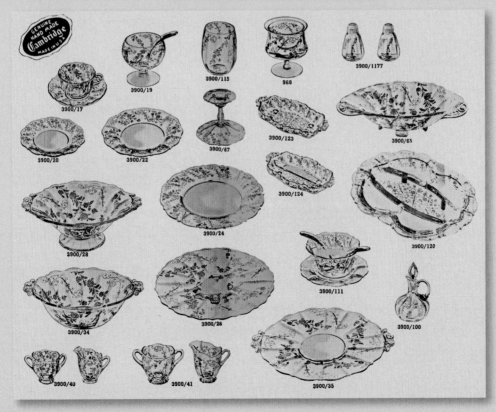

3900/17

3900/19

3900/115

968

3900/1177

3900/20   3900/22

3900/67

3900/123

3900/65

3900/24

3900/124

3900/28

3900/120

3900/111

3900/26

3900/34

3900/100

3900/40   3900/41

3900/35

3900/54 3900/126 3900/131 3900/165 1309 3900/129

3900/130 3900/72 3900/166 1603 1617 1237 6004-6 6004-8

3900/62 3900/74 3900/125 1238 278 279

3900/33 3900/136 3900/671 274 1299

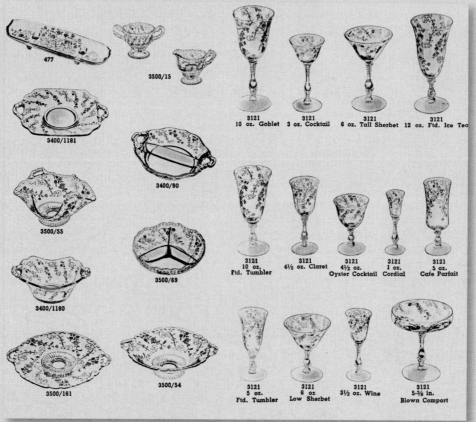

477

3500/15

3400/1181

3400/90

3500/55

3500/69

3400/1180

3500/161 3500/54

3121
10 oz. Goblet

3121
3 oz. Cocktail

3121
6 oz. Tall Sherbet

3121
12 oz. Ftd. Ice Tea

3121
10 oz.
Ftd. Tumbler

3121
4½ oz. Claret

3121
4½ oz.
Oyster Cocktail

3121
1 oz. Cordial

3121
5 oz.
Cafe Parfait

3121
5 oz.
Ftd. Tumbler

3121
6 oz
Low Sherbet

3121
3½ oz. Wine

3121
5-⅜ in.
Blown Comport

COLORS: CRYSTAL, AND W/EBONY FILAMENT STEM, AZURE, AQUAMARINE AND W/CRYSTAL STEM, SPANISH RED W/CRYSTAL STEM

This is another of Morgantown's smaller patterns that can be found on two different stem lines. A sample of each is pictured. The twisted stem cocktail is from the #7994 Queen Anne line and the water goblet is #7630 Ballerina line commonly referred to as a "lady leg" stem. As with most Morgantown lines, stems can be uncovered but other than that, you will have to dig very deeply into the recesses of every shop you enter.

		Crystal
2	Plate, 7½", salad	20.00
	Stem, #7630, 1½ oz., cordial	75.00
	Stem, #7630, 2½ oz., wine	35.00
	Stem, #7630, 4 oz., cocktail	25.00
	Stem, #7639, 5 oz., parfait	35.00
	Stem, #7630, 6 oz., low sherbet	20.00
	Stem, #7630, 7 oz., 6¼" champagne	25.00
	Stem, #7630, 9 oz., 7¾", water goblet	35.00
	Stem, #7664, 1½ oz., cordial	75.00
	Stem, #7664, 2½ oz., wine	35.00
3	Stem, #7664, 4 oz., cocktail	25.00
	Stem, #7664, 6 oz., low sherbet	20.00
	Stem, #7664, 7 oz., 6¼" champagne	25.00
1	Stem, #7664, 10 oz., 8¼", water goblet	35.00
	Tumbler, #7664, 9 oz, 4¼", flair edge	30.00
	Vase, #7602, 6"	100.00
	Vase, #36 Uranus bud, 10"	75.00

* Add 50% for any color

COLORS: CRYSTAL, GREEN, ROSE

Empire is mostly found in Rose (pink), although cataloged as produced in green and crystal. We've heard this pattern referred to as "one of those Tiffin bird patterns" more than once. As we searched for this pattern the last few years, we only found pink and not much of that. Jugs are listed as coming only with lid, so this may be one Tiffin pattern where jugs were not sold without a lid. You will see mostly stems with creamer, sugar, and cup and saucers in short supply. Although the #15018 stem line is pictured, you may find Empire etched on two other lines (#15024 and #15070).

		All Colors
	Bowl, finger, ftd.	45.00
	Comport, 7¼"	50.00
	Creamer	65.00
	Cup	65.00
	Jug w/cover	495.00
2	Plate, 8"	25.00
	Saucer	20.00
	Stem, #15018, 3 oz.., wine	65.00
	Stem, #15018, 4 oz., cocktail	50.00
1	Stem, #15018, 5 oz., café parfait	65.00
	Stem, #15018, 5 oz., claret	75.00
	Stem, #15018, 6 oz., champagne	50.00
	Stem, #15018, 6 oz., sherbet	40.00
3	Stem, #15018, 9 oz., goblet water	75.00
	Sugar	65.00
	Tumbler, water, ftd., 9 oz.	45.00

COLORS: FLAMINGO PINK, SAHARA YELLOW, MOONGLEAM GREEN, COBALT, AND ALEXANDRITE; SOME TANGERINE

During the time colors were made, this pattern was called Empress; but later on, when crystal was produced, the pattern's name was changed to Queen Ann. Some nitpicking Heisey people want to make great observational differences in these patterns so we will let them do it their way.

Notice that Empress can be found on both round and square mould blanks as illustrated on page 94. Many collectors have always favored square plates because they are unusual.

Empress is shown in Sahara on page 93 and Alexandrite on page 94. Alexandrite is Heisey's purple/pink color that changes colors depending upon the lighting source. Under natural light, it appears pink; under florescent light, it appears blue. Our photographers and printers have always done an extraordinary job in showing it correctly. That is not easily achieved and hopefully that statement did not jinx our photos.

		Flamingo	Sahara	Moongleam	Cobalt	Alexandrite
9	Ashtray	175.00	185.00	250.00	300.00	225.00
	Bonbon, 6"	20.00	25.00	30.00		
	Bowl, cream soup	30.00	30.00	50.00		110.00
4	Bowl, cream soup, with liner	40.00	40.00	55.00		175.00
	Bowl, frappe, w/center	45.00	60.00	75.00		
24	Bowl, nut, dolphin ftd., indiv.	30.00	32.00	45.00		170.00
	Bowl, 4½", nappy	40.00	40.00	60.00		
	Bowl, 5", preserve, 2 hdld.	20.00	25.00	30.00		
	Bowl, 6", ftd., jelly, 2 hdld.	20.00	25.00	30.00		
5	Bowl, 6", dolphin ftd., mint	35.00	40.00	45.00		275.00
	Bowl, 6", grapefruit, sq. top, ground bottom	12.50	20.00	25.00		
	Bowl, 6½", oval, lemon, w/cover	100.00	100.00	150.00		
	Bowl, 7", 3 pt., relish, triplex	40.00	45.00	50.00		200.00
	Bowl, 7", 3 pt., relish, ctr. hand.	45.00	50.00	75.00		

		Flamingo	Sahara	Moongleam	Cobalt	Alexandrite
	Bowl, 7½", dolphin ftd., nappy	65.00	65.00	80.00	300.00	350.00
	Bowl, 7½", dolphin ftd., nasturtium	130.00	130.00	150.00	350.00	425.00
	Bowl, 8", nappy	35.00	37.00	45.00		
	Bowl, 8½", ftd., floral, 2 hdld	45.00	50.00	70.00		
	Bowl, 9", floral, rolled edge	40.00	42.00	50.00		
	Bowl, 9", floral, flared	70.00	75.00	90.00		
	Bowl, 10", 2 hdld., oval dessert	50.00	60.00	70.00		
	Bowl, 10", lion head, floral	550.00	550.00	700.00		
	Bowl, 10", oval, veg.	50.00	55.00	75.00		
	Bowl, 10", square, salad, 2 hdld.	55.00	60.00	80.00		
	Bowl, 10", triplex, relish	50.00	55.00	65.00		
	Bowl, 11", dolphin ftd., floral	65.00	75.00	100.00	400.00	500.00
	Bowl, 13", pickle/olive, 2 pt.	35.00	45.00	50.00		
	Bowl, 15", dolphin ftd., punch	900.00	900.00	1,250.00		
	Candlestick, low, 4 ftd., w/2 hdld.	100.00	100.00	170.00		
	Candlestick, 6", #135		50.00	190.00		275.00
23	Candlestick, 6", dolphin ftd.	170.00	125.00	155.00	260.00	400.00
	Candy, w/cover, 6", dolphin ftd.	150.00	150.00	350.00	600.00	
	Comport, 6", ftd.	110.00	70.00	100.00		
	Comport, 6", square	70.00	75.00	85.00		
16	Comport, 7", oval	85.00	80.00	90.00		
	Compotier, 6", dolphin ftd.	260.00	225.00	275.00		
6	Creamer, dolphin ftd.	30.00	45.00	40.00		200.00
26	Creamer, indiv.	45.00	45.00	50.00		210.00

		Flamingo	Sahara	Moongleam	Cobalt	Alexandrite
7	Cup	30.00	30.00	35.00		115.00
21	Cup, after dinner	60.00	60.00	70.00		
	Cup, bouillon, 2 hdld.	35.00	35.00	45.00		
	Cup, 4 oz., custard or punch	30.00	35.00	45.00		
	Cup, #1401½, has rim as demi-cup	28.00	32.00	40.00		
	Grapefruit, w/square liner	30.00	30.00	35.00		
	Ice tub, w/metal handles, dolphin ftd.	100.00	150.00	350.00		2,500.00
	Hors d'oeuvre, 10", 7 compartments		75.00			
18	Jug, 3 pint, ftd.	200.00	210.00	250.00		
	Jug, flat			175.00		
	Marmalade, w/cover, dolphin ftd.	200.00	200.00	225.00		
10, 11	Mayonnaise, 5½", ftd. with ladle	85.00	90.00	110.00		400.00
19	Mustard, w/cover	85.00	80.00	95.00		
	Oil bottle, 4 oz.	125.00	125.00	135.00		
	Plate, bouillon liner	12.00	15.00	17.50		25.00
	Plate, 4½"	10.00	15.00	20.00		
	Plate, 6"	11.00	14.00	16.00		40.00
	Plate, 6", sq.	10.00	13.00	15.00		40.00
	Plate, 7"	12.00	15.00	17.00		50.00
12	Plate, 7", sq.	12.00	15.00	17.00	60.00	65.00
17	Plate, 8", sq.	18.00	22.00	35.00	80.00	75.00
1	Plate, 8"	16.00	20.00	24.00	70.00	75.00
	Plate, 9"	25.00	35.00	40.00		
	Plate, 10½"	100.00	100.00	140.00		335.00
3	Plate, 10½", sq.	100.00	100.00	140.00		335.00
	Plate, 12"	45.00	55.00	65.00		
	Plate, 12", muffin, sides upturned	55.00	80.00	90.00		
	Plate, 12", sandwich, 2 hdld.	35.00	45.00	60.00		180.00
	Plate, 13", hors d'oeuvre, 2 hdld.	50.00	60.00	70.00		
	Plate, 13", sq., 2 hdld.	40.00	45.00	55.00		
	Platter, 14"	40.00	45.00	80.00		
25	Salt & pepper, pr.	100.00	140.00	135.00		400.00
	Saucer, sq.	10.00	10.00	15.00		25.00
22	Saucer, after dinner	10.00	10.00	15.00		
8	Saucer, rnd.	10.00	10.00	15.00		25.00
	Stem, 2½ oz., oyster cocktail	20.00	25.00	30.00		
	Stem, 4 oz., saucer champagne	35.00	40.00	60.00		
	Stem, 4 oz., sherbet	22.00	28.00	25.00		
	Stem, 9 oz., Empress stemware, unusual	55.00	65.00	75.00		
27	Sugar, indiv.	45.00	45.00	50.00		210.00
14	Sugar, dolphin ftd., 3 hdld.	30.00	45.00	40.00		200.00
28	Tray, condiment & liner for indiv. sugar/creamer	75.00	75.00	85.00		
20	Tray, condiment & liner for cream & sugar	50.00	50.00	55.00		
	Tray, 10", 3 pt., relish	50.00	55.00	65.00		
	Tray, 10", 7 pt., hors d'oeuvre	160.00	150.00	200.00		
13	Tray, 10", celery	25.00	35.00	40.00		150.00
	Tray, 12", ctr. hdld., sandwich	48.00	57.00	65.00		
	Tray, 12", sq. ctr. hdld., sandwich	52.00	60.00	67.50		
	Tray, 13", celery	30.00	40.00	45.00		
	Tray, 16", 4 pt., buffet relish	75.00	75.00	86.00		160.00
	Tumbler, 8 oz., dolphin ftd., unusual	150.00	180.00	160.00		
15	Tumbler, 8 oz., ground bottom	60.00	50.00	70.00		
	Tumbler, 12 oz., tea, ground bottom	60.00	50.00	75.00		
	Vase, 8", flared	140.00	150.00	190.00		
2	Vase, 9", dolphin ftd.	200.00	200.00	220.00		850.00

COLORS: BLUE, CRYSTAL, AZURE BLUE, ORCHID, AMBER, ROSE, GREEN, TOPAZ; SOME RUBY, EBONY, AND WISTERIA

Fairfax (the name of this Fostoria #2375 mould blank) was the mould shape used for many of their most popular etchings, including June, Versailles, and Trojan. Illustrated below is Rose (pink) and on page 97 amber and Topaz are depicted. Orchid and Azure blue are the colors most desired in Fairfax. Amber and Topaz (yellow) are readily available, but by and large have had fewer collectors seeking them which make them less expensive to gather. Some collectors of blue or pink June or Versailles are buying Fairfax to plug gaps in their sets. Many Fairfax substitute pieces can be obtained for 25% – 40% of the cost of an etched piece. Some collectors prefer to have a non-etched piece than none at all.

Fortunately, Fairfax collectors have a choice of two stemware lines. The Fostoria stems and shapes shown on page 98 are the #5298 stem and tumbler line (albeit the pieces shown are etched June and Versailles). More collectors embrace this line especially in pink and blue. The other stem line, #5299, is commonly found in Topaz with Trojan etch and is shown at the bottom of the page. Collectors refer to this stem as "waterfall." All Wisteria stems are found only on the #5299 line. Some collectors mix stems, but tumblers are more difficult to mix because they have a noticeably different silhouette. The #5299 tumblers (oyster cocktail on page 98) are more flared at the top than the #5298 (all other tumblers on page 98).

We have shown an array of Fostoria's stemware on page 98 so that all shapes can be seen. The claret and high sherbets are major concerns. Each measures 6" high. The claret is shaped like the wine. We recently had to show that difference to someone who told me he had some blue June clarets, which turned out to be crystal high sherbets. When people identify stems, they tend to look for the highest priced and assume that is what they have. The parfait is also taller than the juice, although shaped similarly.

		Rose, Blue Orchid	Amber	Green Topaz
	Ashtray, 2½"	14.00	5.00	10.00
	Ashtray, 4"	16.00	6.00	11.00
	Ashtray, 5½"	18.00	10.00	12.00
	Baker, 9", oval	45.00	16.00	30.00
	Baker, 10½", oval	50.00	20.00	30.00
	Bonbon	12.50	9.00	10.00
23	Bottle, salad dressing	210.00	75.00	110.00
12	Bouillon, ftd.	15.00	8.00	10.00
	Bowl, 9", lemon, 2 hdld.	20.00	10.00	13.00
	Bowl, sweetmeat	22.00	12.00	16.00
	Bowl, 5", fruit	18.00	8.00	10.00
15	Bowl, 6", cereal	30.00	10.00	15.00
16	Bowl, 6⅞", 3 ftd.	25.00	15.00	20.00
	Bowl, 7", soup	50.00	24.00	33.00
	Bowl, 8", rnd., nappy	45.00	20.00	30.00
18	Bowl, 8½", 2 pt., relish	45.00	20.00	30.00

		Rose, Blue Orchid	Amber	Green Topaz
	Bowl, lg., hdld., dessert	45.00	20.00	30.00
	Bowl, 12"	50.00	25.00	35.00
10	Bowl, 12", ctrpiece, #2394	50.00	25.00	35.00
	Bowl, 13", oval, ctrpiece	50.00	25.00	35.00
	Bowl, 15", ctrpiece	55.00	30.00	40.00
14	Butter dish, w/ cover	150.00	70.00	100.00
	Candlestick, flat top	25.00	12.00	15.00
	Candlestick, 3"	22.00	12.00	16.00
	Candy w/cover, flat, 3 pt.	85.00	45.00	55.00
	Candy w/cover., ftd.	95.00	50.00	65.00
	Celery, 11½"	30.00	15.00	18.00
6	Cheese comport (2 styles), #2368	25.00	10.00	12.50
	Cheese & cracker set (2 styles)	45.00	20.00	25.00
	Cigarette box	30.00	20.00	25.00

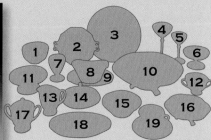

		Rose, Blue Orchid	Amber	Green Topaz
	Comport, 5"	35.00	15.00	25.00
11	Comport, 7"	40.00	15.00	25.00
	Cream soup, ftd.	23.00	10.00	15.00
20	Creamer, flat		10.00	14.00
13	Creamer, ftd.	15.00	7.00	10.00
31	Creamer, tea	20.00	8.00	12.00
32	Cup, after dinner	25.00	10.00	15.00
	Cup, flat		3.00	5.00
19	Cup, ftd.	12.00	4.00	6.00
	Flower holder, oval, window box w/frog	125.00	60.00	75.00
	Grapefruit	35.00	18.00	25.00
	Grapefruit liner	30.00	12.00	20.00
	Ice bucket	95.00	50.00	65.00
1	Ice bowl, #2451	25.00	15.00	20.00
	Ice bowl liner	20.00	10.00	*15.00
2	Lemon dish, 6¾", 2 hndl.	25.00	15.00	20.00
	Mayonnaise	25.00	12.00	15.00
	Mayonnaise ladle	30.00	15.00	20.00
	Mayonnaise liner, 7"	10.00	5.00	6.00
28	Nut cup, blown	25.00	12.00	15.00
25	Oil, ftd.	175.00	85.00	110.00
	Pickle, 8½"	25.00	8.00	12.00
21	Pitcher, #5000	220.00	90.00	150.00
	Plate, canape	20.00	10.00	10.00
	Plate, whipped cream	11.00	8.00	9.00
	Plate, 6", bread/butter	8.00	3.00	4.00
	Plate, 7½", salad	10.00	4.00	5.00
	Plate, 7½", cream soup or mayonnaise liner	10.00	5.00	6.00
	Plate, 8¾", salad	14.00	7.00	8.00

* topaz $10.00

		Rose, Blue Orchid	Amber	Green Topaz
24	Plate, Mah Jongg (w/ sherbet), #2321	50.00	28.00	35.00
	Plate, 9½", luncheon	17.00	7.00	10.00
22	Plate, 10¼", dinner	40.00	15.00	28.00
3	Plate, 10¼", grill	40.00	15.00	28.00
	Plate, 10", cake	22.00	13.00	15.00
	Plate, 12", bread, oval	45.00	25.00	27.50
	Plate, 13", chop	30.00	15.00	20.00
	Platter, 10½", oval	33.00	15.00	25.00
	Platter, 12", oval	50.00	20.00	35.00
	Platter, 15", oval	100.00	30.00	50.00
	Relish, 3 part, 8½"	30.00	10.00	15.00
	Relish, 11½"	22.00	11.00	13.00
8	Sauce boat	50.00	20.00	30.00
9	Sauce boat liner	20.00	10.00	15.00
32	Saucer, after dinner	5.00	2.00	4.00
19	Saucer	4.00	2.50	3.00
29	Shaker, ftd., pr	60.00	30.00	40.00
	Shaker, indiv., ftd., pr.		20.00	25.00
33	Stem, 4", ¾ oz., cordial, #5098	60.00	20.00	40.00
7	Stem, 5½ oz., oyster cocktail	16.00	9.00	11.00
	Stem, 4¼", 6 oz., low sherbet	14.00	9.00	11.00
5	Stem, 5¼", 3 oz., cocktail	20.00	12.00	16.00
27	Stem, 5½", 3 oz., wine, #5098	28.00	16.00	18.00
	Stem, 6", 4 oz., claret	35.00	22.00	28.00
4	Stem, 6", 6 oz., high sherbet, #5098	20.00	10.00	15.00
	Stem, 8¼", 10 oz., water	28.00	12.00	18.00
	Sugar, flat		10.00	12.00
17	Sugar, ftd.	15.00	6.00	8.00

FOSTORIA STEMS AND SHAPES

All are on #5098 "Petal" stems unless otherwise indicated.

Top Row: Left to Right
1. Water, 10 oz., 8¼", #5098
2. Claret, 4 oz., 6", #5098
3. Wine, 3 oz., 5½", #5098
4. Cordial, ¾ oz., 4", #5098
5. Sherbet, low, 6 oz., 4¼", #5098
6. Cocktail, 3 oz., 5¼", #5098
7. Sherbet, high, 6 oz., 6", #5098

Bottom Row: Left to Right
1. Grapefruit and liner, #877
2. Ice tea tumbler, 12 oz., 6", #5098
3. Water tumbler, 9 oz., 5¼", #5098
4. Parfait, 6 oz., 5¼", #5098
5. Juice tumbler, 5 oz., 4½", #5098
6. Oyster cocktail, 5½ oz., #5099 "Waterfall" stemline
7. Bar tumbler, 2½ oz., #5098

Cordial, 3⅞", #5099 "Waterfall" stemline

		Rose, Blue Orchid	Amber	Green Topaz
17	Sugar cover	35.00	20.00	25.00
	Sugar pail	70.00	30.00	45.00
30	Sugar, tea	20.00	8.00	12.00
	Tray, 11", ctr. hdld.	30.00	20.00	25.00
	Tumbler, 2½ oz., ftd.	28.00	12.00	18.00
34	Tumbler, 4½", 5½ oz., ftd., oyster cocktail, #5099	16.00	10.00	11.00
	Tumbler, 5¼", 9 oz., ftd.	20.00	12.00	13.00
26	Tumbler, 6", 12 oz., ftd., #5098	25.00	13.50	18.00
	Vase, 8" (2 styles)	95.00	40.00	60.00
	Whipped cream pail	60.00	30.00	40.00

COLOR: CRYSTAL

First Love is possibly the most well-known Duncan & Miller etching. An assortment of mould lines were integrated into this copious pattern. Among those are #30 (Pall Mall), #111 (Terrace), #115 (Canterbury), #117 (Three Feathers), #126 (Venetian), and #5111½ (Terrace blown stemware). Canterbury can be found on pages 42 to 44 and Terrace can be seen on pages 225 and 226.

Earlier editions of this book illustrated details of those other lines. New patterns have been added which leaves little room for those catalog pages now. Most pieces of First Love will be found on lines #111 or #115.

This etching harmonized with Roger Bros. First Love silver-plate.

1

	Ashtray, 3½", sq., #111	15.00
	Ashtray, 3½" x 2½", #30	15.00
	Ashtray, 5" x 3", #12, club	30.00
	Ashtray, 5" x 3¼", #30	20.00
	Ashtray, 6½" x 4¼", #30	30.00
	Basket, 9¼" x 10" x 7¼", #115	175.00
2	Basket, 10" x 4¼" x 7", oval hdld., #115	185.00
	Bottle, oil w/stopper, 8", #5200	50.00
	Bowl, 3" x 5", rose, #115	35.00
	Bowl, 4" x 1½", finger, #30	32.00
	Bowl, 4¼", finger, #5111½	35.00
	Bowl, 6" x 2½", oval, olive, #115	25.00
	Bowl, 6¾" x 4¼", ftd., flared rim, #111	30.00
	Bowl, 7½" x 3", 3 pt., ftd., #117	35.00
	Bowl, 8" sq. x 2½", hdld., #111	60.00
	Bowl, 8½" x 4", #115	37.50
	Bowl, 9" x 4½", ftd., #111	42.00
	Bowl, 9½" x 2½", hdld., #111	45.00
	Bowl, 10" x 3¾", ftd., flared rim, #111	55.00
	Bowl, 10" x 4½", #115	45.00
	Bowl, 10½" x 5", crimped, #115	44.00
	Bowl, 10½" x 7" x 7", #126	62.00
	Bowl, 10¾" x 4¾", #115	42.50
	Bowl, 11" x 1¾", #30	55.00
	Bowl, 11" x 3¼", flared rim, #111	62.50
	Bowl, 11" x 5¼", flared rim, #6	70.00
	Bowl, 11½" x 8¼", oval, #115	45.00
	Bowl, 12" x 3½", #6	70.00
	Bowl, 12" x 3¼", flared, #115	60.00
	Bowl, 12" x 4" x 7½", oval, #117	65.00
	Bowl, 12½", flat, ftd., #126	75.00
	Bowl, 13" x 3¼" x 8¾", oval, flared, #115	55.00
	Bowl, 13" x 7" x 9¼", #126	67.50
	Bowl, 13" x 7", #117	62.50
	Bowl, 14" x 7½" x 6", oval, #126	65.00
	Box, candy w/lid, 4¾" x 6¼"	55.00
	Butter or cheese, 7" sq. x 1¼", #111	120.00
	Candelabra, 2-lite, #41	35.00
	Candelabrum, 6", 2-lite w/prisms, #30	60.00
8	Candle, 3", 1-lite, #111	25.00
	Candle, 3", low, #115	25.00
	Candle, 3½", #115	25.00
	Candle, 4", cornucopia, #117	25.00
	Candle, 4", low, #111	25.00

	Candle, 5¼", 2-lite, globe, #30	37.50
	Candle, 6", 2-lite, #30	37.50
	Candy box, 6" x 3½", 3 hdld., 3 pt., w/lid, #115	85.00
	Candy box, 6" x 3½", 3 pt., w/lid, crown finial, #106	90.00
	Candy jar, 5" x 7¼", w/lid, ftd., #25	85.00
	Candy, 6½", w/5" lid, #115	75.00
	Carafe, w/stopper, water, #5200	195.00
	Cheese stand, 3" x 5¼", #111	25.00
5	Cheese stand, 5¾" x 3½", #115	25.00
	Cigarette box w/lid, 4" x 4¼"	32.00
	Cigarette box w/lid, 4½" x 3½", #30	35.00
	Cigarette box w/lid, 4¾" x 3¾"	35.00
	Cocktail shaker, 14 oz., #5200	120.00
	Cocktail shaker, 16 oz., #5200	120.00
	Cocktail shaker, 32 oz., #5200	155.00
	Comport w/lid, 8¾" x 5½", #111	135.00
	Comport, 3½"x 4¾"w, #111	30.00
	Comport, 5" x 5½", flared rim, #115	32.00
	Comport, 5¼" x 6¾", flat top, #115	32.00
	Comport, 6" x 4¾", low, #115	37.50
	Creamer, 2½", individual, #115	18.00
	Creamer, 3", 10 oz., #111	18.00
11	Creamer, 3¾", 7 oz., #115	15.00
	Creamer, sugar w/butter pat lid, breakfast set, #28	75.00
	Cruet, #25	90.00
	Cruet, #30	90.00
	Cup, #115	12.50
	Decanter w/stopper, 16 oz., #5200	150.00
4	Decanter w/stopper, 32 oz., #30	175.00
	Decanter w/stopper, 32 oz., #5200	175.00
	Hat, 4½", #30	395.00
	Hat, 5½" x 8½" x 6¼", #30	350.00
	Honey dish, 5" x 3", #91	30.00
13	Ice bucket, 6", #30	110.00
	Lamp, hurricane, w/prisms, 15", #115	165.00
	Lamp shade only, #115	110.00
	Lid for candy urn, #111	35.00
	Mayonnaise, 4¾" x 4½", div. w/7½" underplate	35.00
	Mayonnaise, 5¼" x 3", div. w/6½" plate, #1153	5.00
	Mayonnaise, 5½" x 2½", ftd., hdld., #111	35.00
12	Mayonnaise, 5½" x 2¾", #115	35.00
	Mayonnaise, 5½" x 3½", crimped, #111	32.00
	Mayonnaise, 5¾" x 3", w/dish hdld. tray, #111	35.00

Mayonnaise, w/7" tray hdld, #111	35.00	
Mustard w/lid & underplate	57.50	
Nappy, 5" x 1", w/bottom star, #25	20.00	
Nappy, 5" x 1¾", one hdld., #115	18.00	
Nappy, 5½" x 2", div., hdld., #111	18.00	
Nappy, 5½" x 2", one hdld., heart, #115	28.00	

Nappy, 6" x 1¾", hdld., #111	22.00	
Perfume tray, 8" x 5", #5200	25.00	
Perfume, 5", #5200	85.00	
Pitcher, #5200	175.00	
15	Pitcher, 9", 80 oz., ice lip, #5202	195.00
Plate, 6", #111	12.00	

Ref	Item	Price	Ref	Item	Price
16	Plate, 6", #115, mayonnaise liner	12.00		Stem, 5¼", 5 oz., ftd. juice, #5111½	18.00
	Plate, 6", hdld., lemon, #111	14.00		Stem, 5¾", 10 oz., low luncheon goblet, #5111½	16.00
	Plate, 6", sq., #111	14.00		Stem, 6", 4½ oz., claret, #5111½	38.00
	Plate, 7", #111	17.50		Stem, 6½", 12 oz., ftd. ice tea, #5111½	25.00
	Plate, 7½", #111	18.00		Stem, 6¾", 14 oz., ftd. ice tea, #5111½	25.00
	Plate, 7½", #115	18.00		Stem, cordial, #111	18.00
	Plate, 7½", mayonnaise liner, hdld., #115	15.00		Sugar, 2½", individual, #115	15.00
	Plate, 7½", sq., #111	19.00	10	Sugar, 3", 7 oz., #115	14.00
	Plate, 7½", 2 hdld., #115	19.00		Sugar, 3", 10 oz., #111	15.00
	Plate, 8½", #30	20.00		Tray, 8" x 2", hdld. celery, #111	17.50
	Plate, 8½", #111	20.00		Tray, 8" x 4¾", individual sugar/cream, #115	17.50
	Plate, 8½", #115	20.00		Tray, 8¾", celery, #91	30.00
	Plate, 11", #111	47.50		Tray, 11", celery, #91	40.00
	Plate, 11", 2 hdld., sandwich, #115	30.00		Tumbler, 2", 1½ oz., whiskey, #5200	50.00
	Plate, 11", hdld., #111	40.00		Tumbler, 2½" x 3⅜", sham, Teardrop, ftd.	45.00
6	Plate, 11", hdld., cracker w/ring, #115	40.00		Tumbler, 3", sham, #5200	30.00
	Plate, 11", hdld., cracker w/ring, #111	40.00		Tumbler, 4¾", 10 oz., sham, #5200	33.00
	Plate, 11", hdld., sandwich, #111	40.00		Tumbler, 5½", 12 oz., sham, #5200	33.00
	Plate, 11¼", dinner, #115	55.00		Tumbler, 6", 14 oz., sham, #5200	33.00
3	Plate, 12", egg, #30	135.00		Tumbler, 8 oz., flat, #115	25.00
	Plate, 12", torte, rolled edge, #111	40.00		Urn, 4½" x 4½", #111	25.00
	Plate, 13", torte, flat edge, #111	50.00		Urn, 4½" x 4½", #115	25.00
	Plate, 13", torte, rolled edge, #111	60.00		Urn, 4¾", rnd ft.	25.00
	Plate, 13¼", torte, #111	60.00		Urn, 5", #525	35.00
	Plate, 13½", cake, hdld., #115	50.00		Urn, 5½", ring hdld., sq. ft.	55.00
	Plate, 14", #115	50.00		Urn, 5½", sq. ft.	35.00
	Plate, 14", cake, #115	50.00	9	Urn, 7", sq. hdld., #545	65.00
	Plate, 14½", cake, lg. base, #30	55.00		Urn, 7", #529	35.00
	Plate, 14½", cake, sm. base, #30	55.00		Vase, 4", flared rim, #115	25.00
	Relish, 6" x 1¾", hdld., 2 pt., #111	20.00		Vase, 4½" x 4¾", #115	30.00
	Relish, 6" x 1¾", hdld., 2 pt., #115	20.00		Vase, 5" x 5", crimped, #115	35.00
	Relish, 8" x 4½", pickle, 2 pt., #115	25.00	1	Vase, 6", green, #400	65.00
	Relish, 8", 3 pt., hdld., #115	25.00		Vase, 6", #507	55.00
	Relish, 9" x 1½", 2 pt. pickle, #115	25.00		Vase, 8" x 4¾", cornucopia, #117	65.00
	Relish, 9" x 1½", 3 hdld., 3 pt., #115	32.50		Vase, 8", ftd., #506	90.00
	Relish, 9" x 1½", 3 hdld., flared, #115	32.50		Vase, 8", ftd., #507	90.00
	Relish, 10", 5 pt. tray, #30	65.00		Vase, 8½" x 2¾", #505	100.00
	Relish, 10½" x 1½", hdld., 5 pt., #111	85.00		Vase, 8½" x 6", #115	90.00
	Relish, 10½" x 1¼", 2 hdld, 3 pt., #115	60.00		Vase, 9" x 4½", #505	95.00
	Relish, 10½" x 7", #115	37.50		Vase, 9", #509	90.00
	Relish, 11¾", tray, #115	45.00		Vase, 9", bud, #506	80.00
	Relish, 12", 4 pt., hdld., #111	40.00		Vase, 9½" x 3½", #506	125.00
14	Relish, 12", 5 pt., hdld., #111	55.00		Vase, 10" x 4¾", #5200	90.00
	Salt and pepper pr., #30	25.00		Vase, 10", #507	95.00
	Salt and pepper pr., #115	35.00		Vase, 10", ftd., #111	115.00
	Sandwich tray, 12" x 5¼", ctr. handle, #115	80.00		Vase, 10", ftd., #505	115.00
	Saucer, #115	5.00		Vase, 10", ftd., #506	115.00
	Stem, 3¾", 1 oz., cordial, #5111½	50.00		Vase, 10½" x 12 x 9½", #126	155.00
	Stem, 3¾", 4½ oz., oyster cocktail, #5111½	18.00		Vase, 10½", #126	175.00
	Stem, 4", 5 oz., ice cream, #5111½	12.00		Vase, 11" x 5¼", #505	145.00
	Stem, 4¼", 3 oz., cocktail, #115	16.00		Vase, 11½" x 4½", #506	140.00
	Stem, 4½", 3½ oz., cocktail, #5111½	16.00		Vase, 12", flared #115	145.00
	Stem, 5", 5 oz., saucer champagne, #5111½	16.00		Vase, 12", ftd., #506	145.00
7	Stem, 5¼", 3 oz., wine, #5111½	25.00			

COLORS: CRYSTAL, PINK, YELLOW, AND RARE IN GREEN

We find that Tiffin's Flanders is often mistakenly displayed as Cambridge's Gloria and vice versa. Look at Gloria on pages 110 – 112 to see its curved stem floral design.

New collectors have been exposed to Elegant patterns via the Internet. This is influencing prices on already scarce wares and revealing some that we thought rare as being more bountiful. More glassware has been assembled into collections through the Internet than by any other means in the last few years. If you want any Elegant pattern, do not delay gathering it. We don't feel the unexpected Internet "supply" is going to continue perpetually.

Flanders stems are routinely found on Tiffin's #17024 blank. Normally these have a crystal foot and stem with tops of crystal, pink, or yellow. Color blending that is seen occasionally includes green foot with pink stems, and pink tumblers as well as pitchers with crystal handle and foot. A green Flanders vase was unearthed several years ago and is pictured on the right. Round plates are Tiffin's line #8800 and each size plate has a different number. Scalloped plates are line #5831. We find more of the round plates than we do the scalloped ones with dinners rarely witnessed in either shape.

Shakers are being found in crystal once in a while, but seldom in pink. We have had a few reports of yellow, but have never seen one. Lamps are found only in crystal. That cylindrical shade is occasionally found over a candlestick and designated as a Chinese hurricane lamp. We have pictured one with an electric insert in previous editions. As with most Tiffin pitchers of this time, Flanders was sold with or without a cover. Keep in mind that the pitcher top is plain with no pattern etched on it.

1

		Crystal	Pink	Yellow
	Almond, ftd., nut, blown	30.00	60.00	50.00
	Ashtray, 2¼ x 3¾", w/cigarette rest	50.00		
	Bowl, 2 hdld., bouillon	50.00	135.00	85.00
2	Bowl, 2 hdld., cream soup	60.00		
4	Bowl, finger, ftd., 8 oz., #185	35.00	95.00	60.00
	Bowl, 2 hdld., bonbon	30.00	100.00	65.00
	Bowl, 8", ftd., blown	125.00	325.00	
	Bowl, 11", ftd., console	75.00	175.00	95.00
	Bowl, 12", flanged rim, console	65.00	175.00	95.00
	Candle, 2 styles, #5831 & #15360 shown	40.00	75.00	50.00
	Candy box, w/cover, flat, #329	135.00	350.00	250.00
	Candy jar, w/cover, ftd.	100.00	250.00	185.00

2

		Crystal	Pink	Yellow
	Celery, 11"	40.00	95.00	60.00
	Cheese & cracker	55.00	130.00	100.00
	Comport, 3½"	40.00	95.00	60.00
	Comport, 6"	65.00	175.00	95.00
	Creamer, flat	40.00	110.00	75.00
	Creamer, ftd.	30.00	100.00	50.00
9	Cup, 2 styles, #8869 shown	50.00	100.00	65.00
	Decanter	150.00	350.00	250.00
	Electric lamp w/Chinese style shade	295.00		
	Grapefruit, w/liner	65.00	165.00	110.00
	Hurricane lamp, Chinese style	295.00		
	Mayonnaise, w/liner	50.00	125.00	80.00
	Oil bottle & stopper	110.00	295.00	195.00
	Parfait, 5⅝", hdld.	60.00	150.00	100.00
	Pitcher & cover, 54 oz., #194	250.00	395.00	295.00
11	Plate, 6"	6.00	15.00	10.00
7	Plate, 8", #8833	10.00	20.00	12.50
16	Plate, 10¼", dinner, #8818	50.00	110.00	70.00
	Relish, 3 pt.	60.00	125.00	80.00
	Salt & pepper, pr., #2 (rare)	200.00	450.00	300.00
	Sandwich server, center hdld., octagon, #337		165.00	
9	Saucer, #8869 shown	6.00	12.00	8.00
	Stem, 4½", oyster cocktail	18.00	50.00	22.00
3	Stem, 4½", sherbet/sundae, 6 oz.	15.00	30.00	17.50
6	Stem, 4¾", cocktail, 3½ oz., #15024	20.00	40.00	28.00

		Crystal	Pink	Yellow
	Stem, 5", cordial, 1½ oz., #15024	50.00	110.00	75.00
14	Stem, 5⅝", parfait, cafe, 4½ oz., #15024	35.00	100.00	60.00
	Stem, 6⅛", wine, 3 oz.	30.00	75.00	40.00
12	Stem, 6¼", saucer champagne, 6 oz.	16.00	38.00	20.00
	Stem, 7 oz., hdld., parfait		125.00	
18	Stem, claret, 5 oz., #15024	30.00	100.00	60.00
5	Stem, 8¼", water, 9 oz., #15024	30.00	55.00	35.00
	Stem, cordial, #15047	50.00	110.00	75.00
	Stem, sundae/sherbet, low ft., #15047	16.00	35.00	25.00
	Stem, sundae/sherbet, high ft., #15047	18.00	40.00	28.00
15	Stem, 9 oz., water, #15047	30.00	55.00	35.00
	Sugar, flat, #6	40.00	110.00	75.00
	Sugar, ftd., #185	30.00	100.00	50.00
	Tumbler, 2¾", 2½ oz., ftd., whiskey, #020	30.00	80.00	40.00
8	Tumbler, 4¾", 9 oz., ftd., water	20.00	45.00	22.00
13	Tumbler, 4¾", 10 oz., ftd.	20.00	45.00	22.00
10	Tumbler, 5⅞", 12 oz., ftd., tea, #020	30.00	80.00	35.00
	Tumbler, 12 oz., tea, #14185	25.00	60.00	35.00
	Tumbler, 12 oz., ftd., tea, #15071	30.00	80.00	35.00
17	Vase, bud, 8" or 10", #14185	50.00	125.00	70.00
1	Vase, ftd., 8", #2	80.00	195.00	125.00
	Vase, 10½", Dahlia, cupped, ftd., #151	150.00	275.00	200.00
	Vase, fan, #15151	100.00	250.00	150.00

COLORS: CRYSTAL W/GREEN, TWILIGHT, TWILIGHT W/CRYSTAL, PINK, CRYSTAL W/AMBER

Fontaine is a Tiffin pattern that more collectors would love to find, but they rarely have that opportunity. The purple color shown below is Tiffin's earlier Twilight color that does not change colors when placed under different light sources. Tiffin's later Twilight (1949 to 1980) changes from pink to purple depending upon fluorescent or natural light. We are having difficulty finding new Twilight pieces to picture. We spotted some Twilight in a shop in Arkansas last year. They didn't even know the pattern name, but priced it about triple a normal selling price. We are often baffled as to how some dealers come up with their prices.

We were able to purchase several pieces in other colors for our pictures. The covered pitcher with green accoutrements was spotted the same day as the wildly priced Twilight, but we were happy to find it priced reasonably. Although Tiffin sold pitchers with or without a lid, we have seen only three Fontaine pitchers and all have been with lids.

A fountain motif was popular (even on earlier carnival glass) and used by several companies of this era. As with all Tiffin patterns, cups and saucers are rarely spotted. We bought the set pictured over 20 years ago, before we even considered this pattern a contender for the book. We knew cups and saucers were hard to find in Tiffin patterns. We have never spotted cups and saucers in any other Fontaine colors. Have you?

Water goblets seem to be easier to find than other stemware. Remember that these are often sold as wine goblets to today's wine connoisseurs.

1   1

		Amber Green Pink	Twilight
	Bowl, 8", deep, ftd., #14194	85.00	175.00
	Bowl, 13" ctrpc., #8153	75.00	175.00
	Candlestick, low, #9758	40.00	75.00
	Creamer, stem. ftd., #4	50.00	75.00
4	Cup, #8869	75.00	135.00
	Finger bowl, #022	45.00	85.00
	Grape fruit, #251 & footed liner, #881	65.00	195.00
8	Jug & cover, #194	495.00	1,095.00
	Plate, 6", #8814	10.00	15.00
	Plate, 8", #8833	15.00	30.00
	Plate, 10", #8818	75.00	150.00
	Plate, 10", cake w/ctr. hdld., oct., #345	65.00	150.00
4	Saucer, #8869	10.00	20.00
6	Stem, cafe parfait, #033	65.00	140.00
	Stem, claret, #033	60.00	110.00
	Stem, cocktail, #033	35.00	60.00
3	Stem, cordial, #033	145.00	250.00
	Stem, saucer champagne, #033	30.00	60.00
2	Stem, sundae, #033	25.00	50.00
1	Stem, water, #033	75.00	110.00
	Stem, wine, 2½ oz., #033	65.00	110.00
	Sugar, ftd., #4	50.00	75.00
5	Tumbler, 9 oz. table, #032	35.00	65.00
7	Tumbler, 12 oz.		
	Vase, 8" ftd., #2 (shown in Flanders)	95.00	250.00
	Vase, 9¼", bowed top, #7	125.00	250.00

COLORS: CRYSTAL AND CRYSTAL W/WISTERIA BASE

Fostoria's Fuchsia was included in this book to help differentiate it from all the other Fuchsia patterns. Be sure to look at Tiffin's Fuchsia pattern on the next page so you do not confuse these. Many other companies made a Fuchsia pattern, so you need to be aware of this when shopping. This Fuchsia pattern is mostly etched on Fostoria's Lafayette mould blank #2244, which can be seen on page 136. Stemware line #6044 was featured for Fuchsia. Notice that champagne with the Wisteria stem. Most of those were sold to go with Lafayette Wisteria tableware that was non-etched. We have come across several sets of Lafayette that had Wisteria etched Fuchsia stems included with the plain Wisteria cups, saucers, plates, and creamers and sugars.

We have met a couple of collectors who collect everything Fuchsia, including Fostoria's and Tiffin's as well as Cambridge's Marjorie, which is a Fuchsia design. One even has several pottery designs highlighting Fuchsia.

The large center surface areas of plates are easily scratched from use or from stacking due to the flat, ground bottoms. We have detected dinner plates that were cloudy looking from all the marks. These will not sell for much in that condition, if at all.

Collectors do put a premium on mint condition and some will not buy any glassware that is not mint. We have been told that a few people around the country are trying their hand at buffing out the scratches from these plates; but we understand it is expensive and time consuming. Often it is unsuccessful since most glassware made at that time is very soft compared to highly polished glass of later years.

		Crystal	Wisteria
	Bonbon, #2470	33.00	
	Bowl, 10", #2395	95.00	
	Bowl, 10½", #2470½	75.00	
	Bowl 11½", "B," #2440	75.00	
	Bowl, 12" #2470	90.00	150.00
	Candlestick, 3", #2375	30.00	
5	Candlestick, 5", #2395½	45.00	
	Candlestick, 5½", #2470½	55.00	
4	Candlestick, 5½", #2470	55.00	175.00
	Comport, 6", low, #2470	35.00	100.00
	Comport, 6", tall, #2470	60.00	125.00
	Creamer, ftd., #2440	20.00	
7	Cup, #2440	20.00	
	Finger bowl, #869	30.00	
	Lemon dish, #2470	32.00	
	Oyster cocktail, 4½ oz., #6004	14.00	30.00
	Plate, 10", cake	60.00	
	Plate, 6", bread & butter, #2440	8.00	
	Plate, 7", salad, #2440	12.00	
1	Plate, 8", luncheon, #2440	20.00	

		Crystal	Wisteria
2	Plate, 9", dinner, #2440	50.00	
7	Saucer, #2440	5.00	
	Stem, ¾ oz., cordial, #6004	65.00	195.00
	Stem, 2½ oz., wine, #6004	30.00	50.00
	Stem, 3 oz., cocktail, #6004	22.00	50.00
	Stem, 4 oz., claret, #6004	40.00	65.00
	Stem, 5 oz., low sherbet, #6004	18.00	35.00
	Stem, 5½ oz., 6" parfait, #6004	30.00	75.00
3	Stem, 5½ oz., 5⅝", saucer champagne, #6004	22.00	50.00
	Stem, 9 oz., water, #6004	30.00	85.00
8	Sugar, ftd., #2440	20.00	
	Sweetmeat, #2470	30.00	
	Tumbler, 2 oz., #833	25.00	
	Tumbler, 2½ oz., ftd. whiskey, #6004	30.00	65.00
	Tumbler, 5 oz., #833	20.00	
	Tumbler, 5 oz., ftd. juice, #6004	18.00	45.00
	Tumbler, 8 oz., #833	20.00	
	Tumbler, 9 oz., ftd., #6004	16.00	50.00
6	Tumbler, 12 oz., #833	25.00	
	Tumbler, 12 oz., ftd., #6004	28.00	65.00

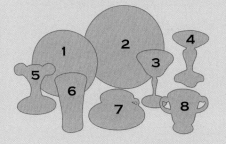

COLORS: CRYSTAL; A FEW EXPERIMENTAL TWILIGHT PIECES WHICH WERE NEVER MARKETED

Be sure to check out Fostoria's Fuchsia pattern listed before this one. The designs are similar, but the shapes are not. You need to be aware that pattern names were not exclusive to any particular company. Remember to state which company made the Fuchsia you collect.

Additional pieces of Fuchsia continue to be revealed. As with Cambridge's Rose Point that emerges etched on almost every line that Cambridge made, Tiffin's Fuchsia seems to have followed this same avenue. Fuchsia has always attracted collectors; and because of this, dealers are searching every nook and cranny, which explains why so many new pieces are being uncovered.

There are many rarely seen pieces including the bitters bottle, icers with inserts, cocktail shaker, salt and pepper shakers, hurricane and electric lamps as well as the tall #17457 stems of all varieties. A hurricane lamp consists of an etched shade over an etched candle. As with most Tiffin patterns, cups, saucers, and dinner plates are not found often enough to supply every collector's desires. There are footed as well as flat finger bowls; and there are three styles of double candlesticks.

You should be able to find an assortment of serving bowls in Fuchsia unlike most other Tiffin patterns where serving pieces come at a premium. The large handled urn vase must have found favor with customers for years as we see that particular vase more than any other Tiffin vase made. We have also seen some amazingly high prices on it. Our selling experience has been that they have a hard time realizing more than $100.00 on a good day.

	Ashtray, 2¼" x 3¾", w/cigarette rest	30.00		9	Candlestick, 2-lite, w/pointed center, #5831	65.00
14	Bell, 5", #15083	80.00			Candlestick, 2-lite, tapered center, #15306	65.00
	Bitters bottle	595.00		24	Candlestick, 5", 2-lite, ball center	65.00
5	Bowl, 4", finger, ftd., #041	50.00			Candlestick, 5⅝", 2-lite, w/fan center, #5902	65.00
15	Bowl, 4½" finger, w/#8814 liner	65.00		4	Candlestick, single, #348	30.00
	Bowl, 5³⁄₁₆", 2 hdld., #5831	30.00			Celery, 10", oval, #5831	35.00
	Bowl, 6¼", cream soup, ftd., #5831	50.00			Celery, 10½", rectangular, #5902	37.50
	Bowl, 7¼", salad, #5902	35.00			Cigarette box, w/lid, 4" x 2¾", #9305	125.00
18	Bowl, 8⅜", 2 hdld., #5831	60.00			Cocktail shaker, 8", w/metal top	250.00
	Bowl, 9¾", deep salad	75.00			Comport, 6¼", #5831	30.00
20	Bowl, 10", salad, #5831	70.00			Comport, 6½", w/beaded stem, #15082	35.00
	Bowl, 10½", console, fan shaped sides, #319	65.00			Creamer, 2⅞", individual, #5831	40.00
	Bowl, 11⅞", console, flared, #5902	75.00			Creamer, 3⅜", flat w/beaded handle, #5902	18.00
27	Bowl, 12", flanged rim, ftd., console, #5831	65.00		26	Creamer, 4½", ftd., #5831	20.00
	Bowl, 12⅝", console, flared, #5902	85.00		3	Creamer, pearl edge	40.00
25	Bowl, 13", crimped, #5902	85.00		22	Cup, #5831	95.00

	Electric lamp	350.00
11	Hurricane, 12", Chinese style	250.00
6	Icer, with insert	165.00
	Mayonnaise, flat, w/6¼" liner, #5902 w/ladle	50.00
	Mayonnaise, ftd., w/ladle, #5831	50.00
	Nut dish, 6¼"	40.00
	Pickle, 7⅜", #5831	40.00
	Pitcher & cover, #194	395.00
	Pitcher, flat	395.00
	Plate, 6¼", bread and butter, #5902	8.00
	Plate, 6¼", sherbet, #8814	9.00
	Plate, 6⅜", 2 hdld., #5831	10.00
8	Plate, 7", marmalade, 3-ftd., #310½	27.50
	Plate, 7½", salad, #5831	14.00
	Plate, 7⅞", cream soup or mayo liner, #5831	10.00
	Plate, 7⅞", salad, #8814	12.00
	Plate, 8⅛", luncheon, #8833	20.00
	Plate, 8¼", luncheon, #5902	15.00
	Plate, 8⅜", bonbon, pearl edge	25.00
	Plate, 9½", dinner, #5902	75.00
19	Plate, 10½", 2 hdld., cake, #5831	65.00
	Plate, 10½", muffin tray, pearl edge	50.00
	Plate, 13", lily rolled and crimped edge	60.00
	Plate, 14¼", sandwich, #8833	60.00
	Relish, 6⅜", 3 pt., #5902	30.00
	Relish, 9¼", sq., 3 pt.	45.00
28	Relish, 10½" x 12½", hdld., 3 pt., #5902	50.00
23	Relish, 10½" x 12½", hdld., 5 pt.	70.00
1	Salt and pepper, pr., #2	175.00
22	Saucer, #5831	10.00
	Stem, 4¹⁄₁₆", cordial, #15083	30.00
	Stem, 4⅜", sherbet, #15083	10.00
	Stem, 4¼", cocktail, #15083	12.00
	Stem, 4⅝", 3½ oz., cocktail, #17453	28.00

	Stem, 4⅞", saucer champagne, hollow stem	125.00
	Stem, 5¹⁄₁₆", wine, #15083	28.00
	Stem, 5¼", claret, #15083	30.00
	Stem, 5⅜", cocktail, "C" stem, #17457	55.00
7	Stem, 5⅜", cordial, "C" stem, #17457	135.00
	Stem, 5⅜", 7 oz., saucer champagne, #17453	25.00
	Stem, 5⅜", saucer champagne, #15083	14.00
	Stem, 5⅜", saucer champagne, "C" stem, #17457	40.00
	Stem, 5⁵⁄₁₆", parfait, #15083	35.00
	Stem, 6¼", low water, #15083	22.00
12	Stem, 7⅜", 9 oz., water, #17453, cupped bowl	35.00
	Stem, 7½", water, high, #15083	25.00
	Stem, 7⅝", water, "C" stem, #17457	75.00
	Sugar, 2⅞", individual, #5831	35.00
	Sugar, 3⅜", flat, w/beaded handle, #5902	18.00
	Sugar, 4½", ftd., #5831	20.00
2	Sugar, pearl edge	40.00
21	Tray, sugar/creamer, ind.	50.00
	Tray, 9½", 2 hdld. for cream/sugar	40.00
17	Tumbler, 2⁷⁄₁₆", 2 oz., bar, flat, #506	65.00
	Tumbler, 3⁵⁄₁₆", oyster cocktail, #14196	12.00
	Tumbler, 3⅜", old-fashioned, flat, #580	50.00
	Tumbler, 4³⁄₁₆" flat, juice	35.00
	Tumbler, 4⁵⁄₁₆", 5 oz., ftd., juice, #15083	22.00
	Tumbler, 5⅛", water, flat, #517	30.00
	Tumbler, 5⁵⁄₁₆", 9 oz., ftd., water, #15083	22.00
	Tumbler, 6⁵⁄₁₆", 12 oz., ftd., tea, #15083	30.00
13	Vase, 6½", bud, #14185	30.00
	Vase, 8¹³⁄₁₆", flared, crimped	110.00
	Vase, 8¼", bud, #14185	35.00
	Vase, 10½", bud, #14185	45.00
	Vase, 10¾", bulbous bottom, #5872	195.00
	Vase, 10⅞", beaded stem, #15082	75.00
10	Vase, 11¾", urn, 2 hdld., trophy.	110.00
16	Whipped cream, 3-ftd., #310	30.00

COLORS: BLACK, BLUE, CRYSTAL, GREEN, RED, AND YELLOW

Gazebo and another Paden City pattern, Utopia, are two very comparable designs, which we are combining for the time being. In the pattern shot at right, Utopia is on the left and Gazebo on the right. The etchings on Utopia are larger and more meticulous than those of Gazebo. Utopia may have been transformed from Gazebo for use on larger items or Gazebo downsized from Utopia. Speculation today is just that, as no one knows why the glass companies did most of the things they did. Over 30 years ago when we first started researching, we believed all of the interviews from retired workers' memories and anecdotal testimonies. Time has proved not all of those were accurate.

The insufficient supplies of Paden City's patterns generate major concerns for collectors today. There is barely enough available to whet your appetite. Thankfully, there seems to be an adequate supply of crystal Gazebo for the present. Before we added Gazebo to our book, you could find pieces priced around $45.00, mostly due to size. People selling Gazebo had no idea what they had. It was old, elegant, and rarely priced inexpensively.

Several different Paden City mold lines were used for this etching. All measurements in our listing are taken from actual pieces. We have yet to find a punch bowl to go with our punch cups. However, it was the fashion of the day to include "custard" cups with a set, so there may be no punch bowl.

		Crystal	Blue
	Bowl, 9", fan handles	35.00	
	Bowl, 9", bead handles	35.00	70.00
	Bowl, 13", flat edge	45.00	
	Bowl, 14", low flat	45.00	
	Cake stand	45.00	
	Candlestick, 5¼"	33.00	
	Candlestick, double, 2 styles, #555	40.00	50.00
	Candy dish, flat, clover	75.00	
	Candy dish, flat, square	75.00	
1	Candy dish w/lid, "heart"	90.00	250.00
4	Candy w/lid, 10¼", small, ftd., #444	65.00	125.00
	Candy w/lid, 11", large, ftd.	75.00	
3	Cheese dish and cover, #555	95.00	275.00
	Cocktail shaker, w/glass stopper	125.00	

		Crystal	Blue
	Creamer	15.00	
	Mayonnaise liner	10.00	
	Mayonnaise, bead handles	25.00	
	Plate, 10¾"	40.00	
	Plate, 12½", bead handles	45.00	85.00
	Plate, 13", fan handles	50.00	
2	Plate, 16", beaded edge, #555		90.00
6	Relish, 9¾", three part, #555	30.00	65.00
	Server, 10", swan handle	45.00	
5	Server, 11", center handle, #555	33.00	85.00
	Sugar	15.00	
	Tumbler, ftd. juice	16.00	
	Vase, 10¼"	80.00	395.00*
	Vase, 12"	80.00	450.00

*Black or yellow

COLOR: CRYSTAL SUNRAY WITH SILVER MIST RIBBING (SEE PAGE 215)

	Item	Price		Item	Price
	Ashtray, individual	20.00		Plate, 8½"	10.00
	Ashtray, square	15.00		Plate, 9½"	20.00
	Bowl, 5" fruit	15.00		Plate 11", torte	35.00
9	Bowl, 5", hdld., round or square	18.00		Plate 12", sandwich	35.00
	Bowl, 5", hdld., triangular	16.00		Plate, 15", torte	42.50
	Bowl, 10", hdld.	35.00		Plate, 16"	42.50
	Bowl, 12", salad	40.00		Relish, 6½", 3-part	27.50
	Bowl, 13", rolled edge	40.00		Relish, 8", 4-part	35.00
	Bowl, custard or frozen dessert	15.00		Relish, 10", 2-part	25.00
	Butter w/lid, ¼ lb.	40.00		Salt dip	18.00
	Candelabra. 2-lite w/prisms	95.00		Saucer	3.00
4	Candlestick, 3"	20.00		Shaker, pr.	37.50
	Candlestick, 5½"	32.50		Stem, 3½", 5½ oz., sherbet	11.00
	Candlestick, duo	55.00		Stem, 3¼", 3½", fruit cocktail	12.00
	Candy w/lid	65.00		Stem, 4⅞", 4½ oz., claret	15.00
5	Celery, 10", hdld.	32.50		Stem, 5¾", 9 oz., water	17.50
	Cigarette & cover	60.00		Sugar, ftd.	15.00
	Comport, 5" w. x 4" h.	32.50		Sugar, ind., ftd.	15.00
1	Cream soup	20.00		Sweetmeat, 6", divided	25.00
	Creamer, ftd.	15.00		Tray, 6½" for cream/sugar	22.50
	Creamer, ind., ftd.	15.00		Tray, 7", oval hdld.	27.50
	Cup	10.00		Tray, 8½", condiment	60.00
	Decanter, rectangular	100.00		Tray, 10", square	55.00
2	Ice bucket	65.00		Tray, 10½", oblong	50.00
	Jelly w/cover, 7¼"	50.00		Tumbler, 2¼", 2 oz., whiskey	10.00
	Mayonnaise, 3-pc. set	50.00		Tumbler, 3½", 5 oz., juice	12.00
	Mustard w/cover and ladle	40.00		Tumbler, 3½", 6 oz., old-fashion	12.00
	Oil bottle w/stopper, 3 oz.	50.00		Tumbler, 3", 4 oz., ftd. cocktail	12.50
	Onion soup w/cover	50.00		Tumbler, 4⅛", 9 oz., water	10.00
8	Pickle, 6"	20.00	6	Tumbler, 4¾", 9 oz., ftd. water	12.50
	Pitcher, 2-quart	75.00		Tumbler, 4⅝", 5 oz., ftd. juice	15.00
	Plate, 6"	7.00		Tumbler, 5¼", 13 oz., ftd. ice tea	15.00
7	Plate, 6½", hdld.	55.00		Tumbler, 5⅛", 13 oz., ice tea	15.00
	Plate, 7½"	10.00		Vase, 3½, rose bowl	33.00

20

COLORS: CRYSTAL, TOPAZ (YELLOW), PEACH-BLO, GREEN, EMERALD GREEN (LIGHT AND DARK), AMBER, BLUE, HEATHERBLOOM, EBONY WITH WHITE GOLD

Cambridge's Gloria pattern is time and again mixed up with Tiffin's Flanders. Look closely at our photos and notice that the flower on Gloria bends the stem. Both are portrayals of poppies, a flower reminiscent of WWI and European poppy fields.

We have tried for a variety of colors and items in our photos here. Observe the seven colors of ice buckets etched on Decagon blanks. The blue and Ebony with white gold are uncommon.

20

Gloria can be assembled in large sets of Topaz (yellow) or crystal; any other color will frustrate you. Our experiences have shown yellow Gloria is more available than is crystal, so if you like that color, buy it when you can. A luncheon set in blue or Peach-Blo (pink) may turn up sporadically, but larger sets appear impossible to pull together. For some inexplicable reason, the dark Emerald green, though quite striking, is very elusive.

Gold encrusted items bring 20% to 25% more than those without gold. However, pieces with worn gold are not easy to sell at present. That may possibly change with all the touting of the "shabby chic" look.

Gloria might make an ideal candidate for merging colors, since there are so many from which to choose. As with other Cambridge patterns in this book, not all Gloria pieces are listed. A more complete listing of Cambridge etched pieces is found under Rose Point. Prices for crystal Gloria will run 30% to 40% less than the prices listed for Rose Point, an exceedingly popular Cambridge pattern.

20

		Crystal	Green Pink Yellow
	Basket, 6", 2 hdld. (sides up)	30.00	50.00
	Bowl, 3", indiv. nut, 4 ftd.	50.00	70.00
	Bowl, 3½", cranberry	35.00	60.00
	Bowl, 5", ftd., crimped edge, bonbon	30.00	50.00
	Bowl, 5", sq., fruit, "saucer"	22.00	35.00
	Bowl, 5½", bonbon, 2 hdld.	25.00	40.00
	Bowl, 5½", bonbon, ftd.	25.00	35.00
	Bowl, 5½", flattened, ftd., bonbon	25.00	35.00
	Bowl, 5½", fruit, "saucer"	22.00	35.00
	Bowl, 6", rnd., cereal	35.00	55.00
	Bowl, 6", sq., cereal	35.00	55.00
	Bowl, 8", 2 pt., 2 hdld., relish	35.00	45.00
	Bowl, 8", 3 pt., 3 hdld., relish	38.00	50.00
	Bowl, 8¾", 2 hdld., figure "8" pickle	30.00	50.00
	Bowl, 8¾", 2 pt., 2 hdld., figure "8" relish	30.00	50.00
	Bowl, 9", salad, tab hdld.	50.00	100.00
	Bowl, 9½", 2 hdld., veg.	75.00	125.00
	Bowl, 10", oblong, tab hdld., "baker"	65.00	110.00
	Bowl, 10", 2 hdld.	55.00	90.00
	Bowl, 11", 2 hdld., fruit	65.00	110.00
	Bowl, 11", ped. ft., #3400/3	70.00	115.00
	Bowl, 12", 4 ftd., console	65.00	110.00
	Bowl, 12", 4 ftd., flared rim	65.00	110.00
	Bowl, 12", 4 ftd., oval	85.00	150.00
	Bowl, 12", 5 pt., celery & relish	60.00	90.00
	Bowl, 13", flared rim	70.00	115.00
10	Bowl, cream soup, w/rnd. liner	50.00	75.00
	Bowl, cream soup, w/sq. liner	50.00	75.00
	Bowl, finger, flared edge, w/rnd. plate	35.00	65.00
	Bowl, finger, ftd.	35.00	60.00
	Bowl, finger, w/rnd. plate	40.00	65.00
8	Butter, w/cover, 2 hdld.	225.00	450.00
	Candlestick, 6", ea., keyhole	40.00	65.00
	Candlelabra, 3 lite, keyhole, #638	45.00	65.00
	Candy box, w/cover, 4 ftd., w/tab hdld.	145.00	225.00

		Crystal	Green Pink Yellow
18	Cheese compote w/11½" cracker plate, tab hdld.	60.00	95.00
	Cocktail shaker, ground stopper, spout (like pitcher)	150.00	250.00
	Comport, 4", fruit cocktail	18.00	33.00
	Comport, 5", 4 ftd.	25.00	75.00
	Comport, 6", 4 ftd.	30.00	80.00
	Comport, 7", low	40.00	100.00
	Comport, 7", tall	45.00	125.00
	Comport, 9½", tall, 2 hdld., ftd. bowl	80.00	195.00
	Creamer, 6 oz., ftd., #3400/16	20.00	30.00
	Creamer, tall, ftd.	20.00	35.00
11	Cup, rnd. or sq.	18.00	30.00
	Cup, 4 ftd., sq.	50.00	100.00
	Cup, after dinner (demitasse), rnd. or sq.	80.00	125.00
	Fruit cocktail, 6 oz., ftd. (3 styles), #3135 shown	15.00	25.00
20	Ice pail, metal handle w/tongs, #3400/851	75.00	160.00
12	Icer, w/insert	55.00	100.00
	Mayonnaise, w/liner & ladle (4 ftd. bowl)	45.00	95.00
15	Oil, w/stopper, 6 oz., tall, ftd., hdld.	110.00	250.00
	Oyster cocktail, #3035, 4½ oz.	18.00	26.00
	Oyster cocktail, 4½ oz., low stem	18.00	26.00
6	Pitcher, 64 oz., #935		
	Pitcher, 67 oz., middle indent	225.00	395.00
16	Pitcher, 80 oz., ball	295.00	495.00
	Pitcher, w/cover, 64 oz.	295.00	695.00
	Plate, 6", 2 hdld.	12.00	18.00
	Plate, 6", bread/butter	10.00	14.00
	Plate, 7½", tea, #3400/60	12.00	16.00
13	Plate, 8½", salad, #3400/62	14.00	22.00
	Plate, 9½", dinner	60.00	90.00
	Plate, 10", tab hdld., salad	45.00	65.00
14	Plate, 11", 2 hdld.	50.00	70.00
	Plate, 11", sq., ftd. cake	110.00	265.00
	Plate, 11½", tab hdld., sandwich	60.00	80.00

	Crystal	Green Pink Yellow			Crystal	Green Pink Yellow
Plate, 14", chop or salad	65.00	100.00		Salt & pepper, ftd., metal tops	60.00	125.00
Plate, sq., bread/butter	12.00	15.00	11 Saucer, rnd.	3.00	5.00
Plate, sq., dinner	55.00	85.00	Saucer, rnd. after dinner	10.00	18.00
Plate, sq., salad	14.00	20.00	Saucer, sq., after dinner (demitasse)	12.00	20.00
Plate, sq., service	50.00	90.00	Saucer, sq.	3.00	5.00
Platter, 11½"	75.00	150.00	Stem, #3035, 2½ oz., wine	28.00	55.00
Salt & pepper, pr., short	45.00	100.00	Stem, #3035, 3 oz., cocktail	18.00	30.00
Salt & pepper, pr., w/glass top, tall	70.00	125.00	Stem, #3035, 3½ oz., cocktail	18.00	30.00

20

20

20

20

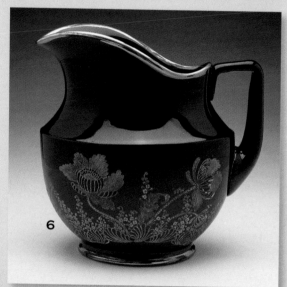

6

7

1 2 3 4 5

		Crystal	Green Pink Yellow
	Stem, #3035, 4½ oz., claret	40.00	65.00
19	Stem, #3035, 6 oz., low sherbet	16.00	22.00
	Stem, #3035, 6 oz., tall sherbet	18.00	28.00
	Stem, #3035, 9 oz., water	25.00	45.00
	Stem, #3035, 3½ oz., cocktail	18.00	33.00
	Stem, #3115, 9 oz., goblet	25.00	50.00
4	Stem, #3120, 1 oz., cordial	60.00	195.00
2	Stem, #3120, 3 oz., cocktail	18.00	30.00
1	Stem, #3120, 4½ oz., claret	38.00	70.00
	Stem, #3120, 6 oz., low sherbet	16.00	22.00
5	Stem, #3120, 6 oz., tall sherbet	18.00	26.00
3	Stem, #3120, 9 oz., water	25.00	45.00
	Stem, #3130, 1 oz., cordial	65.00	175.00
	Stem, #3130, 2½ oz., wine	28.00	55.00
	Stem, #3130, 6 oz., low sherbet	16.00	22.00
9	Stem, #3130, 6 oz., tall sherbet	18.00	28.00
	Stem, #3130, 8 oz., water	25.00	50.00
	Stem, #3135, 6 oz., low sherbet	16.00	22.00
	Stem, #3135, 6 oz., tall sherbet	18.00	26.00
	Stem, #3135, 8 oz., water	25.00	50.00
	Sugar, ftd., #3400/16	20.00	30.00
	Sugar, tall, ftd.	25.00	35.00
	Sugar shaker, w/glass top	175.00	325.00
	Syrup, tall, ftd.	85.00	175.00
	Tray, 11", ctr. hdld., sandwich	35.00	65.00
	Tray, 2 pt., ctr. hdld., relish	30.00	50.00
	Tray, 4 pt., ctr. hdld., relish	35.00	65.00
	Tray, 9", pickle, tab hdld.	35.00	70.00
	Tumbler, #3035, 5 oz., high ftd.	18.00	30.00
	Tumbler, #3035, 10 oz., high ftd.	20.00	40.00

		Crystal	Green Pink Yellow
	Tumbler, #3035, 12 oz., high ftd.	28.00	50.00
	Tumbler, #3115, 5 oz., ftd., juice	20.00	35.00
	Tumbler, #3115, 8 oz., ftd.	20.00	35.00
	Tumbler, #3115, 10 oz., ftd.	22.00	40.00
	Tumbler, #3115, 12 oz., ftd.	26.00	45.00
	Tumbler, #3120, 2½ oz., ftd. (used w/ cocktail shaker), flat, #1070	28.00	60.00
	Tumbler, #3120, 5 oz., ftd.	20.00	32.00
21	Tumbler, #3120, 10 oz., ftd.	22.00	40.00
17	Tumbler, #3120, 12 oz., ftd.	25.00	45.00
	Tumbler, #3130, 5 oz., ftd.	20.00	35.00
	Tumbler, #3130, 10 oz., ftd.	25.00	45.00
	Tumbler, #3130, 12 oz., ftd.	28.00	45.00
	Tumbler, #3135, 5 oz., juice	20.00	35.00
	Tumbler, #3135, 10 oz., water	22.00	40.00
	Tumbler, #3135, 12 oz., tea	28.00	50.00
	Tumbler, 12 oz., flat (2 styles), one indent side to match 67 oz. pitcher	25.00	45.00
	Tumbler, #3120, 2 oz., whiskey, #3400/92	28.00	60.00
	Vase, 6", #1308	50.00	85.00
	Vase, 9", oval, 4 indent	115.00	235.00
	Vase, 10", keyhole base	95.00	165.00
	Vase, 10", squarish top	150.00	295.00
	Vase, 11"	125.00	210.00
	Vase, 11", neck indent	145.00	225.00
7	Vase, 12", #407	150.00	295.00
	Vase, 12", keyhole base, flared rim	165.00	275.00
	Vase, 12", squarish top	195.00	325.00
	Vase, 14", keyhole base, flared rim	175.00	275.00

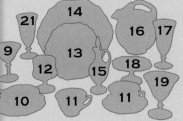

COLORS: CRYSTAL, SPANISH RED, RITZ BLUE, STIEGEL GREEN, 14K TOPAZ, ANNA ROSE, OLD AMETHYST, INDIA BLACK, VENETIAN (SHAMROCK) GREEN, AZURE BLUE, AQUAMARINE, PEACH, CARAMEL, MEADOW GREEN, COPEN BLUE, SMOKE, LIGHT AMETHYST, MISSION GOLD, MILK

Morgantown's Golf Ball pattern is the most established and accumulated design of this company. It is often confused with Cambridge's #1066, which is similar to Golf Ball at first glance; Cambridge's #1066 has cut indentations at intervals around the stem. That can work to your advantage if buying a rare piece such as a candlestick. Candles in #1066 are not nearly as pricey as those of Golf Ball. Morgantown's Golf Ball has symmetrical bumps spread over the surface of the ball of the stem.

As a rule, all pieces of Golf Ball are hard to find except for stems and most vases. Prices for stems have sunk from previous levels due both to quantities found and saturation of collections with stems. The Dupont (inverted two tiers) candle is not easily found. You should note the Irish coffee (row 2, second from right on page 114). It becomes a creamer when a spout is added. The sugar has no handles.

The Harlequin pastel colors, often marketed in sets of eight, include Amethyst, Copen Blue, Gloria Blue, Peach, Smoke, Topaz Mist, Shamrock Green, and Iridized Yellow. Some are illustrated in the top row on page 114. Other Harlequin sets include Coral and Pink Champagne colors.

Note the three Spanish stems in the middle of the next page. The cocktail is first followed by the champagne; the third item is a rarely seen grapefruit. We have only been able to find two collectors who own grapefruits. One has eight and the other only one.

To be consistent in terminology for collectors, my listings have used name designations found in *Gallagher's Handbook of Old Morgantown Glass* that unfortunately is no longer in print.

		Spanish Red *Ritz Blue	Other Colors
	Amherst water lamp, super rare	1,000.00+	
	Bell	125.00	60.00
	Candle, pr., 4⅝", Dupont (inverted 2 tier)	200.00	110.00
	Candle, 6" torch	150.00	90.00
3	Candlestick, 4" Jacobi (top flat rim)	125.00	80.00
	Candy, flat w/golf ball knob cover, 6"x 5½" (Alexandra)	1,000.00	750.00
	Creamer	175.00	
	Compote, 10" diam., 7½" high, w/14 crimp rim (Truman)	475.00	375.00
	Compote w/cover, 6" diam. (Celeste)	750.00	550.00
2	Compote, 6" diam. (Celeste)	450.00	300.00
16	Irish coffee, 5¼", 6 oz.	175.00	125.00
	Pilsner, 9⅛", 11 oz.	165.00	110.00
	Schooner, 8½", 32 oz.	295.00	195.00
	Stem, brandy snifter, 6½", 21 oz.	155.00	125.00

		Spanish Red *Ritz Blue	Other Colors
13	Stem, cafe parfait, 6¼", 4 oz.	85.00	50.00
11	Stem, champagne, 5", 5½ oz.	25.00	15.00
10	Stem, champagne, "Old English"	27.00	16.00
	Stem, claret, 5¼", 4½ oz.	50.00	30.00
8	Stem, cocktail, 4⅛"	18.00	14.00
6	Stem, cordial, 3½", 1½ oz.	40.00	25.00
17	Stem, grapefruit, 4¼", 9 oz.	75.00	
	Stem, oyster cocktail, 4⅜", 4½ oz.	40.00	25.00
	Stem, oyster cocktail, 4¼", 4 oz., flared	35.00	20.00
	Stem, sherbet/sundae, 4⅛", 3½ oz.	16.00	12.00
	Stem, sherry, 4⅝", 2½ oz.	40.00	25.00
9	Stem, water, 6¾", 9 oz.	32.00	20.00
7	Stem, water, 10 oz., "Old English"	30.00	18.00
14	Stem, wine, 4¾", 3 oz.	30.00	20.00
	Sugar, no handles, cone	175.00	
	Tumbler, 4⅜", ftd., wine	25.00	15.00
15	Tumbler, 5", 5 oz., ftd., juice	25.00	15.00
4	Tumbler, 6⅛", 9 oz., ftd., water	28.00	15.00
5	Tumbler, 6¾", 12 oz., ftd., tea	35.00	24.00
	Urn, 6½" high	125.00	65.00
	Vase, 4", Ivy ball, ruffled top	300.00	150.00
12	Vase, 4", Ivy ball w/rim (Kimball)	60.00	40.00
18	Vase, 4", Ivy ball, no rim (Kennon)	55.00	35.00
	Vase, 8" high, Charlotte w/crimped rim	275.00	175.00
1	Vase, 8" high, flair rim flute (Charlotte)	195.00	140.00
	Vase, 10½", #78 Lancaster (cupped w/tiny stand up rim)	425.00	250.00
	Vase, 11", #79 Montague (flair rim)	450.00	300.00

*Add 10% for Ritz Blue.

COLORS: CRYSTAL; FLAMINGO PINK PUNCH BOWL AND CUPS ONLY

Greek Key is an older Heisey pattern that is loved and easily recognized as most pieces are marked with that familiar diamond within an H. Other companies made similar patterns, but Heisey's is the celebrity in the collecting field. Stemware in all sizes is taxing to find and the prices signify that.

1

	Bowl, finger	40.00
	Bowl, jelly, w/cover, 2 hdld., ftd.	145.00
26	Bowl, indiv., ftd., almond	45.00
11	Bowl, 4", nappy	25.00
	Bowl, 4", shallow, low ft., jelly	40.00
	Bowl, 4½", nappy	25.00
	Bowl, 4½", scalloped, nappy	25.00
	Bowl, 4½", shallow, low ft., jelly	40.00
	Bowl, 5", ftd., almond	40.00
	Bowl, 5", ftd., almond, w/cover	110.00
7	Bowl, 5", hdld., jelly	65.00
	Bowl, 5", low ft., jelly, w/cover	75.00
	Bowl, 5", nappy	30.00
	Bowl, 5½", nappy	40.00
	Bowl, 5½", shallow nappy, ftd.	65.00
	Bowl, 6", nappy	30.00
	Bowl, 6", shallow nappy	30.00
	Bowl, 6½", nappy	35.00
	Bowl, 7", low ft., straight side	90.00
	Bowl, 7", nappy	80.00
	Bowl, 8", low ft., straight side	70.00
	Bowl, 8", nappy	70.00
	Bowl, 8", scalloped nappy	65.00
	Bowl, 8", shallow, low ft.	75.00
	Bowl, 8½", shallow nappy	75.00
	Bowl, 9", flat, banana split	45.00
10	Bowl, 9", ftd., banana split	40.00
	Bowl, 9", low ft., straight side	65.00
9	Bowl, 9", nappy	70.00
	Bowl, 9", shallow, low ft.	70.00
	Bowl, 9½", shallow nappy	70.00
	Bowl, 10", shallow, low ft.	85.00
	Bowl, 11", shallow nappy	70.00
	Bowl, 12", orange bowl	500.00
	Bowl, 12", punch, ftd., Flamingo	750.00
	Bowl, 12", orange, flared rim	450.00
	Bowl, 14½", orange, flared rim	500.00
	Bowl, 15", punch, ftd.	400.00
	Bowl, 18", punch, shallow	400.00
	Butter, individual (plate)	35.00
	Butter/jelly, 2 hdld., w/cover	200.00
6	Candy, w/cover, ½ lb.	140.00
	Candy, w/cover, 1 lb.	170.00
	Candy, w/cover, 2 lb.	210.00
	Cheese & cracker set, 10"	175.00
	Compote, 5"	75.00
	Compote, 5", w/cover	130.00
	Creamer	50.00
	Creamer, oval, hotel	45.00
	Creamer, rnd., hotel	40.00

12	Cup, 4½ oz., punch	18.00
	Cup, punch, Flamingo	40.00
	Coaster	20.00
	Egg cup, 5 oz.	80.00
	Hair receiver	170.00
	Ice tub, lg., tab hdld.	150.00
	Ice tub, sm., tab hdld.	130.00
1	Ice tub, w/cover, hotel	225.00
	Ice tub, w/cover, 5", individual, w/5" plate	200.00
27	Jar, 1 qt., crushed fruit, w/cover	400.00
3	Jar, 2 qt., crushed fruit, w/cover	450.00
	Jar, cherry + cover	125.00
	Jar, lg. cover, horseradish	140.00
4	Jar, sm. cover, horseradish	130.00
	Jar, w/knob cover, pickle	160.00
	Oil bottle, 2 oz., squat, w/#8 stopper	90.00
	Oil bottle, 2 oz., w/#6 stopper	100.00
24	Oil bottle, 4 oz., squat, w/#8 stopper	90.00
20	Oil bottle, 4 oz., w/#6 stopper	80.00
21	Oil bottle, 6 oz., w/#6 stopper	80.00
	Oil bottle, 6 oz., squat, w/#8 stopper	80.00
	Pitcher, 1 pint (jug)	130.00
13	Pitcher, 1 quart (jug)	180.00
15	Pitcher, 3 pint (jug)	200.00
	Pitcher, ½ gal. (tankard)	240.00
	Plate, 4½"	15.00
	Plate, 5"	18.00
	Plate, 5½"	20.00
	Plate, 6"	30.00
	Plate, 6½"	30.00
	Plate, 7"	45.00
	Plate, 8"	60.00
	Plate, 9"	90.00
	Plate, 10"	110.00
	Plate, 16", orange bowl liner	180.00
	Puff box, #1, w/cover	175.00
	Puff box, #3, w/cover	175.00
	Salt & pepper, pr.	135.00
2	Sherbet, 4½ oz., ftd., straight rim	25.00
8	Sherbet, 4½ oz., ftd., flared rim	25.00
	Sherbet, 4½ oz., high ft., shallow	25.00
	Sherbet, 4½ oz., ftd., shallow	25.00
	Sherbet, 4½ oz., ftd., cupped rim	25.00
	Sherbet, 6 oz., low ft.	30.00
	Spooner, lg.	110.00
	Spooner, 4½" (or straw jar)	110.00
	Stem, ¾ oz., cordial	225.00
	Stem, 2 oz., wine	100.00
	Stem, 2 oz., sherry	200.00
	Stem, 3 oz., cocktail	40.00

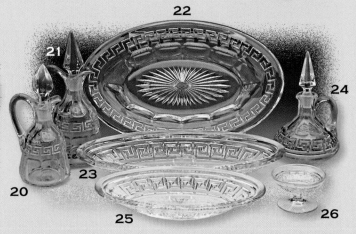

	Stem, 3½ oz., burgundy	125.00		Tray, 15", oblong	300.00
	Stem, 4½ oz., saucer champagne	40.00		Tumbler, 2½ oz. (or toothpick)	900.00
	Stem, 4½ oz., claret	150.00		Tumbler, 5 oz., flared rim	50.00
	Stem, 7 oz.	95.00		Tumbler, 5 oz., straight side	50.00
	Stem, 9 oz.	160.00		Tumbler, 5½ oz., water	50.00
	Stem, 9 oz., low ft.	145.00	19	Tumbler, 7 oz., flared rim	60.00
5	Straw jar, w/cover	425.00	18	Tumbler, 7 oz., straight side	60.00
	Sugar	50.00		Tumbler, 8 oz., w/straight, flared, cupped, shallow	60.00
	Sugar, oval, hotel	45.00	17	Tumbler, 10 oz., flared rim	90.00
	Sugar, rnd., hotel	40.00	16	Tumbler, 10 oz., straight wide	90.00
	Sugar & creamer, oval, individual	100.00		Tumbler, 12 oz., flared rim	100.00
25	Tray, 9", oval celery	50.00		Tumbler, 12 oz., straight side	100.00
23	Tray, 12", oval celery	60.00		Tumbler, 13 oz., straight side	100.00
22	Tray, 12½", French roll	150.00		Tumbler, 13 oz., flared rim	100.00
	Tray, 13", oblong	260.00	14	Water bottle	220.00

COLORS: AMBER, AMETHYST, GREEN, PINK, CRYSTAL, CRYSTAL WITH BLACK, GOLD, AND GREEN TRIM

Central's No. 401 etch was given the name "Harding" when President and Mrs. Harding selected a set of this "Dragon" design for the White House. It was a set of over 300 pieces and etched with gold. Subsequently, Central advertised it as glass "for America's first families."

Few pieces are being found at present, but those that are, are well worth your search. We have bought all six pieces of "Harding" pictured here over the last seven years. We saw a few other pieces, but the price asked became an obstacle. In any case, these few pieces should give you a hint of paucity. You must remember, though, we are discussing 80 year old glassware which nobody dreamed would be worth anything all these years later. It was used, broken, given or thrown away, and replaced by something more modern. It was inexpensive then. The established attitude was that china had value, but glass dishes were "everyday."

4

		*All Colors
	Bowl, 12", console, octagon	80.00
	Bowl, finger, #800	30.00
	Bowl, soup, flat	60.00
	Bowl, soup, 2 hdld. cream	40.00
	Candlestick, octagon collar	45.00
	Candlestick, rnd. collar	40.00
	Candy, ftd. cone w/etched lid	100.00
	Cheese & cracker	35.00
2	Comport, 4½", short stem	35.00
	Comport, 6", short stem	35.00
	Comport, 6", 10 oz., tall stem	45.00
4	Creamer, ftd.	30.00
	Cup, handled custard	20.00
	Decanter, qt., w/cut stop	295.00
	Ice tub, 2 hdld.	395.00
1	Jug, tall, flat bottom	350.00
	Oil & vinegar bottle	165.00
	Plate, 5" sherbet	8.00
	Plate, 6" finger bowl liner	12.00
3	Plate, dinner	65.00

	*All Colors
Plate, lunch	22.00
Server, center handle	50.00
Shaker, ftd. individual	85.00
Stem style, individual, almond	25.00
Stem, 5½ oz. sherbet	15.00
Stem, 6 oz., saucer champagne, #780	20.00
Stem, 9 oz., water, #780	28.00
Stem, cordial	65.00
Stem, oyster cocktail	16.00
Stem, wine	25.00
Sugar, ftd.	30.00
Tumbler, 5 oz	20.00
Tumbler, 8 oz.	22.00
Tumbler, 10 oz., #530	28.00
Tumbler, 12 oz.	28.00
Tumbler, ftd., hdld., tea	40.00
Vase, 8"	150.00
Vase, 10", ruffled top	195.00

* 25% less for crystal

1

3

2

HERMITAGE, #2449, FOSTORIA GLASS COMPANY, 1932 – 1945

COLORS: AMBER, AZURE (BLUE), CRYSTAL, EBONY, GREEN, TOPAZ, WISTERIA

Hermitage currently is collected by a small number of admirers; however, a few of those are beginning to set their sights on Wisteria. Other Fostoria patterns in Wisteria are being priced quite highly. Hermitage prices are affordable right now, so if you like Wisteria this is the time to start gathering a few pieces while you still can.

Our listings are taken out of a Fostoria catalog that had January 1, 1933, entered on the front page in pencil. Pictured are six different colored ice buckets compliments of a collector making the effort to get these shown. Enjoy!

3

		Crystal	Amber, Green Topaz	Azure	Wisteria
	Ashtray holder, #2449	5.00	8.00	12.00	
	Ashtray, #2449*	3.00	5.00	8.00	
5	Bottle, 3 oz., oil, #2449	20.00	40.00		
	Bottle, 27 oz., bar w/stopper, #2449	45.00			
16	Bowl, 4½", finger, #2449½	4.00	6.00	10.00	18.00
	Bowl, 5", fruit, #2449½	5.00	8.00	15.00	
	Bowl, 6", cereal, #2449½	6.00	10.00	20.00	
	Bowl, 6½", salad, #2449½	6.00	9.00	20.00	
15	Bowl, 7", soup, #2449½	8.00	12.00	22.00	40.00
	Bowl, 7½", salad, #2449½	8.00	12.00	30.00	
	Bowl, 8", deep, pedestal, ft., #2449	17.50	35.00	60.00	
1	Bowl, 10", ftd., #2449	20.00	35.00		100.00
	Bowl, grapefruit, w/crystal liner, #2449	20.00	40.00		
	Candle, 6", #2449	12.50	22.00	35.00	
	Coaster, 5⅝", #2449	5.00	7.50	11.00	
6	Comport, 6", #2449	12.00	17.50	27.50	35.00
	Creamer, ftd., #2449	4.00	6.00	10.00	25.00
	Cup, ftd., #2449	6.00	10.00	15.00	18.00
19	Decanter, 28 oz., w/stopper, #2449	35.00	90.00	165.00	
7	Fruit cocktail, 2⅜", 5 oz., ftd., #2449	5.00	7.50	12.00	
3	Ice tub, 6", #2449	17.50	50.00	85.00	195.00
10	Icer, w/insert, #2449	20.00	38.00	55.00	85.00
	Mayonnaise, 5⅝" w/7" plate, #2449	20.00	35.00		
18	Mug, 9 oz., ftd., #2449	15.00			
	Mug, 12 oz., ftd., #2449	17.50			
	Mustard w/cover & spoon, #2449	17.50	35.00		
	Pitcher, pint, #2449	22.50	40.00	60.00	
2	Pitcher, 3 pint, #2449	60.00	90.00	145.00	475.00
	Plate, 6", #2449½	3.00	5.00	8.00	
	Plate, 7", ice dish liner	4.00	6.00	10.00	18.00
	Plate, 7", #2449½	4.00	6.00	10.00	
	Plate, 7⅜", crescent salad, #2449	8.00	15.00	30.00	60.00
21	Plate, 8", #2449½	6.00	10.00	15.00	20.00
	Plate, 9", #2449½	12.50	20.00	30.00	
	Plate, 12", sandwich, #2449		12.50	20.00	
	Relish, 6", 2 pt., #2449	6.00	10.00	15.00	22.00
14	Relish, 7¼", 3 pt., #2449	8.00	11.00	17.50	45.00
	Relish, 8", pickle, #2449	8.00	11.00	17.50	

3   3   3

		Crystal	Amber, Green Topaz	Azure	Wisteria
11	Relish, 11", celery, #2449	10.00	15.00	25.00	45.00
8	Salt & pepper, 3⅜", #2449	20.00	40.00	65.00	90.00
	Salt, individual, #2449	4.00	6.00	10.00	
	Saucer, #2449	2.00	3.50	5.00	6.00
23	Sherbet, 3", 7 oz., low, ftd., #2449	6.00	8.00	12.50	16.00
	Stem, 3¼", 5½ oz., high sherbet, #2449	8.00	11.00	17.50	18.00
	Stem, 4⅝", 4 oz., claret, #2449	10.00	15.00		
22	Stem, 5¼", 9 oz., water goblet, #2449	10.00	15.00	20.00	25.00
4	Sugar, ftd., #2449	4.00	6.00	10.00	25.00
	Tray, 6½", condiment, #2449	6.00	12.00	20.00	25.00
12	Tumbler, 2½", 2 oz., #2449½	8.00	10.00	20.00	35.00
	Tumbler, 2½", 2 oz., ftd., #2449	5.00	10.00		
9	Tumbler, 3", 4 oz., cocktail, ftd., #2449	5.00	7.50	12.00	18.00
13	Tumbler, 3¼", 6 oz. old-fashion, #2449½	6.00	10.00	15.00	28.00
	Tumbler, 3⅞", 5 oz., #2449½	5.00	8.00	12.00	22.00
	Tumbler, 4", 5 oz., ftd., #2449	5.00	8.00	12.00	22.00
20	Tumbler, 4⅛", 9 oz., ftd., #2449	6.00	10.00	15.00	25.00
17	Tumbler, 4¾", 9 oz., #2449½	6.00	10.00	15.00	30.00
	Tumbler, 5¼", 12 oz., ftd., iced tea, #2449	10.00	16.00	28.00	
	Tumbler, 5⅞", 13 oz., #2449½	10.00	16.00	28.00	40.00
	Vase, 6", ftd.	22.00	30.00		

* Ebony – $15.00

COLORS: AMBER, BLACK, CRYSTAL, EMERALD GREEN, PEACH BLO, WILLOW BLUE

Imperial Hunt Scene photographs well when the design is gold encrusted as shown on 121. Gold decoration adds 20% to 25% to the price listed. Be cautious of worn or missing gold; it is not as fascinating for collectors.

Internet auctions have influenced prices on this pattern. Today a piece will fetch a tidy sum due to several bidders wanting it, and tomorrow the same item will receive few bids since the high bidder no longer wants another. That makes for interesting buying and selling as well as our pricing for this book.

Collectors tend to hunt for glassware that depicts animals, but specifically horses. On Imperial Hunt Scene, you get the additional benefit of a fox. Cups, saucers, sugars, and shakers have always been scarce, but presently more collectors are searching for them which increases price. Has anyone found a pink creamer to match the sugar and lid we have pictured previously? None of Cambridge's catalogs show either a sugar or creamer with this etching, but we'd be highly surprised if they made a sugar without a creamer. Sets can be gathered in pink (Peach Blo) and perhaps Emerald green.

Stems are plentiful in most sizes with the exception of cordials and clarets. That is, plentiful in comparison to serving pieces rather than plentiful in comparison to other patterns. We did not claim inexpensive! You may find bi-colored Hunt Scene stemware. Pink bowl with a green stem or foot is the typical form — and the preference of most collectors.

Ebony and Emerald green (dark) with gold decorations retail 25% to 50% higher than prices listed should you encounter any.

		Crystal	Colors
	Bowl, 6", cereal	20.00	40.00
	Bowl, 8"	40.00	95.00
	Bowl, 8½", 3 pt.	45.00	100.00
	Candlestick, 2-lite, keyhole	35.00	70.00
13	Candle 3-lite, keyhole, #638	45.00	90.00
	Comport, 5½", #3085		60.00
	Creamer, flat	15.00	60.00
	Creamer, ftd.	20.00	75.00
	Cup, #933/481	40.00	65.00
5	Decanter		295.00
6	Finger bowl, w/plate, #3085		85.00
	Humidor, tobacco		595.00
	Ice bucket, #851 scallop edge	95.00	195.00
	Ice bucket, #2978 plain edge	90.00	190.00
	Ice tub	55.00	150.00
	Mayonnaise, w/liner	40.00	95.00
	Pitcher, w/cover, 63 oz., #3085		495.00

COLOR: CRYSTAL

June Night stemware is available. We see dozens of stems for every bowl or serving piece. June Night was etched on different stemware lines, but the one most often seen is Tiffin's #17392 that is pictured below. You may find stem line #17378 (prism stem with pearl edge top), #17441 (quadrangle flowing to hexagonal cut), and #17471. That last line has a bow tie stem, but we have never spotted June Night on it. We could use one for photography if you should have one. More of this pattern is being exhibited at shows, but again mostly stems. Evidently, Tiffin advertised this rival of Cambridge's Rose Point for consumers to use with their china. We've noticed that comparable pieces in Cherokee Rose pattern have caused confusion with many novices and part-time dealers. There is a flower encircled on June Night and an urn on Cherokee Rose. Shapes are important, but it is the design that makes the pattern. Since both of these patterns are on the same Tiffin mould blank, pay attention to which one it is before buying or selling it. Just last Monday at a flea market, a dealer was negotiating a price for several June Night juices, which she misidentified as Rose Point. Not only is June Night confused with Cherokee Rose, but even Rose Point.

Pitchers and shakers are the thorniest elements of a set to obtain. We have finally located them to picture. The pitcher has the encircled flower below the ice lip which is shown on the right above the photo. The side of the pitcher does not have this emblem.

Tiffin called gold-trimmed June Night stemware Cherry Laurel. Name altering within same patterns was another glass company attention-grabber. Any distinct process done to a pattern often created a separate name. In the case of gold trim, often they would just add "golden" to the pattern name. Remember that gold trim did not and still does not hold up well with frequent use. Never put gold-trimmed items in the dishwasher especially if you use any soap with lemon in it. Lemon will remove gold trim extremely well — if you so wish.

21	Bowl, 5", finger.	25.00		23	Shaker, pr., #2	200.00
	Bowl, 6", fruit or nut	30.00		15	Stem, 1 oz., cordial	35.00
20	Bowl, 7", salad	35.00		9, 10	Stem, 2 oz., sherry, 10 is Cherry Laurel	28.00
	Bowl, 10", deep salad	70.00		17	Stem, 3½ oz., cocktail	14.00
	Bowl, 12", crimped	75.00			Stem, 3½ oz., wine	20.00
	Bowl, 12½" centerpiece, flared	75.00			Stem, 4 oz., claret	28.00
4	Bowl, 13", centerpiece, #5902, cone	75.00			Stem, 4½ oz., parfait	33.00
14	Candlestick, double branch, #5902	45.00		7	Stem, 5½ oz., sherbet/champagne, #17441	14.00
18	Candlestick, 9", 2-lite	50.00		8	Stem, 9 oz., water, #17441	22.00
22	Celery, 10½", oblong	40.00		13	Sugar	20.00
12	Creamer	20.00		26	Table bell, #9742	85.00
11	Mayonnaise, liner and ladle	45.00		16	Tumbler, 4½ oz., oyster cocktail	18.00
1	Pitcher, #5859	650.00		25	Tumbler, 5 oz., ftd., juice	14.00
6	Plate, 6", sherbet	8.00			Tumbler, 8 oz., ftd., water	16.00
	Plate, 8", luncheon	12.50		19	Tumbler, 10½ oz., ftd., ice tea	20.00
2	Plate, 13½", turned-up edge, lily, #5902	45.00			Vase, 6", bud	25.00
	Plate, 14", sandwich	45.00		5	Vase, 8", bud, #14185	35.00
24	Relish, 6½", 3 pt.	35.00			Vase, 10", bud	45.00
3	Relish, 12½", 3 pt., #5902	65.00				

JUNGLE ASSORTMENT, SATIN DECORATED #14 PARROT, TIFFIN GLASS COMPANY,

ET.AL., C. 1922 – 1934

COLORS: GREEN, PINK, AND CRYSTAL SATIN; VARIOUS FLASHED COLORS

Jungle Assortment is a Tiffin pattern that has fascinated collectors over the last few years. There is a likelihood that the flashed items are from another company. Cathy gathered an exotic colorful display of pieces for our Florida home.

Below is an assortment of various poses which are named for the bird's status. We have orchestrated the photos into various groups on the following pages. The bottom of page 131 shows "Bird on a Bar," the top of page 132 is "Bird on a Branch," and the bottom of page 132 illustrates "Bird on a Perch."

The flashed colors did not hold the hand-painted patterns any better than the satinized versions. This is one pattern where you might like to pick up some slightly worn pieces until mint condition ones appear. You will not find these birds regularly.

The night set, basket, lamp, and vase in metal holder appear to be difficult to find. Notice the 1928 Sears catalog ad for the night set which called it a "Bed Room Water Bottle and Tumbler." They called the bird a cockatoo.

We have found three styles of candleholders. You will undoubtedly find other items not listed, so let us know what you see.

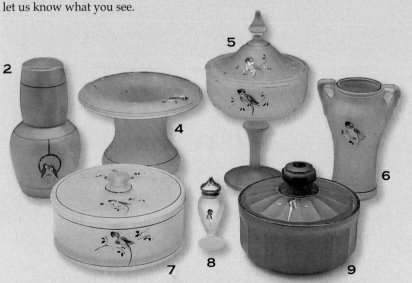

		All Colors
1	Basket, 6", #151	100.00
	Bonbon & cover, 5½" high ftd., #330	60.00
	Bonbon and cover, 5", low ftd., #330	60.00
	Bowl, centerpiece, #320	50.00
12	Candle, hdld., #330	40.00
22	Candle, hdld. tall, octagonal base	65.00
16	Candle, low, #10	30.00
5	Candy and cover, ftd., #15179	75.00
9	Candy box & cover, flat, 5½"	55.00
7	Candy box & cover, flat, 6", #329	65.00
15	Candy jar and cover, ftd., cone, #330	75.00
20	Candy jar and cover, ftd., #179	65.00
27	Candy jar and cover, ftd.	65.00
10	Cologne bottle, #5722	110.00
19	Decanter & stopper	125.00
26	Jug and cover, 2 quart, #127	210.00
24	Lamp	125.00

		All Colors
	Marmalade & cover, 2 hdld., #330	45.00
2	Night cap set, #6712	115.00
14	Puff box and cover, hexagonal, #6772	85.00
21	Puff box	40.00
8	Shaker, ftd., #6205	40.00
	Smoking set, 3 pc., #188	40.00
25	Tumbler, 12 oz., #444	30.00
3	Vase, 5½", ftd., rose bowl	75.00
6	Vase, 6", 2 hdld., #151	45.00
17	Vase, 6⅜", flat	45.00
13	Vase, 7" ftd., flair from base, #330	65.00
11	Vase, 7" ftd., flair rim, #151	65.00
4	Vase, 7" sweet pea, #151	75.00
18	Vase, 8", flat	65.00
	Vase, wall, #320	95.00
23	Vase in metal stand	65.00

COLOR: CRYSTAL

Kalonyal was created in crystal; however, some pieces with ruby stain have emerged which was an old procedure used to get "color" on the glass. Most early Heisey patterns, and this is quite early, are marked with the Heisey insignia, consisting of an H enclosed in a diamond. Because of its pattern number (1776), it became extremely popular with collectors during the bicentennial in 1976, and it has remained in style since that time.

	Bottle, hdld., molasses, 13 oz.	250.00		Cup, punch, 3 oz.	26.00
	Bottle, hdld., oil, 2 oz.	175.00		Cup, punch, 3½ oz.	26.00
	Bottle, hdld., oil, 4 oz.	120.00		Mug, hdld., 8 oz.	175.00
	Bottle, hdld., oil, 6 oz.	120.00		Mustard and cover	235.00
	Bottle, water	300.00		Pickle jar and cover	195.00
	Bowl, 4½", deep	30.00		Pickle tray	65.00
	Bowl, 5", deep	35.00	5	Pitcher, ½ gallon	350.00
8	Bowl, 5", flared	35.00		Plate, 5½"	30.00
	Bowl, 5", hdld.	38.00		Plate, 6"	35.00
	Bowl, 5", crimped	35.00		Plate, 8", fruit	55.00
	Bowl, 6", shallow	35.00		Shaker, salt & pepper, 3 styles, pr.	200.00
	Bowl, 7", deep, straight sided	45.00		Shaker, sugar	145.00
	Bowl, 7", deep, flared	45.00		Spoon tray	60.00
	Bowl, 8", flared	65.00		Spooner, tall	95.00
	Bowl, 9", shallow	65.00		Stem, egg cup, 9½ oz.	55.00
9	Bowl, 10", shallow	70.00	6	Stem, goblet, 9 oz.	150.00
	Bowl, 11", shallow	70.00		Stem, champagne, 6½ oz.	65.00
	Bowl, 12", punch and stand	325.00		Stem, sherbet, 6 oz.	40.00
	Butter and cover, domed	150.00		Stem, sherbet, 5½ oz., straight sided or scalloped	40.00
1	Cake plate, 9", ftd.	275.00		Stem, claret, 5 oz.	100.00
2	Celery, tall	100.00		Stem, sherbet, 4½ oz., scalloped	40.00
	Celery tray, 12"	55.00		Stem, sherbet, 3½ oz., scalloped	40.00
	Comport, deep ftd. jelly, 5"	110.00	4	Stem, burgundy, 3 oz.	60.00
	Comport, shallow ftd. jelly, 5½"	110.00	11	Stem, wine, 2 oz.	110.00
	Comport, deep or shallow, 8", ftd.	225.00	10	Stem, cordial, 1¼ oz.	350.00
	Comport, deep or shallow, 9", ftd.	225.00		Sugar and cover, tall	95.00
3	Comport, deep or shallow, 10", ftd.	300.00		Sugar, hotel (no cover)	70.00
	Creamer, tall	90.00	7	Toothpick	375.00
	Creamer, hotel	70.00		Tumbler, 8 oz.	95.00

COLORS: TOPAZ YELLOW, AZURE BLUE, SOME GREEN

Kashmir was not as widely distributed as other Fostoria patterns, so amassing it will likely take longer than other patterns. Blue Kashmir would be a challenging Fostoria pattern to collect if you like that color. Other Azure Fostoria etched patterns have thousands of collectors searching for them; but a decided lack of attention is given to Kashmir. Of course, finding Azure Kashmir is a dilemma. We decided to sell our accumulation after our last photography session, and the blue sold much faster than we anticipated. The yellow has not sold as well, but there have been a few happy collectors visiting our booth. You could complete a set of yellow Kashmir more economically than any other etched, yellow Fostoria pattern.

We found more Kashmir in the Midwest than anywhere else; you can see from our pictures how green Kashmir has been eluding us, even though we have been searching for it. Supposedly, there are some 6", 7", and 8" plates to be had along with the two styles of cups and saucers, but we have never spotted any plates.

The stemware and tumbler line is #5099, which is the same line on which Trojan is found. This is the so-called cascading "waterfall" stem.

Both styles of after dinner cups are shown in the picture at the bottom of page 135. The square #2419 (Mayfair blank) saucer set is more difficult to find than the round; but we have only encountered it in green.

30

		Yellow Green	Blue
	Ashtray	25.00	30.00
4	Bowl, cream soup	25.00	33.00
	Bowl, finger	15.00	40.00
13	Bowl, 5", fruit	13.00	25.00
	Bowl, 6", cereal	26.00	38.00
	Bowl, 7", soup	35.00	95.00
27	Bowl, 2 hdld., sweetmeat	30.00	
	Bowl, 8½", pickle	20.00	30.00
	Bowl, 9", baker	37.50	85.00
5	Bowl, 10", 2 hdld.	40.00	65.00
7	Bowl, 12", centerpiece	40.00	65.00
	Candlestick, 2"	18.00	28.00
	Candlestick, 3"	22.00	33.00
3	Candlestick, 5", Grecian "Scroll"	25.00	45.00
	Candlestick, 9½"	40.00	75.00
24	Candy, w/cover, #2430	90.00	195.00
	Cheese and cracker set	65.00	85.00
	Comport, 6"	35.00	45.00
14	Creamer, ftd.	16.00	20.00
1	Cup, #2375½	12.00	18.00
2	Cup, #2350½	12.00	18.00
23	Cup, after dinner, flat, #2350	30.00	
25	Cup, after dinner, ftd., #2375	30.00	40.00
	Grapefruit	50.00	
	Grapefruit liner	40.00	
30	Ice bucket, #2375	85.00	125.00
20	Mayo & liner w/spoon	85.00	125.00
	Oil, ftd.	295.00	495.00
18	Pitcher, ftd.	335.00	495.00
12	Plate, cream soup or mayo liner	8.00	10.00
	Plate, 6", bread & butter	5.00	6.00
29	Plate, 7", salad, rnd.	6.00	7.00
	Plate, 7", salad, sq.	6.00	7.00
9	Plate, 8", salad	8.00	10.00

		Yellow Green	Blue
10	Plate, 9", luncheon	9.00	15.00
11	Plate, 10", dinner	40.00	65.00
24	Plate, 10", grill	35.00	50.00
	Plate, cake, 10"	38.00	
	Salt & pepper, pr.	100.00	165.00
21	Sandwich, 11", center hdld., #2375	35.00	40.00
	Sauce boat, w/liner	110.00	155.00
1	Saucer, rnd., #2375	4.00	8.00
2	Saucer, sq., #2419	4.00	8.00
23	Saucer, after dinner, sq.	6.00	
25	Saucer, after dinner, rnd., #2375	6.00	10.00
	Stem, ¾ oz., cordial	75.00	110.00
	Stem, 2½ oz., ftd.	25.00	40.00
	Stem, 2 oz., ftd., whiskey	28.00	45.00
	Stem, 2½ oz., wine	30.00	50.00
	Stem, 3 oz., cocktail	20.00	23.00
15	Stem, 3½ oz., ftd., cocktail	18.00	23.00
	Stem, 4 oz., claret	35.00	60.00
	Stem, 4½ oz., oyster cocktail	14.00	16.00
19	Stem, 5 oz., low sherbet	12.00	18.00
16	Stem, 5½ oz., parfait	30.00	40.00
8	Stem, 6 oz., high sherbet, #5099	16.00	25.00
28	Stem, 9 oz., water, 8½", #5099	22.00	38.00
	Sugar, ftd.	15.00	20.00
	Sugar lid	40.00	75.00
22, 17	Tumbler, 5 oz., 4½", ftd., juice	15.00	22.00
	Tumbler, 9 oz., 5⅜", ftd., water	18.00	28.00
	Tumbler, 10 oz., ftd., water	20.00	33.00
	Tumbler, 11 oz.	20.00	
6	Tumbler, 12 oz., ftd.	22.00	33.00
26	Tumbler, 13 oz., ftd., tea	22.00	
	Tumbler, 16 oz., ftd., tea	33.00	
	Vase, 8"	125.00	185.00

Note: See stemware identification on page 98.

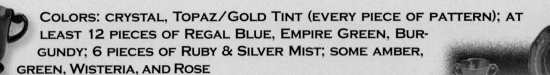

COLORS: CRYSTAL, TOPAZ/GOLD TINT (EVERY PIECE OF PATTERN); AT LEAST 12 PIECES OF REGAL BLUE, EMPIRE GREEN, BURGUNDY; 6 PIECES OF RUBY & SILVER MIST; SOME AMBER, GREEN, WISTERIA, AND ROSE

Lafayette #2440 is the mould line used for most of Fostoria's later etchings, with Navarre and Meadow Rose being the most renown. Colored pieces of Lafayette are admired and gathered for themselves. The preferred color is Wisteria, but yellow can also be accumulated into a large set. We finally found a Regal blue piece (sugar on left). You might intermingle some of the colors with crystal in order to achieve a larger set, but finding crystal without an etching may be a task.

		Crystal Amber	Rose, Green Topaz	Wisteria	Regal Blue	Burgundy	Empire Green
	Almond, individual	12.00	15.00	25.00			
	Bonbon, 5", 2 hdld.	15.00	22.50	40.00	35.00	30.00	33.00
	Bowl, 4½", sweetmeat	18.00	22.50	40.00	35.00	35.00	33.00
	Bowl, cream soup	22.50	35.00	85.00			
	Bowl, 5", fruit		22.50	35.00			
	Bowl, 6", cereal	18.00	22.00	40.00			
	Bowl, 6½", olive	18.00	25.00	50.00			
	Bowl, 6½", 2-pt. relish	22.50	30.00	55.00	55.00	45.00	45.00
	Ruby 50.00; Silver Mist 25.00						
	Bowl, 6½", oval sauce	25.00	35.00	100.00	55.00	50.00	45.00
	Ruby 65.00; Silver Mist 27.50						
	Bowl, 7", "D" cupped	30.00	40.00	100.00			
	Bowl, 7½", 3-pt. relish	25.00	35.00	90.00	55.00	45.00	45.00
	Ruby 55.00; Silver Mist 30.00						
	Bowl, 8", nappy	30.00	40.00	85.00			
	Bowl, 8½", pickle	18.00	30.00	60.00			
	Bowl, 10", oval baker	35.00		75.00	75.00		
	Bowl, 10", "B," flair	35.00	45.00				
	Bowl, 12", salad, flair	38.00	50.00	125.00			
	Cake, 10½", oval, 2 hdld.	40.00	50.00		65.00	65.00	65.00
	Celery, 11½"	30.00	32.00	90.00			
1	Creamer, 4½", ftd.	15.00	22.00	35.00	40.00	40.00	40.00
5	Cup	12.00	15.00	18.00	35.00	35.00	35.00
	Cup, demi	15.00	25.00	60.00			
	Tray, 5", 2-hdld., lemon	17.50	22.50	40.00	35.00	30.00	33.00
	Tray, 8½", oval, 2-hdld.	22.50	30.00	75.00	55.00	45.00	45.00
	Ruby 55.00; Silver Mist 25.00						
	Mayonnaise, 6½", 2 pt.	24.00	30.00	60.00	55.00	55.00	55.00
	Ruby 55.00; Silver Mist 30.00						
	Plate, 6"	8.00	12.00	12.00			
	Plate, 7¼"	8.00	12.00	18.00			
	Plate, 8½"	10.00	15.00	20.00			
3	Plate, 9½"	22.50	27.50	40.00			
	Plate, 10¼"	35.00	45.00	85.00			
4	Plate, 13", torte	40.00	50.00	90.00	115.00	95.00	110.00
	Ruby 110.00; Silver Mist 40.00						
	Platter, 12"	40.00	52.50	110.00			
	Platter, 15"	50.00	65.00				
5	Saucer	3.00	4.00	5.00	8.00	8.00	6.00
	Saucer, demi	6.00	10.00	15.00			
2	Sugar, 3⅜", ftd.	15.00	22.00	35.00	40.00	40.00	40.00
	Vase, 7", rim ft., flair	45.00	60.00				

COLORS: CRYSTAL; RARE IN BLACK AND AMBER

Lariat prices have remained in a slump especially stems, which have apparently saturated the market in recent years. Those highly priced cordials found few buyers at previous levels, but after dropping drastically, they are beginning to be noticed as "bargains." Scarce pieces sell well since there are many collectors looking for seldom-found items. Conversely, the horsehead candy has softened in price since more have been found than there are collectors willing to pay the price. Common Lariat pieces are still available; you can determine scarce pieces by their prices in our listing.

Moonglo is the cutting most often seen on Lariat. Many non-Lariat collectors admire this cut; but surprisingly, few try to round it up. We have tried to beguile you with the number of pieces shown. Enjoy! The ads that we have shown in the past are becoming collectible in their own right. Watch for them in women's magazines of the 1940s and 1950s.

Lariat amber champagnes and black plates have been shown in earlier books but they are rarely found.

1

		Crystal				Crystal
	Ashtray, 4"	15.00	24	Oil bottle, 2 oz., hdld., w/#133 stopper	120.00
	Basket, 7½", bonbon	85.00	18	Oil bottle, 4 oz., hdld., w/#133 stopper	180.00
	Basket, 8½", ftd.	150.00	26	Oil bottle, 6 oz., oval	85.00
	Basket, 10", ftd.	185.00		Plate, 6", finger bowl liner	8.00
	Bowl, 2 hdld., cream soup	50.00	2	Plate, 7", salad	14.00
	Bowl, 7 quart, punch	130.00	4	Plate, 8", salad	22.00
25	Bowl, 4", nut, individual	28.00	3	Plate, 10½", dinner	125.00
	Bowl, 7", 2 pt., mayonnaise	20.00		Plate, 11", cookie	35.00
17	Bowl, 7", nappy	15.00		Plate, 12", demi-torte, rolled edge	40.00
	Bowl, 8", flat, nougat	20.00		Plate, 13", deviled egg, round	225.00
	Bowl, 9½", camellia	22.00		Plate, 14", 2 hdld., sandwich	50.00
	Bowl, 10", hdld., celery	30.00		Plate, 15", deviled egg, oval	290.00
	Bowl, 10½", 2 hdld., salad	32.00		Plate, 21", buffet	70.00
	Bowl, 10½", salad	35.00		Platter, 15", oval	60.00
	Bowl, 11", 2 hdld., oblong, relish	28.00	16	Salt & pepper, pr.	200.00
	Bowl, 12", floral or fruit	36.00	11	Saucer	3.00
	Bowl, 13", celery	40.00	14	Stem, 1 oz., cordial, double loop	175.00
	Bowl, 13", gardenia	30.00	15	Stem, 1 oz., cordial blown, single loop	120.00
	Bowl, 13", oval, floral	30.00		Stem, 2½ oz., wine, blown	20.00
	Candlestick, 1-lite, individual	20.00		Stem, 3½ oz., cocktail, pressed	15.00
8	Candlestick, 2-lite	30.00		Stem, 3½ oz., cocktail, blown	15.00
22	Candlestick, 3-lite	35.00		Stem, 3½ oz., wine, pressed	20.00
	Candy box, w/cover, caramel	75.00		Stem, 4 oz., claret, blown	20.00
	Candy, w/cover, 7"	90.00	13	Stem, 4¼ oz., oyster cocktail or fruit	12.00
	Candy, w/cover, 8", w/horse head finial (rare)	1,400.00		Stem, 4½ oz., oyster cocktail, blown	12.00
	Cheese, 5", ftd., w/cover	45.00		Stem, 5½ oz., sherbet/saucer champagne, blown	10.00
	Cheese dish, w/cover, 8"	50.00		Stem, 6 oz., low sherbet	7.00
	Cigarette box	45.00	10	Stem, 6 oz., sherbet/saucer champagne, pressed	10.00
	Coaster, 4"	8.00		Stem, 9 oz., pressed	16.00
	Cologne	75.00	9	Stem, 10 oz., blown	16.00
19	Compote, 10", w/cover	100.00	5	Sugar	18.00
6	Creamer	18.00		Tray, rnd., center hdld., w/ball finial	165.00
	Creamer & sugar, w/tray, individual	45.00	7	Tray for sugar & creamer, 8", 2 hdld.	24.00
11	Cup	12.00		Tumbler, 5 oz., ftd., juice	20.00
	Cup, punch	8.00		Tumbler, 5 oz., ftd., juice, blown	20.00
23	Ice tub	75.00		Tumbler, 12 oz., ftd., ice tea	25.00
	Jar, w/cover, 12", urn	175.00		Tumbler, 12 oz., ftd., ice tea, blown	25.00
12	Lamp & globe, 7", black-out	120.00	20	Urn jar & cover, 12"	150.00
21	Lamp & globe, 8", candle, hdld.	95.00	1	Vase, 7", ftd., fan	25.00
	Mayonnaise, 5" bowl, 7" plate w/ladle set	60.00		Vase, swung	135.00

COLORS: CRYSTAL, MANDARIN (YELLOW), ROSE (PINK), AND MANDARIN OR ROSE WITH CRYSTAL STEMS

La Fleure is found in Mandarin (yellow) more often than not. It is the obvious color choice for collectors who enjoy this design. We bought a set of yellow glassware in South Florida a couple of years ago. The owners of the set brought us a few sample items to identify along with a listing of their set. The set was identified as yellow Cambridge's Gloria, but we had a gigantic surprise as we were unpacking the boxes of glass. The pitcher, creamer, and sugar were not Gloria, but Tiffin's La Fleure as are pictured here. It gave us a start for a new pattern, but a yellow Gloria pitcher would have been more to our liking.

		All Colors				All Colors
	Bonbon, 2-handled	40.00			Stem, #15022, 3 oz., cocktail	30.00
	Bowl, 12", centerpiece, ftd.	65.00			Stem, #15022, 6 oz., champagne	30.00
	Bowl, finger, 8 oz., ftd.	35.00			Stem, #15022, 6 oz., sherbet	25.00
	Bowl, mayonnaise, ftd.	40.00			Stem, #15022, 9 oz., water goblet	45.00
2	Candle, #5831	35.00			Stem, #15024, 1½ oz., 5", cordial	65.00
	Celery, 10"	60.00			Stem, #15024, 3½ oz., 4¾", cocktail	30.00
	Creamer, #5831, ftd.	45.00			Stem, #15024, 4½ oz., 5⅝", cafe parfait	40.00
4	Creamer, #6, flat	50.00			Stem, #15024, 6 oz., 4½", sherbet	25.00
	Cup	50.00		1	Stem, #15024, 6 oz., 6¼", champagne	30.00
5	Jug	395.00			Stem, #15024, 9 oz., 8¼", water goblet	45.00
	Jug w/cover	495.00			Sugar, #5831, ftd.	45.00
	Plate, 6", mayonnaise	15.00		3	Sugar, #6, flat	50.00
	Plate, 7½"	20.00			Tumbler, 9 oz., ftd.	35.00
	Saucer	15.00			Tumbler, 12 oz., ftd.	40.00

COLOR: CRYSTAL

Duncan's Lily of the Valley is a pattern that even non-collectors treasure. We first noticed its wonderful carved stem when searching for cordials over 25 years ago.

Canterbury #115 and Pall Mall #30 blanks were used for this cutting. The mayonnaise pictured is #30 and the bowl and plate are #115. We have never seen a cup or saucer in this cut.

Stemware has the Lily of the Valley cut into the stem itself, but the bowls on top of the stem are found with or without the cutting. The cutting on the bowl is the icing on the cake for most collectors. Duncan's classification for this stem was D-4 and the cut variety was DC-4. Prices below are for deep cut (DC-4) bowl items; deduct about a third (or more) for plain bowl stems. Once you see this pattern, you will understand why collectors want the cut version.

It does appear from time to time; so keep a sharp eye open.

8	Ashtray, 3"	25.00		5	Plate, 8"	35.00
	Ashtray, 6"	35.00			Plate, 9"	45.00
7	Bowl, 12"	60.00			Relish, 3-part	30.00
3	Candlestick, double, 5"	60.00		12	Stem, cocktail	25.00
15	Candy, w/lid	95.00		10	Stem, cordial	80.00
9	Celery, 10½"	40.00		13	Stem, high sherbet	25.00
	Cheese and cracker	75.00		2	Stem, water goblet	40.00
6	Creamer	30.00		11	Stem, wine	45.00
14	Mayonnaise	30.00		4	Sugar	30.00
14	Mayonnaise ladle	8.00		1	Tumbler, ftd. water	25.00
14	Mayonnaise liner	15.00				

COLORS: AMBER, BLACK, CRYSTAL, GREEN, PINK

We have branded this New Martinsville "coat of arms style" etching as "Lions." We considered calling it "Lions Rampant"; but not being a heraldry expert, we were not quite sure the lions were in the correct posture to be so classified. We will be glad to switch to the original name if one can be ascertained.

We can inform you, hunting "Lions" will be an ordeal. Nearly all "Lions" etch is found on New Martinsville's Line #34 as pictured in black below. The crystal candle and sugar shown are on Line #37 known as "Moondrops" to collectors. We have not seen this etch on colored pieces of Line #37.

You can round up a luncheon set in color, but adding serving pieces may be another matter. We have found two styles of sugar bowls, but no creamer yet. We still need a lid to the pink candy dish we pictured previously.

We are confident that additional pieces not in the list can be found; so let us know what else you have seen.

		Amber Crystal	Pink Green	Black
4	Bowl, creme soup, ftd., 2 hdld., #34	20.00		
3	Candleholder, #37	25.00		
	Candlestick, #34		35.00	
	Candy w/lid		75.00	110.00
	Center handle server		45.00	
	Comport, cheese		25.00	35.00
	Creamer, #34		25.00	35.00
	Creamer, #37	15.00		
6	Cup, #34		25.00	35.00
2	Plate, 8"		20.00	30.00
	Plate, 12", cracker		30.00	40.00
6	Saucer, #34		7.50	10.00
1	Sugar, #34		25.00	35.00
5	Sugar, #37	15.00		

COLORS: CRYSTAL REGULAR OPTIC W/BLACK AND CRYSTAL WIDE OPTIC W/GREEN TRIM

We have found two partial sets of Luciana. A black group with four different pieces was bought in an estate sale in Cincinnati and a few months later we ran into a grouping of seven different pieces of green in Florida. Quite a distance apart, but made for a wonderful variety to picture for this book.

The green plates were well worn, so the original owners obviously enjoyed using them. The plates in the black set are frosted and cut into the plate. Surprisingly, they are not as pleasing to the eye as are the pieces with black etched crystal. The pattern disappears into the black rather than being revealed as on the crystal and green.

The Internet has placed Luciana into the awareness of collectors. The three dancing nymphs caught the eyes of several admirers on an Internet auction and the pursuit of this marvelously decorated Tiffin pattern began.

Prices have stopped soaring for now, but with many aware of this pattern, how long that lull will last is uncertain.

	Bonbon, 5" high	75.00
	Candy w/cover, #9557	145.00
	Creamer, #6	65.00
	Decanter w/stopper, #185	295.00
	Finger bowl, ftd., #002	35.00
	Finger bowl, ftd., #185	35.00
	Pitcher w/cover, 2 qt., ftd., #194	395.00
3	Plate, 6", #8833	12.00
	Plate, 7¼", #8814	15.00
4	Plate, 8", #8833	20.00
1	Plate, 10", #8833	80.00
	Stem, claret, #016	65.00
	Stem, cocktail, 3 oz., #016	35.00
	Stem, oyster cocktail, #043	22.00
	Stem, parfait, #016	55.00
	Stem, parfait, #043	40.00
	Stem, saucer champagne, #016	28.00
7	Stem, sundae, #016	20.00
8	Stem, sundae, #043	22.00

10	Stem, water, #043	50.00
	Stem, water, 11 oz., #016	60.00
	Stem, wine, #043	35.00
9	Stem, wine, 2½ oz., #016	60.00
	Sugar, #6	65.00
6	Tumbler, 5 oz., juice ftd., #194	35.00
5	Tumbler, 9 oz., water ftd., #194	30.00
2	Tumbler, 12 oz., ice tea, ftd., #194	40.00
	Vase, 10½", bud, #004	125.00

COLORS: CRYSTAL, CRYSTAL WITH RUBY OR GOLD, COBALT

Mardi Gras was produced predominantly in crystal, but it may be found with gold trim or ruby flashing and there have been a few rare pieces surface in cobalt. The piece in cobalt that we have seen is a small tray, perhaps a pickle tray, which lies on a metal (chrome) base. There seem to be a profusion of Mardi Gras pieces obtainable and one could put together a small collection rather swiftly if so inclined.

	Bottle, bitters	75.00
	Bottle, molasses, hdld.	85.00
	Bottle, oil, hdld.	40.00
8	Bottle, water	55.00
	Bowl, berry, 4"	20.00
	Bowl, shallow, 6"	24.00
6	Bowl, round, 8"	55.00
	Bowl, fruit, 10"	75.00
	Bowl, punch, 13½", and stand	165.00
	Box, powder and cover	165.00
	Butter and cover, domed	75.00
14	Butter and cover, individual	165.00
	Cake plate, ftd.	110.00
	Celery, tall	65.00
	Cracker jar and cover, tall	145.00
	Creamer, regular	35.00
12	Creamer, individual/child's	80.00
2	Cup, punch	10.00
	Egg cup, ftd.	45.00
	Jug, honey, individual	65.00
	Mustard and cover	75.00
3	Oil bottle	65.00
1	Pitcher, straight sided	125.00
	Pitcher, bulbous	175.00
10	Pitcher, syrup, individual	75.00
7	Plate, 3", butter	26.00

	Plate, 5"	8.00
	Plate, 6"	9.00
	Plate, 7"	9.00
	Plate, 8"	20.00
	Salt & pepper	55.00
11	Salt, open, individual	12.00
	Spooner, tall	65.00
15	Spooner, child's	60.00
	Stem, goblet	45.00
	Stem, claret	50.00
	Stem, champagne/sherbet, 2 styles	22.00
	Stem, cocktail	24.00
9	Stem, wine	28.00
	Stem, sherry, straight sided and flared	35.00
	Stem, cordial	60.00
4	Sugar and cover, regular	50.00
13	Sugar and cover, individual	120.00
	Toothpick	45.00
	Tumbler, water	24.00
	Tumbler, juice	20.00
	Tumbler, bar (2 oz.)	20.00
16	Vase, ball, individual, 1½"	165.00
	Vase, ball, 4"	40.00
	Vase, tall, footed, 10"	55.00
5	Vase, wall, 9½"	100.00

Stemline #3750 (hexagon stem), c. 1940s

Colors: amethyst w/gold, crystal, Emerald green

Cambridge's early Marjorie pattern was altered to Fuchsia in the 1930s; do not confuse it with the Tiffin or Fostoria Fuchsia. The #7606 stems were promoted in the 1927 Sears catalog.

		Crystal				Crystal
3	Bottle, oil & vinegar, 6 oz.	350.00		Stem, 2 oz., creme de menthe, #7606		100.00
6	Candle, 3 lite, #1307	125.00		Stem, 3 oz., cocktail, #7606		25.00
	Comport, #4011	90.00		Stem, 3 oz., wine, #3750		35.00
	Comport, 5", #4004	70.00		Stem, 3½ oz., cocktail, #3750		25.00
	Comport, 5", jelly (sherbet), #2090	70.00		Stem, 4½ oz., claret, #3750		45.00
	Cream, flat, curved in side, #1917/10	100.00		Stem, 4½ oz., claret, #7606		45.00
10	Cream, flat, straight side, #1917/18	125.00		Stem, 5½ oz., cafe parfait, #7606		56.00
	Cup	50.00		Stem, 6 oz., low sherbet, #3750		12.00
	Decanter, 28 oz., cut stop, #17	500.00		Stem, 6 oz., low fruit/sherbet, #7606		12.00
	Decanter, 28 oz. #7606	400.00		Stem, 6 oz., high sherbet, #3750		15.00
	Finger bowl, #7606	40.00		Stem, 6 oz., high sherbet, #7606		15.00
	Grapefruit w/liner inside, #7606	95.00		Stem, 10 oz., water, #3750		22.00
	Jug, 30 oz., #104	265.00		Stem, 10 oz., water, #7606		22.00
	Jug w/cover, 30 oz., #106	325.00	5	Sugar, flat, curved in side, #1917/10		100.00
	Jug, 3 pint, #93	255.00	11	Sugar, flat, straight side, #1917/18		125.00
	Jug, 3½ pint, #108 short, flair bottom	295.00		Syrup & cover, 8 oz., #106		300.00
	Jug, 3½ pint, rim bottom, bulbous, #111	295.00		Tumbler, #8851		20.00
	Jug, 54 oz., flat bottom, #51	325.00	9	Tumbler, 1½ oz. whiskey, #7606		28.00
	Jug w/cover, 66 oz., #106	350.00		Tumbler, 4 oz., 2⁷/₁₆"		20.00
1	Jug, 4 pint, tall, flat bottom, #110	335.00		Tumbler, 5 oz., #8858		15.00
	Jug, guest room 38 oz. w/tumbler fitting inside, #103	450.00		Tumbler, 5 oz., #7606		15.00
	Marmalade & cover, #145	95.00		Tumbler, 5 oz. ftd., #3750		18.00
	Nappie, 4", #4111	32.00		Tumbler, 6 oz., 3⁷/₁₆"		20.00
	Nappie, 4" ftd., #5000	38.00	7	Tumbler, 8 oz., #7606		20.00
	Nappie, 8", #4111	90.00		Tumbler, 9 oz., #8858		20.00
	Nappie, 8" ftd., #5000	95.00		Tumbler, 10 oz., ftd. & hdld., #7606		45.00
	Night bottle, 20 oz. w/tumbler, #4002	450.00		Tumbler, 10 oz., hdld. & ftd., #8023		45.00
2	Oil w/hex cone cut stop, #32	400.00	8	Tumbler, 10 oz., table, #7606		25.00
4	Plate, 7¾", finger bowl liner or salad, #7606	15.00		Tumbler, 10 oz., ftd., #3750		25.00
	Plate, 7¼", finger bowl liner, #7606	15.00		Tumbler, 12 oz., #8858		22.00
	Saucer	30.00		Tumbler, 12 oz., ftd., #3750		25.00
	Stem, ⅞ oz., cordial, #7606	100.00		Tumbler, 12 oz., tea, #7606		22.00
	Stem, 1 oz., cordial, #3750	100.00		Tumbler, 12 oz., hdld., #8858		33.00
	Stem, 2½ oz., wine, #7606	55.00				

COLORS: CRYSTAL AND SOME BLUE

New Martinsville's Meadow Wreath, with few exceptions, is found on Radiance Line #42. Meadow Wreath etching sometimes exasperates Radiance collectors searching for light blue. We see more blue Meadow Wreath etched candles than we do ones without an etching. If a collector were willing to mix the etched Meadow Wreath with non-etched wares, a wider range of blue pieces would be possible.

There is an abundance of bowls and serving pieces available in Meadow Wreath, but essential luncheon items are lacking except for the omnipresent sugars and creamers. We recommend using these serving items to balance some of those other patterns where serving items are almost imaginary. Merging color is already a trend, so blending patterns may not seem such a stretch in this day of ever more expensive and hard to find vintage glassware.

1

		Crystal
4	Bowl, 7", 2 hdld., bonbon	18.00
	Bowl, 7", 2 pt. relish, #4223/26	18.00
5	Bowl, 8", 3 pt. relish, #4228/26	30.00
	Bowl, 10", comport, #4218/26	35.00
	Bowl, 10", crimped, #4220/26	40.00
	Bowl, 10", oval celery, #42/26	30.00
	Bowl, 10", flat, flared	30.00
	Bowl, 11", crimped, ftd. #4266/26	45.00
	Bowl, 11", ftd., flared, #4265/26	45.00
3	Bowl, 12", crimped, flat, #4212	50.00
	Bowl, 12", flat, flared, deep, #42/26	50.00
	Bowl, 12", flat, flared, #4213/26	50.00
	Bowl, 13", crimped, flat	55.00
	Bowl, 5 qt., punch, #4221/26	140.00

		Crystal
	Candle, 2 lite, rnd. ft.	35.00
	Candy box (3 pt.) & cover, #42/26	50.00
	Cheese & cracker, 11", #42/26	40.00
	Creamer, ftd., tab hdld., #42/26	12.00
	Cup, 4 oz., punch, tab hdld.	9.00
	Ladle, punch, #4226	55.00
2	Mayonnaise set, liner & ladle, #42/26	40.00
1	Plate, 11"	30.00
	Plate, 14", #42/26	40.00
	Salver, 12", ftd., #42/26	40.00
	Sugar, ftd., tab hdld., #42/26	12.00
	Tray, oval for sugar & creamer, #42/26	15.00
	Vase, 10", crimped, #4232/26	55.00
	Vase, 10", flared, #42/26	50.00

COLOR: CRYSTAL

Minuet production began in 1939. It is one Heisey pattern where established prices reign. A few price adjustments have been observed for basic pieces like dinner plates, creamers, and sugars. By the way, dinner plates are listed as service plates in Heisey catalogs. That was generally the case in Cambridge and Fostoria catalogs, also — and explains their dearth today. Actual dinner plates were usually cataloged in the 9 – 9½" range, but collectors have always acquired the larger plates to use as dinners.

Minuet stemware is abundant, but most tumblers are obscure. As with most Elegant stemware lines, Minuet was purchased to go with china settings. Serving pieces were also ignored since china was mostly used for serving guests. Only the three-part relish and the three-footed bowls seem to be found without difficulty.

	Bell, dinner, #3408	75.00
11	Bowl, finger, #3309	50.00
	Bowl, 6", ftd., dolphin, mint	45.00
	Bowl, 6", ftd., 2 hdld., jelly	30.00
	Bowl, 6½", salad dressings	35.00
10	Bowl, 7", salad dressings, 2 part	40.00
	Bowl, 7", triplex, relish	60.00
	Bowl, 7½", sauce, ftd.	70.00
	Bowl, 9½", 3 pt., "5 o'clock," relish	50.00
	Bowl, 10", salad, #1511 Toujours	65.00
	Bowl, 11", 3 pt., "5 o'clock," relish	60.00
	Bowl, 11", ftd., dolphin, floral	120.00
	Bowl, 12", oval, floral, #1511 Toujours	65.00
	Bowl, 12", oval, #1514	65.00
	Bowl, 13", floral, #1511 Toujours	60.00
	Bowl, 13", pickle & olive	45.00
5	Bowl, 13½", shallow salad	75.00
	Candelabrum, 1-lite, w/prisms	110.00
	Candelabrum, 2-lite, bobeche & prisms	175.00
	Candlestick, 1-lite, #112	35.00
	Candlestick, 2-lite, #1511 Toujours	130.00
	Candlestick, 3-lite, #142 Cascade	90.00
	Candlestick, 5", 2-lite, #134 Trident	60.00
	Centerpiece vase & prisms, #1511 Toujours	200.00
	Cocktail icer, w/liner, #3304 Universal	125.00
	Comport, 5½", #5010	40.00
	Comport, 7½", #1511 Toujours	60.00
12	Creamer, #1511 Toujours	60.00
	Creamer, dolphin ft. #1509	35.00
	Creamer, indiv., #1509 Queen Ann	37.50
	Creamer, indiv., #1511 Toujours	70.00
	Cup	25.00
	Ice bucket, dolphin ft.	175.00
	Marmalade, w/cover, #1511 Toujours (apple shape)	150.00
	Mayonnaise, 5½", dolphin ft.	50.00
	Mayonnaise, ftd., #1511 Toujours	60.00
	Pitcher, 73 oz., #4164	300.00
	Plate, 7", mayonnaise liner	10.00

	Plate, 7", salad	16.00
	Plate, 7", salad, #1511 Toujours	12.00
	Plate, 8", luncheon	25.00
6	Plate, 8", luncheon, #1511 Toujours	20.00
	Plate, 10½", service	120.00
	Plate, 12", rnd., 2 hdld., sandwich	150.00
	Plate, 13", floral, salver, #1511 Toujours	60.00
	Plate, 14", torte, #1511 Toujours	60.00
	Plate, 15", sandwich, #1511 Toujours	55.00
	Plate, 16", snack rack, w/#1477 center	80.00
	Salt & pepper, pr. (#10)	75.00
	Saucer	8.00
2	Stem, #5010, Symphone, 1 oz., cordial	135.00
	Stem, #5010, 2½ oz., wine	50.00
4	Stem, #5010, 3½ oz., cocktail	35.00
	Stem, #5010, 4 oz., claret	40.00
8	Stem, #5010, 4½ oz., oyster cocktail	25.00
	Stem, #5010, 6 oz., saucer champagne	25.00
	Stem, #5010, 6 oz., sherbet	25.00

	Stem, #5010, 9 oz., water	35.00
	Sugar, individual, #1511 Toujours	70.00
	Sugar, individual, #1509 Queen Ann	37.50
7	Sugar, dolphin ftd., #1509 Queen Ann	35.00
1	Sugar, #1511 Toujours	60.00
	Tray, 12", celery, #1511 Toujours	50.00
	Tray, 15", social hour	65.00
	Tray for individual sugar & creamer	30.00
3	Tumbler, #5010, 5 oz., fruit juice	34.00
9	Tumbler, #5010, 9 oz., low ftd., water	35.00
	Tumbler, #5010, 12 oz., tea	60.00
	Tumbler, #2351, 12 oz., tea	60.00
	Vase, 5", #5013	50.00
	Vase, 5½", ftd., #1511 Toujours	95.00
	Vase, 6", urn, #5012	75.00
	Vase, 7½", urn, #5012	90.00
	Vase, 8", #4196	95.00
	Vase, 9", urn, #5012	110.00
	Vase, 10", #4192	110.00
	Vase, 10", #4192, Saturn optic	115.00

COLORS: AMBER, AMETHYST, BLACK, BLUE, CRYSTAL, GREEN, PINK, LILAC, CRYSTAL STEMS W/COLORED BOWLS

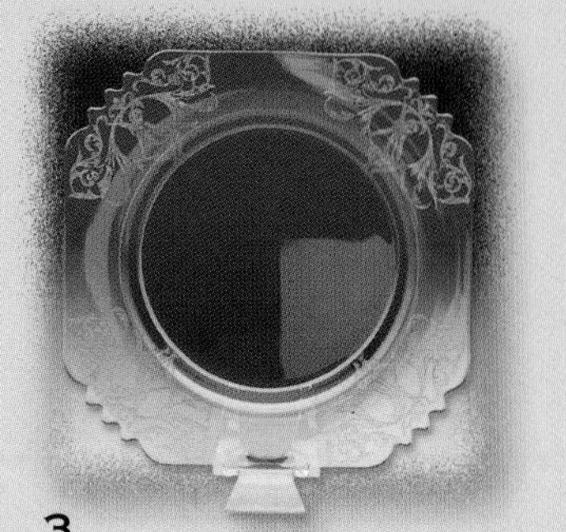

Joseph Balda designed Morgan Etch #412 for Central Glass Works in 1920, although he was widely acknowledged for his designs for Heisey. A family named Morgan allegedly adopted this pattern (Morgan) for use in the West Virginia governor's mansion. Thus, the very masculine pattern name stuck to this seated fairy design.

We found a Morgan pitcher to show you, although it was not an easy task. We have been buying Morgan for about 20 years and this is the first pitcher we had a chance to own. Cathy found the little fairy fascinating about 25 years ago, and we began gathering every piece we could find. We bought some of our most interesting finds at the National Heisey conventions. At that time, Little did we know that Balda had designed the pattern.

3

After introducing it in our book, many new collectors were captivated by this meagerly dispersed pattern. With all the rivalry, it has been more difficult to find auxiliary pieces to include in this book. Notice the three styles of center handled servers and straight and ruffled 10" vases on page 149. The 10" slender bud vases are being found with straight or ruffled tops.

A few pieces of amber are showing up, but there are even fewer collectors buying it. Pieces of black being found include a candy, 6" bonbon, and a bud vase with a gold encrusted fairy. Does anyone have a gold decorated piece other than a bud vase?

The Morgan pattern is found only on the lid of the covered items; so, do not fret too much about condition of the bottom. Other bottoms should turn up. Cups and saucers in color are the items missing from most collections of this Central Glass Works pattern. Crystal ones can be found.

Morgan stemware has become more difficult to find, with blue and lilac stems commanding some royal prices. Internet auctions increased the demand for Morgan tremendously, but prices once commanded have slowed down. There are five styles and shapes of stemware. The beaded stems seem to come in solid colors of crystal, pink, or green. The "wafer" stem is found all pink, green stems with crystal tops, and crystal stems with blue tops. All lilac stems are solid lilac, but the bowls are shaped differently than other colors. This lilac stemware line is the same mould line as "Balda" shown on page 21.

1

		*All Colors
	Bonbon, 6", two hdld.	60.00
	Bonbon, 9", two hdld.	95.00
6	Bowl, 4¼", ftd., fruit	50.00
5	Bowl, 5", finger	55.00
7	Bowl, 10", console	90.00
	Bowl, 13", console	125.00
	Candlestick, 3"	65.00
	Candy, blown, pattern on top	595.00
	Candy w/lid, diamond shaped, 4 ftd.	595.00
	Cheese & cracker	135.00
	Comport, 6½" tall, 5" wide	75.00
	Comport, 6½" tall, 6" wide	85.00
	Creamer, ftd.	65.00
	Cup	150.00
9	Decanter, w/stopper	495.00
	Ice bucket, 4¾" x7½", 2 hdld.	595.00
	Mayonnaise	65.00
	Mayonnaise liner	15.00
	Oil bottle	295.00
20	Pitcher, 75 oz., flat w/optic, #411	995.00
	Plate, 6½", fruit bowl liner	12.00
3	Plate, 6½", squared	30.00
	Plate, 7¼", salad	22.00
	Plate, 8½", luncheon	30.00
	Plate, 9¼", dinner	100.00
	Salt & pepper, pr.	175.00
	Saucer	20.00

		*All Colors
14	Server, 9½", octagonal, center hdld.	100.00
19	Server, 10⅜", round, center hdld.	100.00
17	Server, 11", octagonal, flat, center hdld.	100.00
	Stem, 3¼", sherbet	30.00
	Stem, 4⅜", sherbet, beaded stem	30.00
	Stem, 5⅛", cocktail, beaded stem	35.00
16	Stem, 5⅜", high, sherbet, beaded stem	35.00
4	Stem, 5⅞", high sherbet	45.00
2	Stem, 5⅞", wine	50.00
	Stem, 6", wine, wafer & straight stem	50.00
1	Stem, 7¼", 10 oz., water	65.00
15	Stem, 8¼", water	65.00
	Sugar, ftd.	65.00
	Tumbler, oyster cocktail	35.00
10	Tumbler, 2⅛", whiskey	85.00
	Tumbler, 10 oz., flat water	35.00
	Tumbler, 4⅜", ftd., juice	35.00
12	Tumbler, 5⅜", ftd., 10 oz., water	35.00
18	Tumbler, 5¾", ftd., water	35.00
11	Tumbler, 5⅞", ftd., 12 oz., tea	55.00
	Vase, fan shaped	395.00
	Vase, 8", drape optic	295.00
	Vase, 9⅞", straight w/flared top	395.00
	Vase, 10", bud, straight or ruffled top**	195.00
8	Vase, 10", flared top	295.00
13	Vase, 10", ruffled top	495.00

*Crystal 10% to 20% lower. Blue, lilac 25% to 30% higher.
**Gold decorated $300.00.

COLORS: AMBER, CRYSTAL, CARMEN, ROYAL BLUE, HEATHERBLOOM, EMERALD GREEN (LIGHT AND DARK); RARE IN VIOLET

Sets of Mt. Vernon can only be accumulated in amber or crystal. You may be able to purchase small luncheon sets in red, cobalt blue, or Heatherbloom; but only a few extra pieces were made in those colors. However, prices for any of those colors can more than double the prices listed for amber and crystal. Many collectors are mixing their crystal Mt. Vernon with a splash of color. Indiana's Diamond Point is often confused with Mt. Vernon. See item #12 on page 151 for an example of Diamond Point for comparison.

		Amber Crystal
	Ashtray, 3½", #63	8.00
	Ashtray, 4", #68	12.00
	Ashtray, 6" x 4½", oval, #71	12.00
	Bonbon, 7", ftd., #10	12.50
	Bottle, bitters, 2½ oz., #62	65.00
	Bottle, 7 oz., sq., toilet, #18	75.00
	Bowl, finger, #23	10.00
	Bowl, 4½", ivy ball or rose, ftd., #12	27.50
	Bowl, 5¼", fruit, #6	10.00
	Bowl, 6", cereal, #32	12.50
	Bowl, 6", preserve, #76	12.00
	Bowl, 6½", rose, #106	18.00
	Bowl, 8", pickle, #65	17.50
	Bowl, 8½", 4 pt., 2 hdld., sweetmeat, #105	32.00
	Bowl, 10", 2 hdld., #39	20.00
	Bowl, 10½", deep, #43	30.00
	Bowl, 10½", salad, #120	25.00
	Bowl, 11", oval, 4 ftd., #136	27.50
	Bowl, 11", oval, #135	25.00
2	Bowl, 11½", belled, #128	30.00
	Bowl, 11½", shallow, #126	30.00
	Bowl, 11½", shallow cupped, #61	30.00
	Bowl, 12", flanged, rolled edge, #129	32.50
	Bowl, 12", oblong, crimped, #118	32.50
	Bowl, 12", rolled edge, crimped, #117	32.50
	Bowl, 12½", flanged, rolled edge, #45	35.00
	Bowl, 12½", flared, #121	35.00

		Amber Crystal
	Bowl, 12½", flared, #44	35.00
	Bowl, 13", shallow, crimped, #116	35.00
	Box, 3", w/cover, round, #16	30.00
	Box, 4", w/cover, sq., #17	32.50
9	Box, 4½", w/cover, ftd., round, #15	35.00
5	Butter tub, w/cover, #73	60.00
	Cake stand, 10½", ftd., #150	35.00
	Candelabrum, 13½", #38	150.00
	Candlestick, 4", #130	10.00
	Candlestick, 5", 2-lite, #110	25.00
	Candlestick, 8", #35	27.50
	Candy, w/cover, 1 lb., ftd., #9	90.00
	Celery, 10½", #79	15.00
	Celery, 11", #98	17.50
	Celery, 12", #79	20.00
	Cigarette box, 6", w/cover, oval, #69	32.00
	Cigarette holder, #66	15.00
	Coaster, 3", plain, #60	5.00
	Coaster, 3", ribbed, #70	5.00
	Cocktail icer, 2 pc., #85	30.00
	Cologne, 2½ oz., w/stopper, #1340	40.00
	Comport, 4½", #33	12.00
	Comport, 5½", 2 hdld., #77	15.00
	Comport, 6", #34	15.00
	Comport, 6½", #97	17.50
	Comport, 6½", belled, #96	22.50
	Comport, 7½", #11	25.00

		Amber Crystal
	Comport, 8", #81	25.00
	Comport, 9", oval, 2 hdld., #100	35.00
	Comport, 9½", #99	30.00
	Creamer, ftd., #8	10.00
	Creamer, individual, #4	10.00
	Creamer, #86	10.00
1	Cup, #7	5.00
	Decanter, 11 oz., #47	60.00
	Decanter, 40 oz., w/stopper, #52	85.00
4	Honey jar, w/cover (marmalade), #74	35.00
	Ice bucket, w/tongs, #92	40.00
	Lamp, 9" hurricane, #1607	95.00
	Mayonnaise, divided, 2 spoons, #107	25.00
6	Mug, 14 oz., stein, #84	30.00
	Mustard, w/cover, 2½ oz., #28	25.00
	Pickle, 6", 1 hdld., #78	12.00
	Pitcher, 50 oz., #90	90.00
	Pitcher, 66 oz., #13	95.00
	Pitcher, 80 oz., ball, #95	110.00
	Pitcher, 86 oz., #91	130.00
	Plate, finger bowl liner, #23	4.00
	Plate, 6", bread & butter, #4	3.00
	Plate, 6⅜", bread & butter, #19	4.00
	Plate, 8½", salad, #5	7.00
	Plate, 10½", dinner, #40	30.00
7	Plate, 11½", hdld., #37	20.00
	Relish, 6", 2 pt., 2 hdld., #106	12.00
	Relish, 8", 2 pt., hdld., #101	17.50
	Relish, 8", 3 pt., 3 hdld., #103	20.00
	Relish, 11", 3 part, #200	25.00
	Relish, 12", 2 part, #80	30.00
11	Relish, 12", 5 part, #104	30.00
	Salt, indiv., #24	7.00
	Salt, oval, 2 hdld., #102	10.00
	Salt & pepper, pr., #28	22.50
	Salt & pepper, pr., short, #88	20.00
	Salt & pepper, tall, #89	25.00

		Amber Crystal
17	Salt dip, #24	9.00
	Sauce boat & ladle, tab hdld., #30-445	65.00
1	Saucer, #7	3.00
14	Stem, 3 oz., wine, #27	15.00
	Stem, 3½ oz., cocktail, #26	9.00
	Stem, 4 oz., oyster cocktail, #41	9.00
16	Stem, 4½ oz., claret, #25	13.50
	Stem, 4½ oz., low sherbet, #42	7.50
13	Stem, 6½ oz., tall sherbet, #2	10.00
15	Stem, 10 oz., water, #1	16.00
	Sugar, ftd., #8	10.00
	Sugar, individual, #4	12.00
	Sugar, #86	10.00
18	Tray, 8½", 4 pt., 2 hdld., sweetmeat	8.00
	Tray, for indiv., sugar & creamer, #4	10.00
	Tumbler, 1 oz., ftd., cordial, #87	20.00
8	Tumbler, 2 oz., whiskey, #55	9.00
3	Tumbler, 3 oz., ftd., juice, #22	8.00
	Tumbler, 5 oz., #56	10.00
	Tumbler, 5 oz., ftd., #21	10.00
	Tumbler, 7 oz., old-fashion, #57	14.00
10	Tumbler, 10 oz., ftd., water, #3	15.00
	Tumbler, 10 oz., table, #51	12.00
	Tumbler, 10 oz., tall, #58	12.00
	Tumbler, 12 oz., barrel shape, #13	15.00
	Tumbler, 12 oz., ftd., tea, #20	17.00
	Tumbler, 14 oz., barrel shape, #14	20.00
	Tumbler, 14 oz., tall, #59	22.00
	Urn, w/cover (same as candy), #9	90.00
	Vase, 5", #42	15.00
	Vase, 6", crimped, #119	20.00
	Vase, 6", ftd., #50	25.00
	Vase, 6½", squat, #107	27.50
	Vase, 7", #58	30.00
	Vase, 7", ftd., #54	35.00
	Vase, 10", ftd., #46	65.00

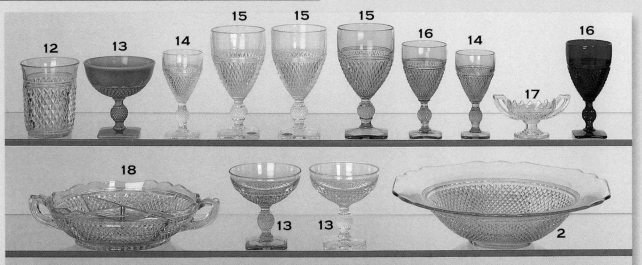

COLOR: CRYSTAL

Narcissus was a cutting applied to glassware by the A.H. Heisey Company, Newark, Ohio, from the early 1940s until its closing in 1957. Narcissus, cutting #965, was utilized on a number of Heisey blanks but more often on the Jamestown stemware line (#3408) and the Waverly general line blanks (#1519) than any others. This cutting was very popular because of its beauty, ease of identity, and the vast production, which offers a complete set of glassware to collect.

	Bell (made from goblet)	55.00		Relish, round, 3-part, 8", #1519	35.00
	Bottle, oil, #1519	175.00		Plate, 7", #1519	12.00
	Bowl, floral, ftd., 11" (#1519	50.00	5	Plate luncheon, 8", #1519	16.00
	Bowl, floral, 13", #1519	45.00		Plate, party, 14", #1519	45.00
	Bowl, gardenia, 13, #1519	40.00	1	Salt & pepper, #1519	75.00
2	Candlestick, 2-lite, #134	35.00	12	Saucer, #1519	10.00
	Candlestick, 3-lite, #1519	65.00		Stem, goblet, 9 oz., #3408	28.00
	Candy and cover, ftd., 5", #1519	140.00	9	Stem, sherbet/saucer-champaign, 6 oz., #3408	16.00
	Celery tray, 12", #1519	35.00		Stem, claret, 4½ oz., #3408	32.00
8	Comport, low ftd., 6", #1519	35.00	4	Stem, cocktail, 3 oz., #3408	18.00
	Comport, ftd. honey, 7", #1519	40.00	7	Stem, wine, 2 oz., #3408	26.00
	Comport, ftd., nut, 7", #1519	70.00	3	Stem, cordial, 1 oz., #3408	85.00
	Creamer, ftd., #1519	30.00		Sugar, #1519	30.00
11	Cup, #1519	30.00	6	Tumbler, ice tea, ftd., 12 oz., #3408	26.00
	Mayonnaise, ftd. and underplate, #1519	55.00		Tumbler, juice, ftd., 5 oz., #3408	24.00
10	Relish, oval, 3-part, 11", #1519	40.00		Vase, round, ftd., 7", #1519	85.00

COLORS: CRYSTAL, BLUE, BLUE AND PINK OPALESCENT

We have received a few letters in the last two years about the stand for the Nautical shakers as pictured below. One collector who has been buying Nautical for 30 years, said he had never known there was a shaker holder; while another said she started collecting the pattern after finding the shakers on a stand — which she thought was "cute." Usually the stand was the one used in Caribbean. This stand has an anchor in the center. (See #5 below.)

Nautical is easily identified; but assorted pieces slip through the cracks. It is difficult to miss items with anchors and rope; however, some pieces do not have the anchor, which means they can elude you unless you are focused.

Blue, and particularly the opalescent, is the most sought color; but collectors are inclined to mix blue with crystal in order to have more pieces. Prices for blue are steady, but opalescent prices have dipped a bit due to the higher limit they attained. Notice the difference in the decanter and covered jar that are pictured side by side in the bottom row on page 154. The jar is listed as a candy jar and the decanter is the taller opalescent covered piece in the row. The decanter is taller and thinner — the lids are not interchangeable as I was once told.

That 7" comport with an anchor for the stem can be found with two different tops. The opalescent one pictured has a pointed edge around the top while the other style has a plain, rounded one.

		*Blue	Crystal	Opalescent
6	Ashtray, 3"	30.00	8.00	
	Ashtray, 6"	40.00	12.50	
19	Bowl, oval, 10"	225.00	60.00	
	Candy jar, w/lid	550.00	295.00	695.00
	Cigarette holder	55.00	15.00	
12	Cigarette jar	75.00	25.00	
17	Cocktail shaker (fish design)	195.00	65.00	
1	Comport, 7"	295.00	110.00	595.00
15	Creamer	45.00	15.00	
18	Decanter	550.00	225.00	695.00
2	Ice bucket	195.00	95.00	300.00
8	Marmalade	75.00	25.00	
9	Plate, 6"	25.00	10.00	
10	Plate, 6½", 2 hdld., cake	35.00	12.00	
3	Plate, 8"	40.00	10.00	
16	Plate, 10"	125.00	25.00	
	Relish, 12", 7 part	75.00	35.00	
11	Relish, 3-part, 2 hdld., tray	45.00	22.50	
4	Shakers, pr., w/tray	350.00	65.00	
	Sugar	45.00	15.00	
14	Tumbler, 2 oz., bar	35.00	12.50	
13	Tumbler, 8 oz., whiskey & soda	30.00	12.00	
	Tumbler, 9 oz., water, ftd.	30.00	15.00	
	Tumbler, cocktail	25.00	12.00	
	Tumbler, ftd., orange juice	30.00	15.00	
	Tumbler, high ball	33.00	18.00	
5	Tray for shakers	150.00		

*Add 10% for satinized.   7 Duncan sailfish added for ambiance

COLORS: CRYSTAL; ALL OTHER COLORS FOUND MADE VERY LATE

Navarre is the most collected pattern of the crystal etchings made by Fostoria. (American is the most widely collected pressed Fostoria crystal pattern; but it was made for about 70 years and several generations came to know it.) Navarre was made for over 40 years; and the thin fragile stems even augment modern day china patterns. Navarre was retailed nationally, but prices on the West Coast were always more costly which was   attributable to shipping costs. With the price of gasoline and postage increasing, transportation costs may have to once again figure into dealers' prices of glassware in today's market.

Only older crystal pieces of Navarre are priced in this book. Pink and blue were made in the 1970s and 1980s as were additional crystal pieces not originally made in the late 1930s and 1940s. These later pieces include carafes, Roemer wines, continental champagnes, and brandies. You can find these later pieces in our *Collectible Glassware from the 40s, 50s, and 60s...*. Most of these later pieces are acid signed on the base "Fostoria" although some carried only a sticker. We are telling you this to make you conscious of the colors made in Navarre. You will even find a few pieces of Navarre that are signed Lenox. These were made after Fostoria closed and Lenox used some Fostoria moulds for a while. Some collectors ignore the colored Lenox pieces since the color is lighter than the original; but it does not seem to make much difference to most Navarre collectors. A few Depression era glass shows have forbidden these pieces or colors to be sold since they were of more recent manufacture. However, most shows are changing these stricter rules to allow patterns to be included as long as production began at an earlier time.

18

		Crystal
	Bell, dinner	75.00
	Bowl, #2496, 4", sq., hdld.	18.00
17	Bowl, #2496, 4⅜", hdld.	16.00
	Bowl, #869, 4½", finger	65.00
	Bowl, #2496, 4⅝", tri-cornered	20.00
16	Bowl, #2496, 5", hdld., ftd.	20.00

		Crystal
	Bowl, #2496, 6", square, sweetmeat	26.00
	Bowl, #2496, 6¼", 3 ftd., nut	23.00
	Bowl, #2496, 7⅜", ftd., bonbon	26.00
	Bowl, #2496, 10", oval, floating garden	65.00
	Bowl, #2496, 10½", hdld., ftd.	80.00
4	Bowl, #2470½, 10½", ftd.	65.00
13	Bowl, #2496, 12", flared	70.00

		Crystal
14	Bowl, #2545, 12½", oval, "Flame"	80.00
	Candlestick, #2496, 4"	22.00
	Candlestick, #2496, 4½", double	35.00
	Candlestick, #2472, 5", double	45.00
	Candlestick, #2496, 5½"	40.00
	Candlestick, #2496, 6", triple	52.00
	Candlestick, #2545, 6¾", double, "Flame"	75.00
1	Candlestick, #2482, 6¾", triple	65.00
	Candy, w/cover, #2496, 3 part	125.00
	Celery, #2440, 9"	35.00
	Celery, #2496, 11"	45.00
	Comport, #2496, 3¼", cheese	30.00
9	Comport, #2400, 4½"	33.00
	Comport, #2496, 4¾"	35.00
	Cracker, #2496, 11", plate	40.00
	Creamer, #2440, 4¼", ftd.	16.00
12	Creamer, #2496, individual	16.00
	Cup, #2440	18.00
	Ice bucket, #2496, 4⅜" high	110.00
	Ice bucket, #2375, 6" high	125.00
	Mayonnaise, #2375, 3 piece	60.00
	Mayonnaise, #2496½, 3 piece	60.00
	Pickle, #2496, 8"	27.50
	Pickle, #2440, 8½"	30.00
18	Pitcher, #5000, 48 oz., ftd.	350.00
	Plate, #2440, 6", bread/butter	8.00
	Plate, #2440, 7½", salad	12.00
	Plate, #2440, 8½", luncheon	18.00
	Plate, #2440, 9½", dinner	45.00
	Plate, #2496, 10", hdld., cake	50.00
	Plate, #2440, 10½", oval cake	60.00

		Crystal
	Plate, #2496, 14", torte	70.00
	Plate, #2464, 16", torte	120.00
10	Relish, #2496, 6", 2 part, sq.	28.00
15	Relish, #2496, 10" x 7½", 3 part	45.00
	Relish, #2496, 10", 4 part	55.00
5	Relish, #2419, 13¼", 5 part	75.00
	Salt & pepper, #2364, 3¼", flat, pr.	75.00
	Salt & pepper, #2375, 3½", ftd., pr.	110.00
	Salad dressing bottle, #2083, 6½"	495.00
	Sauce dish, #2496, div. mayonnaise, 6½"	40.00
	Sauce dish, #2496, 6½" x 5¼"	100.00
	Sauce dish liner, #2496, 8", oval	20.00
	Saucer, #2440	3.00
	Stem, #6016, 1 oz., cordial, 3⅞"	50.00
	Stem, #6106, 3¼ oz., wine, 5½"	30.00
	Stem, #6106, 3½ oz., cocktail, 6"	22.00
8	Stem, #6106, 4 oz., oyster cocktail, 3⅝"	22.00
	Stem, #6106, 4½ oz., claret, 6½"	35.00
2	Stem, #6106, 6 oz., low sherbet, 4⅜"	18.00
	Stem, #6106, 6 oz., saucer champagne, 5⅝"	20.00
	Stem, #6106, 10 oz., wate,r, 7⅝"	35.00
	Sugar, #2440, 3⅝", ftd.	15.00
11	Sugar, #2496, individual	15.00
	Syrup, #2586, metal cut-off top, 5½"	495.00
	Tidbit, #2496, 8¼", 3 ftd., turned up edge	26.00
	Tray, #2496½", for ind. sugar/creamer	20.00
3	Tumbler, #6106, 5 oz., ftd., juice, 4⅝"	20.00
7	Tumbler, #6106, 10 oz., ftd., water, 5⅜"	23.00
6	Tumbler, #6106, 13 oz., ftd., tea, 5⅞"	30.00
	Vase, #4128, 5"	135.00
	Vase, #4121, 5"	120.00
	Vase, #4128, 5"	100.00
	Vase, #2470, 10", ftd.	185.00

COLORS: CRYSTAL, FROSTED CRYSTAL, SOME COBALT WITH CRYSTAL STEM AND FOOT

Since the major production of New Era falls outside the parameters of this book, New Era will be transferred into *Collectible Glassware from the 40s, 50s, and 60s* in the future. Only stems, the celery tray, and candlesticks were made before 1940. The New Era double-branched candelabrum with bobeches is probably the most recognized Heisey candle. Stemware proliferates since it was made before WWII and continued afterwards. Keep your eye peeled for flat pieces of New Era that often goes unidentified as Heisey.

16

		Crystal
12	Ashtray or individual nut	40.00
	Bottle, rye, w/stopper	140.00
1	Bowl, 11", floral	45.00
3	Candelabra, 2-lite, w/2 #4044 bobeche & prisms	140.00
	Creamer	37.50
15	Cup	15.00
	Cup, after dinner	62.50
	Pilsner, 8 oz.	40.00
	Pilsner, 12 oz.	45.00
	Plate, 5½" x 4½", bread & butter	20.00
2	Plate, 9" x 7"	25.00
14	Plate, 10" x 8"	75.00
	Relish, 13", 3 part	35.00
15	Saucer	8.00
	Saucer, after dinner	12.50
9	Stem, 1 oz., cordial	40.00
4	Stem, 3 oz., wine	22.00
16	Stem, 3½ oz., high, cocktail	10.00
11	Stem, 3½ oz., oyster cocktail	9.00
6	Stem, 4 oz., claret	18.00
10	Stem, 6 oz., champagne	11.00
13	Stem, 6 oz., sherbet, low	10.00

		Crystal
8	Stem, 10 oz., goblet	18.00
	Sugar	37.50
	Tray, 13", celery	30.00
	Tumbler, 5 oz., ftd., soda	10.00
	Tumbler, 8 oz., ftd., soda	14.00
	Tumbler, 10 oz., low, ftd.	14.00
7	Tumbler, 12 oz., ftd., soda	20.00
5	Tumbler, 14 oz., ftd., soda	24.00

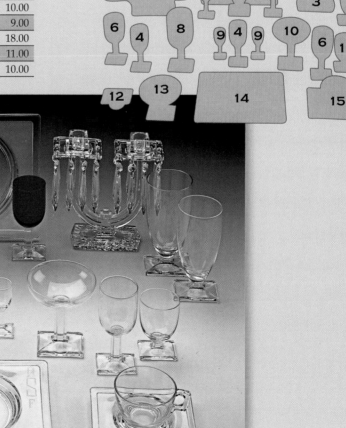

Colors: Amber, Rose, and Topaz

New Garland is a Fostoria pattern that should be genuinely taken into account by new collectors. It is not plentiful, but it can be found with some work either at shows or on the Internet. If you like the older, squared mould shape of Fostoria's #2419 Mayfair line, this pattern is for you. New Garland, by the way, was designed by George Sakier, the man behind many of Fostoria's more avant-garde designs of that era. Notice the ice buckets, which are not often found.

Pink appears to be the color of choice, but we are getting a few requests for Topaz recently. Our problem has been finding more to sell.

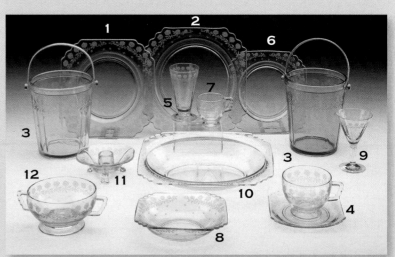

		Amber Topaz	Rose
	Bonbon, 2 hdld.	15.00	20.00
	Bottle, salad dressing	195.00	250.00
	Bowl, 5", fruit	10.00	15.00
	Bowl, 6", cereal	12.00	20.00
8	Bowl, 7", soup	22.00	30.00
	Bowl, 7½"	25.00	40.00
10	Bowl, 10", baker	33.00	48.00
	Bowl, 11", ftd.	50.00	70.00
	Bowl, 12"	55.00	70.00
11	Candlestick, 2"	15.00	20.00
	Candlestick, 3"	17.50	22.50
	Candlestick, 9½"	30.00	40.00
	Candy jar, cover, ½ lb.	50.00	80.00
	Celery, 11"	22.00	30.00
	Comport, 6"	20.00	28.00
	Comport, tall	30.00	40.00
12	Cream soup	16.00	20.00
	Creamer	12.50	15.00
	Creamer, ftd.	15.00	17.50
	Creamer, tea	17.50	20.00
7	Cup, after dinner, #2419	18.00	22.00
4	Cup, ftd., #2419	13.00	15.00
	Decanter	145.00	210.00
	Finger bowl, #4121	12.00	15.00
	Finger bowl, #6002, ftd.	15.00	18.00
3	Ice bucket, #2375	75.00	120.00
	Ice dish	20.00	25.00
	Jelly, 7"	18.00	22.50
	Lemon dish, 2 hdld.	15.00	18.00
	Mayonnaise, 2 hdld.	18.00	22.50
	Mint, 5½"	12.50	16.00
	Nut, individual	10.00	13.00
	Oil, ftd.	125.00	200.00
	Pickle, 8½"	16.00	20.00
	Pitcher, ftd.	225.00	295.00
6	Plate, 6", #2419	4.00	6.00
	Plate, 7"	7.00	10.00
	Plate, 8"	12.00	15.00

		Amber Topaz	Rose
1	Plate, 9", #2419	25.00	35.00
	Plate, 10" cake, 2 hdld.	27.50	35.00
2	Platter, 12"	35.00	50.00
	Platter, 15"	50.00	80.00
	Relish, 4 part	20.00	27.50
	Relish, 8½"	14.00	18.00
	Sauce boat	50.00	75.00
	Sauce boat liner	20.00	25.00
4	Saucer, #2419	3.00	4.00
	Saucer, after dinner	7.00	8.00
	Shaker, pr.	40.00	60.00
	Shaker, pr., ftd.	75.00	100.00
	Stem, #4120, 2 oz., whiskey	20.00	30.00
	Stem, #4120, 3½ oz., cocktail	20.00	24.00
	Stem, #4120, 5 oz., low sherbet	14.00	16.00
	Stem, #4120, 7 oz., low sherbet	15.00	18.00
	Stem, #4120, high sherbet	18.00	20.00
	Stem, #4120, water goblet	22.00	28.00
	Stem, #6002, claret	25.00	35.00
	Stem, #6002, cordial	30.00	40.00
	Stem, #6002, goblet	22.00	28.00
	Stem, #6002, high sherbet	18.00	20.00
	Stem, #6002, low sherbet	14.00	16.00
	Stem, #6002, oyster cocktail	16.00	20.00
9	Stem, #6002, wine	22.00	28.00
	Sugar	12.50	15.00
	Sugar, ftd.	15.00	17.50
	Sugar, tea	17.50	20.00
	Tumbler, #4120, 5 oz.	12.00	18.00
	Tumbler, #4120, 10 oz.	14.00	20.00
	Tumbler, #4120, 13 oz.	15.00	22.00
	Tumbler, #4120, 16 oz.	20.00	28.00
	Tumbler, #6002, ftd., 2 oz.	18.00	25.00
5	Tumbler, #6002, ftd., 5 oz.	12.00	18.00
	Tumbler, #6002, ftd., 10 oz.	14.00	20.00
	Tumbler, #6002, ftd., 13 oz.	15.00	22.00
	Vase, 8"	75.00	95.00

COLORS: AMBER, EMERALD GREEN, PEACH BLO; #3095 COLORED PEACH-BLO W/RIBBED BOWL, CRYSTAL STEM & FOOT, OPTIC, AMBER

Cambridge's Number 520 and Numbers 703 and 704, which follow on the next pages, are usually referred to as "one of those Cambridge numbered patterns," but few dealers outside of those specializing in Cambridge take the trouble to learn which one is which. There are some avid collectors of these lines, and hopefully adding names "Byzantine," "Florentine," and "Windows Border" may help identify the patterns as did "Rosalie" for Number 731.

Collectors like names. Since no factory name has been forthcoming for No. 520, let's adopt one collector's idea. She told us it reminded her of the elaborate designs seen in her travels. "It's very Byzantine," she said.

We see similar quantities of Peach Blo (pink) and Emerald (green), but apparently, there are more fans of the Emerald. We found a few amber pieces that we had never seen before. Enjoy those this time.

		Peach Blo Green Amber				Peach Blo Green Amber
	Bouillon, 2 hdld. soup cup, #934	25.00	3	Plate, 11", club luncheon, grill		30.00
	Bowl, 5¼", fruit, #928	22.50		Plate, finger bowl liner, #3060		12.50
	Bowl, 6½", cereal or grapefruit, #466	33.00	4	Platter for gravy boat, #917		40.00
1	Bowl, 12", oval, #914	45.00	2	Platter, 14½", oval/service, #903		75.00
	Bowl, cream soup	25.00		Saucer, #933		7.00
	Bowl, finger, #3060	28.00		Saucer, cupped, liner for bouillon		12.00
	Butter w/cover	195.00		Stem, 2½ oz., cocktail, #3060		20.00
	Candy box, #300	125.00		Stem, 2½ oz., wine, #3060		30.00
	Comport, 7¼" h., #531	40.00		Stem, 6 oz., high sherbet, #3060		20.00
	Comport, jelly, #2900	35.00		Stem, 7 oz., sherbet, #3060		18.00
	Comport, #3095 (twist stem)	40.00		Stem, 9 oz., water, #3060		28.00
	Creamer, rim ft., #138	20.00		Stem, cocktail, #3095		20.00
	Cup, #933	18.00		Stem, high sherbet, #3095		20.00
4	Gravy or sauce boat, double, #917	95.00		Stem, low sherbet, #3095		18.00
	Oil bottle, #193	195.00		Sugar, rim ft., #138		20.00
	Oil bottle w/cut flattened stop, 6 oz., #197	210.00		Tumbler, 3 oz., ftd., #3060		20.00
	Plate, 6", sherbet	10.00		Tumbler, 5 oz., ftd., #3060		20.00
	Plate, 8", luncheon	18.00		Tumbler, 10 oz., ftd., #3060		22.00
	Plate, 9½" dinner, #810	50.00		Tumbler, 12 oz., low ft., #3095		27.00
	Plate, 10", grill	35.00				

COLORS: GREEN, GREEN W/GOLD

Cambridge's No. 703 is another of the numbered lines that collectors can never recollect what the number is. Maybe the name "Florentine" may stick. Still, even veteran dealers often have to sneak a look at the book to ascertain many of these numbered lines. We have only found "Florentine" in green or green with gold, but have a sneaking suspicion that it was made in other colors. We bought a large set last year and sold most of it the first couple of shows where we had it displayed. You may find additional pieces or colors so keep us informed.

6

		Green
2	Bouillon liner, 6", #934	5.00
3	Bouillon, 2-hdld., #934	15.00
	Bowl, 5¼", fruit, #928	12.50
	Bowl, 6½", cereal, #466	17.50
	Bowl, 8", #1004	55.00
4	Bowl, 8½" soup, #381	25.00
	Candlestick, #625	30.00
6	Creamer, #138	15.00
5	Cup, ftd., #494	12.00
	Finger bowl liner, #3060	6.00
	Finger bowl, #3060	12.50
	Fruit salad, 7 oz., #3060	15.00
	Platter, 12½", oval, #901	65.00
	Platter, 16", oval, #901	85.00
	Sandwich tray, 12" oval, center handle, #173	35.00
5	Saucer, #494	3.00
	Stem, 1 oz., cordial, #3060	45.00
	Stem, 2½ oz., cocktail, #3060	20.00
	Stem, 2½ oz., wine, #3060	22.00
	Stem, 4½ oz., claret, #3060	25.00

		Green
	Stem, 5 oz., low sherbet, #3060	10.00
	Stem, 5½ oz., tall sherbet, #3060	12.50
	Stem, 6 oz., cafe parfait, #3060	22.00
	Stem, 9 oz., water, #3060	22.50
1	Sugar, #138	15.00
	Tumbler, 2 oz., bar, #3060	10.00
	Tumbler, 3 oz., ftd., #3060	12.00
7	Tumbler, 4 oz., oyster cocktail, #3060	12.00
	Tumbler, 5 oz., juice, #3060	12.00
	Tumbler, 5 oz., ftd. juice, #3060	14.00
	Tumbler, 8 oz., table, #3060	15.00
	Tumbler, 8 oz., ftd, #3060	17.50
	Tumbler, 10 oz., ftd., water, #3060	18.00
	Tumbler, 10 oz., water, #3060	17.50
	Tumbler, 12 oz., tea, #3060	20.00
	Tumbler, 12 oz., ftd., tea, #3060	22.50

COLORS: AMBER, BLUEBELL, CRYSTAL, EMERALD, PEACH-BLO

Number 704 is a Cambridge numbered line whose name has been suggested by a collector as "Windows Border" and that might be recalled better than Number 704, which typically is forgotten once it has been looked up.

"Windows Border" is often exhibited in sets in malls without an identifying name, but labeled Cambridge since most pieces are marked with that enlightening C in a triangle indicating Cambridge. We hope this book's exposure will enhance its appeal to collectors and bring it the recognition it justly merits. It's a magnificent etching and above all, it can still be found with searching.

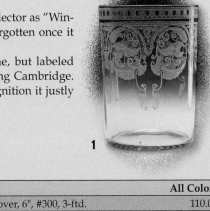

1

		All Colors
	Bottle, decanter, #0315	195.00
	Bottle, decanter, #3075	210.00
	Bowl, 5¼", fruit	18.00
8	Bowl, 6", cereal	25.00
7	Bowl, 7", 3 ftd.	35.00
10	Bowl, 8", rolled edge, #460	35.00
	Bowl, 8½", soup	33.00
	Bowl, 8¾", oval	33.00
	Bowl, 10½", #912 casserole and cover	175.00
	Bowl, 12", oval, #914	50.00
	Bowl, 12", oval w/cover, #915	125.00
	Bowl, 2 hdld. cream soup, #922	20.00
	Bowl, finger, #3060	35.00
	Bowl, finger, #3075	35.00
	Butter and cover, #920	125.00
	Candlestick, 2", #227½	20.00
	Candlestick, 3½", #628	25.00
	Candlestick, 7½", #439	35.00
	Candlestick, 8½", #438	40.00
	Candlestick, 9½", #437	45.00
	Candy box and cover, 5", #98, 3-part, flat	95.00
	Candy box and cover, 5", #299, 3-ftd.	95.00

	All Colors
Candy box and cover, 6", #300, 3-ftd.	110.00
Celery, 11", #908	35.00
Celery tray, 11", #652	45.00
Cheese plate, #468	35.00
Cheese plate & cover, #3075	125.00
Cigarette box, #430	50.00
Cigarette box, #616	50.00
Cologne, 1 oz., #198 or #199	125.00
Comport, 5", #3075	30.00
Creamer, flat, #137	20.00
Creamer, flat, #942	20.00
Creamer, flat, #943	20.00
Creamer, flat, #944	20.00
Cup, #933	12.00
Cup, demi, #925	30.00
Gravy boat, double and stand, #917	125.00
Ice bucket w/bail, short, #970	100.00
Ice bucket w/bail, tall, #957	110.00

		All Colors
	Ice tub, straight up tab hdlds., #394	90.00
	Jug, night set, #103, 38 oz. w/tumbler	250.00
	Jug, #107	195.00
	Jug, #124, 68 oz., w/lid	295.00
	Jug, 62 oz., flat, #955	225.00
	Jug, #3077 w/lid	395.00
	Mayonnaise, 3 pc., #169	70.00
	Mayonnaise, 3 pc., #533	65.00
	Oil, 6 oz., #193	75.00
	Oyster cocktail, 4½ oz., ftd., #3060	12.00
	Pickle tray, 9", #907	30.00
	Plate, 6"	6.00
2	Plate, 7"	8.00
	Plate, 8"	15.00
	Plate, 8½"	18.00
11	Plate, 9½", dinner	55.00
4	Plate, 10½", service	65.00
12	Plate, 12", oval/cracker, #487	30.00
	Plate,13½"	65.00
	Plate, cupped, liner for creme soup, #922	8.00
	Plate, liner for finger bowl, #3060	8.00
	Plate, liner for finger bowl, #3075	8.00
	Platter, 12½", oval service, #901	75.00
	Platter, 16", oval, #904	95.00
	Puff & cover, 3" or 4", #578, blown	85.00
	Puff & cover, 4", #582	55.00
	Saucer, #933	5.00
	Saucer, demi, #925	8.00
5	Stem, 1 oz., cordial, #3075	60.00
9	Stem, 2½ oz., cocktail (wide bowl), #3075	14.00
	Stem, 2½ oz., wine (slender bowl), #3075	28.00
	Stem, 4½ oz., claret, #3075	33.00

		All Colors
	Stem, 5 oz., parfait, #3060	35.00
	Stem, 5½ oz., cafe parfait, #3075	35.00
3	Stem, 6 oz., high sherbet, #3060	18.00
	Stem, 9 oz., #3060	28.00
	Stem, 9 oz., #3075	28.00
	Stem, low sherbet, #3075	12.00
	Stem, high sherbet, #3075	16.00
	Sugar, flat, #137	18.00
	Sugar, flat, #942	18.00
	Sugar, flat, #943	18.00
	Sugar, flat, #944	18.00
	Syrup, 9 oz., w/metal cover, #170	165.00
	Syrup, tall jug, #814	175.00
	Toast dish and cover, 9", #951	250.00
14	Tray, 10", center handle, #140	45.00
13	Tray, 12", oval, center handle, #173	40.00
	Tumbler, 2 oz., flat, #3060	30.00
	Tumbler, 2 oz., whiskey, #3075	30.00
	Tumbler, 3 oz., ftd., #3075	26.00
	Tumbler, 5 oz., ftd., #3075	20.00
	Tumbler, 5 oz., #3075	20.00
	Tumbler, 6 oz., ftd. fruit salad (sherbet)	14.00
	Tumbler, 8 oz., ftd., #3075	18.00
	Tumbler, 10 oz., #3075	20.00
1	Tumbler, 10 oz., flat, #3060	20.00
	Tumbler, 10 oz., ftd., #3075	22.50
	Tumbler, 12 oz., #3075	25.00
6	Tumbler, 12 oz., flat, #3060	25.00
	Tumbler, 12 oz., ftd., #3060	25.00
	Tumbler, 12 oz., ftd., #3075	25.00
	Vase, 6½", ftd., #1005	100.00
	Vase, 9½", ftd., #787	150.00

COLORS: NILE GREEN AND NILE GREEN WITH CRYSTAL

Our first introduction to Nymph was when it was called "Flying Nun" by Fred Bickenheuser. We were curious as to that name as it looked like no nun we had ever seen, but that was the accepted terminology at the time.

We started gathering a few pieces for photography and here it is. We used to attend the National Tiffin show to keep up with that market. About 10 years ago, we stopped going as little dinnerware was being seen, and that was our interest for our books. What was being offered then were colors and mainly a variety of large vases and decorative pieces.

Since we were adding five Tiffin dinnerware lines to this new edition, we went back last year to observe dinnerware prices and see what was now on the table. Things haven't changed. Only four Tiffin dinnerware pieces were being offered for sale, so our trip was not very fruitful in that regard.

		Nile Green
	Candy jar, #9557, ½ lb., w/cover	145.00
1	Creamer	65.00
	Jug w/cover	550.00
	Jug	450.00
3	Plate, 8", salad	20.00
	Plate, 10", service	100.00
	Stem, #15011, 3 oz., cocktail	35.00
7	Stem, #15011, 6 oz., champagne	35.00
	Stem, #15011, 6 oz., sherbet	30.00
6	Stem, #15011, 9 oz., water goblet	50.00
2	Sugar	65.00
5	Tumbler, #14185, 2½ oz., ftd. whiskey	50.00
	Tumbler, #14185, 9 oz., ftd., water	35.00
4	Tumbler, #14185, 12 oz., ftd., iced tea	40.00
	Vase, 10", bud, #15004	75.00

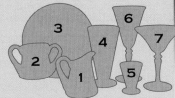

COLORS: CRYSTAL, FLAMINGO PINK, SAHARA YELLOW, MOONGLEAM GREEN, HAWTHORNE ORCHID, MARIGOLD DEEP AMBER/YELLOW, AND DAWN

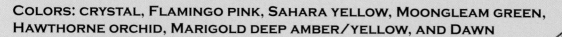

Octagon was commonly marked by Heisey's trademark H within a diamond; so, it is a pattern that anyone can deduce is Heisey. However, few collectors actively hunt for this unadorned pattern, which comes in an array of colors. In the price list below, the only pieces that attract much attention are the basket, ice tub, and the 12" four-part tray. Observe that ice tubs were sometimes cut or etched as shown here. That tray can be found in the rare gray/black color called Dawn. Octagon is sensibly priced for a beginning collector.

Marigold pieces are occasionally found in Octagon, and one piece is shown in the photo at the bottom of next page. This rarely seen Heisey color is prone to peeling and crazing which cannot be undone. If that should happen, it becomes uninviting to collectors.

		Crystal	Flamingo	Sahara	Moongleam	Hawthorne	Marigold
5	Basket, 5", #500	500.00	300.00	300.00	350.00	450.00	800.00
	Bonbon, 6", sides up, #1229	10.00	40.00	25.00	25.00	40.00	
	Bowl, cream soup, 2 hdld.	10.00	20.00	25.00	30.00	40.00	
7	Bowl, 2 hdld, individual nut bowl	15.00	25.00	25.00	25.00	60.00	65.00
	Bowl, 5½", jelly, #1229	15.00	30.00	25.00	25.00	50.00	
	Bowl, 6", mint, #1229	10.00	20.00	25.00	25.00	45.00	30.00
	Bowl, 6", #500	14.00	20.00	22.00	25.00	35.00	
	Bowl, 6½", grapefruit	10.00	20.00	22.00	25.00	35.00	
2	Bowl, 8", #1209	20.00	45.00	45.00	45.00	65.00	
	Bowl, 8", ftd., #1229 comport	15.00	25.00	35.00	45.00	55.00	
	Bowl, 9", flat soup	10.00	15.00	20.00	27.50	30.00	
	Bowl, 9", vegetable	15.00	32.00	25.00	30.00	50.00	
3	Bowl, 12", #1203	25.00	55.00	50.00	55.00	65.00	
	Candlestick, 3", 1-lite	15.00	30.00	30.00	40.00	50.00	
	Cheese dish, 6", 2 hdld., #1229	7.00	15.00	10.00	15.00	15.00	
	Creamer, #500	10.00	30.00	35.00	35.00	50.00	
	Creamer, hotel	10.00	30.00	30.00	35.00	50.00	
	Cup, after dinner	10.00	20.00	20.00	25.00	42.00	
	Cup, #1231	5.00	15.00	20.00	20.00	35.00	
	Dish, frozen dessert, #500	15.00	30.00	20.00	30.00	35.00	50.00
4	Frozen dessert	10.00	22.00		22.00		30.00
1	Ice tub, #500	30.00	75.00	80.00	85.00	129.00	150.00
	Mayonnaise, 5½", ftd., #1229	10.00	25.00	30.00	35.00	55.00	
6	Nut, two hdld.	10.00	25.00	20.00	25.00	65.00	70.00
	Plate, cream soup liner	3.00	5.00	7.00	9.00	12.00	
	Plate, 6"	4.00	8.00	8.00	10.00	15.00	
	Plate, 7", bread	5.00	10.00	10.00	15.00	20.00	
9	Plate, 8", luncheon	7.00	10.00	10.00	15.00	25.00	

	Crystal	Flamingo	Sahara	Moongleam	Hawthorne	Marigold
Plate, 10", sand., #1229	15.00	20.00	25.00	30.00	80.00	
Plate, 10", muffin, #1229, sides up	15.00	25.00	30.00	35.00	40.00	
Plate, 10½"	17.00	25.00	30.00	35.00	45.00	
Plate, 10½", ctr. hdld., sandwich	25.00	40.00	40.00	45.00	70.00	
Plate, 12", muffin, #1229, sides up	20.00	27.00	30.00	35.00	45.00	
Plate, 13", hors d'oeuvre, #1229	20.00	35.00	35.00	45.00	60.00	
Plate, 14"	22.00	25.00	30.00	35.00	50.00	
Platter, 12¾", oval	20.00	25.00	30.00	40.00	50.00	
Saucer, after dinner	5.00	8.00	10.00	10.00	12.00	
Saucer, #1231	5.00	8.00	10.00	10.00	12.00	
Sugar, #500	10.00	25.00	35.00	35.00	50.00	
Sugar, hotel	10.00	30.00	30.00	35.00	50.00	
Tray, 6", oblong, #500	8.00	15.00	15.00	15.00	30.00	
Tray, 9", celery	10.00	20.00	20.00	25.00	45.00	
Tray, 12", celery	10.00	25.00	25.00	30.00	50.00	
8 Tray, 12", 4 pt., #500 variety*	40.00	90.00	110.00	120.00	250.00	*350.00

*Dawn

COLORS: CRYSTAL, FLAMINGO PINK, SAHARA YELLOW, MOONGLEAM GREEN, MARIGOLD DEEP AMBER/YELLOW

Due to the wealth of Sahara (yellow), Old Colony pricing will be based on Sahara as follows: crystal, subtract 50%; Flamingo, subtract 10%; Moongleam, add 10%; Marigold, add 20%. Space does not permit pricing each color separately. If you like Heisey's Sahara, this might be the perfect pattern to collect due to its availability.

		Sahara
	Bouillon cup, 2 hdld., ftd.	25.00
	Bowl, finger, #4075	15.00
	Bowl, ftd., finger, #3390	25.00
	Bowl, 4½", nappy	14.00
	Bowl, 5", ftd., 2 hdld.	24.00
	Bowl, 6", ftd., 2 hdld., jelly	30.00
	Bowl, 6", dolphin ftd., mint	35.00
	Bowl, 7", triplex, dish	40.00
	Bowl, 7½", dolphin ftd., nappy	70.00
	Bowl, 8", nappy	40.00
	Bowl, 8½", ftd., floral, 2 hdld.	60.00
	Bowl, 9", 3 hdld.	90.00
	Bowl, 10", rnd., 2 hdld., salad	60.00
	Bowl, 10", sq., salad, 2 hdld.	55.00
	Bowl, 10", oval, dessert, 2 hdld.	50.00
	Bowl, 10", oval, veg.	65.00
	Bowl, 11", floral, dolphin ft.	80.00
	Bowl, 13", ftd., flared	40.00
	Bowl, 13", 2 pt., pickle & olive	40.00
	Cigarette holder, #3390	44.00
	Comport, 7", oval, ftd.	80.00
	Comport, 7", ftd., #3368	70.00
	Cream soup, 2 hdld.	22.00
1	Creamer, dolphin ft.	45.00
	Creamer, indiv.	40.00
	Cup, after dinner	40.00
9	Cup	32.00
	Decanter, 1 pt.	325.0
	Flagon, 12 oz., #3390	100.0
	Grapefruit, 6"	30.00
	Grapefruit, ftd., #3380	20.00
	Ice tub, dolphin ft.	115.00
	Mayonnaise, 5½", dolphin ft.	50.00
6	Nut dish, individual, dolphin ft.	40.00
	Oil, 4 oz., ftd.	105.00
	Pitcher, 3 pt., #3390	200.00
	Pitcher, 3 pt., dolphin ft.	220.00
	Plate, bouillon	15.00
	Plate, cream soup	12.00
	Plate, 4½", rnd.	5.00

		Sahara
	Plate, 6", rnd.	12.00
	Plate, 6", sq.	12.00
	Plate, 7", rnd.	20.00
8	Plate, 7", sq.	20.00
	Plate, 8", rnd.	26.00
2	Plate, 8", sq.	26.00
	Plate, 9", rnd.	26.00
	Plate, 10½", rnd.	120.00
	Plate, 10½", sq.	110.00
	Plate, 12", rnd.	75.00
	Plate, 12", 2 hdld., rnd., muffin	75.00
	Plate, 12", 2 hdld., rnd., sand.	70.00
	Plate, 13", 2 hdld., sq., sand.	50.00
	Plate, 13", 2 hdld., sq., muffin	50.00
	Platter, 14", oval	55.00
	Salt & pepper, pr.	125.00
	Saucer, sq.	10.00
10	Saucer, rnd.	10.00
5	Stem, #3380, 1 oz., cordial	110.00
	Stem, #3380, 2½ oz., wine	30.00
	Stem, #3380, 3 oz., cocktail	20.00
	Stem, #3380, 4 oz., oyster/cocktail	16.00
	Stem, #3380, 4 oz., claret	34.00
	Stem, #3380, 5 oz., parfait	18.00
	Stem, #3380, 6 oz., champagne	16.00
	Stem, #3380, 6 oz., sherbet	16.00
	Stem, #3380, 10 oz., short soda	16.00
	Stem, #3380, 10 oz., tall soda	20.00
	Stem, #3390, 1 oz., cordial	100.00
	Stem, #3390, 2½ oz., wine	30.00
	Stem, #3390, 3 oz., cocktail	16.00
	Stem, #3390, 3 oz., oyster/cocktail	16.00
	Stem, #3390, 4 oz., claret	26.00
4	Stem, #3390, 6 oz., champagne	20.00
	Stem, #3390, 6 oz., sherbet	20.00
	Stem, #3390, 11 oz., low water	20.00
	Stem, #3390, 11 oz., tall water	22.00
7	Sugar, dolphin ft.	45.00
	Sugar, individual	40.00
	Tray, 10", celery	30.00

		Crystal
	Bowl, finger, w/liner, #3124	45.00
28	Bowl, 10", hndl., #3500/28	60.00
	Bowl, seafood (fruit cocktail w/liner)	45.00
9	Candlestick, 5", keyhole, #3400/646	35.00
24	Candlestick, 5½", double, #502	65.00
	Candlestick, 6", 2-lite, keyhole, #3400/647	45.00
	Candlestick, 6", 3-lite, keyhole, #3400/648	55.00
	Candy box, w/cover, rnd.	135.00
2	Candy box, w/cover, 6", Ram's head, #3500/78	195.00
	Cigarette holder, urn shape	50.00
	Cocktail icer, 2 pt.	65.00
	Cocktail shaker, w/glass stopper	195.00
	Cocktail shaker, 80 oz., hdld. ball w/chrome top	235.00
15	Cologne, 2 oz., hdld. ball w/stopper, #3400/97	195.00
	Comport, 5½"	45.00
	Comport, 5⅜", blown	55.00
11	Creamer, ftd., #3400/68	20.00
	Creamer, hdld. ball	45.00
	Creamer, indiv.	18.00
	Cup, ftd., sq.	25.00
17	Cup, rd., #3400/54	16.00
20	Cup, after dinner, #3400/69	90.00
	Decanter, 29 oz., ftd., sherry, w/stopper	265.00
1	Decanter, 35 oz., flat, hdld., #3400/113	200.00
	Hurricane lamp, candlestick base	195.00
	Hurricane lamp, keyhole base, w/prisms	250.00
	Ice bucket, w/chrome handle	110.00
	Ivy ball, 5¼"	95.00
	Mayonnaise, div. bowl, w/liner & 2 ladles	60.00
23	Mayonnaise, w/liner & ladle, #3400/11	55.00
	Oil, 6 oz., loop hdld., w/stopper	110.00
	Oil, 6 oz., hdld. ball, w/stopper	100.00
	Pitcher, ball, 80 oz., #3400/38	195.00
	Pitcher, Doulton, 76 oz., #3400/152	350.00
6	Pitcher, 76 oz., #3400/100	195.00
	Plate, 6", 2 hdld.	15.00
4	Plate, 6½", bread/butter	7.50
26	Plate, 7", tab hndl., mayonnaise/liner, #3400/15	15.00
	Plate, 8", salad	15.00
	Plate, 8", ftd., 2 hdld.	20.00

1

		Crystal
	Plate, 8", ftd., bonbon, tab hdld.	22.00
	Plate, 8½", sq.	18.00
25	Plate, 10½", dinner	75.00
	Plate, 13", 4 ftd., torte	60.00
	Plate, 13½", 2 hdld., cake	60.00
	Plate, 14", torte	70.00
	Puff box, 3½", ball shape, w/lid	195.00
16	Salt & pepper, pr., ftd., #3400/77	40.00
17	Saucer, rnd., #3400/54	5.00
20	Saucer, after dinner, #3400/69	25.00
	Set: 3 pc. frappe (bowl, 2 plain inserts)	65.00
13	Stem, #3121, 1 oz., cordial	55.00
	Stem, #3121, 1 oz., low ftd., brandy	50.00
	Stem, #3121, 2½ oz., wine	35.00
	Stem, #3121, 3 oz., cocktail	24.00
	Stem, #3121, 4½ oz., claret	38.00
	Stem, #3121, 4½ oz., oyster cocktail	18.00
	Stem, #3121, 5 oz., parfait	35.00
	Stem, #3121, 6 oz., low sherbet	16.00
	Stem, #3121, 6 oz., tall sherbet	18.00
	Stem, #3121, 10 oz., goblet	28.00
7	Stem, #3122, 1 oz., cordial	55.00
18	Stem, #3122, 5 oz., ftd., juice	25.00
	Stem, #3124, 3 oz., cocktail	18.00
	Stem, #3124, 3 oz., wine	28.00
	Stem, #3124, 4½ oz., claret	35.00
	Stem, #3124, 7 oz., low sherbet	16.00
	Stem, #3124, 7 oz., tall sherbet	18.00
	Stem, #3124, 10 oz., goblet	28.00
14	Stem, #3126, 1 oz., cordial	55.00
	Stem, #3126, 1 oz., low ft., brandy	55.00
22	Stem, #3126, 2½ oz., wine	33.00
	Stem, #3126, 3 oz., cocktail	18.00
	Stem, #3126, 4½ oz., claret	35.00

2

		Crystal
	Stem, #3126, 4½ oz., low ft., oyster cocktail	16.00
	Stem, #3126, 7 oz., low sherbet	16.00
3	Stem, #3126, 7 oz., tall sherbet	18.00
	Stem, #3126, 9 oz., goblet	28.00
12	Stem, #3130, 1 oz., cordial	55.00
	Stem, #3130, 2½ oz., wine	35.00
	Stem, #3130, 3 oz., cocktail	18.00
	Stem, #3130, 4½ oz., claret	35.00
27	Stem, #3130, 4½ oz., fruit/oyster cocktail	16.00
	Stem, #3130, 7 oz., low sherbet	16.00
	Stem, #3130, 7 oz., tall sherbet	18.00
	Stem, #3130, 9 oz., goblet	28.00
	Sugar, ftd., hdld. ball	45.00
10	Sugar, ftd., #3400/68	18.00
	Sugar, individual	18.00
	Tray, 11", celery	38.00
8	Tray, 11", hdld., sandwich	38.00
19	Tumbler, 1 oz., cordial, #1344	45.00
	Tumbler, #3121, 2½ oz., bar	38.00
	Tumbler, #3121, 5 oz., ftd., juice	20.00
	Tumbler, #3121, 10 oz., ftd., water	25.00
	Tumbler, #3121, 12 oz., ftd., tea	28.00

		Crystal
	Tumbler, #3124, 3 oz.	18.00
	Tumbler, #3124, 5 oz., juice	20.00
	Tumbler, #3124, 10 oz., water	25.00
	Tumbler, #3124, 12 oz., tea	30.00
	Tumbler, #3126, 2½ oz.	35.00
	Tumbler, #3126, 5 oz., juice	20.00
	Tumbler, #3126, 10 oz., water	24.00
	Tumbler, #3126, 12 oz., tea	28.00
	Tumbler, #3130, 5 oz., juice	22.00
	Tumbler, #3130, 10 oz., water	24.00
	Tumbler, #3130, 12 oz., tea	28.00
29	Tumbler, #3400/38, 12 oz.	30.00
	Vase, 5", globe	55.00
	Vase, 6", ftd.	75.00
	Vase, 8", ftd.	100.00
	Vase, 9", keyhole ft.	85.00
5	Vase, 10", #1242	70.00
	Vase, 11", flower	100.00
	Vase, 11", pedestal ft.	110.00
	Vase, 12", keyhole ft.	130.00
	Vase, 13", flower	165.00

COLOR: CRYSTAL BOWL W/ANNA ROSE (PINK) STEM AND FOOT

Queen Louise continues to mesmerize anyone who sees it. Not everyone can afford this absolutely magnificent silkscreen glassware, but almost all who have seen it, wish to own it.

Queen Louise sells for a substantial price, but may actually be undervalued taking into account its scarcity today. We are not seeing it for sale even at the shows we attend.

Looking for this has been an adventure of almost fourteen years. Apparently, Queen Louise was distributed in the Chicago and St. Louis areas, since that is where it once was being found. Even the Internet auctions have been void of listings of this pattern recently.

Personal observation shows that all stems sell in the same price range with waters being found the most often. Champagnes and parfaits may be the most difficult stems to find. Plates are rare and the footed bowl is seldom seen.

8	Bowl, finger, ftd.	250.00
	Plate, 6", finger bowl liner	110.00
4	Plate, salad	135.00
6	Stem, 2½ oz., wine	400.00
5	Stem, 3 oz., cocktail	400.00
2	Stem, 5½ oz., saucer champagne	360.00
	Stem, 5½ oz., sherbet	310.00
7	Stem, 7 oz., parfait	465.00
3	Stem, 9 oz., water	495.00
1	Tumbler, 9 oz., ftd.	395.00

COLORS: CRYSTAL, SAHARA, ZIRCON, RARE

		Crystal
	Ashtray, rnd.	14.00
10	Ashtray, sq.	10.00
	Ashtray, 4", rnd.	22.00
	Ashtray, 6", sq.	35.00
15	Ashtray, 6", sq. w/oval cig. holder	95.00
	Ashtrays, bridge set (heart, diamond, spade, club)	85.00
	Basket, bonbon, metal handle	25.00
	Bottle, rock & rye, w/#104 stopper	240.00
14	Bottle, 4 oz., cologne	100.00
	Bottle, 5 oz., bitters, w/tube	100.00
19	Bowl, indiv., nut	15.00
13	Bowl, oval, indiv., jelly	20.00
	Bowl, indiv., nut, 2 part	20.00
	Bowl, 4½", nappy, bell or cupped	20.00
	Bowl, 4½", nappy, scalloped	20.00
	Bowl, 5", lemon, w/cover	65.00
	Bowl, 5", nappy, straight	18.00
	Bowl, 5", nappy, sq.	25.00
	Bowl, 6", 2 hdld., div., jelly	40.00
	Bowl, 6", 2 hdld., jelly	30.00
	Bowl, 7", 2 part, oval, relish	30.00
	Bowl, 8", centerpiece	55.00
	Bowl, 8", nappy, sq.	55.00
	Bowl, 9", nappy, sq.	65.00
	Bowl, 9", salad	50.00
	Bowl, 10", flared, fruit	45.00
	Bowl, 10", floral	45.00
	Bowl, 11", centerpiece	50.00
4	Bowl, 11", cone beverage	195.00
	Bowl, 11", punch	175.00
	Bowl, 11½", floral	50.00
8	Bowl, 12", oval, floral	55.00
	Bowl, 12", flared, fruit	50.00
	Bowl, 13", cone, floral	65.00
	Bowl, 14", oblong, floral	70.00
	Bowl, 14", oblong, swan hdld., floral	280.00
	Box, 8", floral	70.00
16	Candle block, 3", #1469½	30.00
	Candle vase, 6"	35.00
	Candlestick, 2", 1-lite	35.00
	Candlestick, 2-lite, bobeche & "A" prisms	80.00
	Candlestick, 7", w/bobeche & "A" prisms	120.00
12	Cheese, 6", 2 hdld.	22.00
	Cigarette box, w/cover, oval	90.00
	Cigarette box, w/cover, 6"	35.00
	Cigarette holder, oval, w/2 comp. ashtrays	70.00
18	Cigarette holder, rnd.	18.00
	Cigarette holder, sq.	18.00
	Cigarette holder, w/cover	30.00
	Coaster or cocktail rest	15.00
	Cocktail shaker, 1 qt., w/#1 strainer & #86 stopper	350.00
	Comport, 6", low ft., flared	25.00
	Comport, 6", low ft., w/cover	40.00

		Crystal
	Creamer	30.00
	Creamer, indiv.	20.00
	Cup	16.00
5	Cup, beverage	24.00
	Cup, punch	12.00
	Decanter, 1 pint, w/#95 stopper	210.00
	Ice tub, 2 hdld.	100.00
	Marmalade, w/cover (scarce)	90.00
	Mayonnaise and under plate	55.00
	Mustard, w/cover	60.00
	Oil bottle, 3 oz., w/#103 stopper	50.00
	Pitcher, ½ gallon, ball shape	380.00
	Pitcher, ½ gallon, ice lip, ball shape	380.00
11	Plate, oval, hors d'oeuvres	850.00
	Plate, 2 hdld., ice tub liner	50.00
	Plate, 6", rnd.	12.00
	Plate, 6", sq.	24.00
	Plate, 7", sq.	28.00
	Plate, 8", rnd.	20.00
	Plate, 8", sq.	32.00
	Plate, 13½", sandwich	45.00
	Plate, 13½", ftd., torte	45.00
	Plate, 14", salver	50.00
6	Plate, 20", punch bowl underplate	140.00
	Puff box, 5", and cover	75.00
	Salt & pepper, pr.	45.00
	Salt dip, indiv.	13.00
	Saucer	5.00
	Soda, 12 oz., ftd., no knob in stem (rare)	50.00
1	Stem, cocktail, pressed	25.00
	Stem, claret, pressed	45.00
	Stem, oyster cocktail, pressed	30.00
	Stem, sherbet, pressed	20.00
2	Stem, saucer champagne, pressed	25.00
	Stem, wine, pressed	40.00
	Stem, 1 oz., cordial, blown	160.00
	Stem, 2 oz., sherry, blown	90.00
	Stem, 2½ oz., wine, blown	80.00
	Stem, 3½ oz., cocktail, blown	35.00
	Stem, 4 oz., claret, blown	55.00
	Stem, 4 oz., oyster cocktail, blown	30.00
	Stem, 5 oz., saucer champagne, blown	25.00

	Crystal
Stem, 5 oz., sherbet, blown	20.00
Stem, 8 oz., luncheon, low stem	30.00
3 Stem, 9 oz., goblet, pressed	35.00
Sugar	30.00
Sugar, indiv.	20.00
Tray, for indiv. sugar & creamer	20.00
Tray, 10½", oblong	40.00
Tray, 11", 3 part, relish	50.00
Tray, 12", celery & olive, divided	50.00
Tray, 12", celery	40.00
17 Tumbler, 2½ oz., bar, pressed	45.00
Tumbler, 5 oz., juice, blown	30.00
Tumbler, 5 oz., soda, ftd., pressed	30.00
Tumbler, 8 oz., #1469¾, pressed	35.00
Tumbler, 8 oz., old-fashion, pressed	40.00

	Crystal
Tumbler, 8 oz., soda, blown	40.00
Tumbler, 10 oz., #1469½, pressed	45.00
Tumbler, 12 oz., ftd., soda, pressed	50.00
Tumbler, 12 oz., soda, #1469½, pressed	50.00
Tumbler, 13 oz., iced tea, blown	40.00
Vase, #1 indiv., cuspidor shape	40.00
Vase, #2 indiv., cupped top	45.00
Vase, #3 indiv., flared rim	30.00
Vase, #4 indiv., fan out top	55.00
Vase, #5 indiv., scalloped top	55.00
Vase, 3½"	25.00
9 Vase, 6" (also flared)	35.00
7 Vase, 8"	75.00
Vase, 8", triangular, #1469¾	110.00

COLOR: CRYSTAL

Rogene, etch #269, is an early Fostoria pattern that has been lately scrutinized by collectors searching for other patterns to collect. There are swarms of pieces that are reasonably priced for their age and beauty, judging by standards of other Fostoria patterns. What other pattern offers five pitchers for your choosing?

	Almond, ftd., #4095	10.00
	Comport, 5" tall, #5078	30.00
	Comport, 6", #5078	30.00
9	Creamer, flat, #1851	30.00
	Decanter, qt., cut neck, #300	95.00
	Finger bowl, #766	20.00
	Jelly, #825	22.50
	Jelly & cover, #825	40.00
	Jug 4, ftd., #4095	100.00
	Jug 7, #318	150.00
	Jug 7, #2270	165.00
	Jug 7, #4095	195.00
	Jug 7, covered, #2270	250.00
	Marmalade & cover, #1968	45.00
	Mayonnaise bowl, #766	28.00
	Mayonnaise ladle	20.00
5	Mayonnaise set, 3 pc., #2138 (ftd. compote, ladle, liner)	60.00
	Nappy, 5" ftd. (comport/sherbet), #5078	17.50
	Nappy, 6" ftd., #5078	25.00
	Nappy, 7" ftd., #5078	30.00
	Night set, 2 pc., #1697 (carafe & tumbler)	145.00
	Oil bottle w/cut stop, 5 oz., #1495	75.00
	Oyster cocktail, ftd., #837	12.50
	Plate, 5"	5.00
	Plate, 6"	6.00
	Plate, 6", #2283	6.00
	Plate, 7", salad, #2283	9.00
4	Plate, 8"	14.00

	Plate, 11"	25.00
	Plate, 11", w/cut star	27.50
	Plate, finger bowl liner	6.00
	Plate, mayonnaise liner, #766	12.50
	Shaker, pr., glass (pearl) top, #2283	55.00
	Stem, ¾ oz., cordial, #5082	40.00
	Stem, 2½ oz., wine, #5082	20.00
10	Stem, 3 oz., cocktail, #5082	14.00
	Stem, 4½ oz., claret, #5082	25.00
	Stem, 5 oz., fruit, #5082	12.50
	Stem, 5 oz., saucer champagne, #5082	15.00
	Stem, 6 oz., parfait, #5082	22.50
1	Stem, 9 oz., #5082	22.50
	Stem, grapefruit, #945½	33.00
	Stem, grapefruit liner, #945½	18.00
6	Sugar, flat, #1851	30.00
	Tumbler, 2½ oz., whiskey, #887	18.00
	Tumbler, 2½ oz., ftd., #4095	18.00
8	Tumbler, 5 oz., flat, #889	12.50
	Tumbler, 5 oz., ftd., #4095	12.50
	Tumbler, 8 oz., flat,, #889	13.00
3	Tumbler, 10 oz., ftd., #4095	14.00
	Tumbler, 12 oz., flat, hdld., #837	25.00
7	Tumbler, 13 oz., flat, #889	17.50
2	Tumbler, 13 oz., ftd., #4095	20.00
	Tumbler, flat, table, #4076	14.00
	Vase, 8½" rolled edge	100.00

COLORS: AMBER, BLUEBELL, CARMEN, CRYSTAL, EBONY, EMERALD GREEN, HEATHERBLOOM, PEACH-BLO, TOPAZ, WILLOW BLUE

Rosalie, Cambridge's #731 line, is a pattern that can be collected in a variety of colors; but completing a set in any one color might take years unless you are exceptionally lucky. The good news is that Rosalie is one of Cambridge's least expensive, etched colored wares, primarily available in pink and green. Conceivably, a small set of Willow Blue is possible; but Carmen, Bluebell, or Heatherbloom are colors that are too seldom seen to be organized into sets. Note how well the pattern shows on the blue pieces that have been highlighted with enamel. These were factory made; and for photography purposes, we wish all patterns were embellished that way.

The Ebony vase at right has Rosalie decoration on black with an additional gold decoration along the rim. Rosalie etching on black is infrequently found.

19

		Blue Pink Green	Amber Crystal
	Bottle, French dressing	210.00	125.00
	Bowl, bouillon, 2 hdld.	30.00	15.00
	Bowl, cream soup	30.00	20.00
1	Bowl, finger, w/liner	70.00	55.00
	Bowl, finger, ftd., w/liner	65.00	50.00
	Bowl, 3½", cranberry	45.00	30.00
	Bowl, 5½", fruit	22.00	15.00
	Bowl, 5½", 2 hdld., bonbon	25.00	15.00
	Bowl, 6¼", 2 hdld., bonbon	25.00	18.00
	Bowl, 7", basket, 2 hdld.	35.00	22.00
	Bowl, 8½", soup	55.00	30.00
	Bowl, 8½", 2 hdld.	75.00	35.00
	Bowl, 8½", w/cover, 3 pt.	150.00	75.00
16	Bowl, 10", rolled edge	75.00	40.00
	Bowl, 10", 2 hdld., #984	75.00	40.00
	Bowl, 11"	80.00	40.00
	Bowl, 11", basket, 2 hdld.	85.00	45.00
	Bowl, 11½"	90.00	55.00
	Bowl, 12", decagon	125.00	85.00

		Blue Pink Green	Amber Crystal
3	Bowl, 13", console	125.00	
	Bowl, 14", decagon, deep	245.00	195.00
	Bowl, 15", oval console	125.00	75.00
	Bowl, 15", oval, flanged	135.00	75.00
	Bowl, 15½", oval	140.00	85.00
18	Candle, 4", #627		30.00
2	Candlestick, 4", #627	35.00	25.00
	Candlestick, 5", keyhole	40.00	30.00
	Candlestick, 6", 3-lite keyhole	60.00	45.00
	Candy and cover, 6", #864	150.00	75.00
14	Candy and cover, 6", #104		130.00
	Celery, 11"	40.00	25.00
	Cheese & cracker, 11", plate	65.00	40.00
	Cigarette jar & cover	90.00	50.00
	Comport, 5½", 2 hdld.	30.00	15.00
	Comport, 5¾"	30.00	15.00
	Comport, 6", ftd., almond	45.00	30.00
	Comport, 6½", low ft.	45.00	30.00
	Comport, 6½", high ft.	45.00	30.00

		Blue Pink Green	Amber Crystal
	Comport, 6¾"	55.00	35.00
7	Creamer, ftd., #867	22.00	15.00
13	Creamer, #979	22.00	15.00
	Creamer, ftd., tall, ewer	65.00	35.00
	Cup	25.00	18.00
	Gravy, double, w/platter, #1147	175.00	100.00
	Ice bucket or pail	110.00	70.00
	Icer, w/liner	75.00	45.00
	Ice tub	110.00	70.00
	Mayonnaise, ftd., w/liner	65.00	35.00
	Nut, 2½", ftd.	65.00	50.00
	Pitcher, 62 oz., #955	295.00	195.00
	Plate, 6¾", bread/butter	8.00	6.00
	Plate, 7", 2 hdld.	15.00	10.00
15	Plate, 7½", salad, #1176	14.00	7.00
	Plate, 8⅜"	18.00	9.00
	Plate, 9½", dinner	60.00	40.00
	Plate, 11", 2 hdld.	45.00	25.00
	Platter, 12"	85.00	50.00
	Platter, 15"	135.00	80.00
	Relish, 9", 2 pt.	45.00	20.00
	Relish, 11", 2 pt.	50.00	30.00
	Salt dip, 1½", ftd.	55.00	30.00
	Saucer	5.00	3.00
4	Stem, 1 oz., cordial		35.00
	Stem, 1 oz., cordial, #3077	90.00	50.00
6	Stem, 3 oz., cocktail	14.00	
	Stem, 3 oz., cocktail, #7606	25.00	15.00

		Blue Pink Green	Amber Crystal
	Stem, 3½ oz., cocktail, #3077	20.00	14.00
11	Stem, 3½ oz., cocktail, #3115	25.00	
	Stem, 4½ oz., claret, #7606	33.00	22.00
	Stem, 6 oz., saucer/champagne, #7606	30.00	20.00
	Stem, 6 oz., low sherbet, #3077	16.00	12.00
5	Stem, 6 oz., high sherbet, #3077	18.00	14.00
	Stem, 9 oz., water goblet, #3077	28.00	20.00
12	Stem, 9 oz., water goblet, #3115	35.00	
	Stem, 10 oz., goblet, #801	33.00	19.00
	Stem, 10 oz., water goblet, #7606	38.00	28.00
8	Sugar, ftd., #867	22.00	13.00
	Sugar shaker	325.00	225.00
	Tray for sugar shaker/creamer	30.00	20.00
	Tray, ctr. hdld., for sugar/creamer	20.00	14.00
	Tray, 11", ctr. hdld.	38.00	28.00
17	Tumbler, 2½ oz., ftd., #3115	40.00	20.00
	Tumbler, 5 oz., ftd., #3077	28.00	18.00
	Tumbler, 8 oz., ftd., #3077	20.00	16.00
10	Tumbler, 8 oz., #3115	33.00	
	Tumbler, 10 oz., ftd., #3077	28.00	18.00
	Tumbler, 12 oz., ftd., #3077	35.00	22.00
9	Tumbler, 12 oz., tea	18.00	
	Vase, 5½", ftd.	85.00	50.00
	Vase, 6"	90.00	55.00
	Vase, 6½", ftd.	125.00	60.00
19	Vase, 12", w/rim (black), #402	195.00	
	Wafer tray	125.00	75.00

LIST OF ROSE POINT ITEMS

3500	10 oz. Goblet
3500	7 oz. Tall Sherbet
3500	7 oz. Low Sherbet
3500	3 oz. Cocktail
3500	2½ oz. Wine
3500	4½ oz. Claret
3500	4½ oz. Oyster Cocktail
3500	1 oz. Cordial
3500	5 oz Cafe Parfait
3500	12 oz. Ftd. Ice Tea
3500	10 oz. Ftd. Tumbler
3500	5 oz. Ftd. Tumbler
477	9½ in. Pickle
3400/1180	5¼ in. 2 Hdl. Bonbon
3400/1181	6 in. 2 Hdl. Plate
3400/90	6 in. 2 part Relish
3500/15	Ind. Sugar & Cream
3500/54	6 in. 2 Hdl. Ftd. Bonbon
3500/55	6 in. 2 Hdl. Ftd. Basket
3500/69	6½ in. 3 part ·Relish
3500/161	8 in. 2 Hdl. Ftd. Plate
3400/91	8 in. 3 part Relish
3500/57	8 in. 3 part Candy Box & Cover
3500/101	5⅜ in. Tall Comport
3900/17	Cup & Saucer
3900/19	2 pc. Mayonnaise Set
3900/20	6½ in. Bread & Butter Plate
3900/22	8 in. Salad Plate
3900/24	10½ in. Dinner Plate
3900/26	12 in. 4 Ftd. Plate
3900/28	11½ in. Ftd. Bowl
3900/33	13 in. 4 Ftd. Torte Plate, R. E.
3900/34	11 in. 2 Handled Bowl
3900/35	13½ in. 2 Handled Cake Plate
3900/40	Ind. Sugar & Cream
3900/41	Sugar & Cream
3900/54	10 in. 4 Ftd. Bowl, flared
3900/62	12 in. 4 Ftd. Bowl, flared
3900/65	12 in. 4 Ftd. Oval Bowl
3900/67	5 in. Candlestick
3900/72	6 in. 2 lite Candlestick
3900/74	6 in. 3 lite Candlestick
3900/100	6 oz. Oil, g. s.
3900/111	4 pc. Mayonnaise Set
3900/115	13 oz. Tumbler
3900/120	12 in. 5 part Celery & Relish
3900/123	7 in. Relish or Pickle
3900/124	7 in. 2 part Relish
3900/125	9 in. 3 part Celery & Relish
3900/126	12 in. 3 part Celery & Relish
3900/129	3 pc. Mayonnaise Set
3900/130	7 in. 2 handled Ftd. Bonbon
3900/131	8 in. 2 handled Ftd. Bonbon Plate
3900/136	5½ in. Comport
3900/165	Candy Box & Cover
3900/166	14 in. Plate, r. e.
3900/671	Ice Bucket
3900/671	Ice Bucket with chrome Handle Chrome Ice Tongs (long)
3900/1177	Salt & Pepper Shaker (doz. pr.)
274	10 in. Bud Flower Holder
278	11 in. Ftd. Flower Holder
279	13 in. Ftd. Flower Holder
968	2 pc. Cocktail Icer
1237	9 in. Ftd. Flower Holder
1238	12 in. Ftd. Flower Holder
1299	11 in. Ftd. Flower Holder
1309	5 in. Glode Flower Holder
1603	Hurricane Lamp (Etch. Chimney only)
1617	Hurricane Lamp (Etch. Chimney only)
6004	6 in. Ftd. Flower Holder
6004	8 in. Ftd. Flower Holder
P. 101	Cocktail Shaker (Patent—D133,198)

COLORS: CRYSTAL; SOME CRYSTAL WITH GOLD; EBONY, CARMEN, CROWN TUSCAN, AND AMBER, ALL WITH GOLD

Undeniably, Rose Point is the most stockpiled Cambridge pattern and most likely the most collected pattern in this book. Only Fostoria's American might come close to the collecting numbers of Rose Point; but American has a benefit of being produced for over 70 years.

There were so many mould lines used to etch Rose Point that individual collectors can choose what they prefer. As a result, not all are always searching for the same pieces. Take note of the two gold encrusted nude stem goblets pictured on page 194. These were the first Rose Point Statuesque table stems to be found gold decorated. Some collectors are becoming quite enthusiastic toward gold "encrusted" items of late.

Pages 191 and 192 show a Rose Point brochure with a listing where pieces are identified by number that should aid in distinguishing pieces. There are space limitations to how much catalog information we can do and still show you the actual glass. A challenge to new collectors is distinguishing the different mould blanks on which Rose Point is discovered. Be sure to examine the brochure to see the different line numbers of #3400, #3500, and #3900. These are the major mould lines upon which Rose Point was etched.

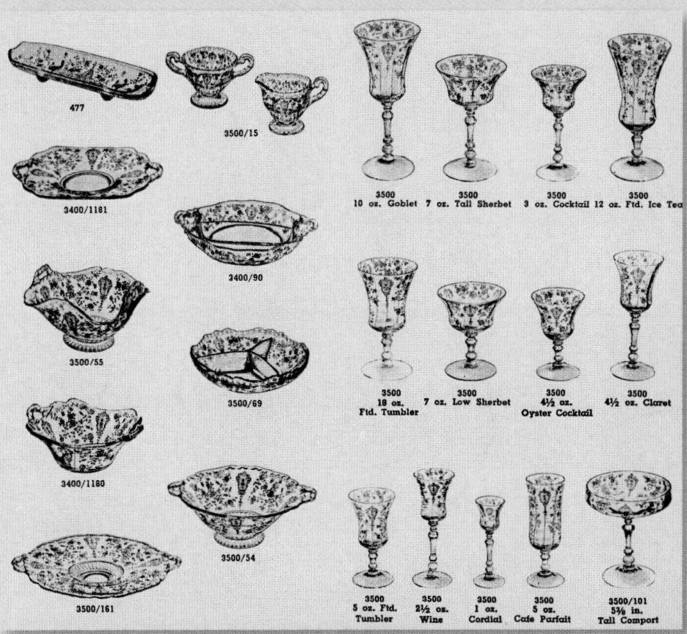

	Crystal
Ashtray, stack set on metal pole, #1715	265.00
Ashtray, 2½", sq., #721	30.00
Ashtray, 3¼", #3500/124	35.00
Ashtray, 3¼", sq., #3500/129	50.00
Ashtray, 3½", #3500/125	35.00
Ashtray, 4", #3500/126	40.00
Ashtray, 4", oval, #3500/130	75.00
Ashtray, 4¼", #3500/127	40.00
Ashtray, 4½", #3500/128	50.00
Ashtray, 4½", oval, #3500/131	60.00
Basket, 3", favor, #3500/79	475.00
Basket, 5", 1 hdld., #3500/51	375.00
Basket, 6", 1 hdld., #3500/52	395.00
Basket, 6", 2 hdld., #3400/1182	35.00
Basket, 6", sq., ftd., 2 hdld, #3500/55	42.00
Basket, 7", 1 hdld., #119	650.00
Basket, 7", wide, #3500/56	55.00
Basket, sugar, w/handle and tongs, #3500/13	350.00
Bell, dinner, #3121	135.00
Bowl, 3", 4 ftd., nut, #3400/71	60.00
Bowl, 3½", bonbon, cupped, deep, #3400/204	85.00
Bowl, 3½", cranberry, #3400/70	75.00
Bowl, 5", hdld., #3500/49	45.00
Bowl, 5", fruit, #3500/10	75.00

	Crystal
Bowl, 5", fruit, blown, #1534	85.00
Bowl, 5¼", fruit, #3400/56	75.00
Bowl, 5½", nappy, #3400/56	65.00
Bowl, 5½", 2 hdld., bonbon, #3400/1179	40.00
Bowl, 5½", 2 hdld., bonbon, #3400/1180	40.00
Bowl, 6", bonbon, crimped, #3400/203	75.00
Bowl, 6", bonbon, cupped, shallow, #3400/205	75.00
Bowl, 6", cereal, #3400/53	100.00
Bowl, 6", cereal, #3400/10	100.00
Bowl, 6", cereal, #3500/11	100.00
Bowl, 6", hdld., #3500/50	42.00
Bowl, 6", 2 hdld., #1402/89	42.00
Bowl, 6", 2 hdld., ftd., bonbon, #3500/54	38.00
Bowl, 6", 4 ftd., fancy rim, #3400/136	150.00
Bowl, 6½", bonbon, crimped, #3400/202	75.00

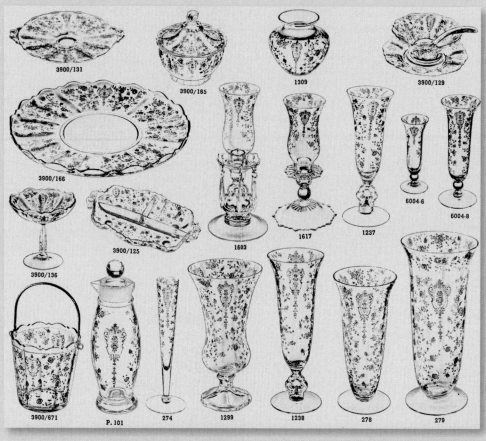

3900/131
3900/165
1309
3900/129
3900/166
3900/136
3900/125
1603
1617
1237
6004-6
6004-8
3900/671
P. 101
274
1299
1238
278
279

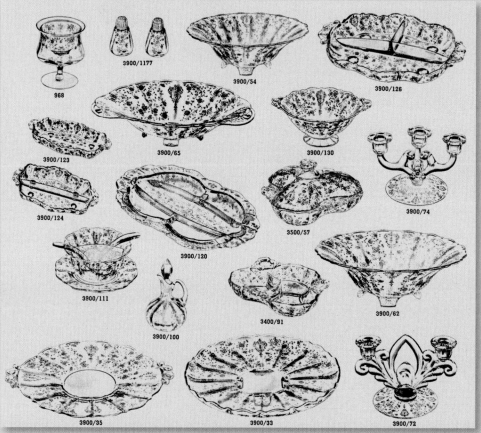

968
3900/1177
3900/54
3900/126
3900/123
3900/65
3900/130
3900/74
3900/124
3500/57
3900/120
3900/111
3900/100
3400/91
3900/62
3900/35
3900/33
3900/72

		Crystal
	Bowl, 7", bonbon, crimped, shallow, #3400/201	110.00
	Bowl, 7", tab hdld., ftd., bonbon, #3900/130	35.00
	Bowl, 8", ram's head, squared, #3500/27	495.00
	Bowl, 8½", rimmed soup, #361	250.00
	Bowl, 8½", 3 part, #221	225.00
	Bowl, 9", 4 ftd., #3400/135	250.00
	Bowl, 9", ram's head, #3500/25	495.00
	Bowl, 9½", pickle like corn, #477	45.00
	Bowl, 9½", ftd., w/hdl., #115	150.00
	Bowl, 9½", 2 hdld., #3400/34	75.00
	Bowl, 9½", 2 part, blown, #225	550.00
	Bowl, 2 hdld., #3400/1185	90.00
	Bowl, 10", 2 hdld., #3500/28	90.00
	Bowl, 10", 4 tab ftd., flared, #3900/54	75.00
	Bowl, 10", salad, Pristine, #427	195.00
	Bowl, 10½", crimp edge, #1351	100.00
	Bowl, 10½", flared, #3400/168	85.00
	Bowl, 10½", 3 part, #222	375.00
	Bowl, 10½", 3 part, #1401/122	375.00
	Bowl, 11", ftd., #3500/16	110.00
	Bowl, 11", ftd., fancy edge, #3500/19	175.00
	Bowl, 11", 4 ftd., oval, #3500/109	375.00
	Bowl, 11", 4 ftd., shallow, fancy edge, #3400/48	110.00
	Bowl, 11", fruit, #3400/1188	110.00
	Bowl, 11", low foot, #3400/3	165.00
	Bowl, 11", tab hdld., #3900/34	85.00
	Bowl, 11½", ftd., w/tab hdl., #3900/28	85.00
	Bowl, 12", crimped, pan, Pristine, #136	395.00
	Bowl, 12", 4 ftd., oval, #3400/1240	135.00
	Bowl, 12", 4 ftd., oval, w/"ears" hdl., #3900/65	100.00
	Bowl, 12", 4 ftd., fancy rim oblong, #3400/160	95.00
	Bowl, 12", 4 ftd., flared, #3400/4	90.00
	Bowl, 12", 4 tab ftd., flared, #3900/62	90.00
	Bowl, 12", ftd., #3500/17	135.00
	Bowl, 12", ftd., oblong, #3500/118	175.00
	Bowl, 12", ftd., oval w/hdld., #3500/21	225.00
	Bowl, 12½", flared, rolled edge, #3400/2	175.00
	Bowl, 12½", 4 ftd., #993	95.00
	Bowl, 13", #1398	150.00
	Bowl, 13", 4 ftd., narrow, crimped, #3400/47	145.00
	Bowl, 13", flared, #3400/1	90.00
	Bowl, 14", 4 ftd., crimp edge, oblong, #1247	150.00
	Bowl, 18", crimped, pan Pristine, #136	695.00
	Bowl, cream soup, w/liner, #3400	195.00
5	Bowl, cream soup, w/liner, #3500/2	195.00
	Bowl, finger, w/liner, #3106	100.00
	Bowl, finger, w/liner, #3121	100.00
3	Butter, w/cover, round, #506	195.00
	Butter, w/cover, 5", #3400/52	195.00
	Butter dish, ¼ lb., #3900/52	450.00
	Candelabrum, 2-lite w/bobeches & prisms, #1268	225.00
	Candelabrum, 2-lite, #3500/94	150.00
	Candelabrum, 3-lite, #1338	75.00
	Candelabrum, 5½", 3-lite w/#19 bobeche & #1 prisms, #1545	175.00

	Crystal
Candelabrum, 6½", 2-lite, w/bobeches & prisms Martha, #496	195.00
Candle, torchere, cup ft., #3500/90	275.00
Candle, torchere, flat ft., #3500/88	250.00
Candlestick, Pristine, #500	150.00
Candlestick, sq. base & lites, #1700/501	225.00
Candlestick, 2½", #3500/108	35.00
Candlestick, 3½", #628	40.00
Candlestick, 4", #627	65.00
Candlestick, 4", ram's head, #3500/74	125.00
Candlestick, 5", 1-lite keyhole, #3400/646	50.00
Candlestick, 5", inverts to comport, #3900/68	65.00
Candlestick, 5½", 2-lite Martha, #495	110.00
Candlestick, 6", #3500/31	135.00
Candlestick, 6", 2-lite keyhole, #3400/647	50.00
Candlestick, 6", 2-lite, #3900/72	55.00
Candlestick, 6", 3-lite, #3900/74	65.00
Candlestick, 6", 3-lite keyhole, #3400/638	65.00
Candlestick, 6", 3-tiered lite, #1338	75.00
Candlestick, 6½", Calla Lily, #499	135.00
Candlestick, 7", #3121	100.00
Candlestick, 7½", w/prism, Martha, #497	145.00
Candy box, w/cover, 5", apple shape, #316	1,250.00
Candy box, w/cover, 5⅜", #1066 stem	225.00
Candy box, w/cover, 5⅜", tall stem, #3121/3	185.00
Candy box, w/cover, 5⅜", short stem, #3121/4	175.00
Candy box, w/cover, blown, 5⅜", #3500/103	225.00
Candy box, w/cover, 6", ram's head, #3500/78	325.00
Candy box, w/rose finial, 6", 3 ftd., #300	325.00
Candy box, w/cover, 7", #3400/9	165.00
Candy box, w/cover, 7", rnd., 3 pt., #103	175.00
Candy box, w/cover, 8", 3 pt., #3500/57	110.00
Candy box, w/cover, rnd., #3900/165	140.00
Celery, 12", #3400/652	55.00
Celery, 12", #3500/652	55.00
Celery, 12", 5 pt., #3400/67	75.00
Celery, 14", 4 pt., 2 hdld., #3500/97	175.00
Celery & relish, 9", 3 pt., #3900/125	55.00
Celery & relish, 12", 3 pt., #3900/126	65.00
Celery & relish, 12", 5 pt., #3900/120	85.00
Cheese, 5", comport & cracker, 13", plate, #3900/135	135.00
Cheese, 5½", comport & cracker, 11½", plate, #3400/6	135.00
Cheese, 6", comport & cracker, 12", plate, #3500/162	155.00
Cheese dish, w/cover, 5", #980	595.00
Cigarette box, w/cover, #615	165.00
Cigarette box, w/cover, #747	175.00
Cigarette holder, oval, w/ashtray ft., #1066	175.00
Cigarette holder, rnd., w/ashtray ft., #1337	150.00
Coaster, 3½", #1628	50.00
Cocktail icer, 2 pc., #3600	70.00
Cocktail shaker, metal top, #3400/157	210.00
Cocktail shaker, metal top, #3400/175	200.00
Cocktail shaker, 12 oz., metal top, #97	400.00
Cocktail shaker, 32 oz., w/glass stopper, #101	295.00
Cocktail shaker, 46 oz., metal top, #98	225.00

ROSE POINT

	Crystal
Hurricane lamp, candlestick base, #1617	300.00
Hurricane lamp, keyhole base, w/prisms, #1603	300.00
Hurricane lamp, 8", etched chimney, #1601	300.00
Hurricane lamp, 10", etched chimney & base, #1604	400.00
Ice bucket, #1402/52	195.00
Ice bucket, w/chrome hdld., #3900/671	175.00
Ice bucket, P.672	175.00
Ice bucket, #3400 & #3900	175.00
Ice pail, P.1705	250.00
Ice pail, #3400/851	175.00
Ice tub, Pristine, P.671	295.00
Icer, cocktail, #968 or, #18	70.00
Marmalade, 8 oz., #147	195.00
Marmalade, w/cover, 7 oz., ftd., #157	215.00
Mayonnaise sherbet type w/ladle, #19	70.00
Mayonnaise, div., w/liner & 2 ladles, #3900/111	85.00
Mayonnaise, 3 pc., #3400/11	75.00
Mayonnaise, 3 pc., #3900/129	75.00
Mayonnaise, w/liner & ladle, #3500/59	75.00
Mustard, 3 oz., #151	185.00
Mustard, 4½ oz., ftd., #1329	400.00
Oil, 2 oz., ball, w/stopper, #3400/96	130.00
Oil, 6 oz., ball, w/stopper, #3400/99	185.00
Oil, 6 oz., hdld., #3400/193	125.00
Oil, 6 oz., loop hdld., w/stopper, #3900/100	165.00
Oil, 6 oz., w/stopper, ftd., hdld., #3400/161	275.00
Pickle, 9", #3400/59	65.00
Pickle or relish, 7", #3900/123	40.00
Pitcher, 20 oz., #3900/117	395.00
Pitcher, 20 oz., w/ice lip, #70	395.00
Pitcher, 32 oz., #3900/118	400.00
Pitcher, 32 oz., martini slender, w/metal insert, #3900/114	579.00
Pitcher, 60 oz., martini, #1408	1,995.00
Pitcher, 76 oz., #3900/115	325.00
Pitcher, 76 oz., ice lip, #3400/100	225.00
Pitcher, 76 oz., ice lip, #3400/152	400.00
Pitcher, 80 oz., ball, #3400/38	250.00
Pitcher, 80 oz., ball, #3900/116	250.00
Pitcher, 80 oz., Doulton, #3400/141	345.00
Pitcher, nite set, 2 pc., w/tumbler insert top, #103	995.00
Plate, 6", bread/butter, #3400/60	12.00
Plate, 6", bread/butter, #3500/3	12.00
Plate, 6", 2 hdld., #3400/1181	18.00
Plate, 6⅛", canape, #693	195.00
Plate, 6½", bread/butter, #3900/20	12.00
Plate, 7½", #3500/4	15.00
Plate, 7½", salad, #3400/176	15.00
Plate, 8", salad, #3900/22	18.00
Plate, 8", 2 hdld., ftd., #3500/161	45.00
Plate, 8", tab hdld., ftd., bonbon, #3900/131	42.00
Plate, 8½", breakfast, #3400/62	20.00
Plate, 8½", salad, #3500/5	18.00
Plate, 9½", crescent salad, #485	225.00
Plate, 9½", luncheon, #3400/63	30.00

	Crystal
Cocktail shaker, 48 oz., glass stopper, #102	225.00
Comport, 5", #3900/135	40.00
Comport, 5", 4 ftd., #3400/74	55.00
Comport, 5½", scalloped edge, #3900/136	65.00
Comport, 5⅜", blown, #3500/101	75.00
Comport, 5⅜", blown, #3121 stem	80.00
Comport, 5⅜", blown, #1066 stem	75.00
Comport, 6", #3500/36	140.00
Comport, 6", #3500/111	175.00
Comport, 6", 4 ftd., #3400/13	55.00
Comport, 7", 2 hdld., #3500/37	150.00
Comport, 7", keyhole, #3400/29	145.00
Comport, 7", keyhole, low, #3400/28	100.00
Creamer, #3400/68	22.00
Creamer, #3500/14	25.00
Creamer, flat, #137	135.00
Creamer, flat, #944	150.00
Creamer, ftd., #3400/16	90.00
Creamer, ftd., #3900/41	22.00
Creamer, indiv., #3500/15, pie crust edge	25.00
Creamer, indiv., #3900/40, scalloped edge	22.00
Cup, 3 styles, #3400/54, #3500/1, #3900/17	28.00
Cup, 5 oz., punch, #488	40.00
Cup, after dinner, #3400/69	300.00
Decanter, 12 oz., ball, w/stopper, #3400/119	395.00
Decanter, 14 oz., ftd., #1320	500.00
Decanter, 26 oz., sq., #1380	695.00
Decanter, 28 oz., tall, #1372	795.00
Decanter, 28 oz., w/stopper, #1321	425.00
Decanter, 32 oz., ball, w/stopper, #3400/92	495.00
Dressing bottle, flat, #1263	425.00
Dressing bottle, ftd., #1261	395.00
Epergne candle w/vases, #3900/75	395.00
Grapefruit, w/liner, #187	125.00
Hat, 5", #1704	500.00
Hat, 6", #1703	535.00
Hat, 8", #1702	695.00
Hat, 9", #1701	900.00
Honey dish, w/cover, #3500/139	395.00
Hot plate or trivet	110.00
Hurricane lamp, w/prisms, #1613	400.00

		Crystal
	Plate, 10½", dinner, #3400/64	150.00
	Plate, 10½", dinner, #3900/24	150.00
	Plate, 11", 2 hdld., #3400/35	60.00
	Plate, 12", 4 ftd., service, #3900/26	65.00
	Plate, 12", ftd., #3500/39	85.00
	Plate, 12½", 2 hdld., #3400/1186	65.00
	Plate, 13", rolled edge, ftd., #3900/33	65.00
	Plate, 13", 4 ftd., torte, #3500/110	125.00
	Plate, 13", ftd., cake, Martha, #170	225.00
	Plate, 13", torte, #3500/38	175.00
	Plate, 13½", #242	150.00
	Plate, 13½", rolled edge, #1397	70.00
	Plate, 13½", tab hdld., cake, #3900/35	75.00
	Plate, 14", rolled edge, #3900/166	80.00
	Plate, 14", service, #3900/167	80.00
	Plate, 14", torte, #3400/65	145.00
	Plate, 18", punch bowl liner, Martha, #129	695.00
	Punch bowl, 15", Martha, #478	4,500.00
	Punch set, 15-pc., Martha	6,000.00
	Relish, 5½", 2 pt., #3500/68	28.00
	Relish, 5½", 2 pt., hdld., #3500/60	38.00
	Relish, 6", 2 pt., #3400/90	38.00
	Relish, 6", 2 pt., 1 hdl., #3400/1093	90.00
	Relish, 6½", 3 pt., #3500/69	60.00
	Relish, 6½", 3 pt., hdld., #3500/61	65.00
	Relish, 7", 2 pt., #3900/124	40.00
	Relish, 7½", 3 pt., center hdld., #3500/71	135.00
	Relish, 7½", 4 pt., #3500/70	60.00
	Relish, 7½", 4 pt., 2 hdld., #3500/62	80.00
	Relish, 8", 3 pt., 3 hdld., #3400/91	35.00
	Relish, 10", 2 hdld., #3500/85	90.00
	Relish, 10", 3 pt., 2 hdld., #3500/86	80.00
	Relish, 10", 3 pt., 4 ftd., 2 hdld., #3500/64	65.00
	Relish, 10", 4 pt., 4 ftd., #3500/65	85.00
	Relish, 10", 4 pt., 2 hdld., #3500/87	85.00
	Relish, 11", 2 pt., 2 hdld., #3400/89	90.00
	Relish, 11", 3 pt., #3400/200	65.00
	Relish, 12", 5 pt., #3400/67	80.00
	Relish, 12", 5 pt., Pristine, #419	295.00
	Relish, 12", 6 pc., #3500/67	250.00
	Relish, 14", w/cover, 4 pt., 2 hdld., #3500/142	1,200.00
	Relish, 15", 4 pt., hdld., #3500/113	225.00
	Salt & pepper, egg shape, pr., #1468	125.00
	Salt & pepper, individual, rnd., glass base, pr., #1470	125.00
	Salt & pepper, individual, w/chrome tops, pr., #360	75.00
	Salt & pepper, lg., rnd., glass base, pr., #1471	135.00
	Salt & pepper, w/chrome tops, pr., ftd. #3400/77	55.00
	Salt & pepper w/chrome tops, pr., flat, #3900/1177	55.00
	Sandwich tray, 11", center handled, #3400/10	145.00
	Saucer, after dinner, #3400/69	60.00
	Saucer, 3 styles, #3400, #3500, #3900	6.00
1	Statusque, cocktail	3,000.00
2	Statusque, banquet goblet	4,000.00
	Stem, #3104, 3½ oz., cocktail	325.00
	Stem, #3106, ¾ oz., brandy	125.00

	Crystal
Stem, #3106, 1 oz., cordial	125.00
Stem, #3106, 1 oz., pousse cafe	125.00
Stem, #3106, 2 oz., sherry	55.00
Stem, #3106, 2½ oz., wine	55.00
Stem, #3106, 3 oz., cocktail	30.00
Stem, #3106, 4½ oz., claret	50.00
Stem, #3106, 5 oz., oyster cocktail	28.00
Stem, #3106, 7 oz., high sherbet	28.00
Stem, #3106, 7 oz., low sherbet	20.00
Stem, #3106, 10 oz., water goblet	38.00
Stem, #3121, 1 oz., brandy	125.00
Stem, #3121, 1 oz., cordial	65.00
Stem, #3121, 3 oz., cocktail	25.00
Stem, #3121, 3½ oz., wine	50.00
Stem, #3121, 4½ oz., claret	70.00
Stem, #3121, 4½ oz., low oyster cocktail	28.00
Stem, #3121, 5 oz., low ft. parfait	80.00
Stem, #3121, 6 oz., low sherbet	16.00
Stem, #3121, 6 oz., tall sherbet	19.00
Stem, #3121, 10 oz., water	32.00
Stem, #3500, 1 oz., cordial	65.00
Stem, #3500, 2½ oz., wine	55.00
Stem, #3500, 3 oz., cocktail	30.00
Stem, #3500, 4½ oz., claret	80.00
Stem, #3500, 4½ oz., low oyster cocktail	28.00
Stem, #3500, 5 oz., low ft. parfait	85.00
Stem, #3500, 7 oz., low ft. sherbet	16.00
Stem, #3500, 7 oz., tall sherbet	22.00
Stem, #3500, 10 oz., water	35.00
Stem, #7801, 4 oz., cocktail, plain stem	35.00
Stem, #7966, 1 oz., cordial, plain ft.	135.00
Stem, #7966, 2 oz., sherry, plain ft.	110.00
Sugar, #3400/68	20.00
Sugar, #3500/14	22.00
Sugar, flat, #137	135.00
Sugar, flat, #944	150.00
Sugar, ftd., #3400/16	90.00
Sugar, ftd., #3900/41	22.00
Sugar, indiv., #3500/15, pie crust edge	25.00
Sugar, indiv., #3900/40, scalloped edge	20.00
Syrup, w/drip stop top, #1670	395.00
Tray, 6", 2 hdld., sq., #3500/91	175.00
Tray, 12", 2 hdld., oval, service, #3500/99	250.00
Tray, 12", rnd., #3500/67	195.00
Tray, 13", 2 hdld., rnd., #3500/72	195.00
Tray, sugar/creamer, #3900/37	25.00
Tumbler, #498, 2 oz., straight side	120.00
Tumbler, #498, 5 oz., straight side	42.00
Tumbler, #498, 8 oz., straight side	42.00
Tumbler, #498, 10 oz., straight side	42.00
Tumbler, #498, 12 oz., straight side	75.00
Tumbler, #3000, 3½ oz., cone, ftd.	100.00
Tumbler, #3000, 5 oz., cone, ftd.	110.00
Tumbler, #3106, 3 oz., ftd.	35.00
Tumbler, #3106, 5 oz., ftd.	32.00

	Crystal
Tumbler, #3106, 9 oz., ftd.	35.00
Tumbler, #3106, 12 oz., ftd.	38.00
Tumbler, #3121, 2½ oz., ftd.	65.00
Tumbler, #3121, 5 oz., low ft., juice	35.00
Tumbler, #3121, 10 oz., low ft., water	30.00
Tumbler, #3121, 12 oz., low ft., ice tea	38.00
Tumbler, #3400/1341, 1 oz., cordial	100.00
Tumbler, #3400/92, 2½ oz.	100.00
Tumbler, #3400/38, 5 oz.	100.00
Tumbler, #3400/38, 12 oz.	60.00
Tumbler, #3900/115, 13 oz.	65.00
Tumbler, #3500, 2½ oz., ftd.	65.00
Tumbler, #3500, 5 oz., low ft., juice	35.00
Tumbler, #3500, 10 oz., low ft., water	28.00
Tumbler, #3500, 13 oz., low ftd.	35.00
Tumbler, #3500, 12 oz., tall ft., ice tea	35.00
Tumbler, #7801, 5 oz., ftd.	40.00
Tumbler, #7801, 12 oz., ftd., ice tea	65.00
Tumbler, #3900/117, 5 oz.	65.00
Tumbler, #3400/115, 13 oz.	50.00
Urn, 10", w/cover, #3500/41	695.00
Urn, 12", w/cover, #3500/42	795.00
Vase, 5", #1309	100.00
Vase, 5", globe, #3400/102	90.00
Vase, 5", ftd., #6004	65.00
Vase, 6", high ftd., flower, #6004	65.00
Vase, 6", #572	180.00

		Crystal
4	Vase, 6½", globe, #3400/103	100.00
	Vase, 7", ivy, ftd., ball, #1066	325.00
	Vase, 8", #1430	295.00
	Vase, 8", flat, flared, #797	210.00
	Vase, 8", ftd., #3500/44	195.00
	Vase, 8", high ftd., flower, #6004	75.00
	Vase, 9", ftd., keyhole, #1237	110.00
	Vase, 9", ftd., #1620	195.00
	Vase, 9½" ftd., keyhole, #1233	125.00
	Vase, 10", ball bottom, #400	265.00
	Vase, 10", bud, #1528	135.00
	Vase, 10", cornucopia, #3900/575	265.00
	Vase, 10", flat, #1242	185.00
	Vase, 10", ftd., #1301	120.00
	Vase, 10", ftd., #6004	125.00
	Vase, 10", ftd., #3500/45	225.00
	Vase, 10", slender, #274	65.00
	Vase, 11", ftd., flower, #278	165.00
	Vase, 11", ped. ftd., flower, #1299	225.00
	Vase, 12", ftd., #6004	135.00
	Vase, 12", ftd., keyhole, #1234	185.00
	Vase, 12", ftd., keyhole, #1238	195.00
	Vase, 13", ftd., flower, #279	295.00
	Vase 18", #1336	2,750.00
	Vase, sweet pea, #629	395.00

5   5

3

COLORS: AMBER, EBONY, BLUE, GREEN

Fostoria's Royal is occasionally identified as Vesper, since both etchings are similar, are found on the #2350 blank, and were distributed in the same colors. Royal does not entice as many collectors as Vesper, possibly due to an inadequate distribution. Inexperienced collectors should find Royal's cost more to their liking since there is less demand. Remember that demand inflates prices more than scarcity.

Enough amber or green can be gathered to acquire a set; but only a very small number of pieces can be found in blue or black. Fostoria's blue color found with the Royal etching was called Blue as opposed to the Azure blue which is a lighter hue found etched with June or other patterns. It has taken us 25 years to gather the Blue shown on page 198.

We have found a few unusual pieces in green, which are identified in the legend. We hope you appreciate everyone's efforts to enhance this book by labeling every piece. It was time-consuming, tedious work and added nearly a month to the production; readers have been pleading for this.

Uncommon and hard to find pieces of Royal include both styles of pitchers, covered cheese and butter dishes, cologne bottles, and sugar lids. The cologne bottle is a combination powder jar and cologne. The stopper is the hardest part of the three-piece set to find. It has a pointed end and is often absent.

Published material indicates production of Royal continued until 1934, although the January 1, 1933, Fostoria catalog no longer listed Royal as being for sale. We have changed our cutoff date of production to 1932. If you can locate a May 1928 copy of *House and Garden*, there is a pleasant Fostoria Royal advertisement displayed.

		*Amber Green				*Amber Green
14	Almond, #4095	28.00		Bowl, #2350, 9", oval, baker		40.00
	Ashtray, #2350, 3½"	20.00	24	Bowl, #2324, 10", ftd.		45.00
	Bowl, #2350, bouillon, flat	15.00		Bowl, #2350, 10", salad		35.00
	Bowl, #2350½, bouillon, ftd.	18.00		Bowl, #2350, 10½", oval, baker		50.00
	Bowl, #2350, cream soup, flat	18.00		Bowl, #2315, 10½", ftd.		45.00
11	Bowl, #2350½, cream soup, ftd.	20.00		Bowl, #2329, 11", console		22.00
10	Bowl, #869, 4½", finger	22.00		Bowl, #2297, 12", deep		22.00
13	Bowl, #2350, 5½", fruit	14.00		Bowl, #2329, 13", console		30.00
	Bowl, #2350, 6½", cereal	25.00		Bowl, #2324, 13", ftd.		50.00
	Bowl, #2267, 7", ftd.	30.00		Bowl, #2371, 13", oval, w/flower frog		150.00
	Bowl, #2350, 7¾", soup	30.00		Butter, w/cover, #2350		295.00
	Bowl, #2350, 8", nappy	30.00		Candlestick, #2324, 4"		20.00
	Bowl, #2350, 9", nappy	32.00		Candlestick, #2324, 9"		65.00

* Add up to 50% more for blue or black.

		*Amber Green
	Candy, w/cover, #2331, 3 part	85.00
	Candy, w/cover, ftd., ½ lb.	150.00
	Celery, #2350, 11"	25.00
	Cheese, w/cover/plate, #2276 (plate 11")	175.00
	Cologne, #2322, tall	135.00
	Cologne, #2323, short	110.00
	Cologne/powder jar combination	295.00
	Comport, #1861½, 6", jelly	22.00
	Comport, #2327, 7"	25.00
	Comport, #2358, 8" wide	28.00
16	Creamer, flat	15.00
	Creamer, #2315½, ftd., fat	15.00
17	Creamer, #2350½, ftd.	12.00
4	Cup, #2350, flat	9.00
20	Cup, #2350½, ftd.	10.00
	Cup, #2350, demi	20.00
	Egg cup, #2350	30.00
	Grapefruit, w/insert	75.00
15	Grapefruit, #2315	30.00
12	Grapefruit, #2350	40.00
	Ice bucket, #2378	65.00
	Mayonnaise, #2315	25.00
	Pickle, 8", #2350	20.00
	Pitcher, #1236	350.00
	Pitcher, #5000, 48 oz.	295.00
	Plate, 8½", deep soup/underplate	32.00
9	Plate, #2350, 6", bread/butter	3.00
	Plate, #2350, 7½", salad	4.00
18	Plate, #2350, 8½", luncheon	8.00
21	Plate, #2321, 8¾", Maj Jongg (canape)	30.00
	Plate, #2350, 9½", small dinner	12.00
	Plate, #2350, 10½", dinner	25.00

		*Amber Green
3	Plate, #2350, 13", chop	30.00
	Plate, #2350, 15", chop	40.00
	Platter, #2350, 10½"	25.00
	Platter, #2350, 12"	35.00
	Platter, #2350, 15½"	75.00
	Salt and pepper, #5100, pr.	65.00
	Sauce boat, w/liner	125.00
5	Saucer, #2350/#2350½	3.00
	Saucer, #2350, demi	7.00
	Server, #2287, 11", center hdld.	25.00
	Stem, #869, ¾ oz., cordial	60.00
	Stem, #869, 2¾ oz., wine	25.00
	Stem, #869, 3 oz., cocktail	15.00
25	Stem, #869, 5½ oz., oyster cocktail	15.00
1	Stem, #869, 5½ oz., parfait	25.00
6	Stem, #869, 6 oz., low sherbet	10.00
8	Stem, #869, 6 oz., high sherbet	12.00
22	Stem, #869, 9 oz., water	25.00
	Sugar, flat, w/lid	175.00
	Sugar, #2315, ftd., fat	15.00
19	Sugar, #2350½, ftd.	12.00
	Sugar lid, #2350½	135.00
	Tumbler, #869, 5 oz., flat	18.00
	Tumbler, #859, 9 oz., flat	20.00
7	Tumbler, #859, 12 oz., flat	25.00
2	Tumbler, #5000, 2½ oz., ftd.	30.00
	Tumbler, #5000, 5 oz., ftd.	10.00
23	Tumbler, #5000, 9 oz., ftd.	12.00
	Tumbler, #5000, 12 oz., ftd.	20.00
	Vase, #2324, urn, ftd.	100.00
	Vase, #2292, flared	110.00

COLORS: SMOKEY TOPAZ, JUNGLE GREEN, FRENCH CRYSTAL, SILVER GRAY, LILAC, SUNSHINE, JADE; SOME MILK GLASS, APPLE GREEN, BLACK, FRENCH OPALESCENT

Ruba Rombic has seen a few price corrections, and surprisingly not as much on the downhill side as has happened to some patterns. Mostly prices have remained uniform, but Ruba Rombic items are way beyond the expenditure limits set by most collectors of glass. There are some who feel this is the most wonderful pattern in the book, while others ridicule anyone who thinks it is. If you see a piece, inexpensively priced, buy it in spite of your feelings. Someone will find it irresistible.

The color most prominent in the photo is Smokey Topaz, priced below with the Jungle Green. Both of these colors are transparent as opposed to the other colors that are cased (layered). Smokey Topaz will be the color you are most likely to find if you are lucky enough to spot a piece. Not long ago, we spotted a Smokey Topaz decanter. Both top and bottom were badly damaged and the inside was cloudy to the point of looking frosted. While turning it around to see the price, we were told that we could buy it for only $1,500.00 since it was worth $1,800.00. Damaged glassware has value if rare, but not close to mint price under any circumstances.

1

The cased color column below includes three colors. They are Lilac (lavender), Sunshine (yellow), and Jade (green). French crystal is a white, applied color except that the raised edges are crystal with no white coloring at all. Silver is sometimes called Gray Silver.

Once a piece of glass reaches four digit prices, there are a limited number of collectors willing, or able to pay that price. Once five digit prices are attained, there are only a handful who can afford it, and then you have to find one of those who wants it that badly. You can buy a good used car or a new import in that range.

Ruba Rombic has always sold in a specialized market that eluded most dealers who did not have a special outlet. The Internet is changing that.

The frosted powder jar shown is often thought to be, but is only a Ruba Rhombic look-alike (10).

		Smokey Topaz Jungle Green	Cased Color	French Opal French Crystal Silver
	Ashtray, 3½"	600.00	750.00	850.00
	Bonbon, flat, 3 part	250.00	350.00	400.00
2	Bottle, decanter, 9"	1,800.00	2,200.00	2,500.00
	Bottle, perfume, 4¾"	1,800.00	1,500.00	1,950.00
	Bottle, toilet, 7½"	1,200.00	1,500.00	1,800.00
	Bowl, 3", almond	275.00	300.00	375.00
9	Bowl, 8", cupped	975.00	1,200.00	1,300.00
8	Bowl, 9", flared	950.00	1,200.00	1,300.00
5	Bowl, 12", oval	1,500.00	1,800.00	1,800.00
	Bowl, bouillon	175.00	250.00	275.00
4	Bowl, finger	110.00	135.00	145.00
	Box, cigarette, 3½" x 4¼"	850.00	1,250.00	1,500.00
	Box, powder, 5", round	850.00	1,250.00	1,500.00
	Candlestick, 2½" high, pr.	500.00	650.00	750.00
	Celery, 10", 3 part	850.00	950.00	1,000.00
	Comport, 7", wide	850.00	950.00	1,000.00
3	Creamer	200.00	250.00	300.00
	Light, ceiling fixture, 10"		1,500.00	1,500.00
	Light, ceiling fixture, 16"		2,500.00	2,500.00
	Light, table light		1,200.00	1,200.00

		Smokey Topaz Jungle Green	Cased Color	French Opal French Crystal Silver
	Light, wall sconce		1,500.00	1,500.00
	Pitcher, 8¼"	2,500.00	3,000.00	4,000.00
	Plate, 7"	75.00	100.00	150.00
	Plate, 8"	75.00	100.00	150.00
	Plate, 10"	250.00	275.00	300.00
	Plate, 15"	1,275.00	1,500.00	1,500.00
	Relish, 2 part	350.00	450.00	500.00
	Sugar	200.00	250.00	300.00
	Sundae	100.00	135.00	150.00
	Tray for decanter set	2,000.00	2,250.00	2,500.00
1	Tumbler, 2 oz., flat, 2¾"	120.00	140.00	160.00
	Tumbler, 3 oz., ftd.	130.00	155.00	175.00
	Tumbler, 9 oz., flat	130.00	175.00	200.00
	Tumbler, 10 oz., ftd.	170.00	300.00	350.00
	Tumbler, 12 oz., flat	195.00	300.00	350.00
	Tumbler, 15 oz., ftd., 7"	350.00	450.00	500.00
7	Vase, 6"	850.00	1,000.00	1,500.00
6	Vase, 9½"	1,500.00	2,500.00	3,000.00
	Vase, 16"	10,000.00	12,000.00	12,000.00

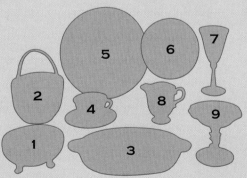

COLORS: EBONY, RITZ BLUE

Sparta is Morgantown Decoration #769 that appeared in gold or platinum on several of their line blanks. Golf Ball, #7643, is the most known decorated line. In that line we can account for a water goblet; sherbet, wine, and a footed water tumbler with Sparta etch on Ritz blue. If there are any commonly found pieces in this pattern, it would be the Lynward decanter pictured. It will not be found priced inexpensively; but we have seen at least three over the years. Barware collectors are latching onto these as well as Morgantown admirers. That cross collecting keeps the supply well in check so that demand is always ahead and the price keeps rising.

The Majesty candleholder is often confused with a sherbet. These were offered with a 13" console bowl, but the unusual thing was that the bowl came with two pairs of candles as opposed to the normally offered single pair.

		All Colors
	Bowl, #4355 Janice, 13", console	195.00
4	Candle, #7662 Majesty, 4"	150.00
2	Decanter, 10½", Lynward	295.00
3	Plate, 8"	40.00
	Stem, #7643, 4⅛", 3½ oz., sherbet	75.00
	Stem, #7643, 4¾", 3 oz., wine	110.00
	Stem, #7643, 5", 5½ oz., champagne	85.00
	Stem, #7643, 6¾", 9 oz., water	125.00
5	Tumbler, #7643, 6⅛", 9 oz., water	100.00
1	Tumbler, #9051, 1½ oz., bar	75.00
	Tumbler, #8701 Garrett, 9 oz.	100.00
	Vase, #67 Grecian, 6"	175.00

COLORS: CRYSTAL, SOME BLOWN STEMWARE IN ZIRCON

Heisey's Stanhope is a Deco pattern that more than Heisey collectors are pursuing. Deco admirers have a high esteem for the red or black "T" knobs, which were incorporated into all the open round handles of Stanhope. "T" knobs, in the price listings, are insert handles (black or red, round, wooden knobs) which are like wooden dowel rods that act as horizontal handles. The insert handles are whimsical to some; but others think them magnificent and will not purchase a piece needing them. Although items are listed with or without the knobs, you can expect items to fetch a minimum of 20% to 25% less when they are missing. We had a challenging time of marketing that rarely seen candy in the photo below since it was missing the insert on the top. If you ever see these inserts offered for sale, buy them even if you do not own any Stanhope, someone will want them.

Notice that prices have held their own except for the omnipresent stemware. Some people mistake the 11" salad bowl shown at the bottom of page 211 for a punch bowl; it would not hold much punch, but enough salad for a small family.

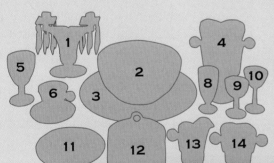

		Crystal
	Ashtray, indiv.	65.00
19	Bottle, oil, 3 oz., w or w/o rd. knob	325.00
	Bowl, 6", mint, 2 hdld., w or w/o rd. knobs	35.00
	Bowl, 6", mint, 2 pt., 2 hdld., w or w/o rd. knobs	35.00
2	Bowl, 11", salad	90.00
15	Bowl, 11", floral, 2 hdld.	75.00
	Bowl, finger, #4080 (blown, plain)	10.00
	Bowl, floral, 11", 2 hdld., w or w/o "T" knobs	80.00
1	Candelabra, 2-lite, w bobeche & prisms	225.00
12	Candy box & lid, rnd., w or w/o rd. knob	180.00
	Cigarette box & lid, w or w/o rd. knob	95.00
13	Creamer, 2 hdld., w or w/o rd. knobs	45.00
6	Cup, w or w/o rd. knob.	25.00
17	Ice tub, 2 hdld., w or w/o "T" knobs	70.00
	Jelly, 6", 1 hdld., w or w/o rd. knobs	30.00
7	Jelly, 6", 3 pt., 1 hdld., w or w/o rd. knobs	30.00
20	Mayonnaise, 2 hdld.	35.00
	Nappy, 4½", 1 hdld., w or w/o rd. knob	30.00

		Crystal
	Nut, indiv., 1 hdld., w or w/o rd. knob	60.00
11	Plate, 7"	25.00
16	Plate, 12", torte, 2 hdld., w or w/o "T" knobs	45.00
3	Plate, 15", torte, rnd. or salad liner	65.00
21	Relish, 11", triplex buffet, 2 hdld., w or w/o "T" knobs	45.00
	Relish, 12", 4 pt., 2 hdld., w or w/o "T" knobs	55.00
	Relish, 12", 5 pt., 2 hdld., w or w/o "T" knobs	55.00
	Salt & pepper, #60 top	140.00
6	Saucer	10.00
	Stem, 1 oz., cordial, #4083 (blown)	70.00
	Stem, 2½ oz., pressed wine	35.00
9	Stem, 2½ oz., wine, #4083	25.00
10	Stem, 3½ oz., cocktail, #4083	20.00
	Stem, 3½ oz., pressed cocktail	25.00
	Stem, 4 oz., claret, #4083	25.00
	Stem, 4 oz., oyster cocktail, #4083	10.00
	Stem, 5½ oz., pressed saucer champagne	20.00
	Stem, 5½ oz., saucer champagne, #4083	15.00
	Stem, 9 oz., pressed goblet	45.00
5	Stem, 10 oz., goblet, #4083	*22.50
	Stem, 12 oz., pressed soda	45.00
14	Sugar, 2 hdld., w or w/o rd. knobs	45.00
	Tray, 12" celery, 2 hdld., w or w/o "T" knobs	55.00
8	Tumbler, 5 oz., soda, #4083	20.00
	Tumbler, 8 oz., soda, #4083	22.50
18	Tumbler, 12 oz., soda, #4083	**25.00
	Vase, 7", ball	100.00
4	Vase, 9", 2 hdld., w or w/o "T" knobs	125.00

*Limelight – 125.00
**Limelight – 95.00

COLOR: CRYSTAL

This early Heisey pattern was produced in crystal only. You might find a piece or two with gold accoutrements, but usually that is well worn to the point of being distracting. Sunburst items may have a variant in the pattern consisting of punties (thumbprints) around the item just above the sunburst. This is not considered a separate pattern although some collectors might argue that point.

	Bottle, molasses, 13 oz.	175.00
	Bottle, oil, 2 oz.	85.00
	Bottle, oil, 4 oz.	85.00
	Bottle, oil, 6 oz.	85.00
2	Bottle, water	90.00
	Bridge set: approx. 5" each	
	Club	65.00
	Diamond	75.00
	Heart	75.00
	Spade	65.00
	Bowl, 4", round, scalloped top	22.00
18	Bowl, 4½", round, scalloped top	22.00
6	Bowl, 5", round, scalloped top, flared	25.00
15	Bowl, 5", finger	25.00
	Bowl, 5", hdld.	25.00
	Bowl, 5", three corner, hdld.	30.00
	Bowl, 6", round	30.00
	Bowl, 7", round	35.00
9	Bowl, 7", oblong	35.00

	Bowl, 8", round	40.00
	Bowl, 8", round, ftd.	40.00
	Bowl, 9", round	40.00
	Bowl, 9", round, ftd.	65.00
	Bowl, 9", oblong	45.00
	Bowl, 10", round	50.00
	Bowl, 10", round, ftd.	85.00
	Bowl, 10", oblong	45.00
13	Bowl, 10", round punch, pegged bottom & stand	400.00
	Bowl, 12", round, punch & stand	225.00
	Bowl, 12", oblong	55.00
	Bowl, 14", round, punch & stand	250.00
	Bowl, 15", round, punch & stand	275.00
8	Butter and domed cover	125.00
	Cake plate, 9", ftd.	165.00
	Cake plate, 10, ftd.	165.00
	Celery tray, 12"	65.00
	Comport, 5", ftd.	45.00
1	Comport, 6", ftd.	45.00

	Creamer, lg.	45.00
	Creamer, hotel	40.00
	Creamer, individual	45.00
14	Cup, punch, two styles	20.00
11	Egg cup, ftd.	65.00
4	Goblet, water	150.00
	Mayonnaise and underplate	55.00
16	Pickle jar and stopper	145.00
	Pickle tray, 6"	35.00
	Pitcher, 1 qt., upright	145.00
	Pitcher, 1 qt., bulbous	145.00
	Pitcher, 3 pt., upright	150.00
	Pitcher, 3 pt., bulbous	150.00
	Pitcher, ½ gal., upright	175.00
	Pitcher, ½ gal., straight sided	175.00

12	Pitcher, ½ gal., bulbous	185.00
	Pitcher, 3 qt., upright	225.00
	Plate, torte, 13"	35.00
	Pitcher, 3 qt., bulbous	235.00
10	Plate, 9", oval underliner	30.00
3	Rose bowl, 3", footed	225.00
	Salt & pepper, 3 styles	125.00
	Spooner	100.00
	Sugar, lg.	45.00
	Sugar, hotel	40.00
	Sugar, individual	45.00
7	Toothpick holder	135.00
17	Tumbler, 2 styles	40.00
5	Vase, orchid, 6"	125.00

COLORS: CRYSTAL, RED, BLUE, GREEN, YELLOW

Added listings of Fostoria's Sunray have been integrated. Pricing is still thorny due to the inconsistency we are seeing. Be sure to see Glacier (page 109) which consists of frosted panels added to Sunray. Some Sunray enthusiasts are willing to mix the two, but most gather one or the other. Both patterns sell in the same price range, although Glacier's supply is more limited.

We price only crystal; but be aware of pieces that are found in red, blue, green, and yellow. We rarely see colored Sunray; so it is doubtful that you could assemble a set in any color. A few colored pieces dispersed in the midst of your crystal would likely enhance its appeal.

The cream soup is tab handled, but by adding a lid on it, it becomes an onion soup according to Fostoria's catalogs. The condiment tray with cruets and mustards is shaped like a cloverleaf analogous to the one in Fostoria's American. It is evidently in shorter supply than the American one, but not as many collectors are on mission to find one.

If you are a novice, you should know that Duncan & Miller made a similar pattern, and if you see a punch set that you assume is Sunray, it is not. There is no Sunray punch set. The item pictured as #23 is also a Duncan piece, and often mistaken labeled as Sunray.

		Crystal				Crystal
24	Almond, ftd., ind.	12.00		5	Pitcher, 64 oz., ice lip	105.00
	Ashtray, ind., 2510½	8.00			Plate, 6"	6.00
	Ashtray, sq.	12.00		6	Plate, 7½"	8.00
	Bonbon, 6½", hdld.	16.00		17	Plate, 8½"	12.00
	Bonbon, 7", 3 toed	17.50			Plate, 9½"	25.00
	Bowl, 5", fruit	10.00			Plate, 11", torte	30.00
	Bowl, 9½", flared	30.00			Plate, 12", sandwich	32.00
	Bowl, 12", salad	35.00			Plate, 15", torte	50.00
	Bowl, 13", rolled edge	40.00			Plate, 16"	60.00
	Bowl, custard, 2¼", high	10.00		13	Relish, 6½", 3 part	22.00
12	Bowl, 10", hdld.	35.00			Relish, 8", 4 part	24.00
	Butter, w/lid, ¼ lb.	35.00			Relish, 10", 2 part	18.00
	Candelabra, 2-lite, bobeche & prisms	85.00			Salt dip	12.50
	Candlestick, 3"	20.00		14	Saucer	3.00
4	Candlestick, 5½"	27.50		22	Shaker, 4", pr.	45.00
8	Candlestick, duo	40.00			Shaker, individual, 2¼", #2510½, pr.	40.00
16	Candy jar, w/cover	55.00			Stem, 3½", 5½ oz., sherbet, low	10.00
	Celery, hdld.	25.00			Stem, 3¼", 3½ oz., fruit cocktail	10.00
15	Cigarette and cover	20.00			Stem, 3", 4 oz., cocktail, ftd.	10.00
	Cigarette box, oblong	25.00			Stem, 4⅞", 4½ oz., claret	22.00
	Coaster, 4"	8.00		1	Stem, 5¾", 9 oz., goblet	17.50
9	Comport	22.00			Sugar, ftd.	10.00
	Cream soup	27.50			Sugar, individual	10.00
	Cream soup liner	6.00			Sweetmeat, hdld., divided, 6"	25.00
	Cream, ftd.	10.00			Tray, 6½", ind. sugar/cream	10.00
	Cream, individual	10.00			Tray, 10½", oblong	38.00
14	Cup	12.00			Tray, 10", sq.	40.00
	Decanter, w/stopper, 18 oz.	70.00		18	Tray, condiment, 8½", cloverleaf	45.00
	Decanter, w/stopper, oblong, 26 oz.	85.00			Tray, oval hdld.	25.00
	Ice bucket, no handle	55.00			Tumbler, 2¼", 2 oz., whiskey, #2510½	10.00
3	Ice bucket, w/handle	65.00			Tumbler, 3½", 5 oz., juice, #2510½	10.00
	Jelly	16.00		20	Tumbler, 3½", 6 oz., old-fashion, #2510½	12.00
7	Jelly, w/cover	45.00			Tumbler, 4⅛", 9 oz., table, #2510½	12.00
11	Mayonnaise, w/liner, ladle	35.00		2	Tumbler, 4¾", 9 oz., ftd., table	12.00
19	Mustard, w/cover, spoon	45.00			Tumbler, 4⅝", 5 oz., ftd., juice	13.00
	Nappy, hdld., flared	13.00			Tumbler, 5¼", 13 oz., ftd., tea	16.00
	Nappy, hdld., reg.	12.00			Tumbler, 5⅛", 13 oz., tea, #2510½	18.00
	Nappy, hdld., sq.	14.00			Vase, 3½", rose bowl	25.00
	Nappy, hdld., tri-corner	15.00			Vase, 5", rose bowl	32.50
10	Oil bottle, w/stopper, 3 oz.	35.00			Vase, 6", crimped	40.00
21	Onion soup, w/cover	45.00			Vase, 7"	50.00
	Pickle, hdld.	20.00			Vase, 9", sq. ftd.	60.00
	Pitcher, 16 oz., cereal	50.00			Vase, sweet pea	75.00
	Pitcher, 64 oz.	80.00				

COLORS: CRYSTAL, AMBER, COBALT, RED

Terrace is a Duncan pattern that had been pretty much ignored over the years by collectors outside the Pittsburgh area due to limited distribution and lack of information being found. The Internet auctions have disseminated more information over the last few years than the few books on Duncan glassware ever did.

Red and cobalt are the colors being sought with little collector interest being shown for amber or crystal. Little amber is available and most of that found has a gold decoration on it. Those desiring crystal openly look for First Love or some other etching rather than Terrace itself.

Be aware of the crystal bowls and plates with cobalt or red bases. Learn to recognize that base pattern so you do not pass one of these.

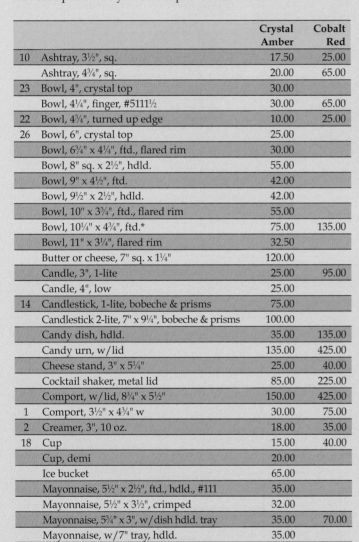

1

		Crystal Amber	Cobalt Red
10	Ashtray, 3½", sq.	17.50	25.00
	Ashtray, 4¾", sq.	20.00	65.00
23	Bowl, 4", crystal top	30.00	
	Bowl, 4¼", finger, #5111½	30.00	65.00
22	Bowl, 4¾", turned up edge	10.00	25.00
26	Bowl, 6", crystal top	25.00	
	Bowl, 6¾" x 4¼", ftd., flared rim	30.00	
	Bowl, 8" sq. x 2½", hdld.	55.00	
	Bowl, 9" x 4½", ftd.	42.00	
	Bowl, 9½" x 2½", hdld.	42.00	
	Bowl, 10" x 3¾", ftd., flared rim	55.00	
	Bowl, 10¼" x 4¾", ftd.*	75.00	135.00
	Bowl, 11" x 3¼", flared rim	32.50	
	Butter or cheese, 7" sq. x 1¼"	120.00	
	Candle, 3", 1-lite	25.00	95.00
	Candle, 4", low	25.00	
14	Candlestick, 1-lite, bobeche & prisms	75.00	
	Candlestick 2-lite, 7" x 9¼", bobeche & prisms	100.00	
	Candy dish, hdld.	35.00	135.00
	Candy urn, w/lid	135.00	425.00
	Cheese stand, 3" x 5¼"	25.00	40.00
	Cocktail shaker, metal lid	85.00	225.00
	Comport, w/lid, 8¾" x 5½"	150.00	425.00
1	Comport, 3½" x 4¾" w	30.00	75.00
2	Creamer, 3", 10 oz.	18.00	35.00
18	Cup	15.00	40.00
	Cup, demi	20.00	
	Ice bucket	65.00	
	Mayonnaise, 5½" x 2½", ftd., hdld., #111	35.00	
	Mayonnaise, 5½" x 3½", crimped	32.00	
	Mayonnaise, 5¾" x 3", w/dish hdld. tray	35.00	70.00
	Mayonnaise, w/7" tray, hdld.	35.00	
	Nappy, 5½" x 2", div., hdld.	18.00	
21	Nappy, 6" x 1¾", hdld.	22.00	35.00
	Pitcher	295.00	995.00
	Plate, 6"	10.00	20.00
25	Plate, 6", hdld., lemon	12.00	28.00
13	Plate, 6", sq.	12.00	28.00
	Plate, 7"	15.00	30.00
	Plate, 7½"	15.00	30.00
16	Plate, 7½", sq.	15.00	30.00

		Crystal Amber	Cobalt Red
	Plate, 8½"	18.00	22.00
15	Plate, 9", sq.	22.00	100.00
6	Plate, 11", sq.	28.00	125.00
	Plate, 11", hdld.	28.00	
	Plate, 11", hdld., cracker w/ring	28.00	100.00
	Plate, 11", hdld., sandwich	28.00	
	Plate, 12", torte, rolled edge	32.50	
24	Plate, 13", cake, ftd., crystal top*		195.00
	Plate, 13", torte, flat edge	35.00	
	Plate, 13", torte, rolled edge	37.50	
	Plate, 13¼", torte	35.00	175.00
	Relish, 6" x 1¾", hdld., 2 pt.	20.00	50.00
	Relish, 9", 4 pt.	35.00	100.00
	Relish, 10½" x 1½", hdld., 5 pt.	65.00	
20	Relish, 12", 4 pt., hdld.	40.00	100.00
	Relish, 12", 5 pt., hdld.	40.00	
	Relish, 12", 5 pt., w/lid	100.00	325.00
19	Salad dressing bowl, 2 pt., 5½" x 4¼"	45.00	75.00
18	Saucer, sq.	6.00	12.00
	Saucer, demi	5.00	
	Stem, 3¾", 1 oz., cordial, #5111½	42.50	
	Stem, 3¾", 4½ oz., oyster cocktail, #5111½	20.00	
	Stem, 4", 5 oz., ice cream, #5111½	14.00	
	Stem, 4½", 3½ oz., cocktail, #5111½	22.50	
	Stem, 5", 5 oz., saucer champagne, #5111½	15.00	50.00
	Stem, 5¼", 3 oz., wine, #5111½	32.50	
	Stem, 5¼", 5 oz., ftd. juice, #5111½	20.00	
	Stem, 5¾", 10 oz., low luncheon goblet, #5111½	22.00	
	Stem, 6", 4½ oz., claret, #5111½	45.00	
	Stem, 6½", 12 oz., ftd. ice tea, #5111½	32.50	
	Stem, 6¾", 10 oz., tall water goblet, #5111½	25.00	
	Stem, 6¾", 14 oz., ftd. ice tea, #5111½	32.50	
4	Sugar, 3", 10 oz.	15.00	35.00
4	Sugar lid	12.50	90.00
17	Tumbler, 2 oz., shot	15.00	40.00
27	Tumbler, 4", 9 oz., water	17.50	65.00
	Tray, 8" x 2", hdld., celery	17.50	
	Urn, 4½" x 4½"	27.50	
	Urn, 10½" x 4½"	135.00	350.00
	Vase, 10, ftd.	115.00	

*Colored foot

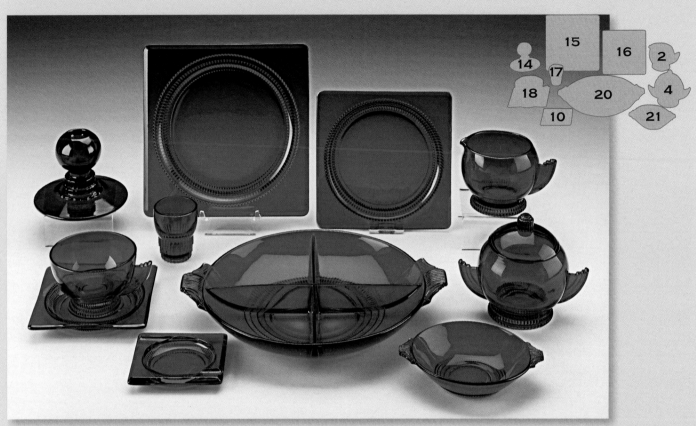

COLOR: CRYSTAL

Both Tiffin and Central made this precise Thistle etching. The designs are unerringly alike so you only have the mould shapes to help you decide which company made a specific piece. The good news is that there ought to be more of this pattern accessible with two different makers marketing Thistle over the years.

6

1	Bowl, 14 oz. finger	12.50
	Bowl, 8½", soup	20.00
	Comport, 5" high	22.00
	Comport, 6" high	25.00
	Comport, low, 4½" diameter	15.00
	Comport, low, 6" diameter	18.00
	Comport, low, 7" diameter	22.00
	Cup, 4½ oz. handled custard	12.00
	Decanter, 32 oz., w/stopper	90.00
	Marmalade, 8 oz., w/lid	35.00
	Marmalade liner/coaster, 4½"	4.00
	Night bottle	75.00
	Night set tumbler	15.00
5	Pitcher w/cover., 80 oz.	95.00
6	Plate, 5", sherbet	4.00
	Plate, 6", finger bowl liner	5.00
	Stem, 3 oz., cocktail	12.50
3	Stem, 3 oz., wine	16.00
	Stem, 4 oz. or 5 oz., claret	16.00
	Stem, 4 oz., small sherbet	8.00
	Stem, 6 oz., large sherbet	10.00
	Stem, 6 oz., saucer champagne	12.00
	Stem, 10 oz., water	18.00
	Teapot with lid	125.00

	Tumbler, 2½ oz., flared shot	10.00
4	Tumbler, 3¼ oz., flared	7.00
	Tumbler, 5 oz., flared	8.00
	Tumbler, 5½ oz., flared	10.00
	Tumbler, 6½ oz., ale (like vase)	25.00
	Tumbler, 7 oz., flared	10.00
	Tumbler, 8 oz., flared	12.00
	Tumbler, 8 oz., narrow, high ball	12.00
2	Tumbler, 9 oz., flared	12.00
	Tumbler, 9 oz., straight	12.00
	Tumbler, 10 oz., flared	12.00
	Tumbler, 11 oz., handled tea	20.00
	Tumbler, 11 oz., flared	14.00
	Tumbler, 12 oz., flared	14.00
	Tumbler, 14 oz., flared	15.00

1   3   4   5   2

COLORS: BLUE, GREEN, AND PINK

Thistle Cut appears on two separate Fry dinnerware lines, which are both demonstrated in the photo below. Line #3101 is shown by the round pieces; and Line #3104 by the octagon shaped ones. The stems with the disc connectors (bee-hive shape) are usually found with the round line. You can find this cutting on pink (Rose), green (Emerald), or blue (Azure). There are other cuttings showing up, so be sure to study this pattern to identify this Thistle design. Most collectors have acknowledged the blue as "Cornflower" in the past rather than Azure.

We bought this set almost 30 years ago at Washington Court House, Ohio, because of the blue color, which we found appealing. At that time, no one seemed to know what it was, so it sat packed away incognito until Cathy was researching our first *Glassware Pattern Identification Guide*. She exhumed the set and the maker. As with Duncan patterns, we rarely find Fry patterns outside a circle of 100 miles of Pittsburgh.

7

		All Colors
8	Bowl, 9", round, ftd.	65.00
4	Candlestick	40.00
6	Cup	25.00
5	Plate, 6", round, bread & butter	10.00
	Plate, 8", octagonal, luncheon	15.00
7	Plate, 8", round, luncheon	15.00
2	Plate, 10½", octagonal, dinner	45.00
	Plate, 10", round, dinner	45.00
6	Saucer	5.00
1	Stem, high sherbet	20.00
	Stem, juice, ftd.	22.00
	Stem, low sherbet	16.00
3	Stem, water goblet	30.00

COLORS: CRYSTAL AND CRYSTAL W/PALE BURGUNDY, CHAMPAGNE (YELLOW), AND GREEN-BLUE LUSTRE STAIN; MORE INTENSE RUBY COLOR REPLACED PALE BURGUNDY LATER; BLACK TURTLES IN 1952

Thousand Eye is probably Westmoreland's most well-known non milk glass pattern and had one of their greatest production runs except for English Hobnail. It was introduced in 1934 and concluded, except for turtles, in 1956. The turtle cigarette box was reissued, but those decorated turtles pictured are an earlier production. Obviously these were customers' favorite pieces as there are so many uncovered today. Fairy lamps, both footed and flat, were created into the late 1970s.

We often run into a 13" bowl on an 18" plate which are regularly attributed to Westmoreland's Thousand Eye line, but are actually Canton's Glass Line 100. They are usually found in crystal, but are seen in blue, red, or amber. These colored wares were evidently Paden City, but Canton did advertise in 1954 that they would make standard colors as well as special colors if the customer so desired. They acquired many of Paden City's moulds after that company closed.

Numerous Thousand Eye pieces are suggestive of previous pattern glass items. It seems to be another one of the patterns that collectors really revere or cannot stomach. Stemware abounds and like some of the Duncan patterns, you can buy these older pieces and use them less expensively than scores of today's glassware lines sold in department stores. Thousand Eye is durable, but it was used extensively, and it shows. You need to check plates and other flat pieces for wear. Mint condition flatware is more challenging to find than any of the stems and tumblers.

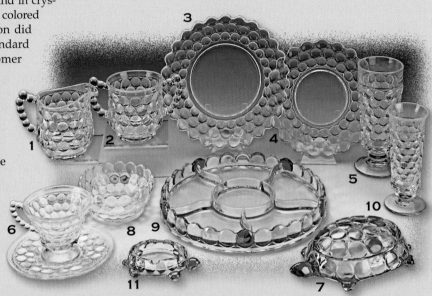

		Crystal
11	Ashtray (sm. turtle)	8.00
	Basket, 8", hdld., oval	48.00
8	Bowl, 4½", nappy	8.00
	Bowl, 5½", nappy	12.00
	Bowl, 7½", hdld.	20.00
	Bowl, 10", 2 hdld.	35.00
	Bowl, 11", belled	33.00
	Bowl, 11", crimped, oblong	40.00
	Bowl, 11", triangular	40.00
	Bowl, 11, round	40.00
	Bowl, 12", 2 hdld., flared	45.00
	Candelabra, 2 light	35.00
7	Cigarette box & cover (lg. turtle)	30.00
	Comport, 5", high ft.	22.50
	Creamer, high ft.	12.50
1	Creamer, low rim	10.00
6	Cup, ftd., bead hdld.	6.00
	Fairy lamp, flat	45.00
	Fairy lamp, ftd.	50.00
	Jug, ½ gal.	95.00
	Mayonnaise, ftd., w/ladle	30.00
	Plate, 6"	5.00
	Plate, 7"	6.00
4	Plate, 8½"	9.00
3	Plate, 10", service	20.00
	Plate, 16"	30.00

		Crystal
	Plate, 18"	45.00
9	Relish, 10", rnd., 6 part	30.00
6	Saucer	2.00
	Shaker, ftd., pr.	30.00
	Stem, 1 oz., cordial	14.00
	Stem, 2 oz., wine	10.00
	Stem, 3 oz., sherry	10.00
	Stem, 3½ oz., cocktail	8.00
	Stem, 5 oz., claret	10.00
	Stem, 8 oz.	12.00
	Stem, high ft., sherbet	9.00
	Stem, low ft., sherbet	6.00
	Stem, parfait, ftd.	12.50
	Sugar, high ft.	12.50
2	Sugar, low rim	10.00
	Tumbler, 1½ oz., whiskey	10.00
	Tumbler, 5 oz., flat ginger ale	8.00
	Tumbler, 5 oz., ftd.	8.00
	Tumbler, 6 oz., old-fashion	10.00
10	Tumbler, 7 oz., ftd.	9.00
	Tumbler, 8 oz., flat	9.00
	Tumbler, 9 oz., ftd.	10.00
5	Tumbler, 12 oz., ftd., tea	12.50
	Vase, crimped bowl	30.00
	Vase, flair rim	30.00

"TINKERBELL," ETCH #756, MORGANTOWN GLASS WORKS, C. 1927

COLORS: AZURE, GREEN, PINK

We automatically dubbed this etch "Tinkerbell," when we first bought 16 stems about 30 years ago. About 10 years later we found that they were Morgantown's #7631 Jewel stem. After talking to Jerry Gallagher, we found that Morgantown collectors were also calling them "Tinkerbell."

We displayed our goblets and champagnes at the Heisey show, and found they sold very fast. We kept two of each and finally added a wine to our set. Last year we were able to add the bottle from the medicine bottle/night set, but the rest of that four-piece set has eluded us so far. The only complete set we've seen was in a not-for-sale display.

That green bud vase is 10" tall and was found in an antique mall in Ohio. It remains the only piece of green "Tinkerbell" we have seen.

		Azure Green
	Bowl, finger, ftd.	100.00
5	Night or medicine set bottle, 4 pc. (med. bottle w/stop, night glass, w/water bottle)	750.00
	Plate, finger bowl liner	30.00
	Stem, 1½ oz., cordial	225.00
3	Stem, 2½ oz., wine	150.00
	Stem, 3½ oz., cocktail	110.00
4	Stem, 5½ oz., saucer champagne	110.00
	Stem, 5½ oz., sherbet	90.00
2	Stem, 9 oz., goblet	175.00
6	Tumbler, 9 oz., ftd.	90.00
	Vase, 10", plain top, ftd., #36 Uranus	395.00
1	Vase, 10", ruffled top, ftd., #36 Uranus	495.00

COLORS: ROSE PINK, TOPAZ, YELLOW

Reserves of Topaz and Rose Trojan are becoming progressively sparse. Topaz sells quite well, and has always been more abundant than pink in the market. A few years ago, there was a surplus of Topaz being offered for sale due to the thinning out of some large collections. Now collectors are once again having trouble finding pieces other than stems. The smaller supply of pink has discouraged collectors; so that lesser supply has been adequate for demand.

You need to be familiar with the following Fostoria facts: liner plates for cream soup and mayonnaise are the same piece; two-handled cake plates come with and without an indent in the center (the indented version also serves as a plate for one of two styles of cheese comports); bonbon, lemon dish, sweetmeat, and whipped cream bowls all come with loop or bow handles; and sugars come with a straight or ruffled edge. Unpredictably, it is the ruffled top sugar that takes a lid.

Trojan stemware can be found except for cordials and clarets in either color. Clarets are nearly impossible to find in most Fostoria patterns. If you want them, you had better buy them whenever you find them. The claret has the same shape as the wine, but holds four ounces as opposed to the three ounces of the wine. Yes, wine glasses in those days held 2 to 3½ ounces of liquid. This confuses today's collector who is used to wine goblets holding eight ounces or more. In those days, that capacity was reserved for water. Due to the propensity of the public to buy water goblets to use as wines, prices for clarets and the original wines are slipping due to lack of demand.

Soup and cereal bowl scarcities have been noted by the increasingly rising prices. We have only owned a few of each, but one dealer displayed eight soups at a show not long ago. They were highly priced, but it was hard to convince a collector they were rare with eight sitting there. Sometimes it is all about marketing strategy.

12

		Rose	Topaz
	Ashtray, #2350, lg.	30.00	25.00
	Ashtray, #2350, sm.	25.00	20.00
	Bottle, salad dressing, #2983	595.00	395.00
	Bowl, baker, #2375, 9"		75.00
	Bowl, bonbon, #2375		22.50
	Bowl, bouillon, #2375, ftd.		20.00
	Bowl, cream soup, #2375, ftd.	35.00	30.00
	Bowl, finger, #869/2283, w/6¼" liner	50.00	45.00
	Bowl, lemon, #2375	24.00	20.00
	Bowl, #2394, 3 ftd., 4½", mint	25.00	20.00
	Bowl, #2375, fruit, 5"	25.00	20.00
	Bowl, #2354, 3 ftd., 6"	45.00	40.00
	Bowl, cereal, #2375, 6½"	50.00	40.00
	Bowl, soup, #2375, 7"	120.00	100.00
	Bowl, lg. dessert, #2375, 2 hdld.	100.00	80.00
	Bowl, #2395, 10"	115.00	75.00
7	Bowl, #2395, scroll, 10"	110.00	85.00
	Bowl, combination #2415, w/ candleholder handles	250.00	175.00
	Bowl, #2375, centerpiece, flared optic, 12"	75.00	60.00
	Bowl, #2394, centerpiece, ftd., 12"	85.00	75.00
	Bowl, #2375, centerpiece, mushroom, 12"	95.00	70.00
	Candlestick, #2394, 2"	25.00	20.00
11	Candlestick, 3", #2375	27.50	22.50
	Candlestick, #2375, flared, 3"	30.00	25.00
	Candlestick, #2395½, scroll, 5"	60.00	50.00
	Candy, w/cover, #2394, ¼ lb.	295.00	225.00
	Candy, w/cover, #2394, ½ lb.	200.00	175.00
	Celery, #2375, 11½"	45.00	35.00
5	Cheese & cracker, set, #2375, #2368	75.00	60.00

		Rose	Topaz
	Comport, #5299 or #2400, 6"	60.00	45.00
	Comport, #2375, 7"	60.00	45.00
	Creamer, #2375, ftd.	20.00	16.00
9	Creamer, tea, #2375½	50.00	40.00
	Cup, after dinner, #2375	40.00	30.00
10	Cup, #2375½, ftd.	18.00	15.00
	Decanter, #2439, 9"	1,395.00	995.00
	Goblet, claret, #5099, 4 oz., 6"	100.00	65.00
3	Goblet, cocktail, #5099, 3 oz., 5¼"	28.00	22.00
	Goblet, cordial, #5099, ¾ oz., 4"	100.00	60.00
	Goblet, water, #5299, 10 oz., 8¼"	40.00	30.00
	Goblet, wine, #5099, 3 oz., 5½"	50.00	35.00
	Grapefruit, #5282½	50.00	40.00
	Grapefruit liner, #945½	50.00	40.00
12	Ice bucket, #2375	110.00	90.00
	Ice dish, #2451, #2455	45.00	35.00
	Ice dish liner (tomato, crab, fruit), #2451	20.00	10.00
	Mayonnaise ladle	30.00	20.00
	Mayonnaise, w/liner, #2375	55.00	45.00
	Oil, ftd., #2375	395.00	295.00
	Oyster, cocktail, #5099, ftd.	28.00	22.00
	Parfait, #5099	60.00	38.00
	Pitcher, #5000	450.00	325.00
	Plate, #2375, canape, 6¼"	30.00	20.00
	Plate, #2375, bread/butter, 6"	6.00	5.00
	Plate, #2375, salad, 7½"	10.00	8.00
	Plate, 2375, cream soup or mayo liner, 7½"	12.00	8.00
	Plate, #2375, luncheon, 8¾"	18.00	14.00
	Plate, #2375, sm., dinner, 9½"	30.00	25.00
6	Plate, #2375, cake, handled, 10"	60.00	45.00

		Rose	Topaz
	Plate, #2375, grill, rare, 10¼"	90.00	80.00
	Plate, #2375, dinner, 10¼"	70.00	55.00
	Plate, #2375, chop, 13"	70.00	55.00
	Plate, #2375, round, 14"	70.00	60.00
	Platter, #2375, 12"	75.00	60.00
	Platter, #2375, 15"	140.00	110.00
	Relish, #2375, 8½"		40.00
	Relish, #2350, 3 pt., rnd., 8¾"	45.00	40.00
	Sauce boat, #2375	125.00	85.00
	Sauce plate, #2375	35.00	30.00
	Saucer, #2375, after dinner	9.00	9.00
10	Saucer, #2375	5.00	4.00
	Shaker, #2375, pr., ftd.	110.00	90.00
	Sherbet, #5099, high, 6"	28.00	22.00
2	Sherbet, #5099, low, 4¼"	20.00	16.00
	Sugar, #2375½, ftd.	22.50	18.00

		Rose	Topaz
	Sugar cover, #2375½	125.00	95.00
	Sugar pail, #2378	195.00	165.00
8	Sugar, tea, #2375½	50.00	40.00
4	Sweetmeat, #2375	22.00	18.00
1	Tray, 11", ctr. hdld., #2375	50.00	40.00
	Tray, #2429, service & lemon insert		250.00
	Tumbler, #5099, ftd., 2½ oz.	50.00	40.00
	Tumbler, #5099, ftd., 5 oz., 4½"	30.00	24.00
	Tumbler, #5099, ftd., 9 oz., 5¼"	22.00	17.50
	Tumbler, #5099, ftd., 12 oz., 6"	40.00	30.00
	Vase, #2417, 8"	200.00	150.00
	Vase, #4105, 8"	275.00	195.00
	Vase, #2369, 9"		250.00
	Whipped cream bowl, #2375	32.00	24.00
	Whipped cream pail, #2378	135.00	100.00

COLORS: AMBER, AMBER W/GREEN, AMBER W/RED, ROSE W/GREEN

Turkey Tracks is what this pattern has been called for years. It tends to turn up in quantities when it is found. We certainly opened a Pandora's Box with this inclusion in the last book. Our prices were gathered from dealers who were selling it. These have been drastically overhauled due to our experiences in selling Turkey Tracks.

The color combinations are rather eye-catching with the colors fluorescing. Amber is usually not a color we notice, but this amber is quite different from most ambers in that it even glows under a black light, not the normal circumstance. Wonder if all the people calling green glass "vaseline" will add this to the mix also? "Vaseline" is canary yellow, not green, which fluoresces because of uranium in its composition.

You will find some highly priced bi-colored stems and footed tumblers in Turkey Tracks, but then, two-tone items have many admirers by themselves — without the added unusual design. Flat tumblers and plates seem to be available in all amber, but you could find other colors. If you find additional pieces or colors, please let us know.

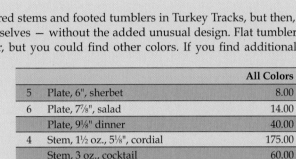

		All Colors
5	Plate, 6", sherbet	8.00
6	Plate, 7⅞", salad	14.00
	Plate, 9⅛" dinner	40.00
4	Stem, 1½ oz., 5⅛", cordial	175.00
	Stem, 3 oz., cocktail	60.00
3	Stem, 3 oz., wine	65.00
	Stem, 6 oz., 4", high sherbet	50.00
2	Stem, 6 oz., low sherbet	40.00
	Tumbler, 3 oz., bar	40.00
	Tumbler, 6 oz., old-fashion	55.00
8	Tumbler, 6 oz., 4", ftd., juice	30.00
	Tumbler, 9 oz., ftd.	35.00
1	Tumbler, 10 oz., 4¼" ftd. water	50.00
	Tumbler, 12 oz., 5½", ftd. tea	55.00
7	Tumbler, 13 oz., 5⅞", ftd. ice tea	55.00

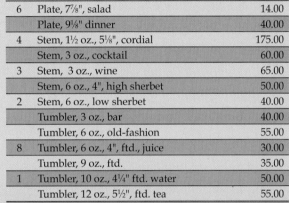

COLORS: CRYSTAL, FLAMINGO PINK, MOONGLEAM GREEN, MARIGOLD AMBER/YELLOW, SAHARA YELLOW, SOME ALEXANDRITE (RARE)

Crystal Twist has been way down the line in collector priorities in the past, but there is a growing contingency paying attention to this Deco influenced pattern. The Moongleam cocktail shaker on the right is one of few to be uncovered, although the mould turned up during the purchase of old moulds by the National Heisey Club several years ago. Cocktail shakers in other Twist colors have never been shaken or stirred insofar as we can determine.

That amber/yellow colored ice bucket to the left is Marigold; and the pink/purple colored bucket on the bottom right is Alexandrite. Both are rare Heisey colors. Be aware that Marigold is arduous to find in mint condition because that applied color has a propensity to flake or peel. Items that are beginning to deteriorate will continue to do so. If you have an option in owning a piece of this rarely seen color that has some problems, ignore it unless it is cheaply priced. Nothing can be done to renew it, but we understand there have been many who have tried.

Few price adjustments have been seen in colored Twist lately. Most Twist items are marked with the H in diamond. When investigating stemmed pieces, check for the mark on the stem itself. Of course, this easily recognized pattern doesn't really need a mark to distinguish it as Heisey.

Oil bottles, large bowls, and the three-footed utility plates have seen price adjustments. The individual sugar and creamer have both disappeared into collections; buy one if you have an opportunity.

2

1

		Crystal	Flamingo	Moongleam	Marigold	Alexandrite	Sahara
	Baker, 9", oval	25.00	35.00	45.00	60.00		
	Bonbon, individual	15.00	35.00	40.00	40.00		
22	Bonbon, 6", 2 hdld.	10.00	20.00	25.00	30.00		
	Bottle, French dressing	50.00	100.00	110.00	135.00		
	Bowl, cream soup/bouillon	15.00	25.00	32.00	50.00		100.00
	Bowl, ftd., almond/indiv. sugar	35.00	45.00	55.00	75.00		
	Bowl, indiv. nut	10.00	25.00	40.00	45.00		
8	Bowl, 4", nappy	10.00	30.00	35.00	40.00		
25	Bowl, 6", 2 hdld.	7.00	20.00	20.00	25.00		
3	Bowl, 6", 2 hdld., jelly	10.00	20.00	28.00	30.00		
	Bowl, 6", 2 hdld., mint	7.00	20.00	35.00	30.00		20.00
	Bowl, 8", low ftd.		80.00	80.00	85.00		
18	Bowl, 8", nappy, ground bottom	20.00	50.00	55.00	60.00		
	Bowl, 8", nasturtium, rnd.	45.00	70.00	90.00	80.00	450.00	80.00
	Bowl, 8", nasturtium, oval	45.00	70.00	90.00	80.00		

1   1   1   1

		Crystal	Flamingo	Moongleam	Marigold	Alexandrite	Sahara
	Bowl, 9", floral	25.00	40.00	50.00	65.00		
	Bowl, 9", floral, rolled edge	30.00	40.00	45.00	65.00		
6	Bowl, 12", floral, oval, 4 ft.	45.00	100.00	110.00	90.00	550.00	85.00
21	Bowl, 12", floral, rnd., 4 ft.	30.00	40.00	50.00	65.00		
5	Candlestick, 2", 1-lite		40.00	50.00	85.00		
	Cheese dish, 6", 2 hdld.	10.00	20.00	25.00	30.00		
	Claret, 4 oz.	15.00	30.00	40.00	50.00		
2	Cocktail shaker, metal top			900.00			
4	Comport, 7", tall	40.00	90.00	120.00	150.00		
19	Creamer, hotel, oval	25.00	40.00	45.00	50.00		
	Creamer, individual (unusual)	30.00	50.00	60.00	65.00		
	Creamer, zigzag handles, ftd.	20.00	40.00	50.00	70.00		
7	Cup, zigzag handles	10.00	25.00	32.00	35.00		
	Grapefruit, ftd.	15.00	25.00	35.00	60.00		
1	Ice bucket w/metal handle	50.00	135.00	115.00	135.00	400.00	125.00
15	Mayonnaise	35.00	65.00	80.00	80.00		
14	Mayonnaise, #1252½	20.00	35.00	45.00	50.00		
26	Mustard, w/cover, spoon	40.00	130.00	150.00	100.00		
	Oil bottle, 2½ oz., w/#78 stopper	50.00	140.00	170.00	200.00		
	Oil bottle, 4 oz., w/#78 stopper	50.00	110.00	120.00	120.00		90.00
16	Pitcher, 3 pint	95.00	175.00	230.00			
	Plate, cream soup liner	5.00	7.00	10.00	15.00		
	Plate, 8", Kraft cheese	20.00	40.00	60.00	50.00		
	Plate, 8", ground bottom	7.00	14.00	20.00	30.00		20.00
9	Plate, 10½", dinner	40.00	80.00	120.00	120.00		90.00
	Plate, 12", 2 hdld., sandwich	30.00	60.00	90.00	80.00		
	Plate, 12", muffin, 2 hdld., turned sides	40.00	80.00	90.00	80.00		
	Plate, 13", 3 part, relish	10.00	17.00	22.00	35.00		
12	Platter, 12"	15.00	50.00	60.00	75.00		
	Salt & pepper, ftd.	100.00	140.00	160.00	200.00		140.00
10	Salt & pepper, flat	50.00	90.00	100.00	60.00		
7	Saucer	3.00	5.00	7.00	10.00	140.00	
	Stem, 2½ oz., wine, 2 block stem	40.00	90.00	110.00	125.00		
	Stem, 3 oz., oyster cocktail, ftd.	10.00	35.00	40.00	50.00		
	Stem, 3 oz., cocktail, 2 block stem	10.00	30.00	45.00	50.00		
	Stem, 5 oz., saucer champagne, 2 block stem	35.00	25.00	30.00			

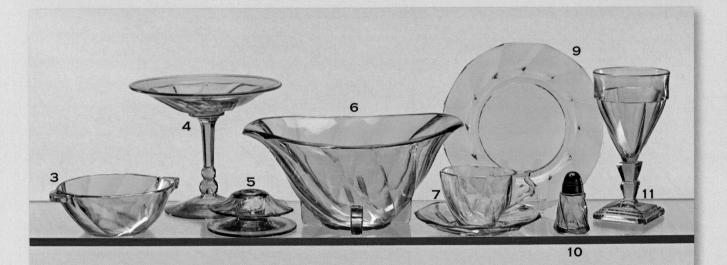

		Crystal	Flamingo	Moongleam	Marigold	Alexandrite	Sahara
	Stem, 5 oz., sherbet, 2 block stem	10.00	18.00	40.00	28.00		
	Stem, 9 oz., luncheon (1 block in stem)	40.00	60.00	70.00	75.00		
11	Stem, 9 oz., goblet (2 block in stem)	35.00	55.00	60.00	65.00		
	Sugar, ftd.	20.00	30.00	37.50	60.00		
20	Sugar, hotel, oval	25.00	45.00	50.00	50.00		
	Sugar, individual (unusual)	30.00	50.00	60.00	65.00		
	Sugar, w/cover, zigzag handles	25.00	40.00	60.00	80.00		
	Tray, 7", pickle, ground bottom	7.00	35.00	35.00	45.00		
24	Tray, 10", celery	30.00	50.00	50.00	50.00		40.00
	Tray, 13", celery	25.00	50.00	60.00	50.00		
17	Tumbler, 5 oz., soda, flat bottom	10.00	35.00	38.00	38.00		
	Tumbler, 6 oz., ftd., soda	10.00	25.00	32.00	36.00		
23	Tumbler, 8 oz., flat, ground bottom	15.00	45.00	70.00	40.00		
	Tumbler, 8 oz., soda, straight & flared	12.00	35.00	40.00	40.00		
13	Tumbler, 9 oz., ftd., soda	20.00	45.00	50.00	60.00		
	Tumbler, 12 oz., iced tea, flat bottom	20.00	50.00	60.00	70.00		
	Tumbler, 12 oz., ftd., iced tea	20.00	45.00	50.00	60.00		

COLORS: CRYSTAL, PINK

There have been at least a half dozen instances in the last year where dealers have asked us if the piece they have is Valencia or Minerva. Although these Cambridge patterns are similar, there is a telltale sign to differentiate them. Notice in the photo of Valencia that the lines in the pattern are perpendicular to each other (think Tic Tac Toe). On Minerva, the lines in the pattern are on a diagonal forming diamonds instead of squares. Valencia had a limited production, so dealers are not as accustomed to seeing it as with many Cambridge patterns.

Valencia has numerous pieces that would be sold for sizeable sums in other Cambridge patterns where demand often exceeds the supply. However, with Valencia, there are so few collectors that rare pieces often are very under valued. Most pieces pictured would be enthusiastically snatched up in Rose Point, but are only just being recognized in Valencia. Valencia items are, unquestionably, rarer than the enormously popular Rose Point. However, rarity is not always as important in collecting as demand, the motivating force.

Some of the more exceptional pieces pictured include the square, covered honey dish, the Doulton pitcher, and that small metal-handled piece that Cambridge called a sugar basket. This is similar to Fostoria's sugar pail, but closer in size to Fostoria's whipped cream pail. Terminology used by glass companies in those days sometimes confuses today's collectors.

		Crystal
16	Ashtray, #3500/16, 3¼", square	10.00
17	Ashtray, #3500/124, 3¼", round	10.00
	Ashtray, #3500/126, 4", round	12.00
18	Ashtray, #3500/128, 4½", round	16.00
3	Ashtray/soapdish, #3500/130, 4", oval	60.00
	Basket, #3500/55, 6", 2 hdld., ftd.	28.00
	Bowl, #3500/49, 5", hdld.	15.00
	Bowl, #3500/37, 6", cereal	25.00
	Bowl, #1402/89, 6", 2 hdld.	18.00
	Bowl, #1402/88, 6", 2 hdld., div.	18.00
	Bowl, #3500/115, 9½", 2 hdld., ftd.	35.00
	Bowl, #1402/82, 10"	45.00
	Bowl, #1402/88, 11"	50.00
	Bowl, #1402/95, salad dressing, div.	35.00
	Bowl, #1402/100, finger, w/liner	40.00
	Bowl, #3500, ftd., finger	30.00
	Candy dish, w/cover, #3500/103	150.00
	Celery, #1402/94, 12"	30.00
	Cigarette holder, #1066, ftd.	60.00
6	Comport, #3500/36, 6"	28.00
	Comport, #3500/37, 7"	42.00
	Creamer, #3500/14	15.00
	Creamer, #3500/15, individual	18.00
21	Cup, #3500/1	15.00
	Decanter, #3400/92, 32 oz., ball	195.00
	Decanter, #3400/119, 12 oz., ball	185.00
20	Honey dish, w/cover, #3500/139	185.00
12	Ice pail, #1402/52	100.00
	Mayonnaise, #3500/59, 3 pc.	40.00
	Nut, #3400/71, 3", 4 ftd.	50.00
	Perfume, #3400/97, 2 oz., perfume	175.00
2	Pitcher, 80 oz., Doulton, #3400/141	350.00
8	Plate, #3500/167, 7½", salad	8.00
	Plate, #3500/5, 8½", breakfast	10.00
	Plate, #1402, 11½", sandwich, hdld.	28.00
4	Plate, #3500/39, 12", ftd.	35.00
	Plate, #3500/67, 12"	35.00
1	Plate, #3500/38, 13", torte	45.00
	Relish, #3500/68, 5½", 2 comp.	28.00
	Relish, #3500/69, 6½", 3 comp.	33.00

		Crystal
10	Relish, #3500/71, 7½", 3 part, hdld.	75.00
	Relish, #1402/91, 8", 3 comp.	50.00
	Relish, #3500/64, 10", 3 comp.	55.00
	Relish, #3500/65, 10", 4 comp.	60.00
19	Relish, #3500/67, 12", 6 pc.	195.00
15	Relish, #3500/112, 15", 3 pt., 2 hdld.	75.00
	Relish, #3500/13, 15", 4 pt., 2 hdld.	75.00
11	Salt and pepper, #3400/18	55.00
21	Saucer, #3500/1	3.00
	Stem, #1402, cordial	60.00
	Stem, #1402, wine	33.00
	Stem, #1402, cocktail	20.00
	Stem, #1402, claret	35.00
	Stem, #1402, oyster cocktail	16.00
	Stem, #1402, low sherbet	12.00
	Stem, #1402, tall sherbet	15.00
	Stem, #1402, goblet	28.00
	Stem, #3500, cordial	60.00
	Stem, #3500, wine, 2½ oz.	33.00
	Stem, #3500, cocktail, 3 oz.	18.00
	Stem, #3500, claret, 4½ oz.	33.00
	Stem, #3500, oyster cocktail, 4½ oz.	16.00
	Stem, #3500, low sherbet, 7 oz.	12.00
	Stem, #3500, tall sherbet, 7 oz.	15.00
	Stem, #3500, goblet, long bowl	28.00
	Stem, #3500, goblet, short bowl	28.00
14	Sugar, #3500/14	14.00
	Sugar, #3500/15, individual	18.00
13	Sugar basket, #3500/13	150.00
9	Tumbler, #3400/92, 2½ oz.	22.00
7	Tumbler, #3400/100, 13 oz.	22.00
	Tumbler, #3400/115, 14 oz.	25.00
	Tumbler, #3500, 2½ oz., ftd.	22.00
	Tumbler, #3500, 3 oz., ftd.	20.00
	Tumbler, #3500, 5 oz., ftd.	18.00
	Tumbler, #3500, 10 oz., ftd.	20.00
5	Tumbler, #3500, 12 oz., ftd.	22.00
	Tumbler, #3500, 13 oz., ftd.	24.00
	Tumbler, #3500, 16 oz., ftd.	28.00

1

3

2

4

5

2

6

8

11

12

13

14

7

9

10

19

20

15

18

21

16

17

COLORS: BLUE, YELLOW, PINK, GREEN

Fostoria line numbers (which also relate to June and Fairfax listings) are cataloged for each piece of Versailles. You can use the listings here to get line numbers for those patterns. All colors of Versailles are in demand with green prices catching up to blue and leaving pink selling nearly the same as yellow. Blue Versailles no longer stands alone at the top of the class since green has attracted hordes of new collectors, particularly on the West Coast. We used to avoid buying green Versailles, as it was difficult to sell, but that is no longer true.

All Fostoria soup and cereal bowls are silently vanishing from the market. There is a green soup bowl in the foreground of that photo. We have never found one in blue.

Be sure to see page 98 for various types of Fostoria stemware. Confusion reigns because stem heights are similar. Here, shapes and capacities are more important. Yellow Versailles is always found on stem line #5099, which has a cascading stem; all other Versailles is found on stem line #5098, which is shown in both photos.

		Green	Blue	Pink Yellow			Green	Blue	Pink Yellow
	Ashtray, #2350	25.00	30.00	22.00	23	Goblet, water, #5098 or #5099, 10 oz., 8¼"	100.00	85.00	50.00
	Bottle, #2083, salad dressing, crystal glass top	695.00	995.00	495.00	30	Goblet, wine, #5098 or #5099, 3 oz., 5½"	65.00	75.00	50.00
					4	Grapefruit, #5082½	50.00	60.00	40.00
	Bottle, #2375, salad dressing, w/ sterling top or colored top	595.00	895.00	495.00	4	Grapefruit liner, #945½, etched	50.00	60.00	40.00
					10	Ice bucket, #2375	100.00	125.00	80.00
	Bowl, #2375, baker, 9"	95.00	150.00	85.00		Ice dish, #2451	45.00	55.00	40.00
	Bowl, #2375, bonbon	28.00	30.00	20.00		Ice dish liner (tomato, crab, fruit), #2451	20.00	20.00	10.00
25	Bowl, #2375, bouillon, ftd.	28.00	40.00	25.00		Mayonnaise, w/liner, #2375	60.00	75.00	50.00
24	Bowl, #2375, cream soup, ftd.	35.00	50.00	30.00		Mayonnaise ladle	20.00	30.00	20.00
5	Bowl, #869/2283, finger, w/6" liner	55.00	75.00	45.00		Oil, #2375, ftd.	495.00	595.00	395.00
	Bowl, lemon	25.00	32.00	25.00		Oyster cocktail, #5098 or #5099	28.00	35.00	26.00
	Bowl, 4½", mint, 3 ftd.	30.00	45.00	30.00		Parfait, #5098 or #5099	65.00	85.00	55.00
	Bowl, #2375, fruit, 5"	30.00	45.00	30.00	14	Pitcher, #5000	495.00	595.00	395.00
	Bowl, #2394, 3 ftd., 6"			40.00		Plate, #2375, bread/butter, 6"	8.00	10.00	7.00
	Bowl, #2375, cereal, 6½"	45.00	65.00	40.00		Plate, #2375, canape, 6"	25.00	30.00	25.00
16	Bowl, #2375, soup, 7"	110.00	140.00	80.00		Plate, #2375, salad, 7½"	12.00	14.00	12.00
	Bowl, #2375, lg., dessert, 2 hdld.	90.00	125.00	80.00		Plate, #2375, cream soup or mayo liner, 7½"	12.00	15.00	12.00
	Bowl, #2375, baker, 10", oval	90.00	125.00	80.00		Plate, #2375, luncheon, 8¾"	18.00	22.00	15.00
	Bowl, #2395, centerpiece, scroll, 10"	90.00	145.00	80.00		Plate, #2375, sm., dinner, 9½"	35.00	40.00	30.00
22	Bowl, #2375, centerpiece, flared top, 12"	80.00	100.00	70.00		Plate, #2375, cake, 2 hdld., 10"	50.00	65.00	40.00
	Bowl, #2394, ftd., 12"	80.00	100.00	70.00	26	Plate, #2375, dinner, 10¼"	85.00	100.00	75.00
	Bowl, #2375½, oval, centerpiece, 13"	85.00	110.00			Plate, #2375, chop, 13"	80.00	90.00	60.00
	Candlestick, #2394, 2"	30.00	35.00	25.00		Platter, #2375, 12"	75.00	100.00	65.00
32	Candlestick, #2395, 3"	33.00	40.00	30.00		Platter, #2375, 15"	125.00	175.00	110.00
15	Candlestick, #2395½, scroll, 3"	50.00	55.00	40.00	28	Relish, #2375, 8½", 2-part			38.00
11	Candy, w/cover, #2331, 3 pt.	200.00	285.00			Sauce boat, #2375	150.00	225.00	100.00
	Candy, w/cover, #2394, ¼ lb.			195.00		Sauce boat plate, #2375	30.00	40.00	25.00
	Candy, w/cover, #2394, ½ lb.			160.00	31	Saucer, #2375, after dinner	12.00	18.00	10.00
29	Celery, #2375, 11½"	75.00	100.00	65.00		Saucer, #2375	4.00	5.00	3.00
	Cheese & cracker, #2375 or #2368, set	85.00	110.00	80.00	27	Shaker, #2375, pr., ftd.	140.00	150.00	110.00
	Comport, #5098, 3"	33.00	45.00	28.00	20	Sherbet, #5098/5099, high, 6"	28.00	33.00	25.00
21	Comport, #5099/2400, 6"	70.00	95.00	70.00	2	Sherbet, #5098/5099, low, 4¼"	24.00	28.00	20.00
9	Comport, #2375, 7½"	45.00	95.00		7	Sugar, #2375½, ftd.	25.00	25.00	20.00
	Comport, #2400, 8"	75.00	125.00			Sugar cover, #2375½	150.00	175.00	125.00
6	Creamer, #2375½, ftd.	25.00	25.00	20.00		Sugar pail, #2378	200.00	275.00	165.00
13	Creamer, #2375½, tea	50.00	55.00	35.00	12	Sugar, #2375½, tea	50.00	55.00	35.00
31	Cup, #2375, after dinner	60.00	75.00	35.00		Sweetmeat, #2375	25.00	25.00	20.00
	Cup, #2375½, ftd.	22.00	25.00	18.00		Tray, #2375, ctr. hdld., 11"	50.00	60.00	40.00
	Decanter, #2439, 9"	1,200.00	2,000.00	895.00	8	Tray, service & lemon	350.00	400.00	250.00
17	Goblet, cordial, #5098 or #5099, ¾ oz., 4"	150.00	150.00	80.00		Tumbler, flat, old-fashion (pink only)			125.00
18	Goblet, #5098 or #5099, claret, 4 oz., 6"	90.00	125.00	80.00		Tumbler, flat, tea (pink only)			135.00
1	Goblet, cocktail, #5098 or #5099, 3 oz., 5¼"	32.00	38.00	28.00		Tumbler, #5098 or #5099 2½ oz., ftd.	60.00	75.00	50.00

VERSAILLES

		Green	Blue	Pink Yellow
3	Tumbler, #5098 or #5099, 5 oz., ftd., 4½"	30.00	35.00	25.00
	Tumbler, #5098 or #5099, 9 oz., ftd., 5¼"	35.00	38.00	25.00
19	Tumbler, #5098 or #5099 12 oz., ftd., 6"	50.00	55.00	35.00
	Vase, #2417, 8"			235.00

	Green	Blue	Pink Yellow
Vase, #4100, 8"	265.00	350.00	
Vase, #2385, fan, ftd., 8½"	295.00	395.00	
Whipped cream bowl, #2375	28.00	33.00	22.00
Whipped cream pail, #2378	200.00	250.00	175.00

Note: See page 98 for stem identification.

COLORS: AMBER, GREEN; SOME BLUE

Amber Vesper is the color most often seen. Today, the popularity of amber is increasing but it wilts a bit when compared to other colors. Obviously, from the abundance of amber glassware made in the late 1920s and 1930s, it was an exceedingly popular color then. I recently sold quite a bit of amber Vesper that had been stored from the late 1970s. As of today, I only have a few pieces left. It wasn't a large dollar volume, but it was quite a quantity to sell in six quick weeks.

There is little blue Vesper to be found for sale at a price collectors are willing to pay. The Fostoria name for the particular blue color of Vesper is simply Blue. Hardly original, I agree; but that does distinguish it from the lighter blue dubbed Azure. Hard to find, attractive, colored glassware often is priced out of the reach of the average collector. Blue Vesper has not reached that point yet, but it is slowly rising in price. Green Vesper is easier to obtain than blue, but it is not capturing many collectors. That lack of collector appeal now over 70 years later makes for more affordable prices for that color than for blue or amber. Difficult to gain are the vanity set (combination perfume and powder jar), moulded and blown grapefruits, egg cup, butter dish, both styles of candy dishes, and the Maj Jongg (8¾" canapé) plate. It is the high sherbet that fits the ring on that plate. All of these have been pictured in earlier editions; but finding them, today, has also been a problem for me. I did manage to round up the two styles of grapefruits and the flat, three-part candy, but that was all for this time.

Vesper comes on stem line #5093 and tumbler line #5100. The shapes are slightly different from those Fostoria etches found on the Fairfax blank (page 98). Cordials, clarets, and parfaits are the most difficult stems to acquire while the footed, 12-ounce iced tea and two-ounce footed bar are the most difficult tumblers.

There will never be a better time to start collecting Vesper, so if this is your cup of tea, better start now.

			Green	Amber	Blue
		Ashtray, #2350, 4"	25.00	25.00	
		Bowl, #2350, bouillon, ftd.	20.00	25.00	36.00
		Bowl, #2350, cream soup, flat	25.00	25.00	
		Bowl, #2350, cream soup, ftd.	22.00	25.00	36.00
16		Bowl, #2350, fruit, 5½"	12.00	16.00	30.00
		Bowl, #2350, cereal, sq. or rnd., 6½"	30.00	30.00	50.00
		Bowl, #2267, low, ftd., 7"	25.00	30.00	
22		Bowl, #2350, soup, shallow, 7¾"	30.00	35.00	65.00
		Bowl, soup, deep, 8¼"		35.00	
		Bowl, 8⅞"	32.00	35.00	
		Bowl, #2350, baker, oval, 9"	65.00	65.00	100.00
		Bowl, #2350, rd.	45.00	50.00	
		Bowl, #2350, baker, oval, 10½"	75.00	75.00	145.00
		Bowl, #2375, flared bowl, 10½"	50.00	50.00	
		Bowl, #2350, ped., ftd., 10½"	55.00	60.00	
20		Bowl, #2329, console, rolled edge, 11"	37.50	35.00	
		Bowl, #2375, 3 ftd., 12½"	50.00	50.00	125.00
		Bowl, #2371, oval, 13"	55.00	55.00	
		Bowl, #2329, rolled edge, 13"	50.00	50.00	
		Bowl, #2329, rolled edge, 14"	55.00	50.00	150.00
		Butter dish, #2350	395.00	750.00	
		Candlestick, #2324, 2"	22.00	22.00	
19		Candlestick, #2394, 3"	23.00	22.00	
		Candlestick, #2324, 4"	24.00	22.00	50.00
		Candlestick, #2394, 9"	85.00	90.00	110.00
		Candy jar, w/cover, #2331, 3 pt.	125.00	125.00	250.00
		Candy jar, w/cover, #2250, ftd., ½ lb.	245.00	195.00	
		Celery, #2350	26.00	25.00	50.00
		Cheese, #2368, ftd.	22.00	20.00	
		Comport, 6"	26.00	25.00	50.00
		Comport, #2327 (twisted stem), 7½"	35.00	35.00	75.00
		Comport, 8"	55.00	50.00	85.00
		Creamer, #2350½, ftd.	16.00	15.00	
		Creamer, #2315½, fat, ftd.	20.00	20.00	35.00

		Green	Amber	Blue
	Creamer, #2350½, flat		22.00	
23	Cup, #2350	14.00	12.00	40.00
24	Cup, #2350, after dinner	42.00	30.00	85.00
17	Cup, #2350½, ftd.	15.00	14.00	35.00
	Egg cup, #2350		35.00	
	Finger bowl and liner, #869/2283, 6"	32.00	30.00	65.00
15	Grapefruit, #5082½, blown	55.00	40.00	90.00
14	Grapefruit liner, #945½, blown	50.00	40.00	65.00
	Grapefruit, #2315, molded	55.00	40.00	
	Ice bucket, #2378	85.00	75.00	250.00
10	Oyster cocktail, #5100	25.00	22.00	40.00
	Pickle, #2350	30.00	25.00	50.00
	Pitcher, #5100, ftd.	295.00	335.00	595.00
	Plate, #2350, bread/butter, 6"	7.00	4.00	12.00
	Plate, #2350, salad, 7½"	10.00	8.00	18.00
	Plate, #2350, luncheon, 8½"	14.00	12.00	25.00
	Plate, #2321, Maj Jongg (canape), 8¾"		30.00	
	Plate, #2350, sm., dinner, 9½"	25.00	25.00	40.00
	Plate, dinner, 10½"	50.00	60.00	
	Plate, #2287, ctr. hand., 11"	30.00	35.00	65.00
21	Plate, chop, 13¾"	40.00	40.00	85.00
	Plate, #2350, server, 14"	55.00	50.00	110.00
	Plate, w/indent for cheese, 11"	25.00	30.00	
	Platter, #2350, 10½"	45.00	45.00	
3	Platter, #2350, 12"	65.00	60.00	150.00
	Platter, #2350, 15",	110.00	95.00	225.00
	Salt & pepper, #5100, pr.	75.00	75.00	
	Sauce boat, w/liner, #2350	160.00	150.00	
24	Saucer, #2350, after dinner	10.00	8.00	25.00
17, 23	Saucer, #2350, #2350½	4.00	3.00	8.00
3	Stem, #5093, high sherbet	18.00	15.00	35.00
4	Stem, #5093, water goblet	28.00	25.00	60.00
1	Stem, #5093, low sherbet	16.00	13.00	30.00
5	Stem, #5093, parfait	40.00	38.00	75.00
8	Stem, #5093, cordial, ¾ oz.	60.00	60.00	150.00
7	Stem, #5093, wine, 2¾ oz.	38.00	30.00	70.00
2	Stem, #5093, cocktail, 3 oz.	25.00	22.00	50.00
6	Stem, #5093, claret, 4 oz.	65.00	60.00	
	Sugar, #2350½, flat		22.00	
	Sugar, #2315, fat, ftd.	20.00	20.00	35.00
	Sugar, #2350½, ftd.	14.00	14.00	
	Sugar, lid	150.00	150.00	
9	Tumbler, #5100, ftd., 2 oz.	35.00	33.00	70.00
11	Tumbler, #5100, ftd., 5 oz.	18.00	16.00	45.00
13	Tumbler, #5100, ftd., 9 oz.	18.00	18.00	50.00
12	Tumbler, #5100, ftd., 12 oz.	30.00	28.00	65.00
	Urn, #2324, small	100.00	110.00	
	Urn, large	115.00	135.00	
18	Vase, #2292, 8"	125.00	115.00	225.00
	Vanity set, combination cologne/powder & stopper	225.00	250.00	395.00

Note: See stemware identification on page 98.

COLORS: CRYSTAL, SAHARA, COBALT, RARE IN PALE ZIRCON

14

Victorian has appeared for sale in a variety of markets recently. All the rarely found items are selling if appropriately priced. Items being priced above market are sitting. Another thing we note is the dust ring after picking up a piece which indicates it has not been handled for a while. It will take a much longer time to find collectors willing to pay outrageous prices on the more commonly observed items even if they were made by Heisey.

Notice the two tumblers used as a pattern shot. The taller one is Victorian while the shorter one is Duncan's Block. Block is an older ware often confused with Victorian and you can understand why. Thankfully, Victorian pieces are usually marked with the Heisey H inside a diamond.

Heisey Victorian was only made in the colors listed. If you see pink (Azalea), green (Verde), or amber Victorian in your travels, then you have Imperial's reissue of the pattern made in 1964 and 1965. These colors are usually also marked with the H in diamond trademark but were made from Heisey moulds after Heisey was no longer in business; Imperial did not remove Heisey's mark at first.

We spotted a set of amber offered at a show a few months ago, with a sign announcing rare Heisey amber at $4.00 each. Rare and $4.00 do not seem to belong in the same sentence. Those pieces had been offered so long the sign has faded. Amber Victorian is striking, but be aware it is Imperial's product and not Heisey's; and, presently collectors of older Heisey tend to spurn Imperial made wares. We suspect that will some day change — but not yet!

Imperial made a few pieces in crystal Victorian, but there is no magical key to separate crystal made by Heisey from Imperial's. These are not as ignored by Heisey collectors, as are the colored Victorian pieces since they are problematic to distinguish.

		Crystal				Crystal
8	Bottle, 3 oz., oil	65.00			Plate, 13", sandwich	90.00
12	Bottle, 27 oz., rye	160.00			Plate, 21", buffet or punch bowl liner	200.00
9	Bottle, French dressing	80.00		10	Relish, 11", 3 pt.	50.00
	Bowl, 10½", floral	50.00		7	Salt & pepper	65.00
	Bowl, finger	25.00		21	Stem, 2½ oz., wine	30.00
	Bowl, punch	250.00		20	Stem, 3 oz., claret	28.00
	Bowl, rose	90.00		17	Stem, 5 oz., oyster cocktail	22.00
	Bowl, triplex, w/flared or cupped rim	125.00		18	Stem, 5 oz., saucer champagne	20.00
3	Butter dish, ¼ lb.	60.00			Stem, 5 oz., sherbet	18.00
	Candlestick, 2-lite	110.00		22	Stem, 9 oz., goblet (one ball)	26.00
	Cigarette box, 4"	80.00			Stem, 9 oz., high goblet (two ball)	30.00
	Cigarette box, 6"	100.00		1	Sugar	30.00
	Cigarette holder & ashtray, ind.	30.00		11	Tray, 12", celery	40.00
	Comport, 5"	60.00		4	Tray, condiment (s/p & mustard)	140.00
	Comport, 6", 3 ball stem	120.00		19	Tumbler, 2 oz., bar	30.00
	Compote, cheese (for center sandwich)	40.00			Tumbler, 5 oz., soda (straight or curved edge)	25.00
2	Creamer	30.00			Tumbler, 8 oz., old-fashion	35.00
	Cup, punch, 5 oz.	10.00		16	Tumbler, 10 oz., w/rim foot	40.00
	Decanter and stopper, 32 oz.	70.00		15	Tumbler, 12 oz., ftd. soda	40.00
13	Jug, 54 oz.	400.00		14	Tumbler, 12 oz., soda (straight or curved edge)	28.00
	Nappy, 8"	40.00			Vase, 4"	50.00
	Plate, 6", liner for finger bowl	10.00			Vase, 5½"	60.00
6	Plate, 7"	20.00			Vase, 6", ftd.	100.00
5	Plate, 8"	35.00			Vase, 7½" (pitcher mold), rare	600.00
	Plate, 12", cracker	75.00			Vase, 9", ftd., w/flared rim	150.00

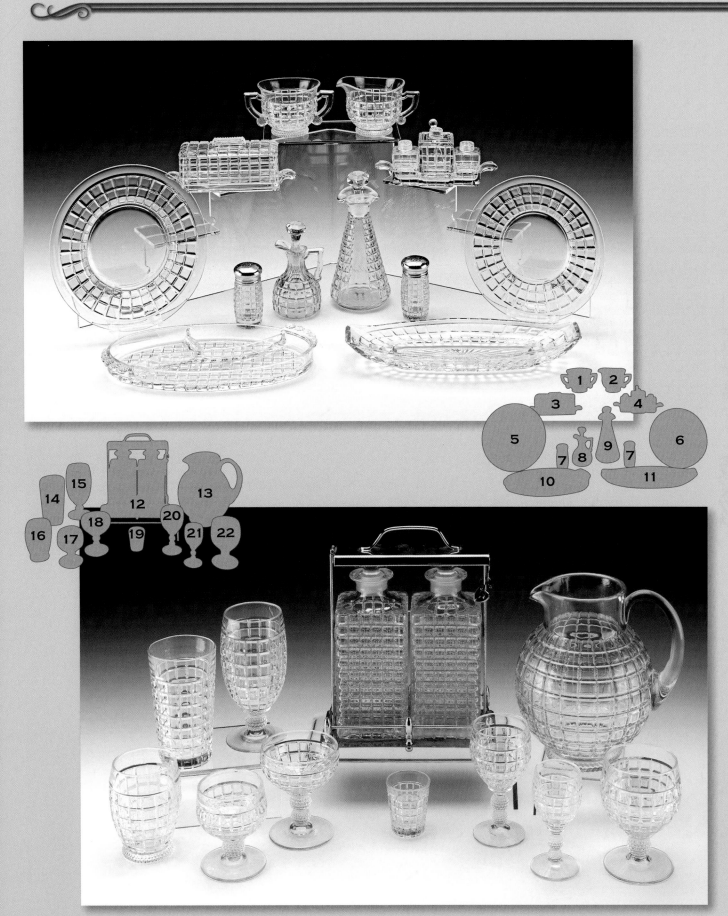

COLORS: CRYSTAL; RARE IN AMBER

Heisey's Waverly #1519 mould blank is better recognized for the Orchid and Rose etchings occurring on it than for itself, even if it's a superb, stylish blank in its own right.

		Crystal
	Bowl, 6", oval, lemon, w/cover	45.00
6	Bowl, 6", relish, 2 part, 3 ftd.	10.00
	Bowl, 6½", 2 hdld., ice	60.00
	Bowl, 7", 3 part, relish, oblong	30.00
	Bowl, 7", salad	20.00
	Bowl, 9", 4 part, relish, round	25.00
	Bowl, 9", fruit	30.00
	Bowl, 9", vegetable	35.00
	Bowl, 10", crimped edge	25.00
	Bowl, 10", gardenia	20.00
7	Bowl, 11", seahorse foot, floral	60.00
	Bowl, 12", crimped edge	35.00
5	Bowl, 13", gardenia, w/candleholder center	75.00
8	Box, 5", chocolate, w/cover	80.00
	Box, 5" tall, ftd., w/cover, seahorse hdl.	90.00
1	Box, 6", candy, w/bow tie knob	45.00
	Box, trinket, lion cover (rare)	700.00

		Crystal
	Butter dish, w/cover, 6", square	55.00
12	Candleholder, 1-lite, block (rare)	100.00
	Candleholder, 2-lite	40.00
	Candleholder, 2-lite, "flame" center	65.00
2	Candleholder, 3-lite	70.00
3	Candle epergnette, 5"	15.00
	Candle epergnette, 6", deep	20.00
	Candle epergnette, 6½"	15.00
	Cheese dish, 5½", ftd.	20.00
	Cigarette holder	60.00
11	Comport, 6", low ftd.	15.00
10	Comport, 6½", jelly	25.00
	Comport, 7", low ftd., oval	40.00
	Creamer, ftd.	15.00
	Creamer & sugar, individual, w/tray	50.00
4	Cruet, 3 oz., w/#122 stopper	75.00
	Cup	14.00

		Crystal
	Honey dish, 6½", ftd.	50.00
	Mayonnaise, w/liner & ladle, 5½"	50.00
	Plate, 7", salad	9.00
	Plate, 8", luncheon	10.00
	Plate, 10½", dinner	80.00
	Plate, 11", sandwich	20.00
	Plate, 13½", ftd., cake salver	60.00
13	Plate, 14", center handle, sandwich	65.00
	Plate, 14", sandwich	35.00
	Salt & pepper, pr.	50.00
	Saucer	4.00
	Stem, #5019, 1 oz., cordial	50.00

		Crystal
	Stem, #5019, 3 oz., wine, blown	20.00
	Stem, #5019, 3½ oz., cocktail	15.00
	Stem, #5019, 5½ oz., sherbet/champagne	9.00
	Stem, #5019, 10 oz., blown	20.00
	Sugar, ftd.	15.00
	Tray, 12", celery	20.00
	Tumbler, #5019, 5 oz., ftd., juice, blown	20.00
	Tumbler, #5019, 13 oz., ftd., tea, blown	22.00
14	Vase, 3½", violet	50.00
9	Vase, 7", ftd.	30.00
	Vase, 7", ftd., fan shape	35.00

COLORS: AMBER, CRYSTAL, EBONY W/GOLD, EMERALD GREEN

Wildflower etchings appear on numerous Cambridge tableware blanks, but it is typically found on #3121 stems. We have attempted to price a sample portion of the pattern, but the list is extensive. You can logically induce that, like Rose Point, almost any Cambridge blank may have been used to etch Wildflower. Price gold encrusted crystal items up to 25% higher. Price colored items about 50% higher, except for gold-encrusted Ebony, which brings double or triple the prices listed. A majority of collectors are searching for crystal because that is what is available.

21

		Crystal
	Basket, #3400/1182, 2 hdld., ftd., 6"	32.00
5	Bowl, #3500/54, 2 hdld., ftd.	30.00
10	Bowl, #3500/69, 3 pt. relish	30.00
4	Bowl, finger, blown, 4½"	30.00
	Bowl, #3400/1180, bonbon, 2 hdld., 5¼"	32.50
	Bowl, bonbon, 2 hdld., ftd., 6"	33.00
18	Bowl, #3400/90, 2 pt., relish, 6"	30.00
	Bowl, #3500/61, 3 pt., relish, hdld., 6½"	50.00
	Bowl, #3900/123, relish, 7"	35.00
	Bowl, #3900/130, bonbon, 2 hdld., 7"	35.00
	Bowl, #3400/88, 2 pt., relish, 8"	35.00
	Bowl, #3400/91, 3 pt., relish, 3 hdld., 8"	37.50
	Bowl, #3900/125, 3 pt., celery & relish, 9"	35.00
	Bowl, #477, pickle (corn), ftd., 9½"	32.50
3	Bowl, #3900/1185, 10"	60.00
	Bowl, #3900/34, 2 hdld., 11"	67.50
	Bowl, #3900/28, w/tab hand., ftd., 11½"	72.50
17	Bowl, #3900/126, 3 pt., celery & relish, 12"	55.00
	Bowl, #3400/4, 4 ft., flared, 12"	70.00
	Bowl, #3400/1240, 4 ft., oval, "ears" hdld., 12"	85.00
	Bowl, #3900/120, 5 pt., celery & relish, 12"	50.00
	Butter dish, #3900/52, ¼ lb.	250.00
	Butter dish, #3400/52, 5"	150.00
6	Cake plate, 13", #170	75.00
	Candlestick, #3400/638, 3-lite, ea.	60.00
	Candlestick, #3400/646, 5"	45.00
	Candlestick, #3400/647, 2-lite, "keyhole", 6"	50.00
19	Candlestick, #3121, 7"	100.00
	Candlestick, P.500	50.00
	Candy box, w/cover, #3400/9, 4 ftd.	135.00
	Candy box, w/cover, #3900/165, rnd.	115.00
2	Candy box, w/cover, #1066, 5½"	125.00
9	Cocktail icer, #968, 2 pc.	65.00
	Cocktail shaker, P.101, w/top	165.00
8	Cocktail shaker, #3400/175	150.00
	Comport, #3900/136, 5½"	50.00
	Comport, #3121, blown, 5⅜"	60.00
	Comport, #3500/148, 6"	40.00
	Creamer, #3900/41	18.00
	Creamer, #3900/40, individual	22.00
14	Creamer, #3500/15, individual	22.00
	Cup, #3900/17 or #3400/54	20.00
	Hat, #1704, 5"	295.00
	Hat, #1703, 6"	395.00
	Hurricane lamp, #1617, candlestick base	195.00
	Hurricane lamp, #1603, keyhole base & prisms	225.00
	Ice bucket, w/chrome hand., #3900/671	125.00

		Crystal
11	Mayonnaise set, 3 pc., #3400/11	55.00
1	Mayonnaise, #3900/19, sherbet style	35.00
	Oil, w/stopper, #3900/100, 6 oz.	125.00
	Pitcher, ball, #3400/38, 80 oz.	195.00
	Pitcher, #3900/115, 76 oz.	225.00
	Pitcher, Doulton, #3400/141	350.00
	Plate, crescent salad	140.00
	Plate, #3900/20, bread/butter, 6½"	10.00
	Plate, #3400/176, 7½"	10.00
	Plate, #3900/161, 2 hdld., ftd., 8"	18.00
	Plate, #3900/22, salad, 8"	18.00
	Plate, #3400/62, 8½"	18.00
	Plate, #3900/24, dinner, 10½"	75.00
	Plate, #3900/26, service, 4 ftd., 12"	55.00
	Plate, #3900/35, cake, 2 hdld., 13½"	75.00
	Plate, #3900/167, torte, 14"	60.00
	Plate, #3900/65, torte, 14"	60.00
	Salt & pepper, #3400/77, pr.	45.00
	Salt & pepper, #3900/1177	45.00
	Saucer, #3900/17 or #3400/54	3.50
	Set: 2 pc. Mayonnaise, #3900/19 (ftd. sherbet w/ladle)	55.00
	Set: 3 pc. Mayonnaise, #3900/129 (bowl, liner, ladle)	60.00
	Set: 4 pc. Mayonnaise, #3900/111 (div. bowl, liner, 2 ladles)	65.00
	Stem, #3121, cordial, 1 oz.	55.00
	Stem, #3121, cocktail, 3 oz.	25.00
	Stem, #3121, wine, 3½ oz.	40.00
	Stem, #3121, claret, 4½ oz.	45.00
	Stem, #3121, 4½ oz., low oyster cocktail	16.00
	Stem, #3121, 5 oz., low parfait	35.00
	Stem, #3121, 6 oz., low sherbet	16.00
	Stem, #3121, 6 oz., tall sherbet	22.00
13	Stem, #3121, 10 oz., water	35.00
20	Stem, #3725, 10 oz., water	30.00
15	Sugar, 3400/16	18.00
	Sugar, 3400/68	18.00
16	Sugar, indiv., 3500/15	22.00
	Sugar, indiv., 3900/40	22.00
	Tray, creamer & sugar, 3900/37	15.00
	Tumbler, #3121, 5 oz., juice	25.00
12	Tumbler, #3121, 10 oz., water	24.00
	Tumbler, #3121, 12 oz., tea	30.00
7	Tumbler, #3900/115, 13 oz.	35.00
	Vase, #3400/102, globe, 5"	55.00
	Vase, #6004, flower, ftd., 6"	65.00

		Crystal
	Vase, #6004, flower, ftd., 8"	75.00
	Vase, #1237, keyhole ft., 9"	110.00
21	Vase, #1528, bud, 10"	110.00
	Vase, #278, flower, ftd., 11"	125.00

	Crystal
Vase, #1299, ped. ft., 11"	150.00
Vase, #1238, keyhole ft., 12"	135.00
Vase, #279, ftd., flower, 13"	225.00

COLOR: CRYSTAL; CRYSTAL WITH GOLD NAMED GOLDWOOD

Woodland is an early Fostoria pattern that is attracting attention from some new collectors. There is a wide range of items found; but per usual, stemware leads the way. The pattern is renamed Goldwood if found with gold trim. We are sure gold trim added some to the production cost; thus, it was a way to provide a new pattern with a higher price and not have to make additional moulds. Today, the gold rim does not add to the price, and to many, it is a distraction.

4

	Bottle, salad dressing w/ stopper, #2083	85.00
	Bowl, 4½", finger, #766	13.00
	Candy jar w/lid, ½ lb., #2250	60.00
	Candy jar w/lid, ¼ lb., #2250	50.00
	Comport, 5"	25.00
	Comport, 6"	25.00
	Creamer, flat, #1851	15.00
	Decanter, 32 oz., #300	75.00
	Jelly w/cover, #825	25.00
	Marmalade w/cover, #4089	37.50
	Mayonnaise liner, 6"	7.00
	Mayonnaise, ftd., #2138	35.00
	Mustard w/cover, #1831	35.00
	Nappy, 5", ftd.	18.00
	Nappy, 6", ftd.	20.00
	Nappy, 7", ftd.	22.50
	Night bottle, 23 oz., #1697	65.00
	Night tumbler, 6 oz., #4023	15.00
	Oil bottle, 5 oz., w/stopper, #1465	45.00
	Oil bottle, 7 oz., w/stopper, #1465	55.00

3	Pitcher, 65 oz., #300	175.00
	Plate, 5", sherbet, #840	5.00
	Plate, 6", fingerbowl liner, #1736	6.00
	Plate, 7", salad, #1897	6.00
	Plate, 8¼", luncheon, #2238	8.00
	Plate, 11", torte, #2238	14.00
	Shaker, pr., #2022	35.00
	Stem, ¾ oz., cordial	20.00
	Stem, 2¾ oz., wine	14.00
	Stem, 3 oz., cocktail	12.50
	Stem, 5 oz., low sherbet	10.00
2	Stem, 5 oz., saucer champagne	10.00
	Stem, 6 oz., parfait	15.00
1	Stem, 9 oz., water	15.00
4	Sugar, flat, #1851	15.00
	Sweetmeat, #766	25.00
	Syrup, 8 oz. w/cut-off top, #2194	95.00
	Tumbler, 3½", 5 oz., juice, #889	8.00
	Tumbler, 4½", 10½", water, #4076	10.00
	Tumbler, 5½", 14 oz., tea, #889	14.00

1

2

3

COLORS: CRYSTAL, FLAMINGO PINK, SAHARA YELLOW, MOONGLEAM GREEN, HAWTHORNE ORCHID/PINK, MARIGOLD DEEP, AMBER/YELLOW; SOME COBALT, AND ALEXANDRITE

Etched designs on Yeoman blank #1184 will bring 10% to 25% more than the prices listed below. Empress is the most frequently found etched pattern on Yeoman, as well as the most desired. Pieces can be found with sterling silver decoration; these were not added at the Heisey factory. Sterling decoration today does not add to the price and often will keep an item from selling at all. Yeoman has some very desirable pieces for item collectors such as cologne and oil bottles as well as sugar shakers.

Hawthorne Yeoman is a consistent pale amethyst, regardless of lighting. It is not the Alexandrite which changes its color in different light sources.

		Crystal	Flamingo	Sahara	Moongleam	Hawthorne	Marigold
11	Ashtray, 4", hdld. (bow tie)	10.00	20.00	22.00	25.00	30.00	35.00
8	Bowl, 2 hdld., cream soup	12.00	20.00	25.00	30.00	35.00	40.00
	Bowl, finger	5.00	11.00	17.00	20.00	27.50	30.00
17	Bowl, ftd., banana split	7.00	23.00	30.00	35.00	40.00	45.00
4	Bowl, ftd., 2 hdld., bouillon, w/liner	10.00	20.00	25.00	30.00	35.00	40.00
	Bowl, 4½", nappy	4.00	7.50	10.00	12.50	15.00	17.00
	Bowl, 5", low, ftd., jelly	12.00	20.00	25.00	27.00	30.00	40.00
	Bowl, 5", oval, lemon and cover	30.00	60.00	65.00	75.00	90.00	90.00
	Bowl, 5", rnd., lemon and cover	30.00	60.00	65.00	75.00	90.00	90.00
	Bowl, 5", rnd., lemon, w/cover	15.00	20.00	25.00	30.00	40.00	50.00
	Bowl, 6", oval, preserve	7.00	12.00	17.00	22.00	27.00	30.00
	Bowl, 6", vegetable	5.00	10.00	14.00	16.00	20.00	24.00
22	Bowl, 6½", hdld., bonbon	5.00	10.00	14.00	16.00	20.00	24.00
	Bowl, 8", rect., pickle/olive	12.00	15.00	20.00	25.00	30.00	35.00
	Bowl, 8½", berry, 2 hdld.	14.00	22.00	25.00	30.00	35.00	50.00
	Bowl, 9", 2 hdld., veg., w/cover	35.00	60.00	60.00	70.00	95.00	175.00
	Bowl, 9", oval, fruit	20.00	25.00	35.00	45.00	55.00	55.00
	Bowl, 9", baker	20.00	25.00	35.00	45.00	55.00	55.00
	Bowl, 10", floral plateau #10	30.00	40.00		45.00	65.00	
	Bowl, 12", low, floral	15.00	25.00	35.00	45.00	60.00	55.00
14	Box, puff w/insert	95.00	150.00		175.00	120.00	
	Candle vase, single, w/short prisms & inserts	90.00			150.00		
13	Candy, hdld., 8½"	25.00	45.00		50.00		90.00
	Cigarette holder (ashtray), bottom	25.00	60.00	65.00	70.00	80.00	100.00
	Cologne bottle, w/stopper	100.00	160.00	160.00	160.00	170.00	180.00
19	Comport, 5", high ftd., shallow	15.00	25.00	37.00	45.00	55.00	70.00
1	Comport, 6", low ftd., deep	20.00	30.00	34.00	40.00	42.00	48.00
3	Comport and cover, #3350	55.00	85.00		85.00	110.00	175.00
	Creamer, #1189	20.00	35.00	35.00	40.00		
9	Creamer	10.00	25.00	20.00	22.00	50.00	28.00
6	Creamer, #1001	40.00	60.00				
	Cruet, 2 oz., oil	20.00	70.00	80.00	85.00	90.00	85.00
10	Cruet, 4 oz., oil	30.00	70.00	80.00	85.00		
	Cup	5.00	20.00	20.00	25.00	22.00	
20	Cup, after dinner	20.00	40.00	40.00	45.00	50.00	60.00
	Cup, coffee, Russian, 5 oz., #3312		45.00				
12	Egg cup	20.00	25.00	35.00	35.00	60.00	35.00
	Goblet, #3325		40.00			65.00	
	Gravy (or dressing) boat, w/underliner	13.00	25.00	30.00	45.00	50.00	45.00
	Marmalade jar, w/cover	25.00	35.00	40.00	45.00	55.00	65.00

		Crystal	Flamingo	Sahara	Moongleam	Hawthorne	Marigold
5	Mustard and cover	60.00	110.00	125.00	125.00		
	Parfait, 5 oz.	10.00	15.00	20.00	25.00	30.00	35.00
	Pitcher, quart	70.00	130.00	130.00	140.00	160.00	180.00
	Plate, 2 hdld., cheese	5.00	10.00	13.00	15.00	17.00	25.00
	Plate, cream soup underliner	5.00	7.00	9.00	12.00	14.00	16.00
	Plate, finger bowl underliner	3.00	5.00	7.00	9.00	11.00	13.00
	Plate, 4½", coaster	3.00	5.00	10.00	12.00		
	Plate, 6"	3.00	6.00	8.00	10.00	13.00	15.00
	Plate, 6", bouillon underliner	3.00	6.00	8.00	10.00	13.00	15.00
	Plate, 6½", grapefruit bowl	7.00	12.00	15.00	19.00	27.00	32.00
	Plate, 7"	5.00	8.00	10.00	14.00	17.00	22.00
	Plate, 8", oyster cocktail	9.00					
	Plate, 8", soup	9.00					
	Plate, 9", oyster cocktail	10.00					
	Plate, 10½"	20.00	50.00		50.00	60.00	
	Plate, 10½", ctr. hdld., oval, div.	15.00	26.00		32.00		
	Plate, 11", 4 pt., relish	20.00	27.00		32.00		
	Plate, 14"	20.00					
	Platter, 12", oval	10.00	17.00	19.00	26.00	33.00	
	Salt and pepper, #49	30.00	40.00				
	Salt, ind. tub (cobalt: $30.00)	10.00	20.00		30.00		
	Salver, 10", low ftd.	15.00	50.00		70.00		
	Salver, 12", low ftd.	10.00	50.00		70.00		
2	Saucer	3.00	5.00	7.00	7.00	6.00	10.00
20	Saucer, after dinner	3.00	5.00	7.00	8.00	10.00	10.00
	Stem, 2¾ oz., ftd., oyster cocktail	4.00	8.00	10.00	12.00	14.00	
	Stem, 3 oz., cocktail	10.00	12.00	17.00	20.00		
	Stem, 3½ oz., sherbet	5.00	8.00	11.00	12.00		
	Stem, 4 oz., fruit cocktail	3.00	10.00	10.00	12.00		
	Stem, 4½ oz., sherbet	3.00	10.00	10.00	12.00		
	Stem, 5 oz., soda	9.00	8.00	30.00	20.00		
	Stem, 5 oz., sherbet	5.00	7.00	9.00	9.00		
	Stem, 6 oz., champagne	6.00	16.00	18.00	22.00		
	Stem, 8 oz.	5.00	12.00	18.00	20.00		
16	Stem, 10 oz., goblet	8.00	15.00	60.00	25.00		
7	Sugar, w/cover	15.00	45.00	45.00	50.00	70.00	40.00
	Sugar and cover, #1189	25.00	45.00	45.00	55.00		
18	Sugar shaker, ftd.	50.00	95.00		110.00		
	Syrup, 7 oz., saucer ftd.	30.00	75.00				
	Tray, 7" x 10", rect.	26.00	30.00	40.00	35.00		
	Tray, 9", celery	10.00	14.00	16.00	15.00		
	Tray, 11", ctr. hdld., 3 pt.	15.00	35.00	40.00			
	Tray, 12", oblong	16.00	60.00	65.00			
	Tray, 13", 3 pt., relish	20.00	27.00	32.00			
	Tray, 13", celery	20.00	27.00	32.00			
	Tray, 13", hors d'oeuvre, w/cov. ctr.	32.00	42.00	52.00	75.00		
	Tray insert, 3½" x 4½"	4.00	6.00	7.00	8.00		
	Tumbler, 2½ oz., whiskey	3.00	20.00	25.00	40.00		
	Tumbler, 4½ oz., soda	4.00	6.00	10.00	15.00		
	Tumbler, 8 oz.	4.00	15.00	20.00	20.00		

		Crystal	Flamingo	Sahara	Moongleam	Hawthorne	Marigold
	Tumbler, 10 oz., cupped rim	4.00	15.00	20.00	22.50		
	Tumbler, 10 oz., straight side	5.00	15.00	20.00	22.50		
	Tumbler, 12 oz., tea	5.00	20.00	25.00	30.00		
	Tumbler cover (unusual)	35.00					
15	Vase, 5½", #4157	40.00	65.00	75.00	70.00	85.00	
	Vase, 6", #516-2		50.00		60.00	75.00	
	Vase, 7", floral bowl, #3480		55.00		65.00	85.00	

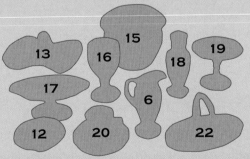

Cambridge Glass Company
Achilles 6
Adonis 7
Apple Blossom 18
Candlelight 33
Caprice 49
Chantilly 57
Cleo 66
Daffodil 76
Decagon 79
Diane 83
Elaine 87
Gloria 110
Imperial Hunt Scene, #718 120
Majorie 144
Mt. Vernon 150
Number 520, "Byzantine" 159
Number 703, "Florentine" 160
Number 704, "Windows Border" 161
Portia 176
Rosalie 189
Rose Point 191
Tally Ho 220
Valencia 235
Wildflower 248

Central Glass Works
"Balda" 21
"Harding" 117
Morgan 148
Thistle 227

Consolidated Lamp & Glass Co.
Catalonian 55
"Dance of the Nudes," Dancing Nymph ...77
Ruba Rombic 199

Duncan & Miller Glass Co.
Canterbury, No. 115 42
Caribbean 52
First Love 99
Lily of the Valley 140
Nautical 153
Plaza 174
Puritan 184
Sandwich 201
"Spiral Flutes" 206
Tear Drop 223
Terrace 225

Duncan Glass Co.
Mardi Gras 143

Fostoria Glass Company
Alexis 9
American 11
Baroque 22

Brocade 28
Colony 69
Fairfax No. 2375 96
  Fostoria Stems and Stems 98
Fuchsia 105
Glacier 109
Hermitage 118
June 127
Kashmir 134
Lafayette 136
Navarre 155
New Garland 158
Oriental 170
Pioneer 173
Priscilla 180
Rogene 188
Royal 197
Seville 205
Shirley 208
Sun Ray 215
Trojan 231
Versailles 239
Vesper 241
Woodland 250

H. C. Fry Glass Company
Thistle Cut 228

Heisey Glass Company
Charter Oak 59
Chintz 62
Crystolite 74
Empress 93
Greek Key 115
Ipswich 122
Kalonyal 133
Lariat 137
Minuet 146
Narcissus 152
New Era 157
Octagon 164
Old Colony 166
Old Sandwich 168
Pleat & Panel 175
Provincial, Whirlpool 181
Ridgeleigh 186
Saturn 203
Stanhope 211
Sunburst 213
Twist 234
Victorian 244
Waverly 246
Yeoman 251

Imperial Glass Company
Candlewick 35
Cape Cod 45

Lotus Glass Company
"Bubble Girl" Etching 31

McKee
Brocade 30
Turkey Tracks 233

Monongah
Bo Peep 27

Morgantown Glass Works
American Beauty 17
Elizabeth 91
Golf Ball 113
Queen Louise 185
Sparta 210
Sunrise Medallion 217
"Tinkerbell" 230

New Martinsville Glass Co.
Janice 123
"Lions" 141
Meadow Wreath 145

Paden City Glass Company
Black Forest 25
Gazebo 108

Tiffin Glass Company
Cadena 32
Cherokee Rose 61
Classic 64
"Columbine Variant," Blueball 73
Empire 92
Flanders 102
Fontaine 104
Fuchsia 106
Julia 126
June Night 127
Jungle Assortment 130
Le Fleur 139
Luciana 142
Nymph 163
Persian Pheasant 172
Psyche 180

U.S. Glass Company
"Deerwood" or " Birch Tree" 81
Psyche 183
Sylvan 219

Viking Glass Co.
Janice 124

Westmoreland Glass Co.
Princess Feather 179
Thousand Eye 229

274

10 oz. 3625 Goblet

4½ oz. 3625 Claret

10 oz. 3625 Ftd. Tumbler

12 oz. Ftd. Ice Tea